"Leslie Baynes has produced a first-rate study that, by turns, chides, challenges, and champions Lewis's various approaches to and engagements with the Bible. Scholarly and spirited, this is easily the best book yet written on Lewis and Scripture."

—**Michael Ward,** University of Oxford,
author of *Planet Narnia: The Seven Heavens in the Imagination of C. S. Lewis*

"This is a marvelous study: scrupulous, illuminating, and much needed. In part, it goes some way toward rescuing Lewis from many of those who admire him but who have a curiously confused notion of how he viewed Scripture and its exegesis within the embrace of Christian faith. But it also provides a portrait of the development of his thinking that, as far as I know, no one else has given us."

—**David Bentley Hart,**
author of *All Things Are Full of Gods: The Mysteries of Mind and Life*

"As a well-informed biblical scholar and a close (also appreciative) reader of C. S. Lewis, Leslie Baynes has provided a masterful study of Lewis on the Bible. The arguments of the book are compelling, both in showing where Lewis stumbled in addressing questions involving technical knowledge of the New Testament and in explaining why so much of Lewis's writing, especially the Narnia tales, puts Scripture to use with consummate effect. Biblical scholars as well as Lewis's many readers will find this a captivating read."

—**Mark Noll,** University of Notre Dame,
author of *C. S. Lewis in America: Readings and Reception, 1935–1947*

"This book is marvelous. I would rank it with Michael Ward's *Planet Narnia* and Alan Jacobs's *The Narnian* in terms of the influence I think it will have on Lewis scholarship, and I place it in my own personal list of best books on Lewis. What an important contribution!"

—**Aubrey Buster,** Wheaton College, author of *Remembering the Story of Israel: Historical Summaries and Memory Formation in Second Temple Judaism*

"Leslie Baynes's comprehensive study of Lewis's view of Scripture is distinguished by its integration of literary criticism, biblical scholarship, and Romantic imagination. Particularly impressive is her exploration of Lewis's major influences, including scholars like James Moffatt and Charles Gore, revealing how their works shaped his imaginative and critical approach to the Bible. Her use of primary sources, including handwritten notes and marginalia from Lewis's personal library, brings a fresh and authoritative perspective that significantly enriches Lewis studies. Baynes also draws extensively on secondary scholarship, including my own study of Lewis's view of biblical inspiration and inerrancy, highlighting how Lewis's view diverges from both evangelical and modern scholarly perspectives. A landmark contribution to Lewis scholarship."

—**Michael J. Christensen,** Northwind Theological Seminary,
author of *C. S. Lewis on Scripture: His Thoughts on the Nature of Biblical Inspiration, the Role of Revelation and the Question of Inerrancy*

"An intellectual feast of the highest order! Part detective story, part reception history of the Bible, part intellectual biography, and part literary analysis, Leslie Baynes's *Between Interpretation and Imagination* is a revelation for C. S. Lewis fans and critics alike. Baynes's knowledge of Lewis is as exhaustive as her knowledge of the Bible, and the result is an eye-opening excavation of Lewis's engagement with both the Bible and biblical scholarship. Her work shows why academic scholarship is so important and why scholars should pay more serious attention to the work of popularizers and apologists."

—**David W. Congdon,** University of Kansas, author of *Who Is a True Christian? Contesting Religious Identity in American Culture*

"In *Between Interpretation and Imagination,* Leslie Baynes takes readers on a fascinating tour of C. S. Lewis's engagement with Scripture, painting a beautiful portrait of Lewis as a complex reader of biblical text and narrative. What emerges is an intellectual whose more formal, restrictive interpretations were offset by an imagination that dared to transform the sacred into storylines that go beyond religious boundaries and speak with life into human experience. At once a captivating and provocative analysis devoted to one of the most influential writers of English literature in the twentieth century!"

—**Loren Stuckenbruck,** LMU Munich, author of *The Myth of Rebellious Angels: Studies in Second Temple Judaism and New Testament Texts*

"Among many books on the work of C. S. Lewis, this one is unique. Written from the perspective of a biblical scholar who is also an Eastern Orthodox Christian, *Between Interpretation and Imagination* offers a challenging reconstruction and critique of the formative influences on Lewis, an intriguing glimpse of his informal musings as judiciously excavated from marginal notes of books that he owned and personal letters, and an exhilarating and often surprising exploration of allusions and echoes from the Bible and other classical sources in the beloved Chronicles of Narnia. Especially welcome are the compelling reading of *The Horse and His Boy* and the exposition of Aslan's lively triumph over death and evil in *The Lion, the Witch and the Wardrobe,* which supplements a more familiar appreciation of his willing death for the 'son of Adam.'"

—**Edith M. Humphrey,** Pittsburgh Theological Seminary, author of *Further Up and Further In: Orthodox Conversations with C. S. Lewis on the Bible and Theology*

BETWEEN INTERPRETATION *and* IMAGINATION

C. S. Lewis and the Bible

Leslie Baynes

William B. Eerdmans Publishing Company
Grand Rapids, Michigan

Wm. B. Eerdmans Publishing Co.
2006 44th Street SE, Grand Rapids, MI 49508
www.eerdmans.com

Published 2025
Printed in the United States of America

31 30 29 28 27 26 25   1 2 3 4 5 6 7

ISBN 978-0-8028-7400-9

Library of Congress Cataloging-in-Publication Data

Names: Baynes, Leslie, author.
Title: Between interpretation and imagination : C. S. Lewis and the Bible / Leslie Baynes.
Description: Grand Rapids, Michigan : William B. Eerdmans Publishing Company, 2025. | Includes index. | Summary: "A study of C. S. Lewis's writings on the Bible, seen within their intellectual, social, and personal contexts"—Provided by publisher.
Identifiers: LCCN 2024026124 | ISBN 9780802874009 (hardcover) | ISBN 9781467469708 (epub)
Subjects: LCSH: Lewis, C. S. (Clive Staples), 1898–1963—Criticism and interpretation. | Lewis, C. S. (Clive Staples), 1898–1963—Religion. | Bible—Study and teaching. | Bible—In literature.
Classification: LCC PR6023.E926 Z58558 2025 | DDC 823/.912—dc23/eng/20240830
LC record available at https://lccn.loc.gov/2024026124

Arguments first presented in Leslie Baynes, "C. S. Lewis's Use of Scripture in the 'Liar, Lunatic, Lord' Argument," *Journal of Inklings Studies* 4, no. 2 (2014): 27–66, are used here by permission.

To James Heft, SM

Of teachers, wisest and best

CONTENTS

PART 3

Beyond Allegory: The Subtle Use of Scripture in the Chronicles of Narnia

INTRODUCTION

In 1944 an Irishman named Arthur Greeves wrote a letter to his friend C. S. Lewis, asking him to recommend some good modern biblical commentaries. The first one Lewis thought of was a huge volume edited by Charles Gore, *A New Commentary on Holy Scripture*,[1] which he calls "probably the best *single* book of modern comment on the Bible." He didn't want to take the time to recommend commentaries on individual books of Scripture because there were so many of them. "Their name is legion," he says.[2]

The allusion to Mark 5:9 tells us two things about Lewis and Scripture that are good to know as we begin. First, his mind was saturated with the Bible. He could burst into apt quotation, even with a clever twist, at any moment. Second, although he did use modern commentaries, his linking them with the spirits that possessed the demoniac in Mark hints at his fraught relationship with biblical scholarship.[3] He probably cited the verse playfully, but he could not have done so thoughtlessly. He knew what it meant, quoting it in the story of his early life and conversion, *Surprised by Joy*, to summarize what he uncov-

1. Charles Gore, Henry Leighton Goudge, and Alfred Guillaume, eds., *A New Commentary on Holy Scripture, Including the Apocrypha* (New York: Macmillan, 1928), hereafter cited as *NCHS*. Although he had the help of Goudge and Guillaume, Gore was the general editor of the volume and thus its guiding force. See Carl Everett Purinton, "*An Anglican Commentary on the Bible*, by Charles Gore, Henry Leighton Goudge, and Alfred Guillaume," *Journal of Religion* 9, no. 3 (1929): 462–65.

2. Lewis to Greeves, Jan. 30, 1944, in *The Collected Letters of C. S. Lewis*, ed. Walter Hooper, vol. 3, *Narnia, Cambridge, and Joy, 1950–1963* (San Francisco: HarperSanFrancisco, 2007), supplement, 3:1548. In this book, shortened references to the *Collected Letters* (*CL*) are by volume and page number.

3. "I usually do my epistles with the aid of separate commentaries." Lewis to Warfield M. Firor, Dec. 5, 1949, in *The Collected Letters of C. S. Lewis*, ed. Walter Hooper, vol. 2, *Books, Broadcasts, and the War, 1931–1949* (San Francisco: HarperSanFrancisco, 2004), 2:1008.

ered in his first spiritual self-examination: "a zoo of lusts, a bedlam of ambitions, a nursery of fears, a harem of fondled hatreds. My name was legion."[4]

Of the making of books there is no end, and that includes commentaries both on the Bible and on Lewis, but few books have been published on Lewis *and* the Bible. This book is a reception history. It not only examines Lewis's reception of the Bible and his readers' reception of his thought, but also sets these topics within the broader history of biblical interpretation in Lewis's era, late nineteenth- through mid-twentieth-century Britain, placing his work on Scripture in its intellectual, social, and personal contexts. It builds upon never-before published notes that Lewis wrote by hand in books from his personal library, ranging from multiple versions of the Bible and tomes in his own field of English literature, to volumes by friends like Austin Farrer and occasional opponents like Alec Vidler, to new biblical scholarship published in 1963, the year he died. These annotations provide unique insight into his thinking as he reads about Scripture in real time. Many people have commented on Lewis's use of the Bible in his most famous books, the Chronicles of Narnia, but this book reveals the subtle beauty of his work with Scripture in the Chronicles as it has never been seen before.

I make three major arguments. First, certain aspects of Lewis's biblical interpretation that may appear unusual to some readers today reflect the views of Charles Gore and James Moffatt, biblical scholars whose work is now largely unknown in the United States. When Lewis returned to Christian faith in 1931, he read Gore and Moffatt to help him understand the Bible, and their opinions influenced him, for better and for worse, to the end of his life. Second, Lewis's most problematic writing on Scripture is rooted in his perceptions of the Gospel of John, particularly when he diverges from Gore, and always when he is focusing on the Gospel's genre and historicity—for example, in his lecture "Modern Theology and Biblical Criticism" and his rendering of the "liar, lunatic, or Lord" argument. The controversies he takes up in these arguments encompass the most fundamental questions in the history of Christian biblical scholarship, and his responses to them have helped form the minds of countless readers for generations. Third, Lewis does his best work on the

4. *Surprised by Joy* (San Diego: Harcourt Brace Jovanovich, 1955), 226. Lewis's poem "Legion" survives in two versions. The one in *Poems* (1964; repr., San Francisco: HarperOne, 2017) includes the line "I am Legion" (181), but the version on p. 390 of *The Collected Poems of C. S. Lewis: A Critical Edition*, ed. Don W. King (Kent, OH: Kent State University Press, 2015; hereafter cited as *Collected Poems*), does not. The latter notes Legion's negative characteristics, but the former does not.

Bible—and especially on the Gospel of John—in the Chronicles of Narnia, where he doesn't have to engage modern biblical scholarship but can rely on his greatest strength, his literary imagination.

Part 1 introduces readers to how Lewis worked with Scripture: what he thought, and why he thought it. It moves chronologically, providing an overview of what he read and wrote that leaves more detailed treatment to the rest of the book. Part 2 applies Lewis's general ideas on Scripture to specific case studies and controversies, setting him first among evangelical Protestants and then modern biblical scholars. Each group has found his work with the Bible problematic for antithetical reasons, and he in turn expressed some objections to them. But Lewis, who was neither an evangelical nor a biblical scholar, also found common ground with both groups, and he was keenly aware of holding what he considered to be a mediating position. This book demonstrates that Lewis shared more in common with academic biblical scholars than he ever imagined, including his bugbear Rudolf Bultmann, the most influential New Testament scholar of his day. Part 3 looks at how he used the Bible in the Chronicles of Narnia. Far from being half-baked "biblical allegory," the Chronicles showcase his most sophisticated employment of Scripture.

Between Interpretation and Imagination: C. S. Lewis and the Bible is written for those who want to learn more about Lewis; for biblical scholars who appreciate him and those who don't; for scholars of Lewis who wish to learn more about his use of the Bible; and for anyone who wants to know how the twentieth century's most influential Christian writer in English worked with the Western world's most influential book. Some chapters will appeal more to one audience than another. The general reader might not initially be attracted to Bultmann, for example, but is urged to give it a go. And I've found that even the tweediest biblical scholars enjoy reading about Narnia.

Lewis fought against the idea that literature should be read in light of the author's biographical context. He once said that if he discovered a new tidbit about a famous writer, he would "throw it in the fire, tell no one, and re-read their works."[5] His opinion is based on a complex of ideas he calls "the personal heresy." There is much more to say about the personal heresy, and I will say it later in the book, but many people have understood it as he expresses it here: that is, we should be interested not so much in authors as in their work—a preference Lewis wished his own readers would apply to his work. He didn't like to talk about himself, but he loved talking about books. After the publication of *The Lion, the Witch and the Wardrobe*, for example, Lewis began to receive fan

5. Lewis to Roy W. Harrington, Jan. 19, 1948, *CL*, 2:831.

mail from children. Their letters delighted him because they wanted to learn more about the story, not the author.[6] However, it seems to me that we read anything better when we put it in as much context as we can, and if I may judge from the number of biographies devoted to Lewis, I'm in good company.

Of course, my own study of Lewis also arises from a personal context. As an undergraduate English major at the University of Dayton, I was disappointed when my favorite professor, Fr. Jim Heft, offered a course on one of my favorite authors, C. S. Lewis, and I wasn't able to take it. I had taken all of Fr. Heft's other courses, but I couldn't take this one. Redeeming that disappointment is the reason why this book exists today. After I earned a PhD in Christianity and Judaism in Antiquity at the University of Notre Dame and was gainfully employed as a professor of New Testament and Second Temple Judaism at Missouri State University, my department head knocked on my office door one day and asked an unexpected question. "If you could teach anything you wanted, what would it be?" "C. S. Lewis," I replied, and I taught the first iteration of the course in 2007. Every time I meet a group of prospective Lewisians, they learn, "You're here because I'm teaching the course I never got to take."

One of those students invited me to speak at an event she was planning, "An Evening with C. S. Lewis," in 2010. When I asked her what she would like me to present upon, she suggested Lewis and the Bible. I knew a fair amount about Lewis, a lot about the Bible, and a few things about how the two fit together, so that sounded good to me. Since it was such a huge topic, I narrowed it down to how Lewis used Scripture in his "liar, lunatic, or Lord" argument for the divinity of Jesus.

The evening featured professors of religion, philosophy, and English. The English professors kept it light and laudatory, and then there was my mildly critical talk (much expanded as chapter 8 here). A question-and-answer session followed, and one woman in the middle of the auditorium directed her voice to me, not with a question, but with a comment. "I came here expecting something fun from people who like Lewis!" she complained. "And I get *this*?" Then she stumbled over the people in her path and left. It was the first—and so far only—time anyone has walked out of one of my presentations. I am happy to report that her reaction was unique in other ways, too. Everyone else has found the "liar, lunatic, or Lord" material compelling, and no one else has ever come away from it thinking I dislike Lewis.

When evaluating Lewis, often the evaluators themselves are judged and found wanting. If they like him, they may be perceived as endorsing tea-and-

6. Lewis to Ruth Pitter, Nov. 28, 1950, *CL*, 3:65–66.

crumpets Anglophilia or talking-beast preciousness, as Lev Grossman portrays readers of the Narnia stand-in Fillory in his novel *The Magicians*. On the other hand, if they criticize him, it may be taken on par with criticizing God, as Samuel Joeckel observes in *The C. S. Lewis Phenomenon*.[7] In this book, I hope it's clear that I love Lewis, even as I criticize some of his work.

Lewis himself relished healthy opposition. He once wrote a correspondent, "Thank you very much indeed for your kind letter, all the more acceptable because of its criticisms: for praise without criticism is rather like an egg without salt."[8] Lewis was a literary critic, and he didn't wield his critical acumen solely upon his peers. After the publication of the Chronicles of Narnia, young readers sent him their own stories, and he didn't pander to them. He took their work seriously, giving them honest feedback.[9] I follow his lead, in hopes of adding some much-needed salt to conversations on Lewis and the Bible.

Unless otherwise noted, all translations of Scripture and other ancient works in Greek and Hebrew are my own, and books from Lewis's personal library discussed here are held in the Marion E. Wade Center in Wheaton, Illinois.

7. Lev Grossman, *The Magicians: A Novel* (New York: Viking, 2009); Samuel Joeckel, *The C. S. Lewis Phenomenon: Christianity and the Public Sphere* (Macon, GA: Mercer, 2013).

8. Lewis to Canon Oliver Chase Quick, Jan. 18, 1941, *CL*, 2:461.

9. Lewis to the Kilmer children, March 19, 1954, *CL*, 3:441–42, and to Joan Lancaster, Aug. 31, 1958, *CL*, 3:970.

1

LEWIS'S LIFE WITH SCRIPTURE

A Brief Biography

1. EARLIEST ENGAGEMENTS

1898–1932

Lord, with what care hast thou begirt us round!
Parents first season us; then schoolmasters
Deliver us to laws; they send us bound
To rules of reason, holy messengers,
Pulpits and Sundayes, sorrow dogging sinne,
Afflictions sorted, anguish of all sizes,
Fine nets and stratagems to catch us in,
Bibles laid open, millions of surprises.

—George Herbert[1]

Lewis was born November 29, 1898, to an Irish Protestant family in Belfast.[2] His parents, he said, "were not notably pious but went regularly to church and took me."[3] In the summer of 1908, when he was nine years old, his mother, Flora, died of cancer. Since he had been taught to pray, he prayed for her healing, and after she died, he continued to pray for a miracle, presumably her rising from the dead.[4] Although his prayers did not produce the desired effect, and the loss was a catastrophe for the survivors—Jack, as he liked to be called; his father, Albert; and his older brother, Warren—his mother's death did not destroy his faith. That occurred several years later when he

1. George Herbert, "Sinne (I)," in *The Poems of George Herbert*, ed. Helen Gardner (Oxford: Oxford University Press, 1961), 38.

2. See Lewis, *That Hideous Strength* (1946; repr., New York: Macmillan, 1965), 33, for his wry take on beginning an essay with "[Surname] was born."

3. Lewis to N. Fridama, Feb. 15, 1946, *CL*, 2:702. They attended the Church of Ireland.

4. *Surprised by Joy* (San Diego: Harcourt Brace Jovanovich, 1955), 20–21.

was at school.[5] Studying for university entrance exams with a beloved atheist tutor, W. T. Kirkpatrick, cemented the edifice of his unbelief.[6]

At the same time, young Lewis knew the Bible. It was read aloud at church, and a record has survived of him studying it at home with his governess, Annie Harper. On January 21, 1908, Miss Harper notes in her calendar that Jack's first task for the day was Psalm 63:1–2. She says no more about it than that, but the way she sets up the assignment with his others in poetry, history, and grammar implies that he was expected to memorize it.[7] In hindsight, the verses tinge prophetic. The KJV reads, "O God, thou art my God; early will I seek thee: my soul thirsteth for thee, my flesh longeth for thee in a dry and thirsty land, where no water is; To see thy power and thy glory, so as I have seen thee in the sanctuary."

All of his schools required church attendance, and one of them, Malvern College, awarded an annual divinity prize.[8] Such prizes were common, as we can see from the books starring Lewis's famous fictional contemporary Bertie Wooster, who won it at his own school—a "fact" his creator P. G. Wodehouse turns into high comedy. Bertie prided himself on his Scripture knowledge, which he used to adorn his writing. On the first page of *The Code of the Woosters*, for example, Bertie wakes up from a night of drunken debauchery feeling, as he puts it, like "some bounder was driving spikes through my head—not just ordinary spikes, as used by Jael the wife of Heber, but red-hot ones."[9]

If Bertie Wooster, who could have won Monty Python's competition for British Upper-Class Twit of Year, can quote Scripture fluidly, how much more so clever Jack? In 1914 he compares a drought of letter writing to "the weeks

5. See Andrew Lazo, ed., "'Early Prose Joy': C. S. Lewis's Early Draft of an Autobiographical Manuscript," *VII: Journal of the Marion E. Wade Center* 30 (2013): 28–29.

6. Lewis to N. Fridama, Feb. 15, 1946, *CL*, 2:702; *Surprised by Joy*, 59–60.

7. In Warren H. Lewis, ed., "Memoirs of the Lewis Family, 1850–1930" (aka the Lewis Family Papers), vol. 3, p. 101, shelf 1, Warren H. Lewis Papers, Wade-A-110, Marion E. Wade Center, Wheaton College, Wheaton, IL.

8. Paul Godsland of the Malvernian Society, email correspondence with author, March 15–16, 2021.

9. Judges 4:21. P. G. Wodehouse, *The Code of the Woosters* (1938; repr., New York: Vintage, 1975), 7. Bertie's school was also named Malvern, but his was in Kent and Lewis's in Worcestershire. In another excellent coincidence, when Bertie went up to Oxford, his college was Magdalen (*Code*, 71). The adult Lewis loved Wodehouse's *Right Ho, Jeeves* (see his letter to his brother, Sept. 2, 1939, *CL*, 2:271). For more on Bertie and Scripture, see Carol Smith, "What Was in the Scripture Knowledge Syllabus at Bertie Wooster's Prep School?," in *Sense and Sensitivity: Essays on Reading the Bible in Memory of Robert Carroll*, ed. Alastair G. Hunter and Phillip R. Davies (Sheffield: Sheffield Academic Press, 2002), 395–415.

'which the locust hath eaten'" (Joel 1:4).[10] In 1915 he pokes fun at the twenty-four elders of Revelation falling on their faces (Rev. 4:10), "which must hurt rather but apparently is the 'thing' up yonder."[11] In 1916 he tells his friend Arthur Greeves, "I suppose I must 'bow myself in the house of Rimmon'" (2 Kings 5:18), quite the obscure passage for a teenaged atheist to drop into casual conversation. The verse stuck with him, as he employs it decades later in *Surprised by Joy*.[12] He consistently calls his father's housekeeper the "Witch of Endor" (1 Sam. 28:7) for reasons we wish he would explain but never does.[13] He can speak of "treasures both old and new" (Matt. 13:52), praise the "ineffably beautiful" language of Job 38:4–7, mention Simon Magus (Acts 8:9–24) and the "smoking flax" of Isaiah 42:3, and satirize 1 Corinthians 13:7 in a complicated riff on a family joke, rejecting Christianity all the while.[14]

Decades later in his heftiest academic tome, *English Literature in the Sixteenth Century, Excluding Drama* (1954), Lewis claims that this sort of self-conscious "quotation, or half-quotation, or parody" of the Bible peaked in the nineteenth and early twentieth centuries. Bits of Scripture "were on everyone's lips," he says, but they stood out from ordinary talk "as something set apart, like plums in a cake or lace on a frock, not like wine mixing in water."[15] He argues much the same thing in a lecture on the literary impact of the Authorized Version (KJV). For centuries everyone knew the Bible because they "heard it read, as a ritual or almost ritual act, at home, at school, at church." Therefore, he observes, most people used Scripture in one of two ways: "with conscious reverence or with conscious irreverence, either religiously or facetiously."[16] Like Bertie Wooster, preconversion Lewis fell into the second camp.

Lewis also imbibed Scripture through his vast reading. If we are to know anything about him at all, we must underline the place reading held in his life. When he introduces his parents in *Surprised by Joy*, Lewis characterizes them by naming the sorts of books they did and didn't like, a mode of description biblio-

10. Lewis to his father, June 22, 1914, in *The Collected Letters of C. S. Lewis*, ed. Walter Hooper, vol. 1, *Family Letters, 1905–1931* (San Francisco: HarperSanFrancisco, 2004), 60.

11. Lewis to Greeves, May 25, 1915, *CL*, 1:121.

12. Lewis to Greeves, July 18, 1916, *CL*, 1:214; *Surprised by Joy*, 162.

13. See Lewis to his father, May 25, 1919, *CL*, 1:450, and subsequent letters.

14. Lewis to Greeves, July 18, 1916, *CL*, 1:214; to Greeves, Aug. 4, 1917, *CL*, 1:333; to Greeves, May 5, 1919, *CL*, 1:447; to his father, June 5, 1926, *CL*, 1:665; to his brother, Aug. 2, 1928, *CL*, 1:776.

15. *English Literature in the Sixteenth Century, Excluding Drama* (Oxford: Clarendon Press, 1954), 214–15.

16. *The Literary Impact of the Authorized Version*, Facet Books Biblical Series 4 (1950; repr., Philadelphia: Fortress, 1963), 28.

philes everywhere will appreciate. He grew up surrounded by books, allowed to read them all, and his omnivorous literary diet built a man made of books who cannot be understood apart from them. His early letters to his father, brother, and best friend Arthur are dominated by reports of what he was reading and writing. Once he landed at a good school, Malvern College (his first school was a Dickensian horror that almost broke him), and studied with a teacher he loved, he can exclaim, "What could be better . . . than reading the greatest masterpieces of all time, under a man who has made them part of himself?"[17] Many of the masterpieces Lewis read for school and on his own, such as the works of Shakespeare and Milton, were permeated with Scripture, and he began to read them when he was a child, finishing *Paradise Lost* when he was nine years old.[18]

However, what the young Lewis cared about most was what he would later call "Joy," an idea that affected his encounters with and writing on Scripture. His conception of Joy is not easy to grasp. The name itself poses a problem, because it has nothing to do with happiness. As he struggles to explain it, he offers synonyms like longing, desire, and the German *Sehnsucht*, but there is more to it than that. The first time he experienced Joy was in the act of remembering. When he was a small boy, he was struck by the memory of a toy garden his brother had made in the lid of a biscuit tin. It was not the original sight of it that brought him Joy but the remembrance of having seen it—a memory that overwhelmed him with "desire; but desire for what?" Not to see the toy garden again but to feel what he felt when he was remembering it, a feeling that had disappeared in a flash.[19]

Lewis recounts two more early glimpses of Joy in *Surprised by Joy*. The first came through Beatrix Potter's little book *Squirrel Nutkin*, which awoke in him what he can articulate only as the "Idea of Autumn."[20] The second was sparked by a chance reading of the lines "Balder the beautiful / Is dead, is dead," which filled him with a desire "of almost sickening intensity" for what he deems "Northernness."[21] But flashes of Joy weren't confined to books.[22] They seized him in nature, art, music, and especially myth. Recalling his years at Malvern (1913–1914), Lewis contrasts the dreary outer world he endured at school to the world inside his head, where satyrs and maenads danced in

17. Lewis to his father, Feb. 16, 1914, *CL*, 1:49.
18. George Sayer, *Jack: A Life of C. S. Lewis* (Wheaton, IL: Crossway, 1994), 51.
19. *Surprised by Joy*, 16.
20. *Surprised by Joy*, 16.
21. *Surprised by Joy*, 17, 73.
22. See "Early Prose Joy," 16.

the company of Brynhild, Sieglinde, Deirdre, and Maeve, a whirl of Greek, Germanic, and Irish divinity.[23]

He didn't talk about Joy with anyone until he met his "First Friend," Arthur Greeves, in 1914. All of Arthur's attempts to socialize with the Lewis boys had been rebuffed until the day Jack reluctantly agreed to visit him when he was ill. As he walked into Arthur's room, he saw *The Myths of the Norsemen* lying on the nightstand, and the resultant meeting of minds established a till-death-do-us-part friendship. Although Lewis wrote to his father and brother for years, he poured his bookish self most freely into his early letters to Greeves, who kept them all.[24] Lewis changed a great deal from his atheist youth to his Christian maturity, but his faith, when it came, did not have the deleterious effect on his writing that it seems to have had with some other authors—for example, the pre- and post-conversion poems of William Wordsworth, in Lewis's judgment.[25] Instead, his turn to God appears to have perfected his writing, and his letters to Arthur document the change, a transition I see beginning around the mid-1930s as he discusses Psalm 95:4.[26]

After a stint fighting in World War I (1917–1918), Lewis earned first-class degrees in Literae Humaniores ("Greats," a combination of classics and philosophy) and English at Oxford.[27] In 1925 he accepted a fellowship at Magdalen College, Oxford, where he remained as tutor in English language and literature until 1954, when he accepted the Chair of Medieval and Renaissance English at Magdalene College, Cambridge. Although Lewis had studied classics and taught philosophy before 1925, from that point forward his professional life centered on English literature. He was never an academic theologian or biblical scholar, a fact he emphasizes repeatedly in his religious writing for a popular audience. There is no false modesty in the disavowal. He was always an amateur, a non-professional who loved the field—gifted in many respects but one who fell prey to his lack of knowledge in others.

Lewis recovered his faith in God gradually in the late 1920s,[28] but Scripture had nothing to do with it if we may judge from what he wrote at the time. Besides

23. *Surprised by Joy*, 118.

24. *Surprised by Joy*, 199. Lewis to Greeves, Sept. 22, 1931, *CL*, 1:971.

25. Lewis to Ruth Pitter, May 12, 1953, *CL*, 2:327.

26. Lewis to Greeves, June 22, 1930, *CL*, 1:909.

27. Walter Hooper, ed., *C. S. Lewis: A Companion and Guide* (London: HarperCollins, 1996), 20, 771.

28. Lewis to N. Fridama, Feb. 15, 1946, *CL*, 2:705–6; *Surprised by Joy*, 199. See also Norbert Feinendegen and Arend Smilde, eds., *The "Great War" of Owen Barfield and*

the clever allusions, he barely mentions Scripture until he becomes a theist in 1930.[29] Then everything changes, and he begins to discuss the Bible in new ways. Looking ahead, we can see him replicate the same pattern of using the Bible when he recounts this period in *Surprised by Joy*. That is, he cites Scripture only a few times until he arrives at the night he surrendered to God in the penultimate chapter of the book. As he describes how God drew near, references to Scripture cluster thick and fast, from John's "know of the doctrine" (John 7:17 KJV) and Mark's "my name is legion" (Mark 5:9), to Ezekiel's valley of dry bones (Ezek. 37) and Exodus's name of God, "I am" (Exod. 3:14), down to the moment when "that which I greatly feared had at last come upon me" (Job 3:25) and Lewis must admit "that God was God." On the last page of the chapter, he describes himself as a figure even more pathetic than Luke's prodigal son, because the prodigal returned to his father under his own volition (Luke 15:17–19), whereas God in his mercy had to compel Lewis (Luke 14:23).[30] In this book, we will see that, consciously or not, Lewis handles Scripture the same way in the Chronicles of Narnia as he does in *Surprised by Joy*: almost always there are only a few biblical allusions when Aslan is not in frame, but they burgeon when he is.

By mid-1930 Lewis is a theist, but he doesn't call himself a Christian—which he defines as someone who acknowledges Jesus as Son of God—until September 1931.[31] He reads and writes more about Scripture during this in-between time than he had earlier. For example, in April 1930 he goes on a ramble with friends, and "according to an excellent custom of our walks," they listen to one of their party read a chapter from the Bible at the lectern of a local church, something it is hard to imagine him tolerating, much less praising, before.[32]

C. S. Lewis: Philosophical Writings, 1927–1930 Inklings Studies Supplements 1, *Journal of Inklings Studies*, 2015.

29. Lewis dates his conversion to theism to Trinity term 1929, but he was mistaken; it was 1930. Andrew Lazo, "Correcting the Chronology: Some Implications of 'Early Prose Joy,'" *VII: Journal of the Marion E. Wade Center* 29 (2012): 55–59; Alister McGrath, *C. S. Lewis: A Life; Eccentric Genius, Reluctant Prophet* (Carol Stream, IL: Tyndale, 2013), 140–46; Brendan Wolfe, "A Note on the Date of C. S. Lewis's Conversion to Theism," *Journal of Inklings Studies* 9, no. 1 (2019): 68–69.

30. *Surprised by Joy*, 226–29. Other references to Scripture in *Surprised by Joy* prior to "Checkmate" include Song of Songs 2:5; 1 Cor. 11:29; 2 Kings 5:18; and Luke 24:5. He follows this pattern even in one of his last books, *An Experiment in Criticism* (Cambridge: Cambridge University Press, 1961), where he quotes Scripture only in the penultimate chapter.

31. *Surprised by Joy*, 237.

32. Lewis to Greeves, April 29, 1930, *CL*, 1:893. Lewis and his friends maintained the custom; e.g., Lewis's letter to his brother, April 11, 1940, *CL*, 2:383.

More significantly for his spiritual development, in June 1930 he tells Greeves that he has just finished reading the Gospel of John in Greek, and "after that most other things are a come down." He went on, "Not that I liked *that* in all respects either."[33] He says no more about John here, and he does not mention it again in the letters leading to his turn to Christ in September 1931 or even when he reflects on his conversion in hindsight. I, however, must jump ahead in our timeline to highlight the impact it made upon him. Like a duckling imprinting on the first thing it sees, Lewis latches on to the Gospel of John. He was familiar with it before, but in 1930 he reads it as an adult who takes it "seriously," a word he uses every time he explains how his encounter with Scripture in this period is different.[34] What he reads in John affects him so indelibly that he will interpret the other Gospels through its lens for the rest of his life.

In the first few months of 1931, Lewis wrote an account of his move to theism that wasn't published until 2013, under the title "Early Prose Joy."[35] This work marks a watershed in how Lewis engages Scripture. He cites the Bible just a few times, but the citations serve neither to adorn his writing nor as the butt of satire. Instead, he takes it seriously. He wonders if his beliefs should affect his actions, and he admits that they should. He tells himself to "cease to do evil; learn to do good" (Isa. 1:16–17). When he tries to do so and fails, he quotes part of Romans 7:23: "I see another law in my members, warring against the law of my mind, and bringing me into captivity to the law of sin which is in my members" (KJV).[36]

Even though Lewis now takes Scripture seriously, it does not seem to have played an outspoken role in his conversion to Christ—but mythology does. From the moment he read "Balder the beautiful / Is dead, is dead," Lewis loved every kind of myth, which paved the way to Joy. However, stories of pagan gods could also serve as an argument against the existence of the Christian God, because he considered all deities equally false. In *Surprised by Joy,* Lewis credits the beginning of his change of mind on the matter to conversations with his "second friend," Owen Barfield. What he does not explicitly discuss

33. Lewis to Greeves, June 1, 1930, *CL,* 1:899.

34. He also uses the word to describe his period of reading the Bible at Oldie's school (*Surprised by Joy,* 34; *Mere Christianity* [1952; repr., San Francisco: HarperSanFrancisco, 2001], 45). Lewis defines "serious" reading much later in *Experiment,* 10–12. "Serious" readers are not grave or humorless but receptive to what the author wants to say, and they approach the text with an open mind.

35. Andrew Lazo, "'Early Prose Joy': A Brief Introduction," *VII: Journal of the Marion E. Wade Center* 30 (2013): 5.

36. "Early Prose Joy," 37–38.

there is an hours-long walk and talk on myth and Christianity he enjoyed late into the night of September 19, 1931, with two other friends, J. R. R. Tolkien and Hugo Dyson.[37] Almost everything we know about this night comes from three letters he wrote to Greeves.

In the first letter, Lewis tells him that the group ate dinner and then went out to Addison's Walk, a tree-lined path around a water-meadow in the Magdalen College grounds. As they strolled, the still autumn evening was suddenly "interrupted by a rush of wind" that showered leaves down on them like rain. They "held their breath" in "the ecstasy of such a thing."[38] I can't help but wonder if Lewis felt this immersion in the "Idea of Autumn" as Joy. He could have told Greeves that in Greek, the language in which the New Testament was written, a single word, *pneuma*, simultaneously means "wind," "breath," and "spirit." These multiple meanings hum beneath his description of the scene in the wood, almost but not quite said, like the incantation Lucy just misses getting right in *Prince Caspian* when she tries to wake the trees—whose leaves rustled even though there was "not a breath of wind."[39]

Lewis contemplates this moment on Addison's Walk over the years, drawing out its implications bit by bit. In November 1939, he uses almost the same words to describe how "real autumn" had arrived "with rocking winds and showers of leaves." The statement appears just after he recounts another talk with Tolkien, this time about "the most distressing text of the Bible," Matthew 7:14: "Narrow is the gate and difficult the road that leads to life, and few are the ones who find it."[40] In his essay "The Weight of Glory" (1941), "the leaves of the New Testament are rustling with the rumor" that the promise of Joy will someday be fulfilled.[41] In the 1950s, he hides a reference to the Holy Spirit in a whisper that was barely audible, "yet it seemed to come from all round you as if the leaves rustled with it."[42]

In his next letter to Greeves, dated October 1, 1931, Lewis casually mentions that he had accepted Christ, much influenced by the talk with Dyson and

37. *Surprised by Joy*, 235–36.

38. Lewis to Greeves, Sept. 22, 1931, *CL*, 1:970.

39. *Prince Caspian* (London: Geoffrey Bles, 1951), ch. 10. Lewis examines the multiple meanings of the Latin *anima* in "Bluspels and Flalansferes: A Semantic Nightmare," in *Selected Literary Essays*, ed. Walter Hooper (1936; repr., Cambridge: Cambridge University Press, 2013).

40. Lewis to his brother, Nov. 5, 1939, *CL*, 2:283.

41. "The Weight of Glory," in *C. S. Lewis Essay Collection: Faith, Christianity and the Church*, ed. Lesley Walmsley (London: HarperCollins, 2002), 104 (hereafter cited as *Essay Collection*).

42. *The Horse and His Boy* (London: Geoffrey Bles, 1954), ch. 11.

Tolkien. After promising to explain more later, he adds a postscript: he had just finished Romans, "the first Pauline epistle I have ever seriously read through. It contains many difficult and some horrible things."[43] He may have read Romans in Greek, just as he did John the year before. He doesn't like everything he reads in either book, but in hindsight, we can see that this state of affairs is a blessing in disguise, for it will goad him to ask *why* he doesn't like it. Some people ignore or reject Scripture they dislike, but Lewis sits with it and struggles through it until he works out the best interpretation he can. The mature Lewis will recommend this strategy to correspondents who ask him for help in reading the Bible, and it will lead to some of his best work on Scripture.

In the third letter, dated October 18, Lewis attempts to clarify his thinking about the Addison's Walk experience both to Greeves and to himself.[44] First, he reflects that what had kept him from Christian faith was not a lack of belief per se but more a lack of understanding of how Christ saved the world. He admits that one can understand how redemption might work in daily life—for example, how a drunkard would not have the power to save himself but would need the help of others.[45] He can even extrapolate the principle to see why a whole world might require some sort of outside aid. But how could someone who died 2,000 years ago help anyone now?

In the Gospels and Paul—that is, in the Scripture he had read over the past year—Lewis had found images like "the blood of the lamb" shocking and repulsive, but now he was ready to rethink them in light of what he learned from his friends on Addison's Walk. They helped him realize that he was "mysteriously moved" by the death and resurrection of any god—he names Balder and Bacchus—except Jesus because, as he writes, "I was prepared to feel the myth as profound and suggestive of meanings beyond my grasp even tho' I could not say in cold prose 'what it meant.'" In other words, Lewis could enjoy pagan myth without feeling compelled to explain it rationally, but he hadn't been able to do so with the Gospels.

Then comes the breakthrough. "Now the story of Christ is simply a true myth: a myth working on us in the same way as the others, but with this tremendous

43. Lewis to Greeves, Oct. 1, 1931, *CL*, 1:975.

44. Lewis to Greeves, Oct. 18, 1931, *CL*, 1:976–77. All quotations in the next three paragraphs are from this letter.

45. Years later, as he dealt with his brother Warren's alcoholism, Lewis wrote that it is a "rule of the universe that others can do for us what we cannot do for ourselves. . . . That is why Christ's suffering *for us* is not a mere theological dodge, but the supreme case of the law that governs the whole world . . . [and] the ultimate law of the spiritual world." Lewis to Greeves, July 2, 1949, *CL*, 2:953.

difference that *it really happened*: and one must be content to accept it in the same way." Many readers have focused on the words Lewis emphasized, but what follows them is just as important: to Lewis, the "same way" of accepting the story of Christ means accepting it as story. He knew that the ancient Greek word *mythos* meant "story," and the story could be true or false. God chose to speak to humanity through the true story embodied in Christ, and this myth, just as it is, will always be better than any abstract formulation built upon it. He continues, "The 'doctrines' we get *out* of true myth are of course *less* true: they are translations into our *concepts* and *ideas*," what God has "expressed in a language more adequate, namely the actual incarnation, crucifixion, and resurrection." Lewis will hold this opinion the rest of his life: human "doctrine" is but a shadow of "true myth," and it is never as good as myth. Story trumps doctrine every time.

The question of what the Gospels are, why they were written, and how they express Christian truth occupies Lewis over the next few months, and by the end of 1931 he comes up with an answer that satisfies. In his opinion, the reason why the abstract doctrine of the atonement, as opposed to the narrative/mythic portrayals of Jesus's death, is not articulated in the Gospels is because the Gospels were written later than Paul's letters, which did teach it. According to Lewis, the Gospels were written for those who had accepted the "*doctrines* and naturally wanted the *story*."[46]

At the beginning of 1932 he takes up the topic again, in response to Greeves's cousin, who argues that the authors of the Gospels would have included the doctrine of the atonement if they had known about it. Since they didn't include it, they didn't know it, and that means Jesus didn't teach it. Lewis will have none of this: the New Testament epistles portray the apostles as teaching about the atonement, and they must have learned about it from Jesus, he retorts.[47]

Some of what Lewis argues above is standard biblical scholarship, but most of it is speculative by any estimation. Everyone agrees that Paul's epistles predate the Gospels and that the epistles discuss the meaning of Jesus's death far more than the Gospels do. The Gospels may (or may not—see John 20:31) have been written for those who already followed Christ. Lewis writes that "nearly everyone" thinks so, an opinion he may have drawn from the biblical scholars James Moffatt and Charles Gore (discussed in the next chapter).[48]

46. Lewis to Greeves, Dec. 6, 1931, *CL*, 2:22 (emphasis in original).

47. Lewis to Greeves, Jan. 10, 1932, *CL*, 2:35.

48. Moffatt, *The Theology of the Gospels* (London: Duckworth, 1912), 4: "But fundamentally [the Gospels'] audience is one of those who believe already." Gore writes that the New Testament was "addressed to men who were already Christians," who had "already received oral instruction." Gore, *The Incarnation of the Son of God*, ed.

But his major conceptual leap—that the Gospel writers purposely left out "doctrine" because their audience already knew it and wanted the story—has no basis in the facts as we know them.

Lewis was only a months-old Christian when he wrote this in private correspondence, but the idea stayed with him, and he published it in his introduction to J. B. Phillips's book *Letters to Young Churches: A Translation of the New Testament Epistles* (1947). Contrasting the Gospels to the Epistles, he notes that the Gospels are not the "statement of the Christian belief. They were written for those who had already been converted. . . . They leave out many of the 'complications' (that is, the theology)" because their readers "have already been instructed in it."[49]

Mere Christianity (1952) repackages the struggles Lewis describes to Greeves in 1931–1932, leading him in a different direction. Before his conversion, Lewis had thought "the first thing Christians had to believe was one particular theory" about Christ's death. But abstract theories are "not themselves the thing you are asked to accept." With this claim, Lewis steps off a traditionally Protestant path and moves into Eastern Orthodox territory, where there is less defined doctrine on the issue, but he still has to answer the question that naturally follows: What must Christians accept, then? He responds, "Christ was killed for us, His death has washed out our sins, and by dying He disabled death itself. That is the formula. That is Christianity."[50]

Here, too, Lewis stands on ground dominated by the Eastern Orthodox, whose paschal liturgy proclaims again and again, "Christ is risen from the dead, trampling down death by death." As he puts it in his book *Miracles*, death is "the thing Christ came to conquer and the means by which He conquered."[51] Lewis was not Eastern Orthodox, but he had friends who were, and he admired many aspects of their faith and especially their practice. After attending part of a church service in Greece with his wife, Joy, in 1960, he said he "preferred the Orthodox liturgy to either the Catholic or Protestant."[52] He gave lectures

---

Christopher Poore, Library of Anglican Theology 2 (Galesburg, IL: Seminary Street, 2021), 145; Lewis to Greeves, Dec. 6, 1931, *CL*, 2:22.

49. C. S. Lewis, introduction to *Letters to Young Churches*, by J. B. Phillips (New York: Macmillan, 1947), ix–x. For more on Phillips and Lewis, see E. H. Robertson, "J. B. Phillips: Translator," *Expository Times* 95, no. 10 (1984): 300–304.

50. *Mere Christianity*, 54–56. Gore addresses this perception in his commentary: "In old-fashioned Evangelical pulpits 'preaching Christ' came to mean preaching what was supposed to be St. Paul's doctrine of justification and atonement." Charles Gore, "The Teaching of Our Lord Jesus Christ," in *NCHS*, part 1, 276.

51. *Miracles* (1947; repr., New York: Macmillan, 1960), 125.

52. Sayer, *Jack*, 378. See also *Letters to Malcolm: Chiefly on Prayer* (New York: Harcourt, Brace & World, 1964), 10.

to the Society of St. Alban and St. Sergius in Oxford, which was founded to promote understanding between Eastern Orthodox and Anglican Christians, clear evidence of his engaging them in dialogue. These conversations may have continued informally—for example, at Lewis's home, where Militza Zernov, one of the founders of the society, took "official" photographs of Jack and Joy after their marriage, and at the Zernov residence, where Militza and her husband Nicolas hosted a salon that Lewis attended regularly, presenting papers and participating enthusiastically in discussion.[53] Nicolas Zernov, the Spalding Lecturer in Eastern Orthodox Culture at Oxford, presented Lewis with a copy of his book on Christian unity "in gratitude for his friendship," and Lewis read it cover to cover.[54] Throughout this book we will hear him echo interpretations of Scripture that lean Eastern Orthodox, whether he knew it or not. I am not the first to notice it,[55] but our focus on the Bible will bring it out in new ways, beginning with the next chapter, where we see Lewis introduced to the work of John Chrysostom as mediated through the scholarship of Charles Gore.

53. Walter Hooper, *Through Joy and Beyond: A Pictorial Biography of C. S. Lewis* (New York: Macmillan, 1982), 138–39. Reports differ as to whether the "Zernov circle" met weekly or monthly, on a Wednesday or a Saturday. See Dwain Tissell, "C. S. Lewis's Most Important Message: The Abolition of Man as Lewis's Self-Conscious Struggle for the Value of Human Persons," *Sehnsucht* 18, no. 1 (2024); James Houston, "Reminiscences of the Oxford Lewis," *The Lamp-Post of the Southern California C. S. Lewis Society* 7, no. 2 (1983): 6–12. Houston, who was part of the "Zernov circle," reports that Anthony Bloom, later Metropolitan Anthony of Sourozh, bishop of the Russian Orthodox diocese of Great Britain and Ireland, was an occasional visitor, as were monks from Mount Athos. Houston, "Reminiscences of the Oxford Lewis," in *We Remember C. S. Lewis: Essays and Memoirs*, ed. David Graham (Nashville: Broadman & Holman, 2001), 131. See also Jason Lepojärvi, "C. S. Lewis on Female Scholars: A Reply to John D. Rateliff," *Journal of Inklings Studies* 14, no. 1 (2024): 76, and Henry Lee Poe, *The Completion of C. S. Lewis: From War to Joy (1945–1963)* (Wheaton, IL: Crossway. 2022), 115–17. Poe notes that the biblical scholar Austin Farrer and theologian Eric Mascall were also regular participants at the Zernov gatherings.

54. Nicolas Zernov, *The Reintegration of the Church: A Study in Intercommunion* (London: SCM, 1952).

55. See Kallistos Ware, "C. S. Lewis, an 'Anonymous Orthodox'?," in *C. S. Lewis and the Church*, ed. Judith Wolfe and Brendan N. Wolfe (London: T&T Clark, 2011), 135–53, and Edith M. Humphrey, *Further Up and Further In: Orthodox Conversations with C. S. Lewis on Scripture and Theology* (Yonkers, NY: St. Vladimir's Seminary Press, 2017).

2. READING ABOUT SCRIPTURE

The 1930s

Thus far a scanty record is deduced
Of what I owed to Books in early life;
Their later influence yet remains untold.

—William Wordsworth[1]

Anyone familiar with Lewis's essay "Modern Theology and Biblical Criticism," a spirited critique of the title subject, may be forgiven for thinking that he rejected contemporary scholarship on the Bible, but in fact, he read a good deal of it from the late 1920s into the 1930s, and it was a practice he maintained throughout his life.[2] *Surprised by Joy* has much to say about the books that led Lewis back to Christ, but nothing about what he read specifically on Scripture. For this, we must consult his letters and his personal library, where we find him perusing the books of Matthew Arnold, Friedrich von Hügel, Gustaf Aulén, James Moffatt, and Charles Gore.[3] Moffatt and Gore, biblical scholars whose prolific output was well known in early

1. *The Prelude,* book 5, lines 630–32, in Wordsworth, *The Prelude, or Growth of a Poet's Mind (Text of 1805),* ed. Ernest de Selincourt (London: Oxford University Press, 1960).

2. Lewis, "Modern Theology and Biblical Criticism," in *Christian Reflections,* ed. Walter Hooper (Grand Rapids: Eerdmans, 1967), 152–66; hereafter cited as "MTBC." This essay will be treated in depth in chapter 7.

3. "Contemporary" biblical scholarship for Lewis would certainly include material written in the prior fifty years, and probably in the prior century. See Arnold, *St. Paul and Protestantism: With Other Essays* (London: Smith, Elder, 1892), which, according to handwriting analysis, Lewis read between January 1929 and July 1930; von Hügel, *Essays and Addresses on the Philosophy of Religion,* series 1 (London: J. M. Dent and Sons, 1928), read shortly after it was published; Aulén, *Christus Victor: An Historical Study of the Three Main Types of the Idea of the Atonement,* trans. A. G. Hebert (London: SPCK, 1931), which Lewis marked as finished in 1936; Moffatt, *The Theology of the Gospels* (London: Duckworth, 1912); and the books by Gore cited below.

twentieth-century Britain, made a particularly strong impact on his thought. In an unconscious gift to future scholars of his work, Lewis often marked up the books he read, underlining, writing marginal notes, and making lists of topics on the flyleaves. What he marks in these books foreshadows how he will interpret the Bible, and especially the Gospel of John, ever after.[4]

James Moffatt

Lewis probably read Moffatt's *The Theology of the Gospels* (1912) around 1930–1931, on the cusp of his conversion, a timeframe that may be estimated by analyzing his handwritten notes in the book. The singular "Theology" of the "Gospels" (plural) in Moffatt's title signals that he will argue for unity across diversity. Although he does acknowledge differences among the four Gospels, Moffatt also insists on their continuity, not only across the three Synoptics—Matthew, Mark, and Luke—but even between the Synoptics and John. For example, Moffatt thinks that John 20:31, "These are written that you may believe that Jesus is the Christ, the Son of God, and that believing you may have life in his name," may "not unfairly" be understood as "the motto for all the four gospels." The problem with this claim is that the Synoptics never use the word "believe" in the context of "believing in Jesus." As a seasoned biblical scholar, Moffatt knew this, a fact he notes later in the book: "It is faith in God rather than faith in Himself which is uppermost in [Jesus's] teaching. His divine authority invests Him with a unique claim, but the explicit allusions to faith in Himself are scanty" in the Synoptics. In fact, the allusions are so scanty that Moffatt can cite only two, both of which dissolve under scrutiny. At the same time, he argues that "The germs of [John's theology] may be found within the theology of the synoptic gospels."[5]

The distinction Moffatt makes between John and the Synoptics is important, and it will be important throughout this book. The three Synoptic Gospels are so called because they often "look the same," setting out many of the same stories of Jesus, sometimes in the same words. John is not counted among them because it differs from them so much.[6] Some Christians, disturbed by

4. Lewis's handwriting changed in distinctive ways over the years. I am indebted to the work of Charlie Starr, "'Villainous Handwriting': A Chronological Study of C. S. Lewis's Script," *VII: Journal of the Marion E. Wade Center* 33 (2016): 73–94, and grateful for his help in dating Lewis's handwriting throughout this book.

5. *Theology of the Gospels*, 3, 173, 29.

6. See Lewis to his brother (Oct. 24, 1931), *CL*, 2:9, where he critiques a sermon that called the Gospel of Luke "artistic" in contrast to the "purely *facty* nature of the other two synoptics, or the mystical nature" of John.

these differences, have tried to harmonize them, weaving the narratives together in an attempt to produce a seamless whole. Depending on one's social circle, harmonization is either a welcome solution to the problem or an abomination to be avoided at all costs. Almost all academic biblical scholars reject it, since it flattens the four unique Gospels with their four distinct portraits of Jesus into a single unified witness.

Harmonizers also set themselves at odds with the decisions of the early church. Fully aware of how each Gospel differs from the others, early Christians canonized all four. Renowned Christian leaders like John Chrysostom (d. 407) did not ignore the issue but placed it front and center in their work. In his first homily on Matthew, for example, Chrysostom asks why there are four Gospels. "Wouldn't one suffice?" he imagines an opponent objecting. Yes, Chrysostom answers, but look: here are four writers who didn't collaborate as they wrote, yet they say the same things about Jesus. This fact is a "great demonstration of their truth." "But," the imagined opponent interrupts, "they actually don't say the same things." Chrysostom responds, "This very thing is a great evidence of their truth." For if they agreed with one another "in all things exactly even to time and place and to the very words," enemies of the faith would accuse the evangelists of colluding to get their stories straight. The differences among them "deliver them from all suspicion and speak clearly on behalf of the character of the writers." Discrepancies as to times and places in the Gospels aren't important, Chrysostom says, because "in the chief subjects, those which constitute our life and make up our doctrine," there is no disagreement.[7] In other words, some contradiction among the Gospels actually serves to underscore their historical reliability.

Centuries later, the woman Lewis would marry, Joy Davidman, employs a similar argument. "Fiction is always congruous, life usually incongruous. . . . Lies, being planned, have that same congruousness and extra effectiveness" that never happen in real life. "The Gospels are full of these little incongruities," she notes, and that is why she trusts them.[8]

Harmonizing the Gospels plasters over the incongruities, suppressing ambiguous, divergent, and difficult passages, thus creating a work that no evangelist actually wrote. Moffatt, himself a respected biblical scholar,[9] was well aware of his peers' hostility to harmonization, but he thought the backlash against it

7. Chrysostom, *Homilies on Matthew* 1.6. Of course, Chrysostom is not altogether correct regarding the Gospels' chief doctrinal subjects, as we will see particularly in chapter 8 of this book.

8. Davidman to Chad Walsh, Jan. 27, 1950, in Don W. King, ed., *Out of My Bone: The Letters of Joy Davidman* (Grand Rapids: Eerdmans, 2009), 112.

9. "Moffatt, James, 1870–1944," *Journal of Biblical Literature* 64 (1945): xi–xii.

had gone too far—so far, in fact, that he imagines the ancient authors rising up to condemn the antiharmonizers![10] As Edward Hincks, who reviewed the book, wrote, Moffatt argues that "Jesus, Mark, Matthew, Luke, and John, give us one theology. . . . There is no essential difference, it is urged, between the various conceptions of Christ. The latest is the earliest in a more developed form."[11] To Moffatt, the through-line that connects and unifies all four Gospels is "the filial consciousness of Jesus": Jesus's knowledge that he is the Son of God.[12]

Moffatt's thesis did not survive peer review. Hincks observes, "If Dr. Moffatt means by this that the Johannine Christology is, to use his own word, 'implicit' in the filial consciousness of Jesus, he makes an assertion which many candid readers of the Gospels will be unable to accept. . . . The unsupported assumption is a serious defect in a book professedly giving results drawn from facts by historical methods." John portrays Jesus's self-understanding as "son" differently than the Synoptics do, and this is not a "little incongruity." But Hincks is not entirely negative. Moffatt's book also has its strong points, and Hincks praises its treatment of Jesus as Son of Man in particular.[13] Moffatt does well with this topic, and chapter 8 of this book will show how Lewis both embraces and ignores his work on it. But Moffatt's argument for harmonizing the Gospels through the "filial consciousness" of Jesus seems to have vanished without a trace—except insofar as it affected C. S. Lewis. On the top of the page where Moffatt begins to address "filial consciousness," Lewis writes "Consciousness of Sonship >< Messianic Consciousness."[14] By this I think he means that Jesus knew he was both son and messiah, a conviction Lewis will defend militantly for the rest of his life. Furthermore, inspired perhaps by Moffatt's argument on the unified theology of John and the Synoptics, Lewis will ignore most of the places where Moffatt contrasted them, and he will harmonize the Gospels' different Christologies, a practice that culminates in his claim that Jesus went about calling himself divine just as much in the Synoptics as he did in John—a claim Moffatt explicitly denies.[15]

10. *Theology of the Gospels*, 29.

11. Edward Y. Hincks, review of *The Theology of the Gospels*, by James Moffatt, *Harvard Theological Review* 7, no. 4 (1914): 601–3.

12. *Theology of the Gospels*, 176.

13. Hincks, review of *Theology of the Gospels*, 602–3.

14. *Theology of the Gospels*, 130.

15. Lewis, "Rejoinder to Dr Pittenger," in *God in the Dock: Essays on Theology and Ethics*, ed. Walter Hooper (Grand Rapids: Eerdmans, 1970), 180; *Theology of the Gospels*, 137. See chapter 8 of this book for Lewis's argument.

The Theology of the Gospels isn't the only book by Moffatt that Lewis owned. He also read and recommended his translations of the Bible,[16] and the preface to his copy of Moffatt's New Testament states another view Lewis held all his life: Scripture should be "freed from the influence of the theory of verbal inspiration."[17] The phrase "verbal inspiration" has been understood variously over time, but Lewis will take it to mean "mechanical inspiration" or "dictation theory," the idea that God dictated the words of Scripture to its human authors, who wrote them down.[18] Arguments against it had emerged in the Anglican world well before Moffatt, and when Lewis was a young adult they were closely associated with Charles Gore.

In 1933, Lewis urges Greeves to drop everything and buy Gore's *Jesus of Nazareth* (1929), which he calls the best theological book he has read yet.[19] Gore's book serves to correct some of Moffatt's deficiencies, including Moffatt's tendency to harmonize the Gospels. Gore states flatly that the relationship between the Synoptics and John is fraught with difficulty. For example, when Gore looks at one of the most consequential differences between them, the discrepancy about the day Jesus was crucified, he sides with John: Jesus was crucified on the day before Passover, as John reports, rather than the day of Passover, as the Synoptic Gospels say (compare Mark 14:14 to John 19:14, 31).[20] Differences between the Synoptics and John don't bother Gore because, he says, when the Gospels were being composed, "plainly there was so far no idea of the literal infallibility of the Gospel records." The Synoptics do not always

16. Lewis to Mary Neylan, March 26, 1940, *CL*, 2:375; his introduction to *Letters to Young Churches: A Translation of the New Testament Epistles*, by J. B. Phillips (New York: Macmillan, 1947), ix; and *Miracles* (1947; repr., New York: Macmillan, 1960), 164.

17. James Moffatt, *The New Testament: A New Translation* (New York: Hodder & Stoughton, 1913), v. Lewis's personal copy that I cite throughout this book is held at the Wilson Special Collections Library at the University of North Carolina–Chapel Hill.

18. See Roland H. Bainton, "The Bible in the Reformation," in *The Cambridge History of the Bible*, vol. 3, *The West from the Reformation to the Present Day*, ed. S. L. Greenslade (Cambridge: Cambridge University Press, 1963), 12–21. Lewis owned and read this book. For brief definitions of "verbal inspiration" and related terms, see Donald K. McKim, *The Westminster Dictionary of Theological Terms* (Louisville: Westminster John Knox, 1996), 144–45.

19. Lewis to Greeves, Sept. 12, 1933, *CL*, 2:125.

20. Charles Gore, *Jesus of Nazareth* (1929; repr., Oxford: Oxford University Press, 1950), 32, 106. For more detail on the differences between the Synoptics and John, see Paula Fredriksen, *Jesus of Nazareth, King of the Jews* (New York: Vintage Books, 1999), ch. 1, "Gospel Truth and Historical Innocence."

agree with each other, and "reconciliations of their apparent discrepancies are often forced and improbable. On such grounds we have felt constrained to give up the theory of miraculous infallibility."[21]

Gore does believe the New Testament contains "good history," and a text that does not enjoy "miraculous infallibility" is divinely inspired.[22] He begs his readers to remember that the church never held a council on scriptural infallibility, a topic that doesn't appear in the creed.[23] Gore never budges on this issue. In the biblical commentary Lewis recommended to Greeves in 1944, Gore insists: "No doubt we need to deal critically with our material. It is mere folly to seek to represent everything in the four Gospels as verbally and infallibly true, or as on the same uniform level of trustworthiness merely because it is there. The facts are against any such view."[24]

While Lewis agrees with Gore and Moffatt in rejecting the verbal infallibility of the Bible, he applies it more consistently to the Old Testament than to the New. Although he does acknowledge a few discrepancies among the Gospels (e.g., in the genealogies of Jesus in Matthew and Luke), he prefers to harmonize them and accept their trustworthiness without question.[25] This tendency might have been encouraged by George MacDonald, one of the most formative influences on his Christian life. The story of teenage Lewis's first encounter with MacDonald, when he picked up the book *Phantastes*, is foundational Lewisian lore. Some thirty years later, he published an anthology of MacDonald's writings, wherein he calls the Scot his "master."[26] MacDonald's nonfiction offers examples of his harmonizing approach to the Synoptics. He sees that the story of the rich young man in Matthew 19:16–22 is "very different" from its parallels in Mark and Luke. But "there is not for that the smallest necessity for rejecting either account; they blend perfectly, and it is to me a joy unspeakable to have both. Put together they give a complete conversation." Likewise, when MacDonald looks at Matthew on the one hand and Luke and Mark on the other regarding the healing of the bleeding woman (Matt. 9:20–22; Luke 8:43–48;

21. *Jesus of Nazareth*, 125–26. The next section on how the idea of verbal inspiration developed is absurd, but his main point stands.

22. *Jesus of Nazareth*, 126; Gore, "The Bible in the Church," in *NCHS*, part 1, 15.

23. *Jesus of Nazareth*, 126.

24. Gore, "The Teaching of Our Lord Jesus Christ with an Outline of His Life," in *NCHS*, part 1, 277.

25. Lewis to Clyde Kilby, May 7, 1959, *CL*, 3:1045.

26. *Surprised by Joy*, 179–81; Lewis, *George MacDonald: An Anthology* (1946; repr., New York: HarperCollins, 2001), xxxvii.

Mark 5:25–34), he writes, "No perplexity arises from the difference between the accounts, for there is only difference, not incongruity: the two tell more than the one."[27] In many other aspects of his biblical interpretation, however, Lewis follows Gore, so it is important to know more about him and his work.

Charles Gore

Charles Gore (1853–1932), Anglican priest, theologian, prolific author, and bishop of Oxford, was and still is best known for the collection of essays he edited in 1889, *Lux Mundi*, which was published in response to the biblical scholarship that began to emerge from Germany in the eighteenth century and became impossible to ignore in the nineteenth.[28] Today the book is remembered mainly for Gore's chapter "The Holy Spirit and Inspiration." This chapter received more attention than the rest of the volume combined, igniting immediate controversy with its claim that there was nothing to fear from German biblical scholarship, even if certain elements of it—such as the argument that Moses didn't write the Pentateuch or doubting the historicity of the book of Jonah—might appear to contradict what Jesus said in the Gospels.

After the controversy died down, the chapter emerged not only unscathed, but even as a hallmark of Anglican thought, so much so that Gore, initially considered a "scandalous radical in connection with biblical criticism," was widely viewed as a conservative long before he died in 1932.[29] Gore had "identified the most controversial issue of the day and encountered the most immediate resistance. However, his ideas won the day, preventing Anglicans from falling into the debacle of Roman Catholicism in the early part of the 20th c[entury]. His positions became 'an unquestionably legitimate, if not the actually definitive, form of Anglicanism.'"[30] As a result, Gore found himself "a great theological power" in the Church of England.[31]

27. MacDonald, *Unspoken Sermons*, series 2 (London: Longmans, Green, 1885), 2; *The Miracles of Our Lord* (London: Longmans, Green, 1896), 25.

28. Charles Gore, ed., *Lux Mundi: A Series of Studies in the Religion of the Incarnation* (London: John Murray, 1889).

29. Peter Waddell, *Charles Gore: Radical Anglican* (Norwich: Canterbury, 2014), xix.

30. John Muddiman, "The Holy Spirit and Inspiration," in *The Religion of the Incarnation: Anglican Essays in Commemoration of "Lux Mundi,"* ed. Robert Morgan (Bristol: Bristol Classical Press, 1989), 119.

31. Michael Ramsey, *An Era in Anglican Theology: From Gore to Temple; The Devel-*

It is hard to overstate how much Gore's work influenced Lewis. He owned a copy of *Lux Mundi*, but such was its ongoing force in the Anglican world that he didn't have to read it to be affected by it. Point by point, ideas about Scripture that may look distinctive to Lewis can be traced back to Gore.

Lux Mundi is subtitled "A Series of Studies in the Religion of the Incarnation," and for both men, Christ's incarnation stands at the center of everything. In Gore's preface to the tenth edition, where he responds to his critics, he writes that one should not think of Christianity as

> a "religion of a book" in such sense that it is supposed to propose for men's acceptance a volume to be received in all its parts as on the same level, and in the same sense, Divine. On the contrary, Christianity is a religion of a Person. . . . The test question of the Church to her catechumens has never been: "Dost thou believe the Bible?" but "Dost thou believe that Jesus Christ is the Son of God?" If we do believe that, then we shall further believe in the Bible: in the Old Testament as recording how God prepared the way for Christ.[32]

There are four points to emphasize relative to Lewis. First is the centrality of the incarnation, the Son of God made flesh, which permeates his work. Second, Gore proposes that the entire Bible is not "divine" in the same way, a conviction Lewis adopts for himself. Third, Gore believes that the Old Testament records "how God prepared the way for Christ," another key idea in Lewis's biblical theology.

Before we move to the fourth point, it will be helpful to discuss the term "Old Testament." The Christian Old Testament, while overlapping in many ways with the Jewish Hebrew Scriptures, is in others quite different. A major difference between them is how they order their constituent books. The Hebrew Scriptures conclude with Chronicles, the last verses of which announce the end of the Babylonian exile, inviting the Jews to go up to Jerusalem and rebuild their temple. The Babylonian exile and the destruction of the first temple are watershed events in Jewish history, and the last book of the Hebrew Scriptures looks forward to restoration. The Christian Old Testament, on the other hand, concludes with Malachi, the final verses of which promise the return of the prophet Elijah before "the great and terrible day of the Lord." The

---

opment of Anglican Theology between "Lux Mundi" and the Second World War, 1889–1939 (New York: Scribner, 1960; repr., Eugene, OR: Wipf & Stock, 2009), 13.

32. *Lux Mundi*, 10th ed. (London: John Murray, 1890), xxxv–xxxvi.

Synoptic Gospels equate Elijah with John the Baptist, the forerunner of Jesus, so this ordering of books encourages Christians to consider, as Gore puts it, "how God prepared the way for Christ." Because they are not entirely the same, "Old Testament" will refer to the Christian version and "Hebrew Scriptures" to the Jewish in this book.

The fourth point is the fact that Jesus, not Scripture, is the word of God. As Gore observes, no baptismal rite ever asked a catechumen, "Do you believe in the Bible?" The question has always been "Do you believe in Jesus?" Lewis gives a similar response to a correspondent who asks if the Bible is infallible, answering, "It is Christ Himself, not the Bible, who is the true word of God."[33] He may also have been influenced by MacDonald on the topic. In his anthology, Lewis quotes MacDonald's insistence that Scripture "nowhere lays claim to be regarded as *the* Word, *the* Way, *the* Truth. The Bible leads us to Jesus, the inexhaustible, the ever unfolding Revelation of God. It is Christ 'in whom are hid all the treasures of wisdom and knowledge,' not the Bible, save as leading to him."[34] We will look at controversies about this claim in chapter 5.

Since Gore argues that God's revelation is not a book, but a person, the real question is "whether the Divine claim made for Jesus Christ by the Church is historically justified. . . . If Christ be God, the Son of God, incarnate, as the Creeds assert, Christianity is true."[35] Incarnational theology is just as important to Lewis as it is to Gore, and Lewis will take it even further. Gore notes that *the church* through its *creeds* proclaims Jesus "God" and "Son of God."[36] Lewis will write that Jesus makes divine claims for *himself* in the Gospels, expressing this most famously in his "liar, lunatic, or Lord" argument.

Gore's emphasis on the incarnation stamped itself on Anglicanism for decades. Archbishop of Canterbury Michael Ramsey explains, "It is almost a commonplace that a theology of Incarnation prevailed in Anglican divinity from the last decade of the reign of Queen Victoria until well into the new century."[37] Like everyone else, Lewis was influenced by his social context, and he

33. Lewis to Mrs. Johnson, Nov. 8, 1952, *CL*, 3:246.

34. MacDonald, *Unspoken Sermons*, series 1 (1867; repr., London: Longmans, Green, 1890), 52–53; Lewis, *George MacDonald*, 6.

35. *Lux Mundi*, 10th ed., xxviii.

36. See Gore, *The New Theology and the Old Religion* (London: John Murray, 1907), 101–6, for how he explains continuity between the New Testament and creedal formulations on the divinity of Jesus. Lewis never addresses the issue; he simply assumes a one-to-one correlation between the New Testament and the creeds.

37. Ramsey, *Era in Anglican Theology*, 16.

was far from alone in emphasizing the incarnation as the key to understanding the world, the "Grand Miracle" that makes sense of everything.[38]

If Jesus was incarnate, he was human, but how human was he? And if, as the Council of Chalcedon asserted in 451, he is both fully human and fully divine, what did the human Jesus know? How did his state of knowledge during the incarnation interact with his divinity? To answer these questions, Gore emphasizes the kenosis, or self-emptying, of Christ. The classic biblical text is Philippians 2:7, where Christ "emptied (Greek *kenoō*) himself, taking the form of a slave." The way Gore applies kenosis to the state of Jesus's knowledge provoked one of the biggest controversies about "The Holy Spirit and Inspiration," and Lewis would follow him exactly.

According to Gore, Jesus did not want to reveal his divinity through any superhuman knowledge he might possess. Rather, "the Incarnation was a self-emptying of God to reveal Himself under conditions of human nature and from the human point of view."[39] Jesus's knowledge was limited. When he talked about the sun "rising," for example, he used "ordinary human knowledge. He willed so to restrain the beams of Deity as to observe the limits of the science of His age, and He puts Himself in the same relation to its historical knowledge." Jesus allowed people to recognize his divinity gradually "by his moral and spiritual claims," not by dazzling them with a show of supernatural knowledge.[40]

When Lewis writes about Jesus for a popular audience, he doesn't use the term "kenosis," but he includes the idea nonetheless. In his first book of apologetics, *The Problem of Pain* (1940)—a title that replicates the title of *Lux Mundi*'s third chapter, "The Problem of Pain: Its Bearing on Faith in God"—Lewis follows Gore's lead on how the kenosis of Christ affects what Jesus knows:

> It might be argued that when He emptied Himself of His glory He also humbled Himself to share, as a man, the current superstitions of His time. And I certainly think that Christ, in the flesh, was not omniscient—if only because a human brain could not, presumably, be the vehicle of omniscient consciousness, and to say that Our Lord's thinking was not really conditioned by the size and shape of His brain might be to deny the real incarnation and become a Docetist. Thus, if Our Lord had committed Himself

38. Ramsey, *Era in Anglican Theology*, 9; Lewis, "The Grand Miracle," in *Essay Collection*; see also *Miracles*, ch. 14.

39. Gore, "The Holy Spirit and Inspiration," in Gore, *Lux Mundi*, 10th ed., 264.

40. Gore, "Holy Spirit," 265.

> to any scientific or historical statement which we knew to be untrue, this would not disturb my faith in His deity.[41]

To Lewis, Jesus was fully human, and therefore not omniscient. To think otherwise flirts with Docetism, the idea that Jesus only *seemed* to be human but really wasn't. God incarnate could be as wrong about history and science as any other human being and still be divine.

Eleven years after publishing *The Problem of Pain,* Lewis builds on the idea in his essay "The World's Last Night." Jesus could make mistakes not only about history and science but even about "religious" things like the timing of the end, as when he said, "This generation will not pass away until all of these things have taken place" (Mark 13:30). Lewis calls it "the most embarrassing verse in the Bible." But—O happy fault!—this verse, along with Mark 15:34 ("My God, my God, why have you forsaken me?"), convince him that the New Testament is "historically reliable." Why would Mark include words that reflect so poorly on Jesus unless Jesus had said them? With this argument Lewis anticipates the "criterion of embarrassment" that biblical scholars have used to evaluate the historicity of the Gospels: if something reflects poorly on Jesus, but the Gospel writers chose to include it anyway, it is more likely to be true.[42]

Although the two men often concur, Gore proves himself a more astute interpreter of Scripture than Lewis will ever be. The most important difference between them is that Gore readily acknowledges discrepancies among the Gospels, but Lewis rarely does. At the same time, Gore insists upon the Gospels' essential historical truth. He can claim solid support from early Christians who held these two concepts, discrepancy and historicity, in tandem, by citing someone we have already noted: "Chrysostom, of the literal school of interpreters, explains quite in the tone of a modern apologist, how the discrepancies in detail

41. *The Problem of Pain* (1940; repr., New York: Macmillan, 1944), 122. The French edition (1950) adds a footnote after "Docetist": "I now consider the conception of the Incarnation implied in this paragraph as gross and the result of ignorance" (*Essay Collection,* 296). The footnote is puzzling in light of how Lewis built upon the paragraph's Christology in "The World's Last Night" (1951). Equally puzzling is what Lewis writes in his "Rejoinder to Dr Pittenger," 177. Pittenger had accused Lewis of Docetism and Apollinarianism. Apollinarians believed that Jesus had a divine mind, not a human one. In his rejoinder, Lewis agrees that there is Apollinarianism in *The Problem of Pain,* but he tried to correct it in a footnote in the French edition (i.e., the one quoted above). But there is no Apollinarianism in the paragraph—quite the opposite.

42. "The World's Last Night," in *Essay Collection,* 45. For the criterion of embarrassment, see John P. Meier, *A Marginal Jew* (New York: Doubleday, 1991), 168–71.

between the different Gospels, assure us of the independence of the witnesses, and do not touch the facts of importance, in which all agree."[43]

When he talks about the historicity of Scripture, Gore relies on Mark and Luke, whom he believes had no agenda other than to "record things as they happened."[44] In reading these two Gospels, Gore says, "we shall find ourselves on the most solid historical ground. Nothing, I think, could resist this conviction, except a dogmatic presupposition that the supernatural things there recorded cannot have actually happened."[45]

Gore published *Lux Mundi* to face up to German scholarship and take as much good from it as he could. He thought the church had more to gain from engaging the Germans than by ignoring or condemning them—even bringing up the Galileo affair as a cautionary tale he did not want to repeat.[46] But he drew the line at denying the possibility of miracles. Gore, and Lewis after him, affirmed New Testament miracles, and both believed that the presence of a miracle in a biblical text did not by itself render it unhistorical. A book like Jonah may be deemed unhistorical on "literary or evidential grounds,"[47] Gore writes, but that was a different thing than rejecting its historicity because of an "*a priori* refusal of the supernatural or miraculous."[48] When Lewis writes his book *Miracles,* responds to personal letters that ask him about the Bible, and delivers his talk "Modern Theology and Biblical Criticism," he will repeat Gore's arguments down to the very books of the Bible he cites as examples.

Gore's assessment of John is more complex than his views on Mark and Luke. He thinks John knew the Synoptics and wrote his own Gospel to "supplement and occasionally correct" them. John preserves "very real and important features in our Lord's teaching" that the Synoptics don't.[49] But Gore "cannot resist the impression" that the Synoptics present the way Jesus taught more accurately than John does. For example, although Gore thinks the *content* of Jesus's long discourses in John comes from Jesus, their *form* reflects the end result of John's "memory and meditation."[50] Thus Gore believes that "the

43. Gore, "Holy Spirit," 263.

44. Gore, *Belief in God* (New York: Charles Scribner's Sons, 1922), 215.

45. Gore, *Belief in God,* 204.

46. Gore, "Holy Spirit," 262, 265–66.

47. Gore, "Holy Spirit," 261.

48. Gore, "Teaching of Our Lord," 277.

49. Gore, *Belief in God,* 203–4.

50. Gore, *The Epistles of St. John* (London: John Murray, 1920), 4–35; see also *Lux Mundi,* 12th ed. (London: John Murray, 1891), 255.

differences between the records of the different evangelists make it impossible to suppose that in all cases we have got the *ipsissima verba* of the Lord."[51] At the same time, the Gospels are true to history on "all essential points"[52] because John is "interpreting and not distorting . . . the claims of Jesus Christ."[53] As an interpretation of Jesus's teaching, John's Gospel doesn't preserve Christ's very words, but its main points are rooted in history.

Gore and Lewis end up in the same vicinity regarding their belief in the historicity of John's content, even while Gore directs a sharper eye to how it differs from that of the Synoptics. To Gore, John's words may be true to history in a general sense without being exactly what Christ said. Gore could never call the words of Jesus in John "reportage," as Lewis does in "Modern Theology and Biblical Criticism" (see chapter 7).[54]

They also converge in their belief that "Scripture must be read in the same spirit in which it was written." The mere presence of a book in the Bible doesn't guarantee its historicity, because its author may have composed it as fiction. However, with the exception of stories like the parables of Jesus, both men think that fiction in the Bible is confined to the Old Testament. Gore, and Lewis after him, highlight Job and Jonah as premier examples, arguing that both are at the same time fictional and inspired. Furthermore, Gore says, although it may be true that no ancient writer called Job or Jonah "fiction," that doesn't mean the idea is an illegitimate new-fangled assertion. Literary criticism, like the scientific method, develops and improves over time, and just because prior generations didn't consider Jonah fiction doesn't mean that it isn't. He can rightly remind his readers of esteemed early Christians like Clement, Origen, and Anselm, who did not take the whole of the Old Testament as historical fact—especially the six days of creation in Genesis.[55]

These six days bring us to the genre of myth. Lewis may have developed his theories on myth and the Bible before reading Gore, and he does much more with them than Gore ever does, but here, too, they agree. Gore explains that "a myth is not a falsehood" but rather "the earliest mode in which the mind of man apprehended truth."[56] Like Lewis, Gore characterizes the first chapters of Genesis as myth. Because it is such an important aspect of how he reads the

51. Gore, "Bible in the Church," 4.
52. Waddell, *Radical Anglican*, xxx.
53. Gore, "Holy Spirit," 255.
54. "MTBC," 155.
55. Gore, "Holy Spirit," 257–63.
56. Gore, "Holy Spirit," 238.

Bible, we will focus on what myth means to Lewis, especially in conversation with Scripture, in chapter 6.

Finally, Gore writes, "If any man comes to us and says that he has studied and assimilated the Christian Creed with all the care and reverence in his ability, and has rejected it because he finds it irrational and false, we cannot complain of him. We cannot ask him to accept it though he thinks it false."[57] Lewis says the same thing in *Mere Christianity*, noting that he does not ask anyone "to accept Christianity if his best reasoning tells him that the weight of the evidence is against it."[58] Both of them, of course, believe that the best reasoning will support it.

The work we have done comparing and contrasting how Gore and Lewis approach the Bible sets up almost everything that follows in this book. Gore exerted a large and lasting influence on Lewis's interpretation of Scripture from the beginning of his adult Christian life, first from his reading *Jesus of Nazareth*, then through his reliance on Gore's biblical commentary, and not least through the impact the essay "The Holy Spirit and Inspiration" made on the Anglican world. Lewis followed Gore (1) in rejecting the theory of the verbal inspiration of Scripture and (2) in identifying the "Word" of God with Christ rather than with Scripture; (3) in his attention to the genre of the books of the Bible, which led him to believe that there were different sorts of biblical inspiration without denying that the canon as a whole was inspired; (4) that the presence of miracles does not automatically disprove historicity; (5) that some books in the Old Testament were composed as fiction, but with a few clear exceptions nothing in the New Testament was; (6) that both testaments could contain errors of fact regarding history and science, and (7) that Jesus could be wrong, even about "religious" things, because the dogma of the incarnation requires his kenosis, which makes the human Jesus fallible. Gore and Lewis share similar views on the overall historicity of the Gospels apart from the momentous difference in their perception of discrepancies among them.

57. Gore, "Holy Spirit," 239.

58. *Mere Christianity* (1952; repr., San Francisco: HarperSanFrancisco, 2001), 140.

3. WRITING ABOUT SCRIPTURE

1932–1949

> *Even in poetry it is the imaginative only, viz., that which is conversant with, or turns upon infinity, that powerfully affects me. . . . I mean to say that, unless in those passages where things are lost in each other, and limits vanish, and aspirations are raised, I read with something too much like indifference—but all great poets are in this view powerful Religionists.*
>
> —William Wordsworth[1]

We have looked at what Lewis read about the Bible early in his adult Christian life, and now we move to what he wrote about it, mainly in his letters and books, but also in his poetry. Young Lewis longed to be a great poet. Although he published many poems, he considered himself a failed poet—an assessment some now dispute.[2] His lifelong love of language colored his interpretation of the Bible, which he read with an eye to a beautiful turn of phrase. In the 1930s, he builds his knowledge of Scripture by talking about what he doesn't understand with friends and by puzzling through it in the way he likes best, through his literary imagination.[3] In the 1940s, he

1. Wordsworth to Walter Savage Landor, Jan. 21, 1824, in *The Letters of William and Dorothy Wordsworth: The Later Years, I: 1821–30*, ed. Ernest de Selincourt (Oxford: Clarendon, 1939), 134–35.

2. Malcolm Guite, "Poet," in *The Cambridge Companion to C. S. Lewis*, ed. Robert MacSwain and Michael Ward (Cambridge: Cambridge University Press, 2010), 294–310.

3. For Lewis's definitions of imagination, see Peter Schakel, "C. S. Lewis: Reason, Imagination, and Knowledge," in *C. S. Lewis and Friends: Faith and the Power of Imagination*, ed. David Hein and Edward Henderson (Eugene, OR: Cascade Books, 2011), 15–17.

works his new insights on the Bible into his apologetics, including *The Problem of Pain* and *Miracles*. The 1940s witnessed the full flowering of his Christian apologetics but only the first buds of his work on Scripture, efforts that would bear fruit in the 1950s.

Letters and Poems, 1932–1939

In 1932 Lewis informs his brother that he had started to read Paul's first letter to the Corinthians, but he "didn't make much of it." In his next letter, however, he can quote 1 Corinthians 1:26 astutely while discussing Christianity in Asia.[4] In spring 1934 he tells his former student Bede Griffiths, who was teaching Greek, that he doesn't find New Testament Greek easy, especially in Luke and Paul. Nevertheless, he is beginning to get a grasp of Paul, who used to be "quite opaque" to him.[5] Lewis will correspond with Griffiths about Scripture, fuss about New Testament Greek, and find Paul perplexing for the rest of his life.[6]

In fall 1934 Lewis tells Greeves that he is reading the Old Testament, and he highlights Numbers 13:33: "And there we saw the giants, the sons of Anak, which come of the giants: and we were in our own sight as grasshoppers, and so we were in their sight" (KJV). Lewis loves how the word "grasshoppers" functions in the passage: "It brings out the monstrosity of the giants so well, because one thinks of the grasshopper as being not only small, but fragile, light and even flimsy. 'Beetles', for example, would not have done nearly so well."[7] He shows no interest in the narrative or historical context of the verse but homes in on the word choice—just as one might expect a poet to do.

Material evidence in Lewis's library suggests that the Old Testament he was reading in 1934 was a huge King James Bible published in 1839. Other than an inscription on the flyleaf, the only marks in it are underlinings in pencil executed just as Lewis underlines his other books, as well as marginal notes that match his handwriting from the period.[8] These marks are confined over-

4. Lewis to his brother, March 20 and April 8, 1932, *CL*, 2:62, 69.

5. Lewis to Bede Griffiths, April 4, 1934, *CL*, 2:136.

6. For more on the friendship between Lewis and Griffiths, see Ron Dart, "C. S. Lewis and Bede Griffiths: Chief Companions on the Contemplative Journey," in *The Inklings and Culture*, ed. Monika B. Hilder, Sara L. Pearson, and Laura N. Van Dyke (Newcastle upon Tyne, UK: Cambridge Scholars Publishing, 2020), 81–94.

7. Lewis to Greeves, Oct. 1, 1934, *CL*, 2:144.

8. *The Holy Bible, containing the Old and New Testaments: translated out of the original tongues: and with the former translations diligently compared and revised, by His Majesty's special command* (Oxford: Oxford University Press, 1839). C. S. Lewis personal library, Marion E. Wade Center, Wheaton College, Wheaton, IL. The 1839 Bible does not ap-

whelmingly to the Old Testament, with every book thereof demonstrating his hand, including Numbers 13:33, where "we were in our own sight as grasshoppers" is underlined. Lewis may have read straight through the Old Testament of this Bible in 1934. Since he didn't know Hebrew, he had to read the Old Testament in English.[9] Since he was fluent in Greek, he could read the New Testament in that language. There are very few marks in the New Testament of the 1839 Bible, perhaps because he wanted to read it in Greek, as he had the Gospel of John several years before.

In 1936, Lewis reflects on the implications of a biblical event by writing a poem about it. Second Kings 18–19 tells the story of King Hezekiah of Judah, who was under threat of attack by Sennacherib of Assyria. Hezekiah prays, and God delivers his people by sending the angel of the Lord to kill 185,000 Assyrians in their sleep. A similar story is recorded by the Greek historian Herodotus. In this version, the monarch under threat is Sethos of Egypt, who is priest of the god Hephaestus. Sethos prays to Hephaestus for deliverance, and the god pledges, "I shall send you champions." As the Assyrian warriors sleep, they are overrun by mice that destroy their bowstrings. Thus deprived of their weapons, the Assyrians are routed.[10]

Lewis writes,

> The Bible says Sennacherib's campaign was spoiled
> By angels: In Herodotus it says, by mice—

and he harmonizes the two accounts:

> But muscular archangels, I suggest, employed
> Seven little jaws at labour on each slender string.[11]

---

pear to be a Lewis family heirloom. The inscription on the flyleaf reads "Elizabeth Warman, Brize Norton, July 19th, 1846." In the census of 1841, she is noted as living with her parents. A dressmaker by that name is registered as having married James Hall in the village of Brize Norton, Oxfordshire, Sept. 5, 1848, when she was twenty-seven years old, and Elizabeth Hall appears as the wife of James Hall in the census of 1851. Elizabeth's brother Edmund Warman, a witness to the marriage, was a colorful character, an itinerant musician who pitched a dancing tent and was repeatedly brought before the magistrate for living in his caravan and allowing his horses to stray. See https://tinyurl.com/2skxjdcu. I have no idea how Warman's Bible came into the possession of Lewis.

9. Lewis to Bede Griffiths, April 24, 1936, *CL*, 2:189.

10. Herodotus 2.141.

11. "Sonnet," in *Collected Poems*, 319. Originally published May 14, 1936, in the *Oxford Magazine* 54.

An omnipotent God, he concludes, can work through small things. Someone reading this poem after the publication of *The Lion, the Witch and the Wardrobe* may find themselves thinking about the mice that chewed through the cords binding Aslan to the stone table. As Aslan tells them later, this is when they became *talking* mice.

In summer 1939 Lewis makes first contact with a woman who will play a large, but until now largely unsung, role in forming his interpretation of Scripture. Penelope Lawson, a religious sister of the Anglican Community of St. Mary the Virgin in Wantage, wrote Lewis a fan letter after she read his book *Out of the Silent Planet.*[12] By 1939 she had published several books of her own, and she must have included a copy of her most recent, *God Persists,* because Lewis discusses it in detail when he replies. Among other delights, he is pleased to learn what the words "Israel" and "glory" mean. Her thoughts on "glory"—it "really means *revealed beauty,* and the verb *to glorify* is the same as *to clarify* or *make clear*"—are reflected two years later in Lewis's sermon "The Weight of Glory."[13] He closes the letter humbly, noting that he is a youngster in Christian years, and he asks for her prayers.[14]

Thus begins a correspondence that blossoms into mutual respect, support, and lifelong collaboration. She sends him another book, and he asks for the title of the one she wrote on the Psalms. Because she read both Greek and Hebrew, he also asks her to recommend a good essay on the "meaning of that momentous little word" *en* (in) in New Testament Greek (e.g., "in Christ") as well as any Hebrew or Aramaic correlates that might help him understand it better.[15] We don't know if she did, but we watch him struggle with the word in *The Problem of Pain,* which he had begun to write that summer.[16] As he tries to work through the phrases "in Adam" and "in Christ," he notes that the "difficulty of the Pauline formula turns on the word 'in,'" and he allows that Paul uses it in ways we can no longer grasp.[17]

12. Walter Hooper, *C. S. Lewis: A Companion and Guide* (London: HarperCollins, 1996), 719.

13. A member of CSMV [Sister Penelope Lawson], *God Persists: A Short Survey of World History in the Light of Christian Faith* (London: Mowbrays, 1939), 63, as cited by Hooper, *CL,* 2:263.

14. Lewis to Sister Penelope, July [Aug.] 9, 1939, *CL,* 2:261–64. For more on Sister Penelope, see Richard James, "Sister Penelope Lawson CSMV: Her Life, Writings and Legacy," in *Inklings Forever: Published Colloquium Proceedings 1997–2016* 10, article 86 (2016): 363–77.

15. Lewis to Sister Penelope, Aug. 24, 1939, *CL,* 2:265–66.

16. Hooper, *Companion,* 295.

17. *The Problem of Pain* (1940; repr., New York: Macmillan, 1944), 74, 127.

If we skip ahead in our timeline, we see that Lewis's problems with Paul, like the God of Sister Penelope's book title, persist. In 1953 he notes that even Peter was "stumped" by Paul's letters (2 Pet. 3:16–17), and in 1958 he muses, "I cannot be the only reader who has wondered why God, having given [Paul] so many gifts, withheld from him (what would seem necessary for the first Christian theologian) that of lucidity and orderly exposition."[18] He is not the only one to wonder. Lewis's lament admits him to a great cloud of witnesses that includes John Chrysostom. Commenting on Hebrews 1:3 (which he thought Paul wrote), Chrysostom exclaims that both God and this verse surpass human understanding. It demonstrates that "even Paul is weak and doesn't write clearly."[19]

Lewis's struggles are all to the good. He works with the Bible well when he knows what he doesn't know and invites his readers to think through it with him. When he does understand what Paul means, he is quick to put it into practice, as we can see from a letter he sends to Sister Penelope at the end of 1939. Discussing tensions between High and Low Church Anglicans, he notes that he doesn't care what he eats on a Friday, but if he is dining with High Church friends who abstain from meat that day, so does he, so as not to "offend my weak brother" (1 Cor. 8:7–12).[20] This small action stands in microcosm for a large and admirable habit of being. Throughout his life, whether Lewis interprets the Bible confidently or hesitantly, he tries to read it to maximize love. Here he follows the advice of Augustine of Hippo, who writes that, if you don't know how to interpret Scripture, take it literally if doing so will lead to love of God and neighbor, thus fulfilling the Great Commandment (Matt. 22:36–40). Do not take it literally if it won't.[21]

When Lewis is uncertain about how to put the Bible into practice, he chooses to err—if it is erring—on the side of love. He may not accept some of the most incontrovertible fruit of biblical scholarship, but this defect pales in comparison to how he lived out parts of Scripture some people try to ignore—for example, Matthew's parable of the sheep and the goats (Matt. 25:31–46). At

18. Lewis to Emily McLay, Aug. 3, 1953, *CL*, 3:354; *Reflections on the Psalms* (New York: Harcourt, Brace & World, 1958), 113.

19. Chrysostom, *Homilies on the Letter to the Hebrews* 2.2.

20. Lewis to Sister Penelope, Nov. 8, 1939, *CL*, 2:285.

21. Augustine, *On Christian Doctrine* 3.55. Cf. what Lewis writes in a letter of Sept. 20, 1956: "the *real* centre of the Christian life . . . [is] love, obedience, and the surrender of one's will to Christ," as Paul writes in 1 Corinthians 13. Quoted in Charlie W. Starr and Crystal Hurd, "C. S. Lewis Manuscripts at the Lanier Theological Library," *Sehnsucht* 15, no. 1 (2021): 51 (emphasis in original).

the end of the parable, the "sheep" who feed, clothe, and welcome "the least of these" inherit God's kingdom, while the "goats" who do not suffer fire.[22] In response to passages that demand care for the poor, which pervade the Bible, start to finish, Lewis created what he called his "agapony" ("agape money") fund. He drew an emphatic double line next to James 1:27 in his Moffatt New Testament: "Pure, unsoiled religion in the judgment of God the Father means this: to care for orphans and widows in their trouble."

The 1940s: *The Problem of Pain* and *Miracles*

Lewis published two books that could be called "Christian" in the 1930s, *The Pilgrim's Regress* (1933) and *Out of the Silent Planet* (1938). The former sold few copies, and hardly anyone noticed the theology in the latter.[23] His career as a recognized Christian writer began in 1940 with *The Problem of Pain*. It caught the eye of the BBC, which invited him to deliver a series of wartime radio talks that would later be collected under the title *Mere Christianity*.[24] With the publication of the wildly popular *Screwtape Letters* in 1942, Lewis's literary star had ascended, but his work on the Bible had just begun. The biblical material in *Mere Christianity* and *Screwtape* is treated in chapters 7–8, and here I focus on *The Problem of Pain* and *Miracles* (1947).

The Problem of Pain

The Problem of Pain employs Scripture copiously, but I will limit myself to four observations that will inform this study as a whole. First, as a small-*c* catholic Christian, Lewis works not only with Scripture but also with tradition. Although he was never an expert on the church fathers, he consulted some of them for guidance, as for example when he probed the significance of the trees of life and knowledge in Genesis 2–3.[25]

His meditation on Genesis leads to the second point: *The Problem of Pain* marks the first publication of his thoughts on the interplay of Scripture and

22. See *Mere Christianity* (1952; repr., San Francisco: HarperSanFrancisco, 2001), 86.

23. George Sayer, *Jack: A Life of C. S. Lewis,* 2nd ed. (Wheaton, IL: Crossway, 1994), 230, 255.

24. Justin Phillips, *C. S. Lewis at the BBC* (London: HarperCollins, 2003).

25. *Problem of Pain,* 74, 63; Mark Edwards, "C. S. Lewis and Early Christian Literature," in *C. S. Lewis and the Church,* ed. Judith Wolfe and Brendan N. Wolfe (London: T&T Clark, 2011), 23–39.

myth. Lewis respects both pagan myth and myths in the Bible such as Genesis 2–3, and he offers what may be his first formal definition of the word in print: a myth is a "not unlikely tale" and "an account of what *may have been* historical fact." Like Gore, he rejects any definition of myth as "non-historical truth."[26]

Third, in a book on God and pain, Lewis can't avoid talking about hell. He will hold the position he articulates here for the rest of his life: he believes the existence of hell is supported through the words of Jesus in the Gospels. He also debuts an idea that has been identified with him ever since, because it appears in almost everything he writes on the topic for a popular audience: the damned are lost not because God rejects them but because they reject God.

This idea is not original to Lewis. He introduces it by purporting to quote a then-famous figure on the British theological scene, Baron Friedrich von Hügel (d. 1925). Lewis says that von Hügel says that damnation results from the lost souls' "rejection of everything that is not simply themselves."[27] In fact, the baron does say something close to that but not in those exact words. He writes that the spirits in hell "will feel, far more fully than they ever felt on earth, the stuntedness, the self-mutilation, the imprisonment involved in this their endless self-occupation and jealous evasion of all reality not simply their own selves."[28]

Lewis's "quotation" of von Hügel leads to the fourth point. Even when he places words in quotation marks and cites a source, as he does here, sometimes he misquotes. Quotation marks are a pledge to the reader that everything between them replicates what an author wrote. Lewis owned von Hügel's book, and he underlined the words as noted above in his copy. He probably thought he was quoting him verbatim, but the words switched up as they made their way from von Hügel's page to his own. It's an easy thing to do, and despite my best efforts, I may have done the same thing in this book. Lewis's misquotation is slight, and the differences don't matter in their new context. But later, in other work, he will misquote Scripture, and it will matter. Like the little girl in the nursery rhyme who "had a little curl, right in the middle of her forehead," when he was good, he was very, very good, and when he was bad, things tend horrid. If he weren't a public figure, his arguments based on misremembered Scripture wouldn't matter. But he was and continues to be a most prominent one, so we must acknowledge where his work goes astray and, more impor-

26. *Problem of Pain*, 59–60, 64 (emphasis in original).

27. *Problem of Pain*, 111.

28. Friedrich von Hügel, *Essays and Addresses on the Philosophy of Religion*, series 1 (London: J. M. Dent and Sons, 1928), 216–17 (underlining added).

tantly, how that slippage affects the validity of the point he bases on it. This occurs most egregiously in the verses he claims to support the "liar, lunatic, or Lord" argument and in two essays, "Modern Theology and Biblical Criticism" and "What Are We to Say about Jesus Christ?" (treated in chapters 7–8).

I am not the first to notice how Lewis sometimes relies on an imprecise memory. In his preface to Lewis's literary essays, Walter Hooper marvels at his ability to remember "almost everything he read," quoting "straight from memory without bothering to check the texts themselves." But when Hooper does check the texts, he discovers that Lewis misquoted his sources nearly five hundred times. Most of these "do not affect the sense," and Hooper praises Lewis for his indifference to "the minutiae precious to strict pedants." But other readers have not dismissed such errors so lightly. Lewis's student A. C. Spearing received a letter from his teacher that misquotes Shakespeare's *Tempest*. As Spearing observes, the misquotation is "an interesting indication of Lewis's reliance not on books but on his well-stocked memory, and a nice tangle of remembering and misremembering. The reliance on memory, with its capacity for creative error, belongs to an older world of scholarship; the unreferenced misrecollection would never do in a modern academic article, but it does not distort Shakespeare's meaning."[29] Lewis produces even more creative error when he writes on the Gospels. Conjuring new "Scripture" out of nothing, he will transform what they say about the divinity of Jesus into something else entirely.

Miracles

Miracles (1947), like *The Problem of Pain*, is full of Scripture, and Lewis frames the book in the first and last chapters with a criticism of a bit of biblical scholarship from his Gore commentary. In the first chapter, Lewis notes that it is vital to identify one's philosophy of miracles because this will determine what one does next. If miracles are impossible, why would anyone bother to investigate them? Therefore, one must address the philosophical question—are miracles possible?—before doing anything else. But some people don't. As a cautionary example, he criticizes a sentence from the Gore commentary's chapter on the Gospel of John.[30]

29. Walter Hooper, preface to *Selected Literary Essays*, by C. S. Lewis, ed. Walter Hooper (1969; repr., Cambridge: Cambridge University Press, 2013), xvii; A. C. Spearing, "C. S. Lewis as a Research Supervisor," *Journal of Inklings Studies* 12, no. 1 (2022): 116. Cf. Alastair Fowler, "C. S. Lewis: Supervisor," *Yale Review* 91, no. 4 (2003): 74.

30. *Miracles* (1947; repr., New York: Macmillan, 1960), 3–4.

The author of the chapter, Walter Lock, is working through the problem of dating the Gospel. Anyone who attempts to do this must deal with John 21, where Jesus predicts how Peter will die. After making his prediction about Peter, Jesus hints that another follower, "the disciple whom he loved," will be alive when Jesus comes again. Then the narrator of the Gospel interjects, "So the rumor spread in the community that this disciple would not die. Yet Jesus did not say to him that he would not die, but 'If it is my will that he remain until I come, what is that to you?'" (John 21:22–23). Many scholars before and after Lock have thought that the narrator's interjection was sparked by the death of the Beloved Disciple before the return of Jesus—which, of course, has not happened to this day. Based on this analysis, Lock notes that John 21 must have been written "after the crucifixion of St. Peter, possibly after the death, certainly after the extreme old age, of the loved disciple."[31] From Lock's line of reasoning, Lewis infers that Lock does not believe in miraculous prediction, and thus not in miracles at all. If he did, he might have dated the Gospel earlier. Therefore, according to Lewis, such biblical scholarship—and such biblical scholars—are not to be trusted.

In the last chapter of *Miracles*, the epilogue, Lewis returns to what he wrote in the first chapter. Readers who encounter scholars like Lock (Lewis never names him) must be aware that they move "as sheep among wolves," even if the wolves are not ravaging sheep on purpose. Lewis goes out of his way to attribute good motives to the scholarly wolves, but he still concludes that lupine "naturalistic assumptions" and question-beggings about miracles hurt sheep.[32] Other than *Screwtape Letters* chapter 23, which was published in the early 1940s, *Miracles* offers Lewis's first critique of modern biblical scholarship in print. In 1959, he will expand upon the sheep simile to structure his lecture "Modern Theology and Biblical Criticism."

Miracles also offers Lewis's first stab at a general theory of Scripture. This appears not in the body of the book but in a footnote on the interplay of myth, truth, history, and the incarnation, all of which reflect the work of Charles Gore. Lewis begins with the idea of God preparing humanity for the incarnation by sowing the world with mythologies that gradually solidify into history. The Jews are God's chosen people, so they receive God's chosen myth, and in the New Testament "truth" becomes "completely historical." Like Gore, Lewis thinks that some parts of the Old Testament are not historical fact, but it can be hard to tell which are and which aren't. For Lewis, the stories of King

31. W. Lock, "The Gospel according to St. John," in *NCHS* part 3, 242.

32. *Miracles*, 164–65.

David are about as historical as the Gospels, while Jonah sits at the other end of the spectrum. As in *The Problem of Pain,* Lewis talks about Christ's kenosis without using the term, here comparing it to myth coming down to earth, a descent that transforms myth into historical fact through the incarnation. He also thinks that, because the New Testament is on the whole more historical than the Old, the New Testament is duller. Revisiting what he wrote to Greeves in 1931, he argues that the story of Jesus demands an imaginative as well as an intellectual response.[33]

This footnote made some readers wonder what Lewis thought about the inspiration of Scripture, and they wrote to ask him. Responding to a 1949 letter from Edward Dell, Lewis replied simply that he had much to learn and "nothing to teach."[34] A letter to Corbin Scott Carnell in 1953 finds Lewis still "uneasy" but more willing than he had been in 1949 to expand upon the topic. He writes that both the position he took on the historicity of the Bible in *Miracles* and the opposite point of view—that everything in the Bible holds the same level of historicity—are debatable. Lewis doesn't doubt the historicity of Jonah because its miracles are improbable, but because its genre is so different from the stories of David and the stories in the New Testament. Jonah isn't even set within a historical framework. The Bible never specifies any narrative as fiction, but Jesus never called his parables "fiction" either, and we know that they are. Lewis's expertise as a literary scholar tells him there are different genres in the Bible, and different genres should be read in different ways. Nonetheless, literary forms like allegory and parable may be just as inspired as those that appear "historical."[35]

The Carnell letter has brought us into the 1950s, the decade in which Lewis produced his most concerted work on the Scriptures.

33. *Miracles,* 133–34.

34. Hooper, *Companion,* 344; Lewis to Edward Dell, Feb. 4, 1949, *CL,* 2:914.

35. Lewis to Corbin Scott Carnell, April 4, 1953, *CL,* 3:318–19.

4. FRUITION

1950–1963

The church with psalms must shout.
No doore can keep them out:
But above all, the heart
Must bear the longest part.

—George Herbert[1]

The 1950s could be called Lewis's "Decade of the Bible," the era in which he produced his most abundant, mature, and confident work on the subject. The decade began with a lecture he delivered in March 1950 and published later that year as *The Literary Impact of the Authorized Version.* His scholarly magnum opus, *English Literature in the Sixteenth Century, Excluding Drama* (1954), includes solid material on the translation of the Bible into English. This volume, produced for the Oxford History of English Literature series, took him so long to write that he referred to it by the series acronym OHEL, with all the implications of authorial agony therein. Shortly thereafter, he reviewed a book on biblical translation that built upon his work in OHEL.[2] In 1958 he published *Reflections on the Psalms,* his only stand-alone book on Scripture, and in 1959 delivered the talk "Modern Theology and Biblical Criticism." He wrote to correspondents who asked him about the Bible, and one of those letters, to Emily McLay, reveals an assumption that—we can see in hindsight—guided his biblical interpretation. From 1950 to 1956, he published the seven Chronicles of Narnia, which I think contain his best work with Scripture. The only other significant piece on the Bible he wrote as sole

1. George Herbert, "Antiphon (I)," in *The Poems of George Herbert,* ed. Helen Gardner (Oxford: Oxford University Press, 1961), 46.

2. C. S. Lewis, review of *Principles and Problems of Biblical Translation,* by Werner Schwarz, in *Image and Imagination: Essays and Reviews,* ed. Walter Hooper (Cambridge: Cambridge University Press, 2013), 68–72.

author before he died was a chapter intended for the book *Letters to Malcolm* (1964), but it was not included there and remained unpublished until 2017. In the last few years of his life, he served on the Anglican Commission to revise the Psalter, a project he loved. Everything Lewis wrote on Scripture in this period, from lectures to letters to essays to books, is consistent with what he had written before. This chapter will focus on his letters and *Reflections on the Psalms*, reserving the *Malcolm* manuscript, "Modern Theology and Biblical Criticism," and the Chronicles of Narnia for parts 2–3.

The Interpretive Principle of Noncontradiction

In 1953 Lewis received a letter from Emily McLay, who was confused about how the Bible discusses salvation. Is one saved by faith, as she understood Paul to say, or works, as in Matthew's parable of the sheep and the goats? It is hard to overstate the importance of Lewis's answer, since it seems to have governed his interpretation of the Bible throughout his adult Christian life and explains why he never acknowledged discrepancies between John and the Synoptics, the blind spot that undermines the quality of his argumentation on Scripture.

He writes, "I take it as a first principle that we must not interpret any one part of Scripture so that it contradicts other parts." For example, one must not pit the letters of Paul against the Gospels as McLay was doing. Lewis admits that he cannot square the circle of the variant passages on faith and works, but this isn't the Bible's fault. Rather, the fault lies with his own inability to grasp the consistency of Scripture. The remedy is to take a cue from scientists, especially the physicists who discovered that light is simultaneously wave and particle; that is, readers of the Bible should hold ideas that appear to contradict each other in creative tension. Like physical reality, Scripture must be internally consistent, even if we can't see how. At the same time, we must not make a fetish of consistency, especially if we're tempted to discard passages that displease us. "It is better to hold two inconsistent views than to ignore one side of the evidence," he advises.[3]

Lewis doesn't mention differences between the Synoptics and John here, and when he does talk about the Gospels elsewhere, he never brings up his "first principle" of biblical interpretation. Nonetheless, it is key to understanding how he interprets the Bible, and especially its narratives on Jesus. As we will see, Lewis is certain that even the Gospels contain contradictions, but like John Chrysostom, he too appears sure that they don't affect matters of significance.

3. Lewis to Emily McLay, Aug. 3, 1953, *CL*, 3:354–55.

Therefore, he can hold two seemingly paradoxical ideas in tandem: material in the Bible sometimes contradicts itself, but we should not interpret one part of Scripture so it contradicts other parts.

McLay wrote him several days later to ask about passages that seem to show God in a bad light, and he rephrases the same argument: she should assume the problem lies with her. She should never ignore these passages but rather set them aside until she is wise enough to understand them—if she ever is.[4]

Of course, Lewis himself struggled to understand divergent passages in the Bible, and he asked others for help. One of the most important of these was his long-distance spiritual advisor, the Roman Catholic priest (and later canonized saint) Don Giovanni Calabria. The two corresponded in Latin because it was the mutual language both felt most comfortable using.

In 1953 Lewis wrote Calabria to inquire about the seemingly contradictory ways Jesus talks about petitionary prayer in the Gospel of Mark. On one hand, Jesus prays for "the cup" of his death to be removed in Gethsemane, but he submits to God's will (Mark 14:36). On the other, Jesus tells his followers, "Whatever you ask for in prayer, believe that you have received it, and it will be yours" (Mark 11:24 NRSV). Trying to reconcile the two passages, Lewis examines Mark 11:24's verb "received" in Greek and Latin. He notes that the Greek has "the past tense[,] . . . which is very difficult." The Latin has the future tense, "will receive," which, Lewis claims, appears in "our vernacular translation."[5] In fact, both of the English translations Lewis read most, the KJV and Moffatt, give the present tense (KJV, "believe that ye receive," and Moffatt, "believe you have got it"). Even Ronald Knox's New Testament, which Lewis recommends in *Miracles*, has the present tense ("believe that it is yours").[6] However, Tyndale's translation, which Lewis praises in OHEL, gives the future tense, so he may have been thinking of it.

All of the above is necessary exegetical prelude to his main question: how can anyone simultaneously believe that he "*will* receive *and* submit himself to the Will of God—Who perhaps is refusing him?"[7] This question haunted Lewis his entire life. When his mother was dying, the heartbroken little boy put into practice what he had been taught—that sincere prayers would be granted—by praying for her healing. But his request was denied. He was still

4. Lewis to Emily McLay, Aug. 8, 1953, *CL*, 3:356–57.
5. Lewis to Calabria, Jan. 14, 1953, *CL*, 3:281.
6. *Miracles* (1947; repr., New York: Macmillan, 1960), 164.
7. Lewis to Calabria, Jan. 14, 1953, *CL*, 3:281 (emphasis in original).

pondering the question in *Letters to Malcolm: Chiefly on Prayer*, which was published posthumously.[8]

Calabria's response has not survived, but Lewis's letter offers an example of how he worked through the thorny problems of biblical and theological interpretation he advised others about. He read the passage in the ancient languages he knew, consulted church tradition, and, when that led nowhere, asked a trusted friend. Oddly, however, Lewis rarely quoted the Vulgate in his letters to Calabria (written 1947–1954). The Vulgate, a Latin version of Scripture translated by Jerome in the fourth century, was the go-to Bible for Western Christians for the next thousand years. One would expect Lewis to keep it close at hand since he wrote to Calabria in Latin, but he didn't. Instead, as Arthur Rupprecht has shown, Lewis relied on his memory of passages in the KJV, and he usually departed from its wording. He then translated these misrecollections into his own Latin, which, more often than not, created new "Scripture," although he usually hewed close to the sense.[9] The Calabria correspondence demonstrates once again how much room the KJV occupied in Lewis's mental library, and it supplies another example of his tendency to rely on faulty memory rather than precise quotation when he worked with the Bible.

Fundamentalism

A letter to Janet Wise in 1955 addresses a topic that Lewis will revisit for the rest of his life: Christian fundamentalism. Wise was disturbed by a growing "disbelief in the authority of the Bible," particularly among clergy. She especially disliked it when her sort of believer was called "fundamentalist." Wise considered herself "an *intelligent* fundamentalist," and she asked Lewis to recommend books to help her understand her opponents.[10]

He felt ill-equipped to make such recommendations, but he did address the topic of fundamentalism. First, he emphasizes the fact that he is not a fundamentalist, and it is important to know how he understood the term. He

8. *Surprised by Joy* (San Diego: Harcourt Brace Jovanovich, 1955), 20–21; *Letters to Malcolm: Chiefly on Prayer* (New York: Harcourt, Brace & World, 1964), 58. Lewis expands on the question in a talk delivered Dec. 8, 1953, to the Oxford Clerical Society, "Petitionary Prayer: A Problem without an Answer" (*Essay Collection*, 197–205), where he says he asked the question of every Christian he knew.

9. Arthur Rupprecht, "The Versatile C. S. Lewis: Latin Scholar," *VII: Journal of the Marion E. Wade Center* 18 (2001): 73–92.

10. *CL*, 3:652 n. 284.

defines fundamentalism as "accepting as a point of faith" that "every statement in the Bible is completely true in the literal, historical sense." He argues against it on literary grounds just as he did in earlier letters: pointing out differences in genre and contrasting material like the book of Acts and the histories of David, which are set in recognizable historical frameworks, to the books of Esther, Jonah, and Job, which are not. In this letter he speaks confidently, asserting that Esther, Jonah, and Job "pretty well *proclaim* themselves to be sacred fiction." He doesn't mention Gore, but rather Calvin and Jerome, and he quotes Jerome as saying that Moses composed his creation story "after the method of a popular poet." The last sentence in the letter roots Lewis in catholic tradition: "The basis of our Faith is not the Bible taken by itself but the agreed affirmation of all Christendom: to wh[ich] we owe the Bible itself."[11]

But not everything in the Wise letter is correct. As we have begun to see, and as chapter 8 will demonstrate in gory detail, Lewis sometimes misquotes his sources. He can also misattribute them, which he does here, for Jerome said no such thing, even though Lewis says six times in his writings that he did. Instead, the dictum comes from John Colet (d. 1519). Lewis scholar Arend Smilde hypothesizes that he made his initial mistake when he wrote about Colet in OHEL. However, removing the attribution to Jerome from the letter does not negate Lewis's argument, because other early church fathers made similar points, even if Jerome did not.

As Smilde notes, "It is reasonable to grant [Lewis] the right to a handful of blunders."[12] This one, like the misquotation of von Hügel in *The Problem of Pain*, is relatively minor, but the blunders do add up over time, pointing to a not-so-admirable habit of being that will mar the quality of his biblical interpretation.

Inspiration

As the 1950s draw to a close, Lewis's thoughts on Scripture are honed to the sharpest edge they will ever attain. He publishes *Reflections on the Psalms* in 1958 and delivers "Modern Theology and Biblical Criticism" in May 1959. Two letters, one penned in 1958 when *Reflections on the Psalms* was in press and the other four days before he presented "Modern Theology and Biblical Criticism," reflect the care he had devoted to thinking about the Bible.

11. Lewis to Janet Wise, Oct. 5, 1955, *CL*, 3:652–53.

12. Arend Smilde, "C. S. Lewis, St Jerome, and the Biblical Creation Story: The Background of a Recurring Misattribution," *Journal of Inklings Studies* 4, no. 2 (2014): 115–24.

In the summer of 1958, Lewis responds to a letter from Lee Turner, who had asked him if the Bible is inspired. By this time, he has much more to say on the topic than he did in 1949. To Lewis, the question is not *if* the Bible is inspired but *how*. It is not inspired through some sort of "automatic writing" where the Spirit overwhelms the human author. He will have none of that, for all one had to do was look at Paul's "I, and not the Lord" (1 Cor. 7:10) and the Hebrew prophets, who record their own feelings and reactions, to dispense with what he calls an "extreme view of inspiration" without ever bringing up modern biblical scholarship. Reading the Bible itself kills that theory. Like Christians from John Chrysostom to Charles Gore, Lewis sees the Bible in all its confusing glory as akin to the incarnation of Christ.[13] Everything human—even the state of being wrong—is intrinsic to the humanity of both Christ and Scripture, and one must not impose modern notions about history and science onto the ancients, who understood them differently than we do.[14]

On May 7, 1959, he writes to a professor of English at Wheaton College, Clyde Kilby, who had sent Lewis a copy of Wheaton's "Statement concerning the Inspiration of the Bible."[15] The letter begins with the disclaimer that Kilby should throw it away if he thinks it will upset anyone. We may be thankful he didn't, because it opens a new window into Lewis's thoughts on the inspiration and historicity of Scripture. First, Lewis confides that he doesn't really think about inspiration when he reads the Bible, because the topic isn't important to him. Neither are questions of historicity, since the Bible is always God's word, and it works upon him as such whether or not everything in it is "historical." Some things like the resurrection must be true for him to keep his faith, but many others—like Lot's wife turning into a pillar of salt—don't matter.

There follows a list of facts Lewis wants to keep in mind when thinking through questions of biblical inspiration and historicity. In addition to Paul's "I, and not the Lord," the parables of Jesus, and Jonah and Job, which we have seen before, he offers new examples. Luke describes how he researched his Gospel carefully (Luke 1:1–4); it was not beamed into his head. Lewis could

13. Bradley Nassif, "John Chrysostom on the Nature of Revelation and Task of Exegesis," in *What Is the Bible? The Patristic Doctrine of Scripture*, ed. Matthew Baker and Mark Mourachian (Minneapolis: Fortress, 2016), 54–55; *Reflections on the Psalms* (New York: Harcourt, Brace & World, 1958), 116.

14. Lewis to Lee Turner, July 19, 1958, *CL*, 3:960–61.

15. Philip Ryken, "Inerrancy and the Patron Saint of Evangelicalism: C. S. Lewis on Holy Scripture," in *The Romantic Rationalist: God, Life, and Imagination in the Work of C. S. Lewis*, ed. John Piper and David Mathis (Wheaton, IL: Crossway, 2014), 44.

have taken this example from Gore's *Jesus of Nazareth*, which makes the same point for the same purpose.[16] In one of the few places where Lewis highlights discrepancies in the New Testament, he notes that Luke's genealogy of Jesus differs from Matthew's, and there are two different accounts of Judas's death in Matthew and Acts. Furthermore, since everything good and true comes from God, whether it appears in Scripture or not, nonscriptural things too "must be *in some sense* inspired." All of this leads him to conclude that every part of the Bible is not inspired in the same way, and requiring ancient writers to conform to modern conceptions of truth and history is misguided.[17]

The Kilby letter was written four days before Lewis delivered "Modern Theology and Biblical Criticism," a scathing attack on New Testament scholars. He finds no common ground with modern scholars in his talk, but he concurs with them in the letter when he highlights passages that speak against certain theories of inspiration and insists that modern conceptions of truth and history should not be applied to the Bible.

Reflections on the Psalms

Lewis was susceptible to the flu. Like the Narnian ape Shift in *The Last Battle*, he had a "weak chest." But this propensity also had its bright side, as recuperating in bed allowed him to indulge in what he dearly loved: reading for hour after uninterrupted hour. During one of these bouts with the flu in 1940, he developed the habit of reading the morning and evening psalms, which, he observed, was an excellent practice for coping with the stress of yet another war.[18]

The only book Lewis devoted strictly to the Bible was *Reflections on the Psalms*. He called it "a very unambitious little work," and some reviewers agreed. Nevertheless, his goals for the book, as summarized in a blurb he sent to his editor, were not small: to look at the Psalms within Judaism, in early Christian interpretation, where they "took on new meanings," and as people use them today.[19] He also employed them as a springboard to launch into

16. *Jesus of Nazareth* (1929; repr., Oxford: Oxford University Press, 1950), 124–25.

17. Lewis to Clyde Kilby, May 7, 1959, *CL*, 3:1044–46.

18. See George Sayer, *Jack: A Life of C. S. Lewis*, 2nd ed. (Wheaton, IL: Crossway, 1994), 40, 49, 65, 330. Lewis to his father, Jan. 25, 1926, *CL*, 1:660, and Feb. 25, 1928, *CL*, 1:745; to his brother, July 12, 1940, *CL*, 2:422.

19. Lewis to Greeves, Nov. 27, 1957, *CL*, 3:900; to Jocelyn Gibb, Jan. 21, 1958, *CL*, 3:916.

related topics, including his views on ancient Jews and his theories on the inspiration and inerrancy of Scripture.

Reflections on the Psalms (1958) is dedicated to Austin and Katharine Farrer. He and Austin had met by 1941, and Katharine became a dear friend of Lewis's wife, Joy, in the 1950s.[20] Katharine was a novelist, and Lewis sought her advice as he wrote *Till We Have Faces*.[21] Austin was the biblical scholar Lewis knew best, but their personal interactions seem to have meant more to him than Farrer's scholarship because, although he admired it, he appears to have used little of it in his own writing on Scripture.[22] Farrer, an Anglican priest, heard Joy's last confession and presided over her funeral, served as lector at Jack's own funeral, and contributed an essay to the first edited volume on Lewis after his death.[23] According to Lewis's friend George Sayer, Farrer was the one who suggested that Lewis write on the Psalms, and he, Jack, and Joy discussed the project throughout the summer of 1957.[24]

When the book appeared, it was reviewed widely and almost entirely positively by Christians on both sides of the Atlantic. More critical reviews came from Jews, for good reason—first among them the fact that Lewis did not read Hebrew, the language in which the Psalms were composed. He faces that problem in the first paragraph of the book, where he admits that he is writing as an amateur for other amateurs. He is no biblical scholar, and he knows no Hebrew.

He was, however, adept in Greek. Although the Psalms were composed in Hebrew, they (and the rest of the Hebrew Scriptures) were translated into Greek well before the birth of Jesus. When psalms are quoted in the New Testament, they often come from the Greek version that, taken as a heterogenous whole, is called the Septuagint (abbreviated LXX). Composed by Jews for Jews, the Septuagint later became the Christian Old Testament. The books that eventually become the New Testament were written in Greek, so their

20. Judith Wolfe, "Austin Farrer and C. S. Lewis," in *Austin Farrer: Oxford Warden, Scholar, Preacher*, ed. Markus Bockmuehl, Nevsky Everett, and Stephen Platten (London: SCM, 2020), 70–85.

21. Walter Hooper, *C. S. Lewis: A Companion and Guide* (London: HarperCollins, 1996), 656.

22. For ways that Lewis and Farrer do intersect, see Philip Irving Mitchell, *The Shared Witness of C. S. Lewis and Austin Farrer: Friendship, Influence, and an Anglican Worldview* (Kent, OH: Kent State University Press, 2021).

23. Robert MacSwain, "A Fertile Friendship: C. S. Lewis and Austin Farrer," *Chronicle of the Oxford University C. S. Lewis Society* 5, no. 2 (2008): 28, 34.

24. Sayer, *Jack*, 390–91.

authors naturally would rely on the Greek rather than the Hebrew version of the Jewish Scriptures. From Matthew to Revelation, wherever Scripture is quoted in the New Testament, it often comes from the Septuagint, and until Latin overtook Greek as the common language of the western Mediterranean world, the Septuagint was the Old Testament for many early Christians.[25] Its wording made a significant impact on Christian biblical interpretation, but Lewis never mentions Septuagint Psalms in his book. He was very familiar with the Septuagint, consulting it to compare its wording to English translations of the Hebrew Bible, as when he scribbled Septuagint Greek in the margins of his 1839 King James Bible—the one he may have read in 1934—and in his copy of *Our Prayer Book Psalter: Containing Coverdale's Version from His 1535 Bible and the Prayer Book Version by Coverdale from the Great Bible 1539–41 Printed Side by Side.*[26] Lewis discusses Miles Coverdale (d. 1568) in OHEL, and he chose Coverdale's translation of the Psalms as the base text for *Reflections on the Psalms* because it was the text in the Anglican Book of Common Prayer and because he thought it the most poetic. But Coverdale, like Lewis, had no Hebrew, so Lewis also consulted Moffatt.[27]

Lewis marked up his copy of *Our Prayer Book Psalter* copiously, and these annotations may stem from his work on OHEL, *Reflections on the Psalms*, or another project he was invited to join as a direct result of publishing the latter—the commission to revise Coverdale's translation of the Psalter for a new edition of the Book of Common Prayer. As one of two literary scholars on the commission (the other was T. S. Eliot), his input helped craft the "clarity, rhythm, alliteration, and figurative language" of the new Psalter. He loved being part of the team, characterizing it as "delightful work, with delightful colleagues," and he especially enjoyed learning from the biblical scholars. Sadly, he was not able to see the project to completion, as poor health forced him to resign in August 1963, several months before he died.[28]

25. For a good introduction, see Timothy Michael Law, *When God Spoke Greek: The Septuagint and the Making of the Christian Bible* (Oxford: Oxford University Press, 2013).

26. *Our Prayer Book Psalter*, ed. Ernest Clapton (London: SPCK, 1934). C. S. Lewis personal library, at the Wilson Special Collections Library, University of North Carolina–Chapel Hill.

27. *Reflections on the Psalms*, 7.

28. George Musacchio, "C. S. Lewis, T. S. Eliot, and the Anglican Psalter," *VII: Journal of the Marion E. Wade Center* 22 (2005): 47, 54; Sayer, *Jack*, 392. See also Francis Warner, "Lewis' Involvement in the Revision of the Psalter," in *C. S. Lewis and the Church*, ed. Judith Wolfe and Brendan N. Wolfe (London: T&T Clark, 2011), 52–63.

After admitting his lack of bona fides in biblical scholarship and his dearth of Hebrew on the first page of *Reflections on the Psalms,* Lewis offers a short paragraph on their dating and authorship before he jumps to the Psalms as poetry, a much more congenial topic, and one more suited to his expertise.[29] Just as he did at the beginning of his adult Christian life in the 1930s, Lewis, a poet and literary critic, would rather enjoy and analyze the lovely language of the Bible than attempt to set it in historical context. Although he doesn't employ the word "genre" in the book, Lewis emphasizes the importance of genre awareness when he writes that the Psalms "must be read as poems" in order to understand them, and he refers to their authors as "poets."[30] He is captivated by ancient Hebrew's use of poetic parallelism (see chapter 14) and loves the idea that God deigned to put the poetry of the chosen people in a form that could be translated relatively easily into other languages. He even thinks it "almost inevitable" that the "great Imagination" that created all things delights in expressing Itself through poetry, "for poetry too is a little incarnation."[31] Lewis imagines Jesus picking up poetry not only from the Psalms but also from his mother, who sang the Magnificat, that great hymn lauding God's justice to the poor (Luke 1:46–55). Here, in one of the few places he writes on Mary, Lewis shines. He compares her to Deborah, the biblical prophet and judge, and he praises both women by calling them "fierce," a word he had used several years earlier to describe Jews in general and Joy Davidman in particular in his foreword to her book *Smoke on the Mountain* (1954).[32]

Lewis on Ancient Jews

Reflections on the Psalms is structured by theme, and the first is "'Judgement' in the Psalms." Modern Christians, Lewis writes, tend to think of themselves as being judged by God and found wanting. In contrast, the psalmists long for God's judgment because they expect to be vindicated. In Lewis's simile, Christians see themselves as guilty defendants in a criminal case, but Jews see themselves as righteous plaintiffs in a civil suit.[33] This juxtaposition points to

29. *Reflections on the Psalms,* 2, 6.

30. *Reflections on the Psalms,* 23, 25, 32, and more.

31. *Reflections on the Psalms,* 2–5.

32. *Reflections on the Psalms,* 6; Judges 4–5; Lewis, foreword to *Smoke on the Mountain: An Interpretation of the Ten Commandments,* by Joy Davidman (Philadelphia: Westminster, 1954), 8–9.

33. *Reflections on the Psalms,* 9–10.

a move he makes throughout the book: contrasting "us," modern Christians, to "them," ancient Jews. From a historical point of view, such a contrast is right and just, because modern Christians and ancient Jews are very different people. But Lewis can take it in a potentially more troubling direction too. Like Christians before and since, he believes Christianity is superior to Judaism both ancient and modern. Granted, such an attitude to some extent may be unavoidable. Why would anyone belong to group A if they thought group B was better? And one can respect and support a forebear, as Lewis does. Jews are "spiritually *senior*" to Christians, he writes, and those who forget it "flirt with anti-Semitism."[34] This statement is both revealing and ironic. Revealing, because Lewis is clearly concerned about antisemitism and wants to speak up against it. Ironic, because he sometimes fails to recognize his own latent antisemitism.

Before we look at passages that appear antisemitic to me, it will be helpful to have a working definition of the term. The Anti-Defamation League, an organization that fights antisemitism, describes it as "belief or behavior hostile toward Jews just because they are Jewish. It may take the form of religious teachings that proclaim the inferiority of Jews, for instance, or political efforts to isolate, oppress, or otherwise injure them. It may also include prejudiced or stereotyped views about Jews."[35] Lewis was never hostile to Jews, and he deplored attempts to oppress or injure them,[36] but he did express stereotyped views about ancient Jews as he discussed Scripture. These views are endemic to so many Christians that they often pass unnoticed.

After he committed to Christ in 1931 until his death, Lewis held a consistent view of Jews.[37] They were and still are God's people, not perfect but chosen. As he writes in *Miracles*, "their mythology was the chosen mythology." He always emphasized the fact that Jesus was a Jew and that this was a good thing.[38] Nevertheless, he deems the Jewish people as a whole deficient because they lack Christ.[39] Lewis didn't have to read Charles Gore to adopt this idea, but

34. Lewis to Mrs. Johnson, May 14, 1955, *CL*, 3:608. This is the only time the term "antisemitism" appears in his currently published letters.

35. "Antisemitism," Glossary of Extremism and Hate, Anti-Defamation League, published Feb. 4, 2017, https://tinyurl.com/cdy4njzs.

36. Lewis to Greeves, Nov. 5, 1933, *CL*, 2:128.

37. For his views before he converted, see P. H. Brazier, *A Hebraic Inkling: C. S. Lewis on Judaism and the Jews* (Eugene, OR: Pickwick, 2021).

38. *Miracles*, 134; *Reflections on the Psalms*, 26–27, and many more.

39. Foreword to *Smoke on the Mountain*, 7.

since we know he did, we can posit influence. As Gore wrote at the beginning of his biblical commentary, "It is of the essence of the Old Testament in all its departments to be imperfect, as St. Augustine says: 'We wrong the New Testament, if we put the Old on the same level with it.' Alike in its teaching and its law of worship it represents an incomplete and, therefore, defective moral and spiritual enlightenment."[40]

For Lewis, the moral and spiritual shortcomings of the Psalms derive from their authors. He can define the word "judge" correctly in the historical context of the book of Judges because he consulted biblical scholars about the term and then opine that "the Christian picture of God's judgement" (in which we are judged by God) is "far safer for our souls than the Jewish" (in which we think we are wronged). But, he notes, Christians should not discard the Jewish picture; instead, they can learn from it. Plaintiffs in a civil suit may be bitter and hateful because that is a natural response to injustice. The lesson is never to be the one who elicits such hatred.[41] On the whole, however, these psalmists tend to think too highly of themselves. Some of them "approach . . . Christian humility and wisely lose their self-confidence," but this doesn't happen much. Therefore, in Lewis's mind, the overconfident psalmist puts himself in "spiritual danger" that "leads into that typically Jewish prison of self-righteousness which Our Lord so often terribly rebuked."[42] In fact, Jesus didn't rebuke Jews in general on the point but scribes and Pharisees (see Matt. 23:1–36). Lewis's sentence exemplifies a far too common conflation: identifying "Pharisee" with "Jew." Therefore, as Philip and Carol Zaleski observe, it is hard not to "wince" at the word "typically."[43] But it is not hard to see what led him to use it: his culture and his reading, both of which were confirmed by his wife.

To Lewis, Jews are typically "self-righteous," a statement he does not defend. It would not have occurred to him to do so, because it was in the air he breathed. In his time and place, "self-righteous" was a synonym for "Pharisee," and "Pharisee" a synecdoche for "Jew." The second definition of "Pharisee" in the *Oxford English Dictionary* (the first, "A member of a religious party within Judaism between the 2nd cent. B.C. and New Testament times," is historical), is "hypocrite" or "self-righteous person." The definition is illustrated by a sentence from

40. Charles Gore, "The Bible in the Church," in *NCHS*, part 1, 8.

41. *Reflections on the Psalms*, 12–16.

42. *Reflections on the Psalms*, 16–17.

43. Philip Zaleski and Carol Zaleski, *The Fellowship: The Literary Lives of the Inklings; J. R. R. Tolkien, C. S. Lewis, Owen Barfield, Charles Williams* (New York: Farrar, Straus & Giroux, 2015), 458.

Bronte's *Wuthering Heights*, "He was, and is . . . the wearisomest, self-righteous pharisee that ever ransacked a bible to rake the promises to himself, and fling the curses on his neighbours," and Malet's *History of Richard Calmady* (1901), "I was a self-righteous little Pharisee—forgive me." The *OED* entry alone demonstrates how much the equation "Pharisee = self-righteous" was baked into British culture. To the end of his life, Lewis defines "Phariseeism" as "self-righteousness and externality," and he refuses to entertain the notion that this view might be wrong. After reading the sentence "modern research has shown that the typical Pharisee was not a pious fraud," Lewis asks sardonically if Jesus was "singularly misinformed. He had not the advantage of modern research."[44]

As always, Lewis's reading on the topic is an important factor to consider. One reason for his urging Greeves to drop everything and buy Gore's *Jesus of Nazareth* in 1933 is that he is glad (finally!) to understand who the Pharisees are.[45] Because he credits the book with teaching him about Pharisees, it is instructive to look at what Lewis learned about them from Gore, by that time a long-established authority among Anglicans, in a book pitched to the general public.

What Gore wrote ranges from insidiously incorrect to poisonous. Pharisees were "legalistic." They were the "people of most importance in society." Their interpretation of Scripture, "which strikes us as quite irrational," had "spread like a net over all the details of human life." They were "self important," and Christians must have "regard[ed] them with horror." He contrasts "the ethical spirit of the old prophets of Israel as against Pharisaic legalism." Gore also contrasts Jesus, "a mere layman," to the Pharisees, "the authorities of an old-established church," who did not want to let "any unauthorized person" interpret Scripture to allow "light into the dungeon of tradition." Pharisees were closer to Jesus "than any other class," which is the only statement here approaching the truth, but it falls apart when he explains why: because both were devoted to "religion."[46] And, of course, they were responsible for the death of Jesus. Gore writes, "Christian Europe has often imagined that the Jews who caused Jesus to be crucified were abnormally wicked people. But that is

44. Marginal note on H. A. Williams, "Theology and Self-Awareness," in *Soundings*, ed. Alec Vidler (Cambridge: Cambridge University Press, 1962), 91. In his preface, Vidler sets the book in the trajectory of *Lux Mundi*.

45. Lewis to Greeves, Sept. 12, 1933, *CL*, 2:125, where Lewis also says he recognizes "a good bit" of Pharisee in himself.

46. On why the word "religion" is problematic here, see Brent Nongbri, *Before Religion: A History of a Modern Concept* (New Haven: Yale University Press, 2013).

not so. He had challenged the Pharisees to change their fundamental ideas and methods in matters of religion; and when have high ecclesiastics been ready to accept this challenge from a 'mere layman'?"[47]

It would take a volume to untangle the errors in the previous paragraph. Luckily for us, there is one: Joseph Sievers and Amy-Jill Levine's *The Pharisees*.[48] To those who don't understand why every bit of the paragraph is wrong, I rephrase what Lewis wrote to Greeves about *Jesus of Nazareth*: drop everything and read *The Pharisees* now.

Young Lewis recommended *Jesus of Nazareth* enthusiastically, and much of the book—for example, its emphasis on Jesus's concern for the poor—stands up well a century later. But it is a relief to find that, after a period of uncritical acceptance, Lewis appears to have outgrown some of what Gore wrote about Pharisees. He repeats Gore's absurd comparison of first-century Pharisees to twentieth-century Christian "high ecclesiastics" in an early letter, but to the best of my knowledge, he never mentions it again.[49]

Joy and Judaism

Lewis imbibed negative views about Pharisees and ancient Jews in general from his culture and his reading, and they were reinforced by his wife, Joy Davidman Gresham Lewis (1915–1960). Davidman, an American Jew who declared herself an atheist at age eight, became a Christian around 1948, in part through reading Lewis. She and her first husband, Bill Gresham, wrote him their first letter in 1949, and she met him for the first time in 1952. After the Greshams' divorce, Davidman and Lewis were married in a civil ceremony (1956) and then by an Anglican priest (1957). She died of cancer in 1960. One might think that Joy, as a Jew and a beloved spouse, would influence her husband's views of Judaism, but if she did, it may not have been for the better.

47. Gore, *Jesus of Nazareth*, 18, 27, 42, 45, 117. Gore felt ill-treated by some members of the Anglican hierarchy, and his biographer paints a tragi-comic portrait of him on Lambeth Bridge "shaking his fist at the Palace and shouting to the open-mouthed amazement of passers-by, 'The Bishops are hopeless! I am done with them!'" See P. D. L. Avis, "Gore and Theological Synthesis," *Scottish Journal of Theology* 28, no. 5 (1975): 462. It is therefore not entirely surprising that he would identify the "high ecclesiastics" of his own tradition with his perception of the Pharisees.

48. Joseph Sievers and Amy-Jill Levine, eds., *The Pharisees* (Grand Rapids: Eerdmans, 2021).

49. Lewis to his brother, April 8, 1932, *CL*, 2:70. The comparison is absurd because Pharisees themselves were "laymen."

Davidman, an award-winning poet and novelist, writes about Jews and Judaism in every genre she takes up, but I will limit my remarks to her nonfiction prose: the autobiographical essay "The Longest Way Round" (1951), the book *Smoke on the Mountain* (1954), and her letters.[50] All of them consistently link Judaism with three concepts: death, hatred, and self-righteousness. For example, the faith of her Eastern European forebears resembles the "taboo system of savages" more than "the prophetic Judaism of the Old Testament or the philosophic and scholarly Judaism" of the Middle Ages. Judaism "was kept going by persecution, as a dead man in a crowd may be kept on his feet by the pressure of those around him. In America, with the persecution removed, the corpse collapsed." This is only the most colorful expression of her thought. She believes the atheism of the Communist party is informed by the atheism of "'enlightened' Jews who are left spiritually bankrupt by the degeneracy of orthodox Judaism into a mixture of insane ritualism and insane nationalist pride." This atheism is "based not on reason but on a combination of disillusion with dead Judaism and hatred of live Christianity." She prefers explaining Jews to Gentiles rather than Gentiles to Jews because "the Jews are too busy hating."[51] She is certainly aware of antisemitism (although she claims to have experienced it personally only once) but feels entitled to make such judgments because, she says, "having been born a Jew, I have the right to say that a man ought to be free to criticize the Jews honestly." Jews who "scream for special immunity" only create more resentment, and "if we want everybody to love us, we'd better devote ourselves to learning to be lovable," implying that "we" are not lovable as we are.[52]

According to Davidman, Jews deserve their suffering. In a 1951 letter to Kenneth Porter, she writes:

50. For Davidman's portrayal of Judaism in her poems, short stories, and novels, see Don W. King, *Yet One More Spring: A Critical Study of Joy Davidman* (Grand Rapids: Eerdmans, 2015). Evaluating Davidman's novel *Anya*, Jeffrey Berman notes, "We cannot equate the author" with the title character, whom he calls a "Jewish anti-Semite," but Davidman's letters support the equation of her antisemitism at least. Berman, *Companionship in Grief: Love and Loss in the Memoirs of C. S. Lewis, John Bayley, Donald Hall, Joan Didion, and Calvin Trillin* (Amherst: University of Massachusetts Press, 2010), 27. See also Andrew Barron, "The Conflicted Jewish Imagination of Joy Davidman," *VII: Journal of the Marion E. Wade Center* 36 (2019): 48–70. I have looked only at Davidman's published letters; more insight into the topic may come from her unpublished work.

51. *Out of My Bone: The Letters of Joy Davidman*, ed. Don W. King (Grand Rapids: Eerdmans, 2009), 84, 102, 118–21.

52. *Out of My Bone*, 102, 107–8.

> The usual Jewish view of "what Christians believe about Jews" is pure paranoia. . . . [Bill Gresham] once said profoundly, "Anti-Semitism is the Jews' religion," and I have seen printed arguments by Jewish rabbis to the effect that it's very bad for the Jews *not* to be persecuted—allows them to forget their racial superiority! . . . Well, we *did* crucify Christ; the Romans wouldn't have given a damn, and what's worse we did, as a people, reject Him—though of course throughout history innumerable Jews have accepted Him and ceased to exist as Jews. . . . For their rejection the Jews have paid and are continuing to pay in the spiritual heartbreak of basing their culture on false premises. The persecutions—horrible enough, though not so unremitting as Jews imagine—are only the result of the Jews' willful self-isolation.[53]

Her endorsements of the claims that some Jews want to be persecuted because it makes them feel superior, that all Jews deserve persecution because they and not the Romans crucified Christ and continue to reject him, and that Jews bring persecution on themselves through their "willful self-isolation" are shocking, especially given when she wrote them, six years after the end of the Holocaust. Lewis proves himself better when he observes, "Hitler silenced all criticism of Jews."[54]

I haven't cherry-picked these statements. Davidman does scatter a few positive crumbs about Jews in *Smoke on the Mountain*, but they are swallowed up by the larger negative whole. *Smoke on the Mountain*, subtitled "An Interpretation of the Ten Commandments," is as close in kind to *Reflections on the Psalms* as it can be. Both books were composed by gifted writers who were nonetheless amateurs regarding their subject matter, and both focus on a discrete section of the Hebrew Scriptures that serves as a springboard for comments on the modern world. Davidman says less about ancient Jews in her book than one might expect given the subject, and when she does, it is almost always to lament their deterioration. She spares a few positive asides for Judaism as it existed before "the rise of an organized and legalistic priesthood," when Jews were savage but "for the most part healthy and brave and sane," a situation that soon changed. As they were defeated by foreign nations, "the sins of the animal . . . were replaced by the sins of the devil: bitterness and pride." Jews became "blind with hatred," dreaming of a messiah who could wreak revenge

53. *Out of My Bone*, 122–23 (emphasis in original).

54. Lewis to Nathan Starr, July 30, 1962, *CL*, 3:1360. I must assume that Lewis is not excusing crimes that individual Jews or the state of Israel may commit.

on their enemies. When Jesus told them instead that "'My kingdom is not of this world,' they crucified him in rage and disappointment," she writes. "Even their law, once a meaningful relation with God, had become corrupted into pointless rituals and taboos, cherished mainly as a reassurance that they were indeed different from other people, a true superrace [*sic*]."[55]

It is hard to watch her regurgitate time-worn anti-Jewish slander.[56] Like Gore's comments on Pharisees, Davidman's recital on Jews ranges from prejudice to error. Here too refutation would require a volume, but I will take the time dispatch one claim. "The Jews" did not crucify Jesus; the Romans did. The Gospels portray certain Jews handing him over to Pontius Pilate, but they had no power to crucify anyone. Answering the question "Who killed Jesus?" is complicated,[57] but evaluating Davidman's belief that "the Jews" wanted him dead because he didn't deliver an earthly kingdom is not, because it is simply fantastical.

Davidman could have absorbed anti-Jewish calumny from any number of sources. Raised in a family dominated by an atheist father, she attended public schools in the Bronx. She rejected all forms of religion until she was rocked by a profound spiritual experience, and "God came in." From 1946 to 1949, Davidman undertook an "unsystematic but intense" study of religion that included the Bible "and its modern interpretation," during the course of which she considered becoming a "good Jew, of the comfortable 'Reformed' persuasion," but reading the New Testament convinced her to become a Christian.[58] Other than mentioning Lewis's books, she divulges nothing of her extrascriptural expository reading about religion in this period, so we don't know what works of modern biblical interpretation she read. We do know that execrable views on Jews like hers had been percolating among influential biblical scholars for quite some time. Davidman's characterization of Judaism as "dead," for exam-

55. *Smoke on the Mountain*, 16, 53, 133, 75–76.

56. Compare Amy-Jill Levine, "Bearing False Witness: Common Errors Made about Early Judaism," in *The Jewish Annotated New Testament*, ed. Amy-Jill Levine and Marc Zvi Brettler, 2nd ed. (Oxford: Oxford University Press, 2017), 759–63.

57. See J. Ramsey Michaels, "John 18:31 and the 'Trial' of Jesus," *New Testament Studies* 36, no. 3 (1990): 474–79; John Dominic Crossan, *Who Killed Jesus? Exposing the Roots of Anti-Semitism in the Gospel Story of the Death of Jesus* (San Francisco: HarperSanFrancisco, 1995).

58. William Gresham, "From Communist to Christian," in *These Found the Way: Thirteen Converts to Protestant Christianity*, ed. David Wesley Soper (Philadelphia: Westminster, 1951), 76–77; Abigail Santamaria, *Joy: Poet, Seeker, and the Woman Who Captivated C. S. Lewis* (Boston: Houghton Mifflin Harcourt, 2015), 176; Davidman, *Out of My Bone*, 93, 96.

ple, is found in the work of Friedrich Schleiermacher and Julius Wellhausen. As Jörg Frey writes, "For Schleiermacher, the 'church father of the 19th century,' contemporary Judaism was a mummy, a dead and merely external religion."[59] Davidman's narrative of Jewish decline from the ethical heights of the prophets to the "ritualism" and "legalism" of the priests could have been written by the nineteenth-century biblical scholar Wellhausen, who identified four main sources for the Pentateuch, abbreviated JEDP. *P* is the Priestly source, the last and, according to Wellhausen, worst stage of ancient Judaism, the one that turned it into a "dead work." His theory sits on a foundation of anti-Judaic bias that went unacknowledged by Christian scholars for far too long.[60]

Closer to home was the impact of her father. Joy's biographer Abigail Santamaria shows that Joseph Davidman was widely known for being "self-righteous"—so much so that it alienated his siblings and even stopped him advancing in his career.[61] At the risk of falling into discredited Freudianism, I speculate that Joy transferred her father's defect to Jews in general. She gives us a lot to work with in her essay "The Longest Way Round," which, like many autobiographies, commences with her parents. Davidman calls herself "an atheist and the daughter of an atheist." Her father insisted that he had "retained the ethics of Judaism, the only 'real' part of it," but she disagreed. An atheist might possess a morality, but it couldn't be a rational one, because without God "nothing is wrong." Therefore, she writes, "What can the best atheist do but turn Pharisee? Since he himself is the only standard of value he recognizes, why shouldn't he be proud?"[62] Davidman considers her father a Pharisee, which she defines as a self-righteous person overcome with spiritual pride. It looks like she imports this fraught relationship with a (by all accounts) maddening man into her writing on Judaism, because she says much the same thing about Pharisees in *Smoke on the Mountain*. Pharisees always think they are right, and when they speak, "God agrees."[63]

59. Jörg Frey, "Anti-Judaism, Philosemitism, and Protestant New Testament Studies: Perspectives and Questions," in *Protestant Bible Scholarship: Antisemitism, Philosemitism and Anti-Judaism*, ed. Arjen Bakker et al. (Leiden: Brill, 2022), 160.

60. Julius Wellhausen, *Prolegomena to the History of Ancient Israel* (1878; repr., New York: Meridian Library, 1957), 425. See Stacy Davis, "Unapologetic Apologetics: Julius Wellhausen, Anti-Judaism, and Hebrew Bible Scholarship," *Religions* 12, no. 8 (2021).

61. Santamaria, *Joy*, 7, 11–13.

62. *Out of My Bone*, 83–85; Santamaria, *Joy*, 33.

63. *Out of My Bone*, 128; *Smoke on the Mountain*, 46.

Outside his foreword to her book, Lewis has little to say about Davidman on Judaism. In 1955 he recommends the book and describes its author as a Jewish convert to Christianity. He says a bit more in a 1959 letter. First, Davidman thinks Gentiles misread the Old Testament because they don't get its humor—as for example in Jonah—but Jews do. Second, Lewis reports without comment her belief that "the only living Judaism is Christianity. Where her own people still have any religion it is archaic, pedantic."[64] If the only living Judaism is Christianity, Judaism itself must be dead. But is that what Lewis himself thought, and, if he did, did he adopt the opinion from Davidman?

At the beginning of the letter, Lewis calls his wife a "Semitic genius." It is hard to know exactly what he means by the phrase. She was a Jew, and she was a verified genius, since her IQ test reportedly broke the charts.[65] But does he mean that she was well-versed in Judaism, and he should therefore defer to her on the topic? He may have considered his wife an expert on Jews, but—and now we don't have to speculate—he didn't always agree with her. He states this explicitly in his foreword to *Smoke on the Mountain*, where he also tries to tamp down some of her anti-Jewish rhetoric. When she calls Jews "My root Who evolve viciously in the east," Lewis tries to soften her language. He counters, "Not perhaps viciously, but without doubt fiercely."[66]

All things considered, then, I disagree with P. H. Brazier's thesis about Davidman's influence on Lewis. In his book *A Hebraic Inkling: C. S. Lewis on Judaism and the Jews*, Brazier states that Davidman "taught him to eschew anti-Semitism."[67] Looking at the available evidence, this does not seem likely. Given what Davidman wrote on Jews throughout her life, if she influenced Lewis on the topic, it probably would have been for the worse.

Jack, Joy, and Supersessionism

Everything we have seen so far leads to the conclusion that Jack and Joy were supersessionists. Neither one of them knew the word, as it was coined in 1972,

64. Lewis to Dorothy L. Sayers: April 6, 1955, *CL*, 3:596; Bede Griffiths, April 30, 1959, *CL*, 3:1042–43.

65. Santamaria, *Joy*, 13.

66. Foreword to *Smoke on the Mountain*, 8. Leslie Baynes, review of *A Hebraic Inkling: C. S. Lewis on Judaism and the Jews*, by P. H. Brazier, *Journal of Inklings Studies* 12, no. 2 (2022): 259–66.

67. Brazier, *Hebraic Inkling*, 202.

almost a decade after Lewis died, but it applies to both of them.[68] That said, they were not equally so. Joy was what David Novak calls a "hard supersessionist," and Jack more of a "soft supersessionist." As Novak defines them, hard supersessionists believe "the old covenant [between God and the Jews] is dead," and they "treat Jews who are not Christians as if they are dead."[69] This definition clearly fits Joy. Judging from what she wrote in the 1951 letter, she was also what Kendall Soulen calls a "punitive supersessionist," someone who thinks God punished the Jews for rejecting Jesus and chose Christians to replace them.[70] Jack, with his more irenic temperament, usually exhibits soft supersessionism, which views the old covenant not as revoked but fulfilled. I say "usually" because in *Reflections on the Psalms* he does claim that Jesus transcends and abrogates Judaism, while he also "fulfils it."[71] Despite his use of "abrogate" here, Lewis gives no indication that he thinks the old covenant is dead anywhere else. Even his essay "The Psalms," which contains the harshest language he ever writes on Jews, never hints at the idea.[72] To the best of my knowledge, he never speculates on their ultimate destiny.

But he always thought Christianity was better than Judaism, an unsurprising thing for a Christian to think. As Amy-Jill Levine observes, "All religions, I suspect, have supersessionistic tendencies"; the challenge is to minimize the harm they may inflict.[73] Even though Lewis was a softer supersessionist than Davidman, his comments on the inferiority of Jews can still stun, as when he asserts that a "converted Jew" is "the only normal human being." To Christians, he continues, the "unconverted Jew (I mean no offense) must appear as a Christian *manqué*; someone very carefully prepared for a certain destiny and then missing it." Apparently attempting to mitigate any offense, he appeals to Romans 11:17–24: Gentile Christians are latecomers, grafted on to the tree of God by grace, and they should remember this fact more often.[74] But he

68. Michael G. Azar, "'Supersessionism': The Political Origin of a Theological Neologism," *Studies in Christian-Jewish Relations* 16, no. 1 (2021): 1–25.

69. David Novak, "The Covenant in Rabbinic Thought," in *Two Faiths, One Covenant? Jewish and Christian Identity in the Presence of the Other*, ed. Eugene B. Korn and John Pawlikowski (Lanham, MD: Rowman & Littlefield, 2005), 66.

70. Kendall R. Soulen, *The God of Israel and Christian Theology* (Minneapolis: Fortress, 1996).

71. *Reflections on the Psalms*, 129.

72. Lewis, "The Psalms," in *Essay Collection*, 218–30.

73. Amy-Jill Levine, "Supersessionism: Admit and Address Rather Than Debate or Deny," *Religions* 13, no. 2 (2022): 4.

74. Foreword to *Smoke on the Mountain*, 7.

can still say that ancient Jews had "far less reason than [Christians] for loving God" because they didn't know Jesus would die for them, and "there is thus a tragic depth in our worship which Judaism lacked." While the section in which these sentiments appear praises ancient Jews, with Lewis noting that Christians should admire and emulate their longing for God, these sentences stagger me. No contemporary Christian reviewer of *Reflections on the Psalms*—and there were dozens—mentioned them, but Jewish reviewers did. Frieda Clark Hyman, writing for the journal *Judaism*, was more than kind when she noted that they must "strike the Jew as downright silly." Another review in *Jewish Social Studies* decries Lewis's "easy assumption of the superiority of Christianity over Judaism."[75]

I think it's a wonder Lewis wasn't more supersessionistic than he was. With Charles Gore marking the beginning of his adult education on ancient Jews and Joy Davidman the end, it could have been worse. But he was always more than a product of his influences, of course. Lest readers take away an incomplete picture of his views on Jews, they must note what he did for his stepson David Gresham when the young man wanted to return to his Jewish roots. Lewis supported him unreservedly, arranging lessons in Hebrew and going to considerable trouble to buy him kosher food.[76] His actions were better than his words.

While it is necessary to identify major problems in *Reflections on the Psalms*, it is just as important to look at the many aspects of ancient Judaism it gets right. We turn to these now.

Jewish Law in the Psalms

Lewis is surprisingly generous on the topic of the Jewish law in *Reflections on the Psalms*, as he tends to be neutral to negative about it elsewhere.[77] Here he accentuates the positive, looking for good even in things that don't initially appeal to him. Hence the title of his chapter on the law is "Sweeter Than Honey," a quotation of Psalm 19:10. At first, he says, he didn't understand the

75. *Reflections on the Psalms*, 50, 52. Frieda Clark Hyman, review of *Reflections on the Psalms*, by C. S. Lewis, *Judaism* 8, no. 2 (1959): 190; Robert Gordis, review of *Book of Job, a Commentary*, by Solomon B. Freehof, *Reflections on the Psalms*, by C. S. Lewis, *Jewish Social Studies* 21, no. 4 (1959): 248.

76. Alister E. McGrath, *C. S. Lewis: A Life; Eccentric Genius, Reluctant Prophet* (Carol Stream, IL: Tyndale, 2013), 352.

77. See his foreword to *Smoke on the Mountain*, 9.

comparison. How could a law be "sweet"? As he puzzles through the problem, he answers the question, but any first-year student of Hebrew could have gotten there quicker.

He knows that Jewish Law—which he capitalizes as a divine entity—is not limited to the Ten Commandments. But he doesn't seem to grasp the full range of the Hebrew word *torah*, which can indeed be translated "law" but equally as "teaching" or "instruction." The weight of centuries of Christian (mis)interpretation hobbled Lewis as he approached the word, but there was a solution close to hand: his Gore commentary. It doesn't employ the word *torah* often, but when it does, it gets it right. "Hence the term *torah* = 'direction' or 'guidance' [is] inadequately translated 'law' in the English versions," notes the chapter on Judges. "The law (*tōrāh*) certainly means parent's or sage's instruction," explains the chapter on Proverbs.[78] Lewis intuits these senses of the word when he imagines an ancient Jew approaching the Law as a subject one might study. He is correct, but he presents the idea as his own insight rather than the actual meaning of the word, something easily found in any Hebrew lexicon.

Psalm 19 is his favorite, and he considers it one of the greatest poems ever written. Taking it as his vantage point, Lewis envisions the "truth" (Hebrew *emeth*) of the Law as a large, luminous thing like the sun. In his foreword to *Smoke on the Mountain*, he can glide from describing the "fierceness" of Davidman and her people to the fierceness of Psalm 19, where "the Sun and the Law become fused in the poet's mind," and nothing can hide from their "disinfectant blaze" (19:5–6). There is "no self-righteousness" here.[79] Even though Lewis paints ancient Jews as "typically" self-righteous, Psalm 19 moves him to a more positive generalization: the "characteristically Jewish feeling that the Law is not only obligatory but beautiful, . . . sweeter than honey."[80] His love for Psalm 19 helps him overcome his typically Christian ignorance about the Law, a development that gratifies even the Jewish reviewers of the book.[81]

The Afterlife

In his chapter "Death in the Psalms," Lewis gets the key terms "soul" and "Sheol" just right, and he makes short work of correcting common misunderstandings

78. L. E. P. Erith, "Judges," in *NCHS*, 211; A. E. Morris, "The Proverbs," in *NCHS*, 398.

79. *Reflections on the Psalms*, 63; foreword to *Smoke on the Mountain*, 8; *Reflections on the Psalms*, 64.

80. Lewis to Mary Van Deusen, Feb. 5, 1956, *CL*, 3:701. See *Reflections on the Psalms*, 56, 60–61.

81. See Hyman, review of *Reflections*, 190; Gordis, review of *Reflections*, 248.

about them. The Hebrew word often translated "soul" (*nephesh*) doesn't refer to the part of a person that survives death, but to one's life on earth. "Sheol," often translated "hell," is not eternal fire, but the place where everyone—good, bad, or indifferent—goes after death. In this chapter, Lewis's facts are correct, his examples astute, his understanding of the evolution of ideas on the afterlife impeccable, and even his characterization of Pharisees unobjectionable.[82]

His reflections on these ideas for his Christian audience stand up well, too. Now, as then, some Christians find it hard to imagine a "religion" that isn't concerned with eternal bliss and punishment, and many of those consider belief in God primarily as a means to attain the one and avoid the other. Lewis, in contrast, considers his year of believing in God before he believed in an afterlife (1930–1931) a great blessing, a time when he learned disinterested love of God because he was not seeking God for personal gain. For Lewis, there is no God and X—that is, some end other than God that attempts to use God as a means. The Lord will not be thus used. Christians who have fallen prey to questionable theology on the afterlife, such as a "rapture" where "true Christians" disappear at the end of the age, may find his words a salutary slap in the face. Lewis never mentions the rapture or its theological kin, dispensationalism, in his published work, perhaps because he took against them in his youth. His friend Arthur Greeves grew up in a household of Plymouth Brethren, a group whose founder, John Nelson Darby, developed dispensationalism less than a century before Greeves and Lewis met. Both boys rejected Darby's theology. Lewis considered the dispensationalist Greeves family poor interpreters of Scripture, and he poked gentle fun at Mrs. Greeves's love of reading books on end-times prophecy.[83]

Babylonian Babies

One of the hardest things to discuss in the Psalms is "The Cursings," as Lewis entitles the third chapter of his book. Among the most infamous of the cursing psalms is 137:8–9: "O daughter of Babylon, wasted with misery: yea, happy shall he be that rewardeth thee, as thou hast served us. Blessed shall he be that taketh thy children: and throweth them against the stones" (Coverdale).[84]

82. *Reflections on the Psalms*, 36–39.

83. *Reflections on the Psalms*, 40–43; Clarence B. Bass, *Backgrounds to Dispensationalism* (Eugene, OR: Wipf & Stock, 2005), 64; Walter Hooper, ed., *They Stand Together: The Letters of C. S. Lewis to Arthur Greeves (1914–1963)* (London: Collins, 1979), 16–18, 28, 432–33. See also Daniel G. Hummel, *The Rise and Fall of Dispensationalism: How the Evangelical Battle over the End Times Shaped a Nation* (Grand Rapids: Eerdmans, 2023).

84. Clapton, *Our Prayer Book Psalter*, 333.

He reserves comment on this passage until the end of the book, where he discusses "second meanings." Up to that point, he had been trying to reflect on the Psalms in their historical context. But most Christians through the ages haven't done this, he says; instead, they have read them Christologically, in light of Christ. Even though the psalmists were not thinking about Jesus, Christians treated them as if they were, producing "second meanings" the ancient authors didn't intend. Christians may arrive at these new meanings through allegorical interpretation. Lewis, an acclaimed expert on allegory, hated his own fiction being allegorized.[85] In *Reflections on the Psalms,* he empathizes with how the psalmists might feel about their words being wrenched out of context before he defends certain forms of allegorizing and applies them to Psalm 137:9 himself.

People allegorize for many reasons. Some do it for fun, and this is probably what motivates readers of Lewis's fiction. More often, readers allegorize a text that is important to them but that has become problematic. They no longer understand it, or they do understand it but don't agree with it, or it's embarrassing, or it no longer seems relevant, and they desperately want it to remain relevant. Because it matters, they can't discard it or leave it to languish as they might another, less fundamental, text. Psalm 137:9 poses all of these problems. It is canonical Scripture for Jews and Christians, but most of them consider a God who blesses baby killers repugnant. Allegory can step in as a salvage operation. It "saves" the Babylonian babies, and thus saves Scripture.

The germ of Lewis's allegory on Psalm 137:9 appears in his booklet *Christian Behaviour* (1942–1943), but I like how he puts it in a 1945 letter to Sister Penelope. She had told him that some plays she had written would not be produced, and he wants to temper his sympathy as he responds, refraining from expressing how badly he feels for her, lest he encourage her to indulge "those very emotions which, no doubt, you are in process of successfully knocking on the head!"[86] That is, he doesn't want to feed any resentment she might have but rather help her overcome it.

Lewis doesn't mention Psalm 137:9 in the letter, but he applies similar language to it in *Reflections on the Psalms,* attempting to redeem what he calls a "devilish" verse.[87] The first time I read the passage, I was bowled over by his adroit

85. See chapter 9 of this book, "Allegory or Otherwise?"

86. *Mere Christianity* (1952; repr., San Francisco: HarperSanFrancisco, 2001), bk. 3, ch. 7, "Forgiveness." See also bk. 4, ch. 8, "Is Christianity Hard or Easy?," where it appears almost identically as in *Reflections on the Psalms.* Lewis to Sister Penelope, Jan. 3, 1945, *CL,* 2:635.

87. *Reflections on the Psalms,* 20.

save—how he made something odious not only spiritually helpful but even rather charming. The Babylonian babies are allegorized as "infantile beginnings" of resentments that whine for attention, dangerous because, if indulged, they will grow up and mature into hatred. But, he continues, "Against such pretty infants (the dears have such winning ways) the advice of the Psalm is the best. Knock the little bastards' brains out." The last line is so memorable that sixty-two years later it was adopted as the title for a scholarly article on the verse.[88]

But Lewis didn't devise this allegorical interpretation of Psalm 137 himself. It goes back to the third century CE, to Origen of Alexandria's *Contra Celsum* (Against Celsus), a book Lewis owned. As Origen thinks through questions about God and violence, he notes that righteous people destroy the evil within themselves, "so that there is not left even an infant sin," and he advises his readers to apply this insight to Psalm 137:8–9. On Origen's allegorical interpretation, "Babylon" means "confusion," and the "infants of Babylon" are "confused thoughts" growing in the soul. Whoever "takes hold of them, so that he breaks their heads by the firmness and solidity of the Word, is dashing the infants of Babylon against the rock, and on this account he becomes blessed." If they think about it like this, Origen concludes, Christians can interpret Psalm 137:9 so it coheres with the gospel.[89] For it does not in fact cohere with the gospel, he claims, and neither do other verses like LXX Psalm 100:8: "Every morning I will kill all the sinners of the earth, to eradicate the lawless from the city of the Lord." No one can take this literally, he says, because the rest of the psalm is so sublime. Centuries later Lewis makes a similar observation, noting that curses pop up "most disquietingly in Psalms we love."[90]

Since Psalm 137:9 is among the most problematic verses in the Bible, Lewis's treatment caught the attention of many reviewers.[91] Most of them approved, but a few did not. Among the latter, the Roman Catholic philosopher Elizabeth

88. *Reflections on the Psalms*, 20, 136. Arie Versluis, "'Knock the Little Bastards' Brains Out': Reception History and Theological Interpretation of Psalm 137:9," in *Violence in the Hebrew Bible*, ed. Jacques van Ruiten and Koert van Bekkum (Leiden: Brill, 2020), 373–96.

89. *Contra Celsum* 7.22, trans. Henry Chadwick (Cambridge: Cambridge University Press, 1953), p. 413. Lewis owned this edition.

90. Origen, *Contra Celsum* 7.19, pp. 410–11; *Reflections on the Psalms*, 21.

91. These include the Hyman review cited above; *Time*, Sept. 22, 1958, 67; M. K. T., "Wise Words in the Psalms," *Amarillo Sunday News-Globe*, Nov. 9, 1958; M. T. R., *Virginia Churchman*, Jan. 1959; J. C. Macaulay, "One Amateur to Another," *Eternity*, March 1959, 38; Stevie Smith, "The Simple Psalms," *Spectator*, Sept. 12, 1958, 352; Jerome Stowell, *Worship* 23, no. 5, 130; and G. E. M. Anscombe, "Some Remarks

Anscombe and the Jewish writer Frieda Clark Hyman stand out. Anscombe is known to many Lewis aficionados through the Socratic Club debate where the two argued about a point in his book *Miracles*.[92] She won that conflict, but, as we will see, he wins this one. Hyman's critique, less adversarial and more historically grounded than Anscombe's, is more successful.

Throughout her short review, Anscombe claims that the translations Lewis chose for *Reflections on the Psalms*—Coverdale informed by Moffatt—are faulty. Had he used others, the unpleasantness of the cursing psalms, and of Psalm 137:9 in particular, might disappear. She especially criticizes his use of Moffatt, whom she describes as "a translator notoriously given to depraving his version to suit his own beliefs."[93] Inflammatory language aside, it is true that Moffatt is prone to idiosyncratic renditions that sometimes look more like paraphrase than translation. Lewis was well aware of the fact. In his copy of Moffatt's New Testament, he not infrequently makes marginal notes to the effect of "that's not in the Greek!" In part 3 of this book, we will see that Moffatt's translation does affect Lewis's reading of Scripture, but it does not appear to do so here. Lewis doesn't quote Psalm 137:9 in any translation in *Reflections on the Psalms*; he paraphrases it in his own words. More importantly, however, Anscombe's accusation is misguided because the choice of translator doesn't matter. The Hebrew of 137:9 is straightforward, and a different translation is powerless to render its content less difficult.[94]

Anscombe doesn't suggest alternative translations, but as a staunch Roman Catholic she was surely familiar with the Douay-Rheims, which was based on the Vulgate and produced by Oxford scholars for English-speaking Catholics. The New Testament (1582), published in Rheims, and the Old Testament (1609–1610, right before the 1611 KJV), published in Douay, served as *the* English translation for Catholics through the mid-twentieth century. Its version of Psalm 137:9 reads, "Blessed be he that shall take and dash thy little ones against the rock," which does not differ substantially from Moffatt: "A blessing on him who snatches your babes and dashes them down on the rocks!"

---

on C. S. Lewis' *Reflections on the Psalms* (1959)," *Journal of Inklings Studies* 9, no. 2 (2019): 177.

92. See chapter 8 of this book.

93. Anscombe, "Some Remarks," 177. For another appraisal of her remarks, see Matthew Wiseman, "A Biblical Scholar's Note on Anscombe's Review of Lewis's *Reflections on the Psalms*," *Journal of Inklings Studies* 9, no. 2 (2019): 178–80.

94. See Marc Zvi Brettler, "Psalm 137:9—a Verse to Criticize," TheTorah.com, 2015, https://tinyurl.com/53bwew3s.

Not everyone admired the Douay. A critique from Hugh Pope (d. 1946), a Roman Catholic biblical scholar, speaks to Anscombe's conflict with Lewis, but not in her favor. Pope remarks that the Douay's "translation of the Psalms is regarded as particularly deplorable, but it must be remembered that the Latin text as it stands is far from satisfactory, and that among Protestants the AV Psalms are equally deplored and compare unfavourably with those of the Prayer Book."[95] In other words, a biblical scholar in Anscombe's own church argues that the translation of the Psalms in the Anglican Prayer Book—Coverdale's—is better than those of both the Authorized Version (KJV) and his own tradition's Douay. Lewis was aware of such issues, having published the chapter "Religious Controversy and Translation" in OHEL. He didn't need Anscombe's tutelage.

The Douay urges its readers to interpret Psalm 137/136:9 exactly as Lewis does. The 1610 edition offers a lengthy note on the verse, explaining that "morally he is blessed" who kills his own passions and small sins so they don't grow strong in his soul and make him commit mortal sin.[96] Richard Challoner (d. 1781), who revised the 1610 edition and its notes, rephrased the comment on Babylonian babies thus: "*Dash thy little ones*, &c. In the spiritual sense, we dash the little ones of Babylon against the rock, when we mortify our passions, and stifle the first motions of them, by a speedy recourse to the rock which is Christ." This note appears in the Douay to the present.[97]

Despite the amount of time I have devoted to it, Anscombe's main objection to Lewis is not his choice of translator, but rather his audacity in thinking he can judge the Bible and find it wanting. She admits Scripture "records much that is mean and beastly," but it is not acceptable to "say that beliefs and attitudes which are circulated by the Bible can be worthy of condemnation." To do so "discredits Christian tradition."[98] It is particularly important to respect

95. Hugh Pope, with revisions by Sebastian Bullough, "The History of the Rheims-Douay Version," in *A Catholic Commentary on Holy Scripture*, ed. Bernard Orchard (Edinburgh: Thomas Nelson and Sons, 1953), 36. At 1,300 pages, this volume looks like a Roman Catholic counterpart to Gore's Anglican *New Commentary on Holy Scripture*. See also Alexandra Walsham, "Unclasping the Book? The Douai-Rheims Bible," in *Catholic Reformation in Protestant Britain* (Surrey: Ashgate, 2014), 285–314.

96. *The holie Bible faithfully translated into English, out of the authentical Latin. Diligently conferred with the Hebrew, Greeke, and other editions in diuers languages. With arguments of the bookes, and chapters: annotations. tables: and other helpes . . . By the English College of Doway*, vol. 2 (1610), https://tinyurl.com/3s23vcz7.

97. https://tinyurl.com/3x64bp87.

98. Anscombe, "Some Remarks," 176.

the Psalms, because they form the Christian prayerbook. If "some disquieting phrase" there puzzles readers, she suggests three responses: to consider it none of their business, to look for a better translation, or to seek instruction.[99]

Anscombe can't believe Lewis takes the psalmist at his word—that the ancient author really does bless baby killers. If Lewis consulted other translations and scholarly commentaries, he might doubt "whether the text meant any such thing." Furthermore, other Scripture also rejoices in the destruction of God's enemies, which makes the emotion right and proper. She highlights passages in the New Testament, especially Revelation, an effective rhetorical move, anticipating as it does the objection that Christian Scripture had left such vindictive rejoicing behind.[100]

Because *Reflections on the Psalms* might make Roman Catholics question God's word, Anscombe thinks they should not read it, and that is why she wrote her review—to warn them off. However, among Catholic reviewers she stands alone. Dom Augustine James calls the book "delectable" and praises the choice of Coverdale. Myles M. Bourke especially enjoys the section on second meanings in the Psalms. Jerome Stowell singles out Lewis's treatment of Psalm 137:9 for special praise, and J. M. Lelen's review is so effusive as to be cringeworthy.[101]

Both Anscombe and Lewis were amateurs when it came to the Bible, but in their skirmish on the Psalms, he won. No translation can soften 137:9. The compulsion to rehabilitate the psalmist, and by extension God and his word, long predates Lewis, and the allegory he highlights is a long-standing component of the established translation of Anscombe's own church. The Douay never calls the verse "devilish," but by offering the allegorical gloss, it quietly admits it is a problem. Anscombe had bested Lewis in the *Miracles* controversy, where her expertise trumped his, but he prevails here.

The Jewish writer Frieda Clark Hyman also critiques Lewis's treatment of the cursing psalms, but more successfully than Anscombe. Like her, she disapproves of the fact that these psalms upset him, and she doesn't approve of his attempts to explain them away. Like Anscombe, she takes Lewis to task for call-

99. Anscombe, "Some Remarks," 177.

100. Anscombe, "Some Remarks," 177.

101. Dom Augustine James, review of *Reflections on the Psalms,* by C. S. Lewis, *Downside Review* 78 (1960): 131–34; Myles M. Bourke, review of *Reflections on the Psalms,* by C. S. Lewis, and *Les Psaumes Commentés Par La Bible I–II,* by Pierre Guichou, *Blackfriars* (1959): 389–91; Jerome Stowell, *Worship* 23, no. 5, 130; J. M. Lelen, review of *Reflections on the Psalms,* by C. S. Lewis, *Priest* 15 (1959): 758–59.

ing 137:9 "devilish," but for quite different reasons. Hyman objects to the word because, as we might say today, it "punches down." The psalm was written by someone "tortured by his memories beyond endurance," and she imagines an author who had "seen his Temple destroyed; his home, family, people put to the sword," and his own children "dashed upon the rocks." Unlike Anscombe, Hyman has no interest in preserving the good repute of the psalmist, the Psalms, the Scriptures, or even God as author of Scripture. "The language is man's," she notes, and "the Bible is man's journey on earth."[102] Lewis would agree up to a point: Scripture was written by humans.[103] But he wouldn't stop there, because to him it is more than that. Unlike Hyman, Lewis will not sit content with reading Psalm 137:9 solely as historical record; he wants it, and its picture of God, to speak to his own image of God, his own ethics, and his own time.

I have devoted several pages to how Lewis works with Psalm 137:9 and contemporary reviews of it because the verse is an infamous crux, the interpretation of which reveals more about its reader than the text. What does Lewis's reading say about him, then? First, he tries to find good even in Scripture that repels him. He holds both that 137:9 is "devilish" and that there are helpful ways to interpret it, offering an example his audience can apply to their lives. Everyone has had to fight resentment. Second, his allegorical reading places him in a long line of interpreters willing to move beyond a "plain meaning" of the text to a "spiritual" one. Third, even though he considers the entire canon inspired, he feels free to criticize and even condemn parts of the Old Testament. Thus he avoids excusing the inexcusable—the idea that God blesses the slaughter of infants—and spouting nonsense like Anscombe does. But he will not make quite so free with the New Testament.

Reflections on Scripture

Chapter 11 of *Reflections on the Psalms*, "Scripture," is the most sustained and sophisticated articulation of the topic Lewis ever published, where clarity, humility, and beauty meet. Before the book appeared in 1958, he had discussed his theories on the Bible chiefly in letters, none of which was published in his lifetime. Chapter 11, in contrast to the letters, is not ad hoc and private, but purposeful and public.

It is positioned in the book as the filling in a literary sandwich, set between chapter 10, "Second Meanings," and chapter 12, "Second Meanings in

102. Hyman, review of *Reflections*, 190, 188.

103. *Reflections on the Psalms*, 116–17.

the Psalms." Chapter 10 argues that pagan texts can elicit second meanings, and before he moves to chapter 12, Lewis wants to explain why Christians believe the Old Testament is even more likely to do so. One reason is because they consider it the "Oracles of God," but he doesn't want anyone to misconstrue how he understands that phrase. He is not a fundamentalist, someone who decides in advance that every bit of the Bible is historically and scientifically accurate. Such a view is an illegitimate a priori assumption, akin to believing that miracles are impossible, and just as likely to stop good thinking dead. Like Charles Gore, Lewis knows that the Old Testament is imperfect, and through his work on the Psalms, he has shown it to contain "naïvety, error, contradiction, even . . . wickedness." That said, he never rejects the Old Testament, because he doesn't approach it with the supposition that its problems invalidate the collection as a whole. The Bible is not "the Word of God," he says, if "Word of God" means every bit of it is "impeccable science or history." Rather, Scripture "carries the Word" as expressed by humans.[104] He is not altogether happy with this conclusion. Sometimes he envies how fundamentalists rely on the Bible and Roman Catholics rely on their church—as unquestioned authorities.[105] Being neither a fundamentalist nor a Catholic, he refuses such comfortable certainty.

However, it is not only the Old Testament that is confusing. In 1958 Lewis is still pondering the question that occupied him when he returned to the Christian fold in 1931: why doesn't the New Testament offer clear, systematic theology, as one might expect a gracious God to provide? Christ's teaching in the Gospels is perfect, but systematic it is not. Sometimes it appears to contradict itself, and anyone who tries to pin it down will discover that Jesus is "the most elusive of teachers." Even Paul, on whose letters so much rests, lacks the gift of clarity. All of this frustrates Lewis, the clearest of writers, but his frustration bears fruit. He concludes that Jesus was elusive on purpose because he didn't want to be approached solely with the intellect. He wanted his followers to steep themselves in his "Personality," and so, with the help of grace and other people, conform their lives to the image of God.[106]

"In the same way," Lewis continues, the imperfections of the Old Testament fortuitously prevent readers from accepting it as is, making them grapple with

104. *Reflections on the Psalms*, 109–12.

105. Lewis may have plucked this idea from Thomas Arnold. See Anthony John Harding, *Coleridge and the Inspired Word* (Kingston, ON: McGill-Queen's University Press, 1985), 100.

106. *Reflections on the Psalms*, 112–14.

God's gradual revelation through "human material." Once again, the incarnation of Christ is key. Jesus was human, and just as humanity with all its faults can be divinized through Christ, so the faulty human words of Scripture can carry the divine. What Lewis calls "the lower," the true humanity of Scripture, is taken up for a higher purpose, and so it can be rife with "second meanings."[107] For Lewis, with his lightning grasp of literature, the Bible presents a rare challenge: a text he cannot master. Therefore, he reasons, mastering it isn't the point. Living it, to the end of conforming himself to the image of God, is.

Conclusion

The present book opens with Lewis recommending Gore's commentary on Scripture, and part 1 has shown that, for better and worse, Gore's scholarship affects Lewis's writing on the Bible. Inasmuch as it follows Gore, Lewis's work sits squarely in the mainstream of mid-twentieth-century Anglicanism, and through Lewis's perennial popularity, it continues to gain traction. At the same time, Lewis's writing on Scripture has also garnered detractors from all sides, and part 2 addresses these ongoing controversies. Lewis located himself between what he called "fundamentalists" and "modernists," but he targeted the bulk of his firepower to the left flank. The "modernists" have paid him little heed, remaining serenely indifferent to the volleys he fired. Such is not the case with the "fundamentalists," who continue to devote more energy to arguing against Lewis on biblical interpretation than he ever spent on them. Some Christians who otherwise adore him deplore his views on the inspiration and inerrancy of Scripture, and because this group comprises a not insignificant portion of those who have written on Lewis and the Bible, we address them first.

107. *Reflections on the Psalms*, 114–17.

2

CASE STUDIES AND CONTROVERSIES

Lewis the "Bonny Fighter"

5. "WE ARE NOT FUNDAMENTALISTS"

Lewis among the Evangelicals

You've got to ac-cent-tchu-ate the positive
Eliminate the negative
And latch on to the affirmative
Don't mess with Mr. In-between

—Johnny Mercer

Early in November 1955, when Lewis had been resident at Cambridge for almost a year, the American evangelist Billy Graham led a mission there. John Stott, who had invited him, set up a meeting between Graham and Lewis, and both men were pleasantly surprised by the quality of conversation that ensued. Graham, who had suffered premeeting jitters, found Lewis "gentle and gracious; . . . genuinely interested" in what he said. As they wrapped up, Lewis told Graham, "You know, you have many critics, but I have never met one of your critics who knows you personally."[1] Lewis later reported that he "liked him very much indeed," and this response, according to historian George Marsden, was the simplest way to identify an evangelical in the 1950s and '60s: "anyone who likes Billy Graham."[2] But whatever truth Marsden's quip might hold, Lewis was not an evangelical, as much as some evangelicals may want to claim him for their own.

"Evangelical" is an unruly term, notoriously difficult to define. A widely accepted attempt to corral it, David Bebbington's "evangelical quadrilateral," sets out four characteristic emphases: conversionism, activism, biblicism, and

1. Billy Graham, *Just as I Am: The Autobiography of Billy Graham*, rev. ed. (San Francisco: HarperOne, 2007), 258.

2. "Heaven, Earth, and Outer Space: Part Two of an Interview with C. S. Lewis," Sherwood E. Wirt, *Decision*, Oct. 1963, 4. George Marden, *Understanding Fundamentalism and Evangelicalism* (Grand Rapids: Eerdmans, 1991), 6.

crucicentrism.[3] The first two apply to Lewis. Christopher Mitchell finds that he was conversionist (convinced of the necessity of personal conversion)[4] and activist (committed to improving people's lives). The last two may apply to Lewis, but not as many North American evangelicals understand them, especially regarding his views on the Bible. He believed Scripture was inspired and authoritative, which places him comfortably among nineteenth-century evangelicals, but he rejected the idea of biblical inerrancy, which puts him outside many—though not all—forms of North American evangelicalism in the twentieth century.[5]

One of the paradoxes of Lewis's popularity in the decades after his death is his often-rapturous reception among North American evangelicals, some of whom root their biblical interpretation in theories of inspiration and inerrancy that Lewis repeatedly rejected.[6] The last four chapters have laid out Lewis's thinking on these matters. Influenced by Charles Gore, whose scholarship was broadly accepted by centrist Anglicans, Lewis believed the Bible was inspired, but not all of it in the same way. He thought some of the Bible's statements regarding what we now call history and science are incorrect, which put him at odds with "Fundamentalists," to use his preferred term, who insist that every bit of the Bible is historically and scientifically accurate. He was careful to distance himself from these ideas. Although he was happy to stand in solidarity with evangelical Christians as fellow supernaturalists, especially to oppose what he considered "liberal" theology, he didn't want to give the impression that he belonged to their number, once rejecting a revision of his book *Miracles*

3. See Bebbington, "Preaching the Gospel: The Nature of Evangelical Religion," in *Evangelicalism in Modern Britain: A History from the 1730s to the 1980s* (1989; repr., London: Routledge, 2003), 1–19.

4. Lewis's understanding of "conversionism" may not match that of some evangelicals. It seems "v[ery] dangerous," he writes, to insist that everyone must experience an instant conversion and possess an assurance of "eternal security" to be counted among the saved. Lewis to Stuart Robertson, May 6, 1962, *CL*, 3:1337.

5. Christopher W. Mitchell, "Lewis and Historic Evangelicalism," in *C. S. Lewis and the Church*, ed. Judith Wolfe and Brendan N. Wolfe (London: T&T Clark, 2011), 154–73; Stephen R. Holmes, "Evangelical Doctrines of Scripture in Transatlantic Perspective," *Evangelical Quarterly* 81, no. 1 (2009): 39.

6. See Molly Worthen, "John Stott, C. S. Lewis, J. R. R. Tolkien: Why American Evangelicals Love the British," *Religion and Politics*, May 1, 2012, https://tinyurl.com/bdh5ectm; Stephanie L. Derrick, *The Fame of C. S. Lewis: A Controversialist's Reception in Britain and America* (Oxford: Oxford University Press, 2018); K. Alan Snyder, *America Discovers C. S. Lewis: His Profound Impact* (Eugene, OR: Wipf & Stock, 2016).

because, he said, the proposed changes made him look like a "fundamentalist and a non-smoker."[7]

Key words in this chapter—*evangelical, fundamentalist, inspiration, inerrancy*—have been understood differently by different people at different times in different parts of the world. It would be easy to get tangled up in terminology, debating what they mean and have meant. Definitions are important, and clarifying them aids fruitful conversation, but I have no desire to rehash a century's worth of scholarship on the terms. Here I will focus on what they meant to Lewis and on several ways they were understood in his social context, mid-twentieth-century Britain, before looking at how his work on the Bible has been received by evangelical Christians who appreciate certain aspects of it but not others. Lewis is a high-profile example of the fact that "mere Christianity" need not include modern notions of biblical inerrancy.

Lewis rarely employed the word "evangelical" in any form (e.g., evangelistic, evangelicalism), preferring the word "fundamentalist," which is why I'm using it here.[8] Many evangelicals have not appreciated being called fundamentalists, but Lewis appears to have used the two terms synonymously.[9] We have seen how he defined "fundamentalism" in his letters and *Reflections on the Psalms*, and he says more about it in a chapter he wrote at the end of his life for the book *Letters to Malcolm* (1964). This manuscript was not included in the book and remained unpublished until 2017.[10]

The Unpublished Chapter of *Letters to Malcolm*

Lewis begins by disagreeing with Alec Vidler, an Anglican priest, author, and editor of the journal *Theology*, to which Lewis contributed from 1939 to 1941. In matters theological, Vidler was a modernist, someone willing to rethink "outdated" ideas of the past in order to speak more cogently to the present.

7. Lewis to Jocelyn Gibb, May 9, 1960, *CL*, 3:1150.

8. "In Britain, 'Evangelicalism' and 'Evangelical' have usually been capitalized," but in the United States they have not. Mark Noll, "Introduction: One Word but Three Crises," in *Evangelicals: Who They Have Been, Are Now, and Could Be*, ed. Mark Noll, David W. Bebbington, and George M. Marsden (Grand Rapids: Eerdmans, 2019), 5.

9. For one midcentury British evangelical reaction to the word, see J. I. Packer, *"Fundamentalism" and the Word of God* (Grand Rapids: Eerdmans, 1958), 29–36.

10. Lewis, "*Letters to Malcolm*: Letter XIIa," *VII: Journal of the Marion E. Wade Center* 34 (2017): 71–74. No one knows why it wasn't included in the book. For possible reasons, see Norbert Feinendegen, "*Letters to Malcolm*: The Lost Chapter," *VII: Journal of the Marion E. Wade Center* 34 (2017): 75–82.

Lewis critiqued his work early and often, and the other essay Lewis devoted to biblical interpretation, "Modern Theology and Biblical Criticism" (1959), his most vituperative on the topic, was also catalyzed by reading Vidler. He was Lewis's unshakable gadfly.[11]

In the unpublished *Malcolm* chapter, Lewis rejects Vidler's proposal to discard doctrines and institutions the Anglican Church has allegedly outgrown.[12] But, Lewis notes, just because he disagrees with Vidler here doesn't mean the opposite stance is valid—namely, that one should accept "inerrancy, and the miraculous purity of the text, and literal inspiration; in a word, Fundamentalism."[13] The first item on the list that Lewis addresses is the oddly phrased "literal inspiration," which is hard not to read as "literal interpretation." But that isn't what he means, as demonstrated by the example he gives to illustrate it: the prologue to the Gospel of Luke, where the evangelist says he gathered his material through the process of normal human research (1:1–4).[14] By "literal inspiration," then, Lewis is referring to what has been called mechanical inspiration or dictation theory, the idea that every word of the Bible was dictated by God with little effort required on the part of the human author beyond writing it down. He uses the same Lukan passage to reject that idea in his letter to Clyde Kilby.[15] Lewis may or may not be correct in thinking that it is constitutive of fundamentalist identity, as J. I. Packer, an evangelical Anglican priest, insisted in 1958 that British evangelicals never held it. The American evangelical Wayne Grudem, author of a widely used seminary textbook, also cites Luke 1:1–4 to refute that view of inspiration. But biblical scholar James Barr notes that "these denials simply ignore the history of the subject," and even if evangelicals reject the phrasing, they rely on the substance of the idea.[16]

Lewis offers two reasons why he doesn't think Scripture is inerrant. The first is "because there are contradictions in the historical parts."[17] He gives

11. For more on Lewis and Vidler, see Joel D. Heck, "Alec Vidler's Permanent Opposition: C. S. Lewis," *Sehnsucht* 13 (2019): 57–79. The surviving evidence indicates that Vidler respected Lewis's work.

12. Vidler, *Soundings* (Cambridge: Cambridge University Press, 1962), 254.

13. Lewis, "Letter XIIa," 71.

14. Lewis, "Letter XIIa," 71.

15. Lewis to Clyde Kilby, May 7, 1959, *CL*, 3:1045.

16. Packer, *"Fundamentalism,"* 178–81. Evangelical denial of mechanical inspiration predates Packer; see Archibald A. Hodge and Benjamin B. Warfield, *Inspiration* (Princeton: Presbyterian Board of Publication and Sabbath-School Work, 1881), 18–19; Wayne A. Grudem, *Systematic Theology*, 2nd ed. (Grand Rapids: Zondervan Academic, 2020), 70–71; James Barr, *Beyond Fundamentalism* (Philadelphia: Westminster, 1984), 154.

17. Lewis, "Letter XIIa," 71.

no examples here, but the Kilby letter does: the variant genealogies of Jesus in Matthew and Luke and the irreconcilable stories of the death of Judas in Matthew and Acts.[18] As we have seen, Lewis is comfortable acknowledging contradictions in the Bible. In *Reflections on the Psalms,* the Kilby letter, and the *Malcolm* manuscript, he states without demur that the Bible contains contradictions. Some readers may think it is Lewis who is contradicting himself if they remember what he wrote to Emily McLay about his "first principle of non-contradiction" (chapter 4), but what he said there is different. He told McLay that one "must not *interpret*" Scripture so it "contradicts other parts" (emphasis mine). If he were asked to clarify, he might say it would be surprising if Scripture, a "leaky vessel" written by humans, did not contain occasional contradictions and errors of fact. He wrote as much to Kilby: Just as all Scripture is not inspired in the same way, so its individual passages are not true to history in the same way. Some passages—for example, the ones exaggerating the number of soldiers in ancient armies—are "religiously irrelevant," and if they are proven incorrect, it doesn't negate such vital matters as the historicity of the resurrection.[19] We may also compare a sentence he writes on Blaise Pascal. The seventeenth-century French intellectual "directly contradict[s]" some biblical passages and therefore "must be wrong."[20] Lewis doesn't specify which passages in Pascal or in Scripture he is referring to, but one thing at least is clear: it is Pascal contradicting Scripture, not Scripture contradicting itself, that is at issue.

The second reason why the Bible is not inerrant, he submits, is more important: it contains fiction like Jonah and Job, the argument he had adopted from Gore. Because Job is untethered from any named time or place, Lewis thinks the book has "once upon a time" written all over it, thus suggesting that it is a fairy tale—one of his favorite genres.[21] Concluding this part of the *Malcolm* chapter, Lewis admits that, through his stand on "literal inspiration" and inerrancy, he aligns himself with modernists and against fundamentalists. Nonetheless, he disagrees heartily with almost everything else he thinks modernists say about Scripture, summarizing his objections to them in a précis of his 1959 lecture "Modern Theology and Biblical Criticism." This critique requires a sizeable section of its own to do it justice, and I will address it in chapter 7. After dispatching the modernists, Lewis finds himself, hermeneutically speaking,

18. Lewis to Clyde Kilby, May 7, 1959, *CL,* 3:1045.

19. Lewis to Clyde Kilby, May 7, 1959, *CL,* 3:1045.

20. Lewis to Bede Griffiths, May 28, 1952, *CL,* 3:195.

21. Lewis, "Letter XIIa," 71; see also Lewis to Mrs. Wise, Oct. 5, 1955, *CL,* 3:708, and chapter 9 of this book.

somewhere in between, neither fish nor fowl, holding views on the authority of the Bible that would satisfy neither fundamentalists nor modernists.

In defending what he considers his centrist position, Lewis typically claims the witness of "mere Christianity," what has been believed "everywhere, always, and by all," the "Vincentian canon," so called because it is attributed to Vincent of Lérins.[22] Lewis appeals to it often, but over the years his opinion on the role of the Bible in determining "mere Christianity" changes. In 1945, when asked how one determines which church's doctrine is correct, he answers that such evaluations should be based on agreement over centuries and among diverse entities, including Scripture, the church fathers, and different Christian denominations, although "whatever can be proved from Scripture" is the final arbiter.[23] At the end of the Malcolm chapter, however, it appears that Lewis has changed his mind. Scripture is not "*the* datum," he writes, but "one of the data" among many, which include tradition, agreements among different churches, the lives of the saints, and the writings of the fathers. At the end of his life, he doesn't set Scripture as the lead actor over the others, even noting that it's not his responsibility to rank them in order of importance. He does think that the better a theology reconciles all "the data," the better it will be.[24]

We have now exhausted what Lewis wrote on fundamentalism, inspiration, and inerrancy. To those who care about the topics, his comments might seem brief and vague, frustratingly insubstantial, and if they are, it is probably because he wasn't much interested in them. This attitude also can be traced back to the influence of Charles Gore on twentieth-century Anglicanism. In his *New Commentary on Holy Scripture,* Gore exclaims, "Mercifully we [Anglicans] have been preserved from any definition of inspiration."[25] After reading Gore and Moffatt in the early 1930s, Lewis rejected inerrancy, and the question was settled. When he read the Bible, he didn't think about theories of inspiration and the historicity of Scripture because, as he told Kilby, they didn't affect his religious life. In fact, Lewis would prefer that ruminating on such theories didn't afflict anyone. In a letter to Lee Turner, he is glad to see that Turner's questions about biblical inspiration and inerrancy have not rattled the man's faith, and he inquires, "Do you see a clear reason why [they] need bother anyone else's?"[26] Lewis discussed these topics because he was asked, and he always answered his correspondents, and because

22. Vincent of Lérins, *Commonitory* 2.6.

23. Lewis to H. Lyman Stebbins, May 8, 1945, *CL,* 2:646–47.

24. *Letter XIIa,* 73.

25. Gore, "The Bible in the Church," in NCHS, part 1, 10.

26. Lewis to Kilby, May 7, 1959, *CL,* 3:1044; to Lee Turner, July 19, 1958, *CL,* 3:961.

he wanted to defend himself against the charge of being a fundamentalist. However, his quiescence did not extend to voicing opinions on modern biblical scholarship, where he took the initiative and played offense, perhaps because, as a scholar himself, he encountered them more often, and perhaps because he thought modernists had the power to inflict more damage than "fundamentalists" could.

Fundamentalism in Midcentury Britain

Lewis rarely discussed fundamentalism unless prodded. He had more occasions to do so in the 1950s and '60s, due in part to the "Fundamentalist Controversy" of 1955, "the only time when Christian fundamentalism became a matter of public debate in post-war Britain."[27] Anyone who studies Lewis on Scripture in these decades should take this controversy into account.

In the early 1950s, some Anglican clergy worried that fundamentalists were gaining traction in their ranks, to the point that the 1953–1954 edition of *Crockford's Clerical Dictionary* complained that many prospective ordinands were "biblical 'Fundamentalists' or so close to being so that no ordinary magnifying glass can detect any significant difference." Institutions connected to Oxford and Cambridge educated many clergy, and John Stott's work with the evangelical Inter-Varsity Fellowship at those universities had, in the opinion of some, been too successful. News of Billy Graham's upcoming mission to Cambridge in November 1955 served to throw a match on the controversy, which exploded in the pages of the *Times* in August.[28]

Henry Kenneth Luce, headmaster of Durham School, was the first to submit an anxious letter to the editor of the *Times* about Graham's visit. Luce, concerned about "the recent increase of fundamentalism among university students," thought no educational institution should accept "an outlook which ignores the conclusions of modern scholarship." Since the purpose of a university is to advance knowledge, why should fundamentalists get a hearing there, especially when Jesus himself told his followers to love God "with mind as well as heart and soul"? Luce predicted that Graham's fundamentalism would lead to "disaster for educated men and women."[29]

27. Alister Chapman, "Evangelical or Fundamentalist? The Case of John Stott," in *Evangelicalism and Fundamentalism in the United Kingdom during the Twentieth Century*, ed. David Bebbington and David Ceri Jones (Oxford: Oxford University Press, 2013), 194.

28. Chapman, "Evangelical or Fundamentalist?," 195–96.

29. *Times*, Aug. 15, 1955, 7.

The *Times* printed dozens of responses to Luce, so many that they were collected and published the same year in a pamphlet entitled *Fundamentalism: A Religious Problem*.[30] Some correspondents supported Luce, and others did not. T. Wigley argues that fundamentalism "ignores the conclusions of modern scholarship" and that readers should listen to Luce, while B. F. C. Atkinson states that Billy Graham's teaching is "in accord with true scholarship illumined by Revelation."[31] Mabel Lazenby accuses Luce both of underestimating the intelligence of Cambridge undergraduates and of being a snob. H. Gresford Jones defends Graham's mission by appealing to the *Oxford English Dictionary*: "'Fundamental' means 'primary' and 'essential,'" and "in this sense every true Catholic, every true Evangelical, is a 'fundamentalist.' The present situation is all part of the age-long battle between 'reason' and 'revelation,'" so Gresford Jones is happy "that Dr. Graham stands so fearlessly for these primary and essential things which modern scholarship has done so much not to disprove but to confirm."[32] Michael Ramsey, then Anglican bishop of Durham and later archbishop of Canterbury, weighs in to support Luce and reprimand Gresford Jones:

> Many will be grateful to Canon Luce for raising in your columns the problem created by the revival of fundamentalist evangelism. The strength of this evangelism lies in its emphasis upon decision and personal conversion to Christ. What causes misgiving is the crudity of the doctrine presented, so that the act of decision and conversion may involve the stifling of the mind instead of its liberation into a new service of God and man. It is not surprising that the successes of this preaching are won, particularly within the universities, at a cost both of moral casualties and of an alienation of thoughtful men and women from the Christian faith. How harmful the new fundamentalist movement has been may be illustrated by the appalling statement in the letter of Bishop Gresford Jones (August 18) that there is an "age-long battle between 'reason' and 'revelation.'" Are we to forget the long line of great evangelists, including within living memory William Temple, whose emphasis upon decision and conversion has gone hand in hand with an insistence upon the duty of thought and the rationality of the Christian revelation?[33]

30. *Fundamentalism: A Religious Problem* (London: The Times Publishing Company, 1955).

31. *Times*, Aug. 17, 1955, 9.

32. *Times*, Aug. 18, 1955, 7.

33. *Times*, Aug. 20, 1955, 7.

Ramsey thinks "fundamentalist evangelism" may stifle the mind, singling out Gresford Jones's comment on the "battle between 'reason' and 'revelation,'" a conflict that, Ramsey notes, need not occur among Anglicans.

John Stott, himself an Anglican priest, enters the fray to clarify the meaning of fundamentalism and respond to Ramsey. He writes: "It is surprising that your correspondents on this subject have not paused to define the term 'fundamentalism.' They have assumed that your readers understood the term, that they understood it in the same sense, and that it accurately describes Dr. Graham. Actually, the term clearly has different meanings, and Dr. Graham has publicly denied on more than one occasion that he is a fundamentalist." After situating the word in its immediate historical context, the American debates of the early twentieth century, Stott says that "fundamentalism" now

> is almost a synonym for obscurantism, and it is generally used as a term of opprobrium. It appears to describe the bigoted rejection of all Biblical criticism, a mechanical view of inspiration and an excessively literalist interpretation of scripture. It is doubtless in this sense that your correspondents have employed the term, and in this sense that Dr. Billy Graham and others associated with him have repudiated it. Clearly a distinction must be drawn between fundamentalism and the traditional, conservative view of scripture. It is neither true nor fair to dub every conservative evangelical a "fundamentalist."[34] The conservative evangelical desires to lay a truly Biblical emphasis on the necessity of divine revelation, to ascribe to the scriptures no meaner an authority than did our Lord and his apostles, and to accept the Biblical doctrine of scripture as they accept the Biblical doctrine of God and Christ and the Church. The real point at issue in this controversy, revealed by an episcopal disagreement in your columns, seems to be the place of the mind in the perception of divine truth. All thoughtful Christians would agree with the Bishop of Durham, whose letter you published on August 20, that God's revelation is essentially reasonable, but would have to add that it is often in conflict with the unenlightened reason of sinful men.[35]

Stott's definition of fundamentalism overlaps with Lewis's on one point. Like Lewis, he identifies it with "a mechanical view of inspiration." Unlike

34. This may be the only instance in the 1955 letters where the word "evangelical" specifies a certain kind of Christian.

35. *Times*, Aug. 25, 1955, 14.

Lewis, Stott distinguishes between fundamentalist and evangelical interpretation of Scripture, rejecting the former and explaining how he thinks it differs from the latter. In making these distinctions, Stott demonstrates that he, like Billy Graham, considers "fundamentalist" a "term of opprobrium." Speaking in Scotland in 1955, Graham had insisted, "I am neither a fundamentalist nor a modernist, but a constructionist," using exactly the same vocabulary and dichotomy, fundamentalist versus modernist, that Lewis employs in the unpublished *Malcolm* chapter.[36] Graham, like Lewis, rejects both labels. However, it is important to emphasize that Lewis doesn't use the term "fundamentalist" pejoratively; to him, it is simply descriptive.

For Stott, the "real point at issue" in the *Times* controversy is the place of the mind in Christian interpretation of Scripture, including the role of modern biblical scholarship. When he writes that fundamentalists reject "all Biblical criticism," Stott implies that his own community, conservative evangelical Anglicans, accepts at least some of it. Lewis, too, was committed to cultivating the life of the mind and the right use of reason, but he rarely encouraged the use of modern biblical criticism in print. Even though he read and employed it, the two essays he devoted to such scholarship—the *Malcolm* chapter and "Modern Theology and Biblical Criticism," neither published in his lifetime—give the impression that he rejected it with prejudice.

Evangelicals on Lewis on the Bible

Since Lewis published little explicitly on biblical interpretation, proportionally little has been written on what he said about it, and much of that has come from Protestants of the evangelical variety, mainly in North America. Few are biblical scholars; rather, they are experts in theology or, like Lewis himself, English literature.[37] Among these responses, pride of place goes to Michael J. Christensen's *C. S. Lewis on Scripture* (1979), not just because it was the first—and up to this time only—book-length treatment of the topic, but also because it is well done.[38] Christensen's project, like Lewis's work on the Bible in the 1950s and '60s, is best understood within its social context. As he explains,

36. Ian M. Randall, "Billy Graham, Evangelism, and Fundamentalism," in Bebbington and Jones, *Evangelicalism and Fundamentalism*, 173.

37. For the purposes of this book, a "biblical scholar" has, at minimum, a PhD or its equivalent in biblical studies from a reputable institution. The study of theology is a different discipline.

38. Michael J. Christensen, *C. S. Lewis on Scripture: His Thoughts on the Nature of*

"The decade of the 70s has seen a surge of debate about the question of biblical inerrancy," the "so-called battle for the Bible," as one prominent combatant, Harold Lindsell, entitled his famous book of 1976. Lindsell declared biblical inerrancy "the most important theological topic of this age," and he defined inerrancy just as Lewis had understood fundamentalists to do, by asserting that Scripture's "science" and "history" are without error. According to Lindsell, naysayers put themselves outside the pale of legitimate Christianity.[39] But some evangelicals disagreed. Christensen's own denomination at the time, the Church of the Nazarene, didn't include inerrancy in its statement of faith when he published the book, so Christensen was primed to read Lewis sympathetically.[40] He writes a successful work of apologetics defending Lewis's theories on Scripture against evangelical dissenters.[41]

Like Christensen, theologian Kevin Vanhoozer takes no umbrage at Lewis's denial of inerrancy in his chapter "On Scripture" in *The Cambridge Companion to C. S. Lewis* (2010). Vanhoozer's work, the best short treatment of Lewis on the Bible, focuses on his understanding of genre and myth and the implications of his certainty that it is Jesus, not the Bible, who is the true word of God. Lewis didn't want so much to look *at* the Bible as *through* it, in order to meet a person, Jesus Christ.[42]

Biblical Inspiration, the Role of Revelation, and the Question of Inerrancy (1979; repr., Waco, TX: Word Books, 1988).

39. Christensen, *Lewis on Scripture*, 19–20. Harold Lindsell, *The Battle for the Bible* (Grand Rapids: Zondervan, 1976), preface (unpaginated), 30–31. Richard Quebedeaux, *The Worldly Evangelicals* (New York: Harper & Row, 1978), surveys the broad diversity of North American evangelicalism at the time; see pp. 87–90 on inerrancy and Lindsell.

40. Andrew Walker, foreword to *Lewis on Scripture*, 12. The 2017–2021 Manual of the Church of the Nazarene (https://tinyurl.com/2rd6z8hp) notes, "We believe in the plenary inspiration of the Holy Scriptures . . . given by divine inspiration, inerrantly revealing the will of God concerning us in all things necessary to our salvation."

41. That said, Walker's and Christensen's respective characterizations of Lewis's neither fundamentalist nor liberal approach to Scripture as "unusual" (Walker, 12) or "unique" (Christensen, 37) in *Lewis on Scripture* are both incorrect because, as we have seen, it is a widespread Anglican approach rooted in Gore's *Lux Mundi*.

42. Kevin J. Vanhoozer, "On Scripture," in *The Cambridge Companion to C. S. Lewis*, ed. Robert MacSwain and Michael Ward (Cambridge: Cambridge University Press, 2010), 75–88. For more from Vanhoozer on inerrancy, see *Five Views on Biblical Inerrancy*, ed. J. Merrick and Stephen Garrett (Grand Rapids: Zondervan, 2013). Like Vanhoozer, Lyle Dorsett writes a primarily descriptive piece that doesn't focus on how

Christensen defends Lewis's views on the Bible, and Vanhoozer takes a more neutral, descriptive stance. Several other evangelicals, including Andrew Wheeler, Donald T. Williams, and Philip Ryken, while appreciating many aspects of Lewis's thought, disagree with his position on inerrancy and his refusal to identify Scripture with the word of God. In his book *C. S. Lewis: Clarity and Confusion*, Wheeler rightly notes that there is a broad range of views among evangelicals on Lewis, from those who accept almost everything he says to those who think he isn't a Christian. Wheeler is sure that Lewis is a Christian, but he finds some of his ideas "deeply troubling," first among them his theories on Scripture. In his opinion, the root of the problem is that Lewis "was never given the sound teaching on the Bible" he desired, so his understanding of Scripture suffered.[43] Donald Williams agrees, calling Lewis's presentation "caricatured," with his broad-brushed concept of inspiration "mak[ing] us suspect that Lewis had never encountered a nuanced statement of the classic doctrine."[44] Both Williams and Philip Ryken think Lewis would have benefited from reading the 1978 Chicago Statement on Biblical Inerrancy, which he couldn't do, since it was published after he died.[45] Even if he could have, however, I doubt it would have changed his mind, because Lewis was consistently cogent in his objections to inerrancy, and well-intentioned evangelicals themselves disagree about how to interpret the Chicago Statement.[46] There is no evidence that Lewis ever read an argument in favor of biblical inerrancy, but he read many good ones against it. In addition to Gore and Moffatt, he evaluated the theory as he marked up his copies of Coleridge's *Aids to Reflection and the Confessions of an Inquiring Spirit*, Austin Farrer's *The Glass of Vision*, and C. H. Dodd's *The Authority of the Bible*.

Samuel Taylor Coleridge, while taking pains to affirm his orthodoxy, argues against the dictation theory of Scripture as pernicious to Christian faith

Lewis's views of Scripture differ from most evangelicals. Dorsett, *Seeking the Secret Place: The Spiritual Formation of C. S. Lewis* (Grand Rapids: Brazos, 2004), 51–67. Gregory S. Cootsona's evenhanded chapter, "The Crisis of the Bible," in *C. S. Lewis and the Crisis of a Christian* (Louisville: Westminster John Knox, 2014), 93–106, mediates Lewis's views of Scripture to evangelicals and mainline Protestants.

43. Andrew Wheeler, *C. S. Lewis: Clarity and Confusion; A Balanced Introduction to His Writings* (Leominster, UK: Day One, 2006), 6, 52.

44. Donald T. Williams, *Deeper Magic: The Theology behind the Writings of C. S. Lewis* (Baltimore, MD: Square Halo Books, 2016), 61.

45. Williams, *Deeper Magic*, 69; Philip Ryken, "Inerrancy and the Patron Saint of Evangelicalism: C. S. Lewis on Holy Scripture," in *The Romantic Rationalist*, ed. John Piper and David Mathis (Wheaton, IL: Crossway, 2014), 50.

46. See Merrick and Garrett, *Five Views*, 131, 147.

because it "plants the vineyard of the Lord with thorns." Why inflict it on anyone when "the passages which can without violence" be found to support it are few and, with one exception (2 Pet. 3:16), refer to the Old Testament? "It is remarkable," he observes, that both proponents and opponents of the idea can appeal to the same verse, 2 Timothy 3:16, to support their position, and he offers a lengthy footnote—marked by Lewis in his copy—detailing different ways the verse has been translated and interpreted through Christian history. Furthermore, inerrantists beg the question, using their predetermined conclusion (the Bible is inerrant) to argue for that conclusion. Coleridge believes the Bible is inspired, but his opponents' account of it is "superstitious and unscriptural," repugnant to "Scripture, Reason, and Common Sense."[47] In order to maintain it, they must invent whimsical harmonies that ignore genre and history. In a word, the doctrine is "Bibliolatry."[48] Lewis underlined that word, and in the index of the book he highlighted and cross-referenced the entries "Bibliolatry, and the mis-interpretation of the Bible" and "Inspiration of every word in the Bible, the doctrine argued against," actions that demonstrate his close study.[49] Judging by some of his handwriting, he seems to have read the book in the late 1940s, and he finished rereading it September 25, 1962.[50]

Lewis's friend Austin Farrer doesn't so much oppose certain concepts of inspiration as transcend them. He sets 2 Timothy 3:15–16 KJV, "Thou hast known the sacred writings which are able to make thee wise until salvation. Every scripture is inspired by God," as the epigraph to the third chapter of his *Glass of Vision* (1948), but he never directly addresses the verse. Being Farrer, he presents a highly subtle argument that defies easy summary, a fact he acknowledges in the end, admitting that he hasn't given "a plain and uniform account of the inspiration of the text of Scripture, comparable with the old doctrine of inerrant supernatural dictation. But this, surely, is no blemish. For a doctrine of the unchallengeable inspiration of the whole text is a burden which our backs will no longer bear. What is vital is that we should have such a doc-

47. Samuel Taylor Coleridge, *Confessions of an Inquiring Spirit*, in *Aids to Reflection and the Confessions of an Inquiring Spirit* (London: George Bell and Sons, 1890), 297–99, 309, 323. Grudem, *Systematic Theology*, 85–103, addresses these and other objections unsuccessfully.

48. Coleridge, *Confessions*, 313.

49. Index to Coleridge, *Aids to Reflection and the Confessions of an Inquiring Spirit*, 366, 372.

50. David Lyle Jeffrey, "C. S. Lewis, the Bible, and Its Literary Critics," *Christianity and Literature* 50, no. 1 (2000): 102, estimates that he read it in the 1920s.

trine of Scripture as causes us to look for the right things in reading Scripture: above all, that we should look for the life-giving inspired word, and make the proper use of it when we have found it." This is exactly what Lewis believed, and when he mentions *Glass of Vision* in 1949, he describes Farrer as "α +."[51]

C. H. Dodd, one of the most respected New Testament scholars of mid-twentieth-century Britain, published *The Authority of the Bible* in 1928, but Lewis read a 1962 reissue. To Dodd, an "extreme" understanding of biblical inspiration considers "all parts of the Canon . . . directly and equally inspired by God," including its science and history, which must be "exactly and literally true." Dodd finds this view so outlandish that he doesn't think anyone could possibly hold it, even if they claim they do. In supporting his argument, he writes a section Lewis marks: "The Bible itself does not make any claim to infallible authority for all its parts. On the contrary, some of its greatest writers contemplate the possibility that they may be mistaken." These writers include Isaiah, Jeremiah, and Paul, the latter of whom "sometimes claims to speak the word of the Lord, but at other times 'gives his opinion' quite tentatively." We have seen Lewis discuss this idea more than once. Dodd continues, "The Protestant who believes in the infallibility of the whole does so on some other grounds, such as the declaration of his own Church—which in this point he accepts as infallible, . . . or something personal to himself."[52] Since Lewis finished reading Dodd in August 1962 and Coleridge a month later, it is reasonable to speculate that he might have done so to check and confirm his antifundamentalist position as he wrote the *Letters to Malcolm* chapter.

In flat contrast to the scholars and poets Lewis read, Andrew Wheeler speaks for many evangelicals when he asserts, "It is dangerous and wrong to admit the possibility of errors in the Bible." He approves Lewis's analogy comparing the humanity and divinity of Christ to the human and divine aspects of the Bible, but in his opinion Lewis doesn't take the analogy far enough. Jesus is perfect, so why doesn't he accept that the Bible must be, too? Wheeler laments that Lewis doesn't think Scripture *is* the word of God but only carries it.[53] As we have seen, Lewis adopted this conviction at least in part through his reading of George MacDonald and Charles Gore (see chapter 2), buttressed once again by Coleridge.[54] In the late nineteenth century, concurrent

51. Farrer, *The Glass of Vision* (Westminster: Dacre, 1948), 52; Lewis to Sister Penelope, Aug. 8, 1949, *CL*, 2:961.

52. Dodd, *The Authority of the Bible* (London: Collins Fontana, 1962), 20–21, 25–26.

53. Wheeler, *Clarity and Confusion*, 6, 52, 56–59.

54. Coleridge, *Confessions*, 294; Anthony John Harding, *Coleridge and the Inspired Word* (Kingston, ON: McGill-Queen's University Press, 1985), 74–75.

with the publication of Gore's *Lux Mundi*, "the claim that 'the Bible is God's word' became a rallying point against the liberal threat of supposing that the Bible merely 'contains' God's word."[55] Archibald Hodge and Benjamin Warfield, nineteenth-century North American redoubts of Protestant inerrancy, asserted that they were "sincerely convinced of the perfect soundness of the great catholic doctrine of biblical inspiration—i.e., that the Scriptures not only contain, but ARE THE WORD OF GOD, and hence that all their elements and all their affirmation are absolutely errorless,"[56] but graphically shouting it from the page in capital letters did not move their opponents, of whom Lewis was a direct descendant.

Philip Ryken calls Lewis "suborthodox" on the point because some of his views on Scripture don't meet what Ryken considers to be even the minimum standard for "mere Christianity."[57] However, many Christians throughout the history of the church have never held any such doctrine of inerrancy. We can go back to the very beginning, to the Gospel writers Matthew and Luke, who rewrote their predecessor Mark, correcting its many infelicities and errors. Yet Mark remains in the biblical canon still. Donald Williams also appeals to "historic Christians" who held "plenary verbal inspiration," arguing that Lewis's failure to accept the Bible as *the* word of God opens up the fatal "gap" that leads him to deny inerrancy. As a result, Lewis "comes short of teaching the historic doctrine of the church" regarding Scripture.[58] The question is, which church? Roman Catholics, Eastern Orthodox, and many Protestants, including evangelicals, can successfully appeal to "historic Christianity" to combat modern shibboleths about inerrancy. Critics of Lewis on the point are parochial, speaking out of an evangelical ghetto, as they proclaim against all evidence that their position is and always has been the only acceptable one.[59]

Conclusion

Since they so heartily disagree with Lewis on what they consider such a foundational belief for Christian thought and practice, why have these evangelicals tolerated him, much less praised him? It is because they hold common ground elsewhere. However mistaken Lewis was about Scripture, Ryken says, he was

55. John Poirier, *The Invention of the Inspired Text* (London: Bloomsbury, 2021), 6.

56. Hodge and Warfield, *Inspiration*, 26.

57. Ryken, "Lewis on Holy Scripture," 46.

58. Williams, *Deeper Magic*, 59–68.

59. See Michael Graves, *The Inspiration and Interpretation of Scripture: What the Early Church Can Teach Us* (Grand Rapids: Eerdmans, 2014).

otherwise orthodox, as he argued for the reality of miracles and the divinity of Christ. Even more, he fought theological liberals.[60] These are the same reasons Lewis gave for finding common cause with evangelicals. In a 1952 letter to the *Church Times*—one of the few places he uses the word "evangelical"—he asserts, "What unites the Evangelical and the Anglo-Catholic against the 'Liberal' or 'Modernist'" is that both accept the supernatural. The differences among supernaturalist Christians pale compared to what they hold in common.[61] The people with whom Lewis found it "hardest to be in charity" were not "extreme Protestants"—he notes Baptists as an example[62]—but "liberal Christians," with Rudolf Bultmann heading the list.[63]

60. Ryken, "Lewis on Holy Scripture," 56, 62–64.

61. To the editor of the *Church Times*, Feb. 8, 1952, *CL*, 3:164. Lewis laments that the letter to which he responds, R. D. Daunton-Fear's "Evangelical Churchmanship," felt the need to "describe the Bishop of Birmingham as an Evangelical."

62. Lewis to Walter Van Der Kamp, July 28, 1962, *CL*, 3:1359.

63. Lewis, "God in the Dock," in *God in the Dock: Essays on Theology and Ethics*, ed. Walter Hooper (Grand Rapids: Eerdmans, 1970), 241.

6. MYTH AS FACT OR FICTION?

Lewis vs. Bultmann

> *"I think magic went out when people began to have steam engines," Billy insisted, "and newspapers, and telephones and wireless telegraphing."*
>
> *"Wireless is rather like magic when you come to think of it," said Gerald.*
>
> *"Perhaps there's given up being magic because people didn't believe in it anymore," said Kathleen.*
>
> *"Well, don't let's spoil the show with any silly old not believing," said Gerald. "I'm going to believe in magic as hard as I can."*
>
> —E. Nesbit, *The Enchanted Castle,* 1907

In April 1941 the biblical scholar Rudolf Bultmann lobbed an intellectual bomb into his academic field when he delivered the lecture "New Testament and Mythology" to a gathering of German Confessing Church theologians, a group formed to resist the Nazis. He hoped it would make the preaching of Jesus more accessible to contemporary Christians, but instead, what people remember most about it is a line that has become infamous: "It is impossible to use electric light and the wireless and to avail ourselves of modern medical and surgical discoveries, and at the same time to believe in the New Testament world of spirits and miracles."[1]

A month later, in May 1941, C. S. Lewis published the first installment of *The Screwtape Letters,* an imagined correspondence between the demons Screwtape, a middle manager in the bureaucracy of hell, and Wormwood, his protégé

1. Rudolf Bultmann, "New Testament and Mythology," in *Kerygma and Myth: A Theological Debate,* ed. Hans Werner Bartsch, trans. Reginald H. Fuller (London: SPCK, 1953; New York: Harper & Row, 1961), 5.

in the subtle art of temptation.[2] The book tells the story of a battle for a human soul so convincingly that some readers didn't understand it was fiction. It is, but it also voices Lewis's belief in the reality of "the New Testament world of spirits" that Bultmann denied.

The working out of their respective ideas shaped each author's legacy. Bultmann's name is bound, for better or worse, to the concept of demythologizing the New Testament.[3] Lewis's *Screwtape Letters* catapulted him to fame in the English-speaking world. Until the Chronicles of Narnia became popular, it was his best-known book, inspiring a 1947 *Time* magazine cover that featured a portrait of Lewis with an angel on one shoulder and a demon on the other.[4] By 1947 the war between their nations had ended, but the intellectual skirmishes on the role of the supernatural that the two men represent raged on, and they continue to this day.

It might be tempting to pit their positions against each other, especially since Lewis did so himself. Both men provoke polarized reactions, and some readers, like the *Time* magazine cover, may assign to each of them either an angel or a demon. However, such judgments are premature, because both Bultmann and Lewis hoped their work would be received in the same spirit: to make Jesus meaningful to what they called "modern man." What follows here suggests that Lewis succeeded, but Bultmann largely did not.

Bultmann toured Great Britain in 1955, when Lewis was at the height of his fame, but they never met, and Bultmann probably never read anything Lewis wrote.[5] Lewis, on the other hand, had read some of Bultmann's work, and he despised it. Every time he brings it up, he is dismissive or sarcastic. He may have heard of demythologizing through his friend Austin Farrer, a biblical scholar who wrote the closing essay for *Kerygma and Myth*, the volume that published the first translation of "New Testament and Mythology" in English in 1953. Farrer's essay, bearing the irenic and likely ironic title "An

2. Installments appeared weekly in the Anglican newspaper the *Guardian*, which ceased publication in 1951.

3. Bultmann did not coin the word "demythologizing"; he found it in the work of his student Hans Jonas. David W. Congdon, *The Mission of Demythologizing: Rudolf Bultmann's Dialectical Theology* (Minneapolis: Fortress, 2015), 592.

4. Sept. 8, 1947, https://tinyurl.com/4rabjtsj.

5. Bultmann was delivering the Gifford Lectures, published in 1957 as *History and Eschatology*. On the way home he visited Durham, York, London, and Canterbury. Konrad Hammann, *Rudolf Bultmann: A Biography*, trans. Philip E. Devenish (Salem, OR: Polebridge, 2013), 440.

English Appreciation," critiques with a feather-light brush what Lewis will hit with a hammer.[6]

Bultmann's essay did not remain the preserve of academic biblical scholars in Britain. A journal for pastors, the *Expository Times*, opened its January 1954 issue with a review of *Kerygma and Myth*. The review begins by observing that biblical mythology is "the most fashionable question just now," and it highlights Bultmann's sentence on the impossibility of believing in the "New Testament world of demons and spirits," exclaiming, "This is 'one in the eye' for contemporary theologians who have been inviting us to revive our belief in the devil!" I can't help but think the anonymous author was referring to Lewis and *The Screwtape Letters*.[7]

The only record of interaction between the two is Lewis writing on Bultmann. I will begin with an overview of Bultmann's work on myth and demythologizing, paying special attention to the issue of cosmology, or how one pictures the universe. Then I will look at Lewis's ideas on those topics and put the two men into conversation with each other before summarizing their ongoing impact.

Bultmann on Demythologizing

Bultmann's most accessible publication on demythologizing, which also happens to be his most mature work on the topic,[8] is a series of lectures he delivered in the United States in 1951 and published in English as *Jesus Christ and Mythology* in 1958. The book opens with a discussion of the coming kingdom of God, an event wherein the Son of Man will descend, the dead will be raised, and the final judgment will begin, resulting in bliss for the righteous and hell for the damned.[9] To Bultmann, every element of this scene is mythological because "it is different from the conception of the world which has been formed and developed by science."[10] This statement raises the question of how Bultmann defines myth and how myth differs from science, questions that must be addressed before we can approach the term "demythologizing."

Myth is difficult to define, and Bultmann "mostly failed in his attempt to clarify [it], if the confusing and contradictory claims made by both his contem-

6. Austin Farrer, "An English Appreciation," in Bartsch, *Kerygma and Myth*, 212–23.

7. "Notes of Recent Exposition," *Expository Times* 65, no. 4 (1954): 97.

8. Congdon, *Mission of Demythologizing*, 614.

9. Rudolf Bultmann, *Jesus Christ and Mythology* (New York: Charles Scribner's Sons, 1958), 13.

10. Bultmann, *Jesus Christ and Mythology*, 15.

poraries and later scholars are any indication," as David Congdon, Bultmann's best contemporary expositor, observes.[11] Farrer says the same in his essay: Bultmann seems to have made little attempt toward, and shows even less interest in, "consistent statement or accurate definition."[12] It is helpful to be as clear as possible when defining key terms, and Bultmann misses the mark.[13]

It's not surprising that Lewis didn't understand what Bultmann wrote about myth, because many specialists in the biblical scholar's own field didn't either. One impediment lies in the fact that Bultmann holds several different ideas about myth together in tension, describing it both as the world-picture (*Weltbild*) of an ancient culture and as an objectifying mode of thinking.[14] He puts it this way: "Mythology is primitive science, the intention of which is to explain phenomena . . . which are strange, curious, surprising, or frightening, by attributing them to supernatural causes, to gods or to demons. . . . Myths give worldly objectivity to that which is unworldly."[15]

Even more, he calls the ancient Jewish world-picture of a three-tiered cosmos—earth here, heaven above, hell below—a myth. God, angels, and spirits good and evil influence human affairs. According to Bultmann, this view is outdated and therefore unacceptable because "nobody reckons with direct intervention by transcendent powers. Of course, there are today some survivals and revivals of primitive thinking and superstition," but "the Church would make a disastrous mistake" if it paid any attention to them because "the nature of man is to be seen in modern literature," as for example the novels of Camus and Hemingway, and in newspapers, which never attribute anything to the agency of God, angels, or demons.[16] Bultmann doesn't explain why he thinks divine powers don't act in the world. He considers it self-evident, thus exemplifying the philosophical presupposition against the supernatural to which Lewis objects in his book *Miracles*.

To Bultmann, Jesus the human being is not a myth in the sense of being a fictional character. Bultmann was never a mythicist, someone who thinks

11. Congdon, *Mission of Demythologizing*, 595–96. Roger A. Johnson, *The Origins of Demythologizing* (Leiden: Brill, 1974), 14, thinks that Bultmann was more interested in demythologizing than in the concept of myth itself.

12. Farrer, "An English Appreciation," 212.

13. Johnson, *Origins of Demythologizing*, 10.

14. David Congdon, "Demystifying the Program of Demythologizing: Rudolf Bultmann's Theological Hermeneutics," *Harvard Theological Review* 110, no. 1 (2017): 12.

15. Bultmann, *Jesus Christ and Mythology*, 18–19.

16. Bultmann, *Jesus Christ and Mythology*, 36–37.

Jesus never existed. He believed Jesus was a historical person, but the Gospel accounts of his begetting by the Holy Spirit, birth from a virgin, miracles, and status as Son of God are mythological.[17] Therefore, he writes, the proclamation of Jesus as Christ is "a unique combination of history and myth."[18] On this last statement, Bultmann and Lewis agree. The devil (perhaps Screwtape or one of his henchmen) is in the details, which consist mainly in how the two men understand myth.

Jesus Christ and Mythology represents Bultmann's argument better than the 1941 essay because, among other things, it responds to his critics. One objection they had raised was the fact that worldviews go in and out of fashion, and the worldview we are least capable of evaluating, or even noticing, is our own. Readers of Lewis will light up when they see this, because the concept was integral to his thought. He calls it "chronological snobbery": "the uncritical acceptance of the intellectual climate common to our own age and the assumption that whatever has gone out of date is on that count discredited."[19] Bultmann defends himself against the charge when he notes that "all the results of science are relative, and no world-view of yesterday or today or tomorrow is definitive."[20]

In fact, his main point about science is not its opposition to mythology, but rather the tendency of people to depend on it for answers, and thus for "security"—a concept that is crucial to Bultmann's thought. He writes, "The scientific world-view engenders a great temptation, namely, that man strives for mastery over the world and over his own life. He knows the laws of nature and can use the powers of nature according to his own plans and desires." Dependence on science may become a sort of worship, a god in itself, an "illusory security" that might be called a form of idolatry.[21] We know that Lewis agreed. In works of fiction (*That Hideous Strength*) and nonfiction (*The Abolition of Man*), he decried the use of technology devoid of morality to manipulate the world to the advantage of those wielding it. On this point, both Bultmann and Lewis have proven prophetic.

For Bultmann, myth "objectifies the transcendent"[22] when it presents something unworldly as worldly; for example, it "represents the transcendence

17. Bultmann, *Jesus Christ and Mythology*, 17.

18. Bultmann, "New Testament and Mythology," 34.

19. *Surprised by Joy* (San Diego: Harcourt Brace Jovanovich, 1955), 241.

20. Bultmann, *Jesus Christ and Mythology*, 37.

21. Bultmann, *Jesus Christ and Mythology*, 40.

22. Bultmann, *Jesus Christus und die Mythologie* (Hamburg: Furche, 1964), 17, as translated by Congdon, *Mission of Demythologizing*, 615.

of God as spatial distance (usually as 'above')."[23] This objectifying is the stimulus for and target of the Lutheran scholar's demythologizing, a project akin to relying on faith rather than works of the law. Indeed, he describes demythologizing as "the radical application of the doctrine of justification of faith to the sphere of knowledge and thought. Like the doctrine of justification, demythologizing destroys every longing for security."[24] The only thing one should rely upon for security, says Bultmann, is God.

To Bultmann, demythologizing—"an unsatisfactory word, to be sure"—is a method of New Testament interpretation. It "tries to recover the deeper meaning behind the mythological conceptions. . . . Its aim is not to eliminate the mythological statements but to interpret them."[25] Demythologizing does not reject Scripture, but it does reject its cosmological worldview, which includes the direct intervention of God, angels, and demons in human life.[26] Far from being a modern imposition on the ancient biblical text, he claims that it began in the Bible itself, in the letters of Paul and the Gospel of John.[27] Bultmann hopes to build upon this allegedly ancient method through a form of existentialism. To put it succinctly, he wants the word of God to speak to the essence of a human being, to make sense of that person's lived experience, and to give it meaning. Through demythologizing, the Bible becomes for Bultmann "a word addressed personally to me, which not only informs me about existence in general, but gives me real existence." One "cannot speak of God's action in general statements," he says, but only "of what He does here and now with me."[28]

But what does he mean when he talks about "God's action," especially in the context of demythologizing? Isn't the statement "God acts" itself mythological language? Bultmann doesn't think so: rather, he says, it is analogical language. For example, we can speak of God as loving because we have lived experience of human love. He insists that "only such statements about God are legitimate

23. Bultmann, "Über den Begriff 'Mythos,'" in Congdon, *Mission of Demythologizing*, 853.

24. Bultmann, *Jesus Christ and Mythology*, 84. Bultmann was rooted more in nineteenth- than sixteenth-century Lutheranism. See Johnson, *The Origins of Demythologizing*, 33.

25. Bultmann, *Jesus Christ and Mythology*, 18.

26. Bultmann, *Jesus Christ and Mythology*, 35–37.

27. Bultmann, *Jesus Christ and Mythology*, 32.

28. Bultmann, *Jesus Christ and Mythology*, 52, 66.

as express the existential relation between God and man. Statements which speak of God's actions as cosmic events are illegitimate."[29]

In light of what Bultmann asserts about demythologizing, it is striking that he concludes his 1941 essay by quoting John 1:14, "And the Word became flesh," a sentence that looks like the epitome of a myth, the myth of God coming down to earth. But, he claims, "The transcendence of God is not as in a myth reduced to immanence. Instead, we have the paradox of a transcendent God present and active in history."[30]

Bultmann says nothing more on John 1:14 here,[31] but the verse may serve as a hinge as we turn to Lewis, who plays with the Latin translation of John 1:14, "Et Verbum caro factum est," when he entitles his own essay on Jesus and mythology "Myth Became Fact." For Lewis, the incarnation, death, and resurrection of Christ are not only true but also myths, not reduced to immanence, but actually made immanent. But this is his mature thinking. It took him decades of grappling with the subject to get there.

Lewis on Mythologizing

Myth played a vital role in Lewis's life. He became an atheist around the same time he discovered Norse mythology, which fed his imagination as nothing else had. Chapter 1 describes how he and Arthur Greeves bonded over their love of these myths, and a letter he wrote to Greeves on October 18, 1916, when he was seventeen, allows us to eavesdrop on the words of Jack Lewis, adolescent atheist, pontificating on Christ and myth. When he uses the word "Christ," he says, he means "the mythological being into whom he was afterwards converted by popular imagination, . . . the legends about his magic performance and resurrection etc." In Jack's opinion, Jesus the human being did exist, "but all the other tomfoolery about the virgin birth, magic healings . . . is on exactly the same footing as any other mythology."[32]

Although he articulates it in a much less sophisticated fashion than Bultmann the biblical scholar, teenaged Lewis understands the application of myth to Christ in a remarkably similar way. The man Jesus did walk the earth, but

29. Bultmann, *Jesus Christ and Mythology*, 69.

30. Bultmann, "New Testament and Mythology," 44.

31. Congdon writes that "it is no accident" that the publication of the last installment of Bultmann's *Gospel of John* appeared within a month of the 1941 essay on the New Testament and mythology (*Mission of Demythologizing*, 483).

32. Lewis to Greeves, Oct. 18, 1916, *CL*, 1:234.

supernatural events such as the virgin birth, his miracles, and his resurrection from the dead are impossible; they never happened. Rather, the followers of Jesus used myth to proclaim him in their preaching.

Around 1929–1930, Lewis the Oxford scholar attempts to define the term in a letter to Owen Barfield: "Will this do as a definition of Myth? A *myth* is a description[x] or a story introducing supernatural personages or things, determined not, or not only, by motives arising from events within the story, but by the supposedly immutable relations of the personages or things[x]: possessing unity: and not, save accidentally, connected with any given place or time."[33]

Here we may observe the effects of academia on a young person's writing and be grateful that Lewis soon shook them off, though not before playfully attempting to coin new terms for the study of myth that rival Bultmann's own tongue-twister "demythologizing." "Would 'mythonomy' do? . . . 'Mytho-logic' (noun) wouldn't be bad, but people w[oul]d read it as an adjective. I have also thought of 'mythopoeics' . . . but that leads to 'a mythopoeician' wh[ich] is frightful: whereas 'a mythonomer' . . . is nice. Or shall we just invent a new word—like 'gas.'"[34]

Lewis's circle of friends continued to stimulate his thinking about myth into the next decade. On October 18, 1931, fifteen years to the day after he sent the "tomfoolery" letter to Greeves, Lewis wrote him again—this time working through the implications of his conversation with Dyson and Tolkien about myth on Addison's Walk (see chapter 1). In one of the many ironies of his life—coincidences too strange for fiction—myth emerges as the key that unlocks Lewis's understanding of Christ and opens the door between Deism and Christianity. Long influenced by James Frazer's *Golden Bough*, rife with tales of dying and rising gods, Lewis had been sure that "pagan stories" discredited the story of Jesus.[35] On this view, all myths were equally false. After the talk on Addison's Walk, however, he flipped the lens: all myths were not equally true, but all expressed some truth, however imperfectly.

Of course, the idea that pagan myths undermine the validity of Christianity long predates Frazer. Justin Martyr fought against it in the second century. In his *First Apology*, Justin writes that wicked demons encouraged many to

33. Lewis to Owen Barfield, Great War Letters, series 1, letter 5 [1929–1930], *CL*, 3:1619. The two superscript *x*'s mark a footnote for Barfield reading "Think it over. You'll see why."

34. Lewis to Owen Barfield, June 8, 1928, *CL*, 1:765. Lewis's most mature definition of myth appears in *An Experiment in Criticism* (Cambridge: Cambridge University Press, 1961), 40–49, but it has surprisingly little to say to his views on demythologizing.

35. "The Grand Miracle," in *Essay Collection*.

be called sons of Zeus specifically to convince people "that statements about Christ were marvelous tales, like the assertion of poets."[36] Lewis took Justin's argument and turned it upside down. For Justin, demons used myths to spread lies, but for Lewis, God seeded the minds of the poets with mythology to anticipate truth. In other words, pagan myth was to the incarnation what John the Baptist was to Jesus, a forerunner to point the way. Stoic philosophers speculated about *logoi spermatikoi,* the seeds of the Logos, the divine principle of reason scattered throughout the cosmos that order creation. As Alister McGrath notes, Lewis suggests a theory of *mythoi spermatikoi,* premeditated acts of God that prepared the ground for true myth, the incarnation of Jesus.[37]

Since myth played such an important role in his life before his conversion to Christ and also helped catalyze the conversion itself, Lewis's negative reaction to Bultmann is unsurprising. But when Lewis addresses demythologizing, a word he could have gotten only from Bultmann or discussions about him, Lewis never mentions his name.

The term "demythologizing" appears for the first time in Lewis's work in a letter he wrote to Mary Van Deusen in January 1959. *Jesus Christ and Mythology* was published in 1958, and Lewis seems to be responding to her questions about it, or at least to questions on demythologizing in general.[38] He begins with the topic of existentialism. Like Queen Victoria, he is not amused, writing, "I am sure 'demythologising' [the New Testament] always really means re-mythologising it: i.e. clothing it in the popular scientific and historical theories of your own period which are in fact transitory and will soon seem as mythological as those of the first century."[39] Without mentioning Bultmann, Lewis voices objections other critics had leveled against his work: the supposed poppycock of existentialist thought and the alleged chronological snobbery of demythologizing. On the latter, Lewis is one of many who have misunderstood Bultmann, even though the two men actually concurred. In

36. Section 54 in L. W. Barnard, *The First and Second Apologies,* Ancient Christian Writers 56 (New York: Paulist, 1997).

37. Alister McGrath, *The Intellectual World of C. S. Lewis* (Chichester, UK: Wiley-Blackwell, 2014), 65.

38. Bultmann was in residence as visiting professor of religion at Syracuse University in New York 1958–1959, which, according to Congdon, "furthered the English-speaking interest in his work." Congdon, "Kerygma and History: Bultmann's Hermeneutical Theology in North America Today," in *Rudolf Bultmann und die Neutestamentliche Wissenschaft der Gegenwart,* ed. Lukas Bormann and Christof Landmesser (Tübingen: Mohr Siebeck, 2022), 97.

39. Lewis to Mary Van Deusen, Jan. 16, 1959, *CL,* 3:1012.

the next chapter, when we examine how Lewis attacks Bultmann in "Modern Theology and Biblical Criticism," we will see—though Lewis never will—how often they agree with one another.

Lewis recycles some of the Van Deusen letter in *Letters to Malcolm*. Giving advice on how to read the Bible, he says:

> I suggest two rules for exegetics. (1) Never take the images literally. (2) When the *purport* of the images . . . seems to conflict with the theological abstractions, trust the *purport* of the images every time. For our abstract thinking is itself a tissue of analogies. . . . Are these likely to be more adequate than the sensuous, organic, and personal images of Scripture—light and darkness, . . . hen and chickens, father and child? . . . Hence what they now call "demythologizing" Christianity can easily be "re-mythologizing" it—and substituting a poorer mythology for a richer.[40]

Here, in one of the last things he writes on Scripture, Lewis revisits an essay he wrote on figurative language in 1936, where he claims, "Those who have prided themselves on being literal . . . about the highest abstractions" are not doing themselves any favors. Almost all truth "is won by metaphor," and if there is not some "psycho-physical" correspondence between pairings like "good and light," then "all our thinking is nonsensical."[41] Like Bultmann, Lewis respects the *purport* of the images but rejects taking the images themselves literally.

But Lewis still misunderstands the application of the term "demythologizing," which does not entail rejecting biblical images taken from nature and does not aim to replace concrete words with spiritualized abstractions. Bultmann quotes John 3:19, "And this is the judgment, that the light has come into the world, and people loved the darkness more than the light," to emphasize the concrete language of light and darkness as a specific example of the process of demythologizing itself.[42] He notes that the joy of the just can be depicted only in "symbolic pictures such as a blessed banquet," which is one of Lewis's own favorite images for expressing communal bliss—so much so that it permeates his work (see part 3 of this book).[43] Bultmann insists that he abhors abstraction, and he claims that it is myth that is abstract, since by its very nature

40. *Letters to Malcolm: Chiefly on Prayer* (New York: Harcourt, Brace & World, 1964), 52 (emphasis in original).

41. Lewis, "Bluspels and Flalansferes," in *Selected Literary Essays*, ed. Walter Hooper (1969; repr., Cambridge: Cambridge University Press, 2013), 265.

42. Bultmann, *Jesus Christ and Mythology*, 33.

43. Bultmann, *Jesus Christ and Mythology*, 29.

myth doesn't speak to "modern man."[44] This is a major crux between Bultmann and Lewis, because Lewis argues the opposite: he thinks myth may be the only thing that speaks to moderns about God.

This argument takes center stage in "Myth Became Fact" (1944), an essay that refutes demythologizing without ever mentioning the word. The essay opens with the same idea that Bultmann's 1941 paper made infamous, here posed as a question from a certain "Corineus."[45] Corineus thinks that "Historic Christianity is something so barbarous that no modern man can really believe it," and he wonders why educated people must express "their deepest thoughts in terms of an archaic mythology which must hamper and embarrass them at every turn."[46] Because, Lewis answers, "It is the myth which is the vital and nourishing element in the whole concern. Corineus wants us to move with the times. Now, we know where times move. They move away. But in religion we find something that does not move away. It is what Corineus calls the myth that abides. . . . It is the myth that gives life."[47]

How does myth give life? By mediating between the abstract and the concrete. Human thought is abstract, but human experience is concrete, and no one can fully engage both at the same time. One cannot think abstractly while immersed in concrete experience.[48] He illustrates his argument about the mediating function of myth by retelling a myth, the story of Orpheus and Eurydice. Orpheus may lead his dead wife out of Hades as long as he doesn't turn around to look at her. The moment he does, she fades away, falling back into realm of the dead.[49] He may not contemplate his wife and have her, too. It is one or the other.

To Lewis, myth bridges the gap between abstract thought and concrete experience through the power of story. As such, it is indispensable. What is to Lewis the historical fact of the incarnation never ceases to be myth, and it is even greater for being so. Christ is more than the ancient gods, and "we must not be ashamed of the mythical radiance resting on our theology. We must

44. See Congdon, *Mission of Demythologizing*, 583.

45. As Arend Smilde notes, "Corineus is, in ancient British legend, the eponymous founder of Cornwall," and the name almost certainly refers to A. L. Rowse, Tudor historian and Fellow of All Souls College, Oxford, who "acquired some fame as a writer and poet about Cornwall." Smilde, "C. S. Lewis's 'Transposition': Text and Context," *Sehnsucht* 13, no. 1 (2019): 38. My thanks to Michael Ward for pointing out this information.

46. "Myth Became Fact," in *Essay Collection*, 138.

47. "Myth Became Fact," 139–40.

48. "Myth Became Fact," 140.

49. "Myth Became Fact," 141.

not be nervous about 'parallels' and 'pagan Christs': they *ought* to be there—it would be a stumbling block if they weren't. We must not, in false spirituality, withhold our imaginative welcome. If God chooses to be mythopoeic—and is not the sky itself a myth—shall we refuse to be *mythopathic*?"[50] God is mythopoeic, a myth maker. Therefore, it is a religious duty to be mythopathic, someone who deeply feels or experiences myth.[51]

Of all the things I could pluck from the last paragraph, I will focus on an unlikely candidate, the parenthetical remark "Is not the sky itself a myth?" because it can be read as countering Bultmann. Bultmann rejects the three-tiered world-picture of the ancient universe, where God is in heaven and "comes down" to earth in the person of Jesus.[52] Such cosmic action expressed in such objectified language is anathema to him. But would changing the language to something less mythic make any difference? Lewis thinks not. "We can . . . say 'God entered history' instead of saying 'God came down to earth.' But, of course, 'entered' is just as metaphorical as 'came down.'"[53] And so it is. But to Bultmann, metaphor is not myth, and trying to make the language of the New Testament less concrete and more abstract is not the purpose of demythologizing.

To address the question "myth as fact or fiction?" in the title of this chapter, we see that the answer is not either-or but both-and. For both Lewis and Bultmann, the kerygma of Jesus is both myth and fact. Their major disagreement lies in the fact that Bultmann thinks it "senseless and impossible" to retain ancient myth when preaching the gospel, while Lewis holds the opposite view. "The Church," Bultmann claims, "can reestablish communication with modern man and speak with an authentic voice only after she has resolutely abandoned mythology."[54] Lewis, on the other hand, insists that there is no way to encounter the gospel without it, in this or any other world. In *Out of the Silent Planet*, the first volume of his Ransom trilogy, the narrator wonders if "the distinction between history and mythology might be itself meaningless outside the earth."[55] In *Perelandra*, the second and most overtly biblical of the

50. "Myth Became Fact," 142 (italics in original).

51. I am grateful to Derek Keefe for his insight on the word "mythopathic." Keefe notes that Lewis's understanding of the word may draw from his correspondence with Owen Barfield, Feb. 2, 1927, *CL*, 3:1507–8.

52. Bultmann, *Jesus Christ and Mythology*, 20.

53. "Is Theology Poetry?," in *Essay Collection*, 18.

54. Bultmann, "New Testament and Mythology," 2–3; "A Reply to the Theses of J. Schniewind," in Bartsch, *Kerygma and Myth*, 123.

55. Lewis, *Out of the Silent Planet* (1938; repr., New York: Macmillan, 1965), 144–45.

three, he realizes that "the triple distinction of truth from myth and of both from fact was purely terrestrial—was part and parcel of that unhappy division between soul and body which resulted from the Fall." Any dichotomy between myth and fact on earth is a primordial tragedy caused by human sin. God intended it otherwise, and on this planet, the divide began to disappear with the incarnation.[56] To Bultmann, like Corineus, ancient myth, understood as an objectifying world-picture, is a stumbling block, an impediment that must be removed from humans' path to God. To Lewis, in stark contrast, myth forms an essential bridge between past and present, abstract and concrete, God and human. He goes so far as to say that someone who does not accept Christianity as fact but who does feed on it as myth may be "more spiritually alive" than a Christian who does nothing but mouth orthodox doctrine and move on.[57] This conviction is likely autobiographical. From the beginning of his life as an adult Christian, Lewis was sure that God-given myth trumped man-made doctrine, even if the myth itself were not "true" in a historical or scientific sense. The old stories were always better than any theological abstraction built upon them.

Conclusion

That Lewis was a Christian apologist isn't news to anyone. But, strange as it may seem, so was Bultmann. Both men wanted to preach Christ so that he became existentially meaningful to their contemporaries, and both tried to deal with objections that kept belief at bay. Both focused on the role of myth in translating Christ's message from antiquity to modernity, but they understood the definition and function of myth differently, diverging most in their responses to supernaturalism, the starting point of Bultmann's 1941 essay. Bultmann insisted that "nobody" believes in the supernatural world anymore, a claim that many, and not just Lewis, could belie. For example, John Macquarrie, a leading scholar of Bultmann's work, wrote him a letter pointing out the thousands of pilgrims at Lourdes, the Roman Catholic shrine in France where devotees pray for healing through the intercession of Mary. Bultmann's response to Macquarrie was "quite simple and very interesting. . . . 'But these are not modern men.'"[58]

56. Lewis, *Perelandra* (1943; repr., New York: Macmillan, 1965), 149.

57. "Myth Became Fact," 141.

58. Macquarrie, *The Scope of Demythologizing: Bultmann and His Critics* (Gloucester, MA: Peter Smith, 1969), 236.

This is a striking reaction, all the more because it replicates exactly what Lewis said about himself: he was not a modern man. In his inaugural address at Cambridge in 1954, he compared himself to a "live dinosaur," a rare specimen that had survived against all odds into the twentieth century.[59] Macquarrie offers an eerily similar riposte to Bultmann that packs the same punch. The supernaturalist, Macquarrie says, is like a coelacanth, a fish long thought to be extinct but discovered still to be alive in 1938. He writes, "The coelacanth can have survived so long after most of its contemporaries became extinct because there is something fundamentally sound in its constitution. Indeed, . . . the coelacanth may still be pursuing its archaic ways . . . [long] after *Homo sapiens* has effaced himself from the planet's side!"[60] Like the coelacanth, Lewis's work on myth abides, while Bultmann's continues to be misunderstood.[61] These facts alone do not make Lewis right and Bultmann wrong. A concept's staying power is no argument for its validity, as enslaved persons throughout the millennia might attest. But Lewis is clear, consistent, and delightful to read, qualities that, on the whole, Bultmann's work on myth lacks. It is easy to see why Lewis is still read with pleasure on the topic, and Bultmann not so much.

Bultmann's questions about making Christ meaningful to "modern man" remain as important as they've ever been, but his answers have probably not improved the existence of individual Christians as much as he hoped they would. As Jonathan Bernier observes, "Bultmann's particular work of translation largely turned out to be a dead end" because the foundations on which he built have been "almost entirely abandoned."[62] Readers who don't know what those foundations were, much less why they were abandoned, might put Bultmann aside for less cerebral reasons—for his unargued rejection of the supernatural and his condescension toward those who don't reject it.

Thus far we have not seen Lewis call out Bultmann or any other biblical scholar by name. Nor have we seen him engage in a sustained critique of academic biblical scholarship. He does both in his essay "Modern Theology and Biblical Criticism."

59. "*De Descriptione Temporum*," in *They Asked for a Paper* (London: Geoffrey Bles, 1962), 24.

60. Macquarrie, *Scope of Demythologizing*, 238.

61. As an example of the need to explain Bultmann's ideas even to contemporary critical scholars, see Congdon, "Demystifying," 1–23.

62. Jonathan Bernier, "Bultmann and Translation," *Critical Realism and the New Testament* (blog), June 7, 2017, https://tinyurl.com/49mcnkdu.

7. "I AM NO HIGHER CRITIC"

Lewis among the Biblical Scholars

The "Higher Critic"! Who is he?
The man who can't in peace abide
The will of the majority,
Who 'gainst his views of truth decide.

—W. R. Reynolds, 1895[1]

In the winter of 1959, Lewis enjoyed a convivial dinner with Kenneth Carey, the principal of Westcott House, Cambridge, an Anglican seminary. In the course of the evening, he picked up Alec Vidler's book *Windsor Sermons* and read "The Sign at Cana" on Jesus turning water into wine (John 2:1–11).[2] He was surprised by what he found there. Vidler, an Anglican priest, proposes that the Cana story "should be read more as a parable than as a miracle" because, as he correctly notes, John never uses the word "miracle" in his Gospel; instead, he uses "sign." A sign isn't important in itself; it points to something else. With this in mind, Vidler interprets the Cana event allegorically, just as he would a parable.[3] But Lewis seems to have misunderstood him. As Carey recounted it later, Lewis took Vidler to mean that "what the Church has always regarded as a miracle was, in fact, a parable!" Much spirited conversation followed, and Carey invited Lewis to expand on it for his seminarians, which he did on May 11, 1959, in the lecture now known as "Modern Theology and Biblical Criticism."[4]

1. "The Higher Critic," *Herald and Presbyter*, Feb. 6, 1895, 11.

2. For more on the circumstances of the talk, see Joel Heck, "'Modern Theology and Biblical Criticism' in Context," *VII: Journal of the Marion E. Wade Center* 31 (2014): 123–39.

3. Alec Vidler, *Windsor Sermons* (London: SCM, 1958), 66–71; "MTBC," 152. Vidler's allegorical reading is supersessionistic and virulently anti-Jewish; would that Lewis had objected to that.

4. Lewis, "Modern Theology and Biblical Criticism," in *Christian Reflections*, ed.

At the beginning of the lecture, Lewis admits that his reaction to Vidler was "hasty & ignorant," although he never explains why. On my reading, his ignorance consists in this: Vidler didn't say the story *was* a parable but only that it should be read as one. The difference is small but important, because there is more at stake for Lewis than the proper application of literary terms. Parables are fiction, and if Jesus's sign at Cana is a parable, then Vidler implies it didn't happen; Jesus never turned water into wine. Lewis says none of this in the lecture, but he does recast his concerns there when he argues that "liberals" misidentify literary forms in the Gospel of John and thus undermine its historical credibility. This complaint is the foundation of his paper on modern biblical criticism.

"Modern Theology and Biblical Criticism" confronts "higher critics" of the New Testament, the "liberals" and "modernists" who are the targets of the essay. Walter Hooper claims that Lewis's friend Austin Farrer, himself a higher critic of the Gospels, called it "the best thing he ever wrote."[5] Farrer's reputation has gone from strength to strength in the decades since his death, but I must disagree with him here. The statement so amazes me that I wonder if he read the essay, because its errors are legion, whether one judges it from the perspective of a biblical or a literary scholar.[6] Lewis misreads almost all the sources he criticizes, from Gore's *New Commentary on Holy Scripture* and Tyrrell's *Christianity at the Cross-Roads* to influential texts in his own field such as Auerbach's *Mimesis*, and these misreadings, coupled with his tendency to rely

---

Walter Hooper (Grand Rapids: Eerdmans, 1967), 152–66. Hooper retitled the essay "Fern-Seed and Elephants" in the 1975 collection of the same name.

5. Hooper, preface to *Fern-Seed and Elephants* (Glasgow: Collins, 1975), 9.

6. To my knowledge, only four biblical scholars have published specifically on "MTBC": T. Francis Glasson (discussed in detail below); Christopher Bryan, "C. S. Lewis and the Art of Reading Scripture," *Sewanee Theological Review* 55, no. 2 (2012): 180–207, a thoughtful but uncritically laudatory essay; Richard Bauckham, "Are We Still Missing the Elephant? C. S. Lewis's 'Fernseed and Elephants' Half a Century On," *Theology* 116, no. 6 (2013): 427–34, which does lightly critique Lewis; and Edith Humphrey, *Further Up and Further In: Orthodox Conversations with C. S. Lewis on Scripture and Theology* (Yonkers, NY: St. Vladimir's Seminary Press, 2017), 71–82. Humphrey has written a valuable book, but I assess "Modern Theology and Biblical Criticism" very differently than she does. Literary scholars and theologians who have engaged the essay invariably accept what Lewis writes without question, and often with schadenfreude. Apologist Josh McDowell simply copies and pastes the entirety of the essay without comment, as if it interprets itself. McDowell, *The New Evidence That Demands a Verdict* (Nashville: Thomas Nelson, 1999), 574–79.

on "feel" rather than fact, produce the worst thing he ever wrote on Scripture. My analysis suggests that, if Lewis had read the works he opposed more carefully, he would have discovered how much they held in common, opening doors to biblical scholarship instead of slamming them shut, and thereby giving his readers the opportunity to understand the Bible better.

Liberals, Modernists, and Higher Critics

Lewis always let his readers know he wasn't a trained theologian or biblical scholar. The second sentence of *Reflections on the Psalms* (1958), for example, informs them that he is "no higher critic," but I imagine few understood what he meant.[7] By 1958 the phrase was decidedly old-fashioned, its usage having peaked at the end of the nineteenth century. Opponents of the higher critics ridiculed the term because they considered it pretentious, as those critics evidently thought themselves superior to simple believers.[8] To Lewis and many others, higher critics were liberals and modernists whose investigation of Scripture undermined traditional belief.

Higher criticism did trouble some of the faithful, but that was not its goal, and the name was not devised to be condescending. It is "higher" only in relation to "lower criticism," what is now called textual criticism. Traditional textual critics compare and contrast variant manuscripts of the same content to try to determine what an author actually wrote, a practice that goes back to the ancient Greco-Roman world.[9] Academics in many fields—literature, history, biblical studies, and classics—use textual criticism, and it is the discipline where Lewis and biblical scholars met most amicably. He taught a course on it early in his career, and he praises the method in "Modern Theology and Biblical Criticism," which is ironic, because the essay would have benefitted mightily from applying it to a key passage in his argument.[10] Once lower criti-

7. *Reflections on the Psalms* (New York: Harcourt, Brace & World, 1958), 1.

8. Jean-Baptiste Michel et al., "Quantitative Analysis of Culture Using Millions of Digitized Books," *n*-gram of "Higher Critic" in British English, *Science* 331 (2010): 176–82; John Barton, "Source Criticism: Old Testament," in *The Anchor Yale Bible Dictionary*, ed. David Noel Freedman (New York: Doubleday, 1992), 6:164.

9. Textual critics today, not so sure about the likelihood of determining "what the author actually wrote," have different goals. See Garrick V. Allen, ed., *The Future of New Testament Textual Scholarship* (Tübingen: Mohr Siebeck, 2019).

10. Lewis to Greeves, Oct. 17, 1929, *CL*, 1:837; "MTBC," 163. His omission in "MTBC" is more understandable if his complaints while engaging in textual criticism

cism has established a working text, scholars move to higher criticism, which at the beginning of the twentieth century was synonymous with source criticism, a method that investigates the sources authors may have used. As the century progressed, the phrase "higher criticism" became a label for academic biblical scholarship as a whole.

Lewis valued the feeling of being part of a band of brothers united against a common foe. At first, the band was two literal brothers, Jack and Warnie, against their father. Then it was the group of abused boarders at his first school, followed by Lewis's stint as a soldier in the Great War. As an adult Christian, he set himself against theological liberals and modernists. "What unites the Evangelical and the Anglo-Catholic against the 'Liberal' or 'Modernist,'" he proposed, is clear and important: the former are "thoroughgoing supernaturalists" who believe in the incarnation, resurrection, and return of Jesus, and in a final judgment followed by heaven or hell.[11] The latter, at least according to Lewis, don't.

Modernists and liberals themselves located their concerns differently. C. W. Emmet, writing in 1922 when Lewis was a student at Oxford, explains that the modernist movement originated among Roman Catholics, embodied particularly in the priests Alfred Loisy and George Tyrrell.[12] Loisy is mentioned in "Modern Theology and Biblical Criticism," and Tyrrell plays a major role in it, as Lewis devotes the final section of the essay to his book *Christianity at the Cross-Roads* (1910). Tyrrell opens that book by placing himself among higher critics, modernists, and liberals, noting, "The hope of a synthesis between the essentials of Christianity and the assured results of [higher] criticism is very widespread nowadays, and those who share it are commonly called Modernists or Liberals."[13] In 1922, Emmet can observe that modernism is no longer confined to Roman Catholics; it now names what used to be called the "broad, liberal school in Anglicanism." Anglican modernists welcome new developments that integrate higher criticism, science, and tradition.[14] This project encapsulates what Charles Gore tried to do in *Lux Mundi*, although Gore rejected the modernist label for himself.[15]

---

one day in 1930 are representative. In a letter to Greeves begun Jan. 30, he calls the practice of textual criticism "beastly," boring, and even physically painful. *CL*, 1:881.

11. Lewis to the editor of *Church Times*, Feb. 8, 1952, *CL*, 3:164.

12. C. W. Emmet, "The Modernist Movement in the Church of England," *Journal of Religion* 2 (1922): 561.

13. Tyrrell, *Christianity at the Cross-Roads* (London: Longmans, Green, 1910), xv.

14. Emmet, "Modernist Movement," 262.

15. Ramsey, *An Era in Anglican Theology: From Gore to Temple; The Development*

The best exposition of the term "liberal" for putting Lewis's lecture in context comes from T. Francis Glasson, a British biblical scholar who published "Who Were the Liberals?" in 1959, the same year Lewis delivered the lecture. The word is "worse than useless," Glasson notes, until someone explains what it means to them. For fundamentalists, liberals are those who reject biblical inerrancy, a definition that makes Christians like Luther, Calvin, and Chrysostom liberals. As we have seen, Lewis himself, who vehemently rejected inerrancy, belongs to this group. "Liberal" could be defined by its opposite, "conservative," a person who "holds fast to tradition," but the same person can be liberal in one area and conservative in another. Furthermore, Glasson writes, to define the word responsibly, one must specify time and place. German liberalism in 1900 is different from German liberalism in 1959, and both differ from liberalism in Great Britain. "The kind of Liberalism dominant in Germany was never generally followed in this country," he observes, a sentence that foreshadows my analysis of Lewis's lecture. To Glasson, contemporary British theological liberalism entails "the reduction of Christ to a human teacher, the Bible as a human production rather than Divine revelation, disbelief in miracle, and the presentation of Christianity as a message of moral ideals."[16] Everything Lewis writes in his essay indicates that he would agree with this characterization of liberalism.

The Sheep Begins to Bleat

The overarching metaphor of "Modern Theology and Biblical Criticism" is the layperson as sheep. Lewis had used the same image in *Miracles* (1947) for the same purpose, to criticize scholars of the New Testament: "When you turn from the New Testament to modern scholars, remember that you go among them as sheep among wolves," he wrote, even if the scholarly wolves are clergy.[17] In "Modern Theology and Biblical Criticism" he personalizes the

of Anglican Theology between "Lux Mundi" and the Second World War, 1889–1939 (New York: Scribner, 1960; repr., Eugene, OR: Wipf & Stock, 2009), 68.

16. T. Francis Glasson, "Who Were the Liberals?," *Expository Times* 70, no. 11 (1959): 342–44.

17. *Miracles* (1947; repr., New York: Macmillan, 1960), 164. Novelist Flannery O'Connor praises this sentence, calling *Miracles* "very fine. Deceptively simple. You really need to read every sentence twice. Go among the Biblical scholars, says he, as a sheep among wolves." *The Habit of Being: The Letters of Flannery O'Connor*, ed. Sally Fitzgerald (New York: Vintage Books, 1979), 572.

imagery. Lewis, a layman and outsider, neither trained theologian nor biblical scholar, calls himself a sheep who has been invited to bleat before an audience of shepherds and shepherds in training—the priests and seminarians at Westcott House—about the "undermining of the old orthodoxy," which, he proposes, is primarily the fault of New Testament scholars who deny the historicity of the Gospels and the reality of miracles. These "experts" think they know better than their predecessors who have kept the faith for millennia. Lewis doesn't trust them, but because he is "ignorantly sceptical," he "may have nothing but misunderstandings" to offer.[18] On this last point, he is correct, and to a far greater extent than he might have imagined.

The First Bleat

Lewis, Lock, and the Genre of the Gospel of John

The lecture is structured as four "bleats," and Lewis begins by wondering if biblical scholars' focus on Scripture has made them myopic. They should broaden their vision and read as many different literary genres as he has, because in his opinion they "lack literary judgment"; they have no feel for literature. To illustrate the deficiency, Lewis pulls out his well-worn copy of Gore's *New Commentary on Holy Scripture* and opens to its chapter on the Gospel of John.

The chapter was written by Walter Lock (1846–1933), who enjoyed a distinguished career at Oxford, serving as Dean Ireland Professor of Holy Scripture before his appointment as Lady Margaret Professor of Divinity and canon of Christ Church. He contributed to *Lux Mundi*, but he was not as sanguine as Gore was about the benefits of critical scholarship. Lock's obituary calls him "timid and hesitating" because he "feared the consequences of Biblical Criticism for the faith of the average man."[19] This judgment might have surprised Lewis, who presents Lock as the very model of a modern major exegete. Lewis writes:

> In what is already a very old commentary I read that the Fourth Gospel is regarded by one school as a "spiritual romance," "a poem not a history," to be judged by the same canons as Nathan's parable, the Book of Jonah, *Paradise Lost* "or, more exactly, *Pilgrim's Progress*." After a man has said that, why need one attend to anything else he says about any book in the world? Note that he regards *Pilgrim's Progress* . . . as the closest parallel.[20]

18. "MTBC," 153–54, 152.
19. G. A. Cooke, "Walter Lock," *Journal of Theological Studies* 35, no. 137 (1934): 1.
20. "MTBC," 154.

The very old commentary is Gore's, the Fourth Gospel is John's, and the man is Lock. Lock did make mistakes in his chapter, but Lewis made more when he misread Lock and misrepresented what he wrote, intertwining Lock's errors with his own. Pulling them apart is intricate work, like picking knots out of a fine chain that tangles itself up over and over before it finally shakes out smooth.

The first knot was unraveled by T. Francis Glasson, whom we met above. His article "C. S. Lewis on St John's Gospel: A Correction and a Protest" was published in 1968, the year after "Modern Theology and Biblical Criticism" appeared in print.[21] Glasson begins by giving Lewis his due. If a "school" of academic biblical scholars really did call John's Gospel a "spiritual romance," it would "understandably excite [Lewis's] scorn." But, Glasson says, no one ever did. How, then, did Lewis come to think someone had?[22] The problem begins with Lock, who made a mistake when he referenced James Drummond's book *An Inquiry into the Character and Authorship of the Fourth Gospel* (1903). I say "reference" rather than "cite" because Lock produces what Glasson calls "a travesty of Drummond's teaching." Drummond never called John a romance. When he uses the word, he is quoting Macaulay, who is not talking about John at all. Macaulay writes that our modern concept of writing history in terms of "strict accuracy was unknown to the ancients," something Lewis himself affirmed.[23] Macaulay observes that ancient histories "may almost be called romances founded in fact. . . . But the numerous little incidents which heighten the interest, the words, the gestures, the looks, are evidently furnished by the imagination of the author."[24] We will return to questions of history and "the numerous little incidents which heighten the interest" soon.

Drummond agrees with Macaulay about the way ancient histories incorporate both fact and fiction and then moves to the idea of John as the spiritual Gospel among the four, a designation that goes back to second-century Christians, who used it to express how John differed from the other three.

21. T. Francis Glasson, "C. S. Lewis on St John's Gospel: A Correction and a Protest," *Theology* 71, no. 576 (1968): 267–69.

22. Gore uses the phrase "spiritual romance" in *The Epistles of St. John* (New York: Charles Scribner's Sons, 1920), 39, but he does not imply that the Gospel is a "romance" or that anyone ever thought it was. There is no record of Lewis reading this book.

23. Lewis to Clyde Kilby, May 7, 1959, 3:1046.

24. Glasson ("Lewis on St John's Gospel") quoting James Drummond quoting Macaulay in Drummond's *An Inquiry into the Character and Authorship of the Fourth Gospel* (London: Williams & Norgate, 1903), 30. The word "romance" appears only two other times in Drummond (pp. 263–64), and neither concerns John.

Drummond never calls John a romance, and he never compares it to *Pilgrim's Progress*, which is an allegory, but he does note how easily the "spiritual" Gospel lends itself to allegorical interpretation—a very different thing from John *being* an allegory.

Glasson's article does not address Drummond's comments on the allegorical interpretation of John or Lock's remark about judging the Gospel by the same standards as *Pilgrim's Progress*, but Lock misread Drummond on these topics too, because Drummond explicitly refutes the idea of John as allegory. Even though it is the "spiritual" Gospel, Drummond says, "this view does not preclude the possibility, or even probability, that much genuine history is mingled with the narrative, and I am very far from supposing that the whole is a tissue of allegories."[25]

Lock may have made the same mistake when he read Drummond's remarks on the allegorical interpretation of John that Lewis did when he read Vidler's sermon and others have made when they read Lewis's Chronicles of Narnia. That is, if a text can be read *as* an allegory, it *is* an allegory. Since Drummond didn't call John an allegory, then, what might lie behind Lock's comments to that effect that so inflamed Lewis? We don't have to look far. In the first quarter of the twentieth century, calling John an allegory was associated with Alfred Loisy, whom Lewis mentions in the second paragraph of his essay, though not on this topic. Loisy was so well known for calling John an allegory that his obituary in *Theological Studies* highlights the fact: "Loisy's thesis, since become famous, was that 'le quatrième Évangile tout entier n'est pas autre chose qu'une grande allégorie théologique et mystique'" (the Fourth Gospel on the whole is nothing other than a grand theological and mystical allegory).[26]

Many British biblical scholars disagreed. B. H. Streeter, whose work would prove far more influential than Drummond's, refutes "the suggestion that John consciously and deliberately composed stories for the sake of their allegorical meaning." The essay that follows Lock's in the Gore commentary also denies

25. Drummond, *Inquiry*, 428. Drummond writes that John's stories are "far too definite in time, place, and circumstances, and above all in their intrinsic meaning and purpose, to be regarded as legends which the writer carelessly accepted as veritable history." Nonetheless, he comes to a completely different conclusion from this data than Lewis does. To Drummond, the Gospels are not "reportage" but the product of an author who, working in "good faith," "deliberately departed from the current tradition" (429).

26. A. C. Cotter, SJ, "Alfred Loisy (1857–1940)," *Theological Studies* 2, no. 2 (1941): 244, quoting Loisy, *Le quatrième Évangile* (Paris: Alphonse Picard et Fils, 1903), 75.

the allegation: "It is further of great importance to realize that recent criticism, both Jewish and Christian, has been strongly reacting against the view that used to prevail, that the Gospel . . . is allegorical rather than historical." Gore himself writes, "It is really monstrous to suggest, as is frequently done, by critics who ought to know better, that when the Alexandrian Clement calls St. John's Gospel the distinctively 'spiritual' one . . . he means that [it] is only intended as allegory and not history."[27]

Glasson summarizes his work on Lock and Drummond as follows:

> The word "romance," as we have seen, occurs in the quotation from Macaulay, and does not represent Drummond's view of the Gospel. One can only conclude that Lock had given the book a cursory examination and finding the word "romance" had wrenched it from its context and developed what he himself would mean by the word. He is the one who is romancing when he implies that Drummond regarded the events of the Fourth Gospel as no more real than those of *Pilgrim's Progress*.[28]

Lewis read the essay on John by Lock, who had read Drummond's book on John and misconstrued what Drummond said about romance and allegory, and he took Lock's errors at face value. That is not necessarily his fault, although checking quotes is simple due diligence, especially if one is basing an argument on them. He was well aware of the issue, once advising a student to "cultivate the wisdom of the serpent," for "there will be misquotations, and misunderstood quotations in the best books, and you must always hunt up all quotations for yourself and find what they are really in situ."[29] Had he done so, he would not have made this error.

Right before the words Lewis quotes from Lock in the first bleat, Lock writes that "some" think John invented scenes that don't appear in the Synoptic Gospels such as the raising of Lazarus in order to exalt Jesus. Lock continues:

> *If this were so*, it would be useless to look for exact chronology, to attempt to identify all local allusions, or to harmonize facts with the Synoptists; the literary character will be that of a spiritual romance, "a poem, not a history" (Drummond), "a pictorial embodiment of spiritual truth" (*ibid.*); it will

27. Streeter, *The Four Gospels: A Study of Origins* (New York: Macmillan, 1925), 386, 390; Charles Harris, "Additional Note on the Authorship of the Gospel [of John]," in *NCHS*, part 3, 275; Gore, *Epistles of St. John*, 36–37.

28. Glasson, "Lewis on St John's Gospel," 269.

29. Lewis to Sister Madeleva, June 7, 1934, *CL*, 2:142.

> rank with and have to be judged by the same canons of interpretation as Nathan's parable or the Book of Jonah in the Old Testament, as *Paradise Lost, Paradise Regained,* or, more exactly, as *Pilgrim's Progress.* This theory is, in some respects, attractive; it gets rid of some historical difficulties.... [Even if this were so] a great deal of the spiritual value of the book will still remain, and the book will show that the impression of the Lord's Personality was so great both in His lifetime and in His subsequent effect upon the Church.... But there are decisive objections to this view. Great stress is laid on the fact that the miracles were wrought before eye-witnesses . . . and all the earlier facts are treated as on the same level as the undoubtedly historical fact of the crucifixion. John shows that he was face to face with Docetic tendencies (4:2, 3) to which the only reply could be historic facts.... The literary character of John is then that of a history; it has to be classed with the Acts or in the classical literature with Tacitus or Thucydides.[30]

I have italicized "If this were so" to emphasize the fact that Lock is writing conditionally. *If* the author of John invented scenes that don't appear in the Synoptics to make Jesus look more powerful, *then* the Gospel of John might be a romance or allegory, as Lock thinks Drummond said. But Lock himself doesn't think so. He does take a moment to play with the idea: it is appealing because it "gets rid of some historical difficulties" like the fact that the raising of Lazarus appears only in John. However, "there are decisive objections" to the idea that the Gospel of John is more fiction than fact, and Lock thinks the Gospel is narrated in the same way as a work of ancient history. Therefore, he calls John "a history" by genre, like the New Testament book of Acts or the Greco-Roman works of Tacitus and Thucydides—which is exactly what Lewis thinks.

I can now set up a conditional statement of my own: *If* Lewis had grasped what Lock said about the literary and historical character of John, *then* he would have seen that he and Lock agreed, and he could never have conceived the first part of his first bleat, the entirety of which consists of nothing but mistake piled upon mistake. Lewis's assessment of himself as "*ignorantly* skeptical" of biblical critics is truer than he realized. And there is more ignorance to come.

30. Lock, "The Gospel according to St. John," in *NCHS*, part 3, 241. The phrase "a poem, not a history" does not seem to appear in Drummond, but "a pictorial embodiment of spiritual truth" appears on p. 427.

Lewis, Lock, and the Historicity of the Gospel of John

In the next part of the bleat, Lewis builds on his mistakes about the Gospel's historicity. We must pause to acknowledge the problems inherent in the word "historicity." What does it mean for a gospel to be "historical"? Mercifully, Lewis leaves us in no doubt about his own definition regarding the Gospel of John. To him, John is "reportage"; it comes about as close to "the facts," he says, as Boswell.[31] The comparison indicates that Lewis believes the Gospel is eyewitness testimony put to paper during the life of Jesus, just as James Boswell recorded conversations with his friend Samuel Johnson and compiled them into the *Life of Johnson*. In writing this, Lewis might have been reacting to a 1950 book on John by the British biblical scholar C. J. Wright. Wright thinks John was "loyal to the mind of Jesus" but also "the reflective disciple with a mind of his own, not the slavish loyalty of a Boswell recording the utterances of Samuel Johnson. It is this fact which makes it so difficult for us to-day to decide what sayings of Jesus recorded in the Gospel were His exact words." Wright also contrasts John to *Pilgrim's Progress*, rejecting the possibility that the entire Gospel is an allegory: "If the authors in the West write allegories—such as *The Pilgrim's Progress* or *Gulliver's Travels*—they make it quite clear that they are not writing history. . . . Here in this Gospel, however, we see revealed an obviously historical intention, with, at least in places, an obviously allegorical method." Wright, like Gore, believes John mingled good history about Jesus with symbolic meditation, and that not all the words of Jesus in John are *ipsissima verba*.[32]

Lewis brings his conviction about John's "reportage" to bear on another misreading of Lock that he writes in the margins of Lock's essay, notes he does not incorporate into his lecture. After Lock concludes "the literary character of John is then that of a history," he addresses its date of composition, focusing on Jesus's prediction of the deaths of Peter and the Beloved Disciple in John 21. Lock writes, "If [chapter] 21 is by the same author as 1–20, the date must be after the crucifixion of St. Peter, possibly after the death, certainly after the

31. For more sophisticated definitions, see Lewis, "Historicism," in *Christian Reflections*, 100–113, esp. 105. K. Alan Snyder and Jamin Metcalf, *Many Times and Many Places: C. S. Lewis and the Value of History* (Hamden, CT: Winged Lion Press, 2023), came to my attention too late to be incorporated into this book.

32. C. J. Wright, *Jesus the Revelation of God: His Mission and Message according to St. John* (London: Hodder & Stoughton, 1950), 50–53. There is no record that Lewis read this book.

extreme old age, of the loved disciple."[33] In chapter 3 of this book, we looked at how Lewis cites the sentence as an example of improper philosophical presuppositions about miracles. In Lewis's marginal notes next to Lock's essay, he comments on biblical history and "truth." Marking the paragraph where Lock explains his rationale for dating the Gospel, Lewis writes, "*unless* Christ really said it [his predictions that Peter and the Beloved Disciple will die]. The whole para[graph] subject to the assumption that the book is untrue."[34]

This judgment is uncalled for. Nothing Lock says indicates that he assumes John to be "untrue," however Lewis understands the word. Lock had already, decisively, deemed the Gospel to be as "historical" as any other contemporary ancient history and even affirmed the historicity of its miracles. Why, then, did Lewis misread him? We will never know, but certainly he, like Lock, was reading carelessly. It is also possible that Lewis's documented bias against higher critics, which he articulated as early as 1947 in *Miracles*, was so severe that it led him to read into Lock the opposite of what Lock actually said. Lewis might have encountered biblical scholars like Loisy whose theories on the historicity of John differed from his own so radically that they left him prejudiced against modern scholarship on the Gospel. Throughout his life, whether reading Gore, Moffatt, or Lock, Lewis ignores, rejects, mischaracterizes, or, as we will soon see, even sneers at scholarship on John that differs from his own views. These are very human reactions when dearly held beliefs are challenged—and nothing is dearer to Lewis than his belief in Christ, which is rooted especially in the Gospel of John. Thus Lewis can twist Lock's remark that "the writer seems to class himself . . . with the eye-witnesses of the human life of Jesus" into what he thought its worst possible shape: Lock was accusing the evangelist of making it up.[35]

Lewis was no stranger to his own work being misread. It happened all the time, and most of the time he let it go. However, he did defend himself against

33. Lock, "Gospel according to St. John," 242.

34. Emphasis Lewis's. Marginal notes in Lewis's copy of *NCHS*, C. S. Lewis personal library, Marion E. Wade Center, Wheaton College, Wheaton, IL.

35. Lock ("Gospel according to St. John," 243) writes of the authorship of John: "All these facts point to the loved disciple as the author of at least 1–20, writing in his old age. If the indications of a later date outweigh them, then the author was probably a disciple of the loved disciple; the latter was, if not the author, at least the authority for the Gospel." Apparently this wasn't good enough for the editors of the commentary, since Lock's article is followed by an "Additional Note on the Authorship of the Gospel" whose author insists that John the apostle composed the Fourth Gospel.

a misreading by W. Norman Pittenger. First Lewis excoriates him, and then he turns on his heel to give Pittenger the benefit of the doubt: "How many times does a man need to say something before he is safe from the accusation of having said exactly the opposite? (I am not for a moment imputing dishonesty to Dr Pittenger; we all know too well how difficult it is to grasp or retain the substance of a book one finds antipathetic)."[36] I propose that something similar happened when Lewis read Lock. The actual substance of Lock's commentary on John wasn't antipathetic to Lewis. In fact, it was sympathetic! But because Lewis read carelessly and anticipated the worst, he pulled out the opposite of what Lock said.

We have untangled several errors in the first bleat, but Lewis isn't finished tying himself into knots about the historicity of John. As he continues, the mistakes twist round about themselves word by word, sentence by sentence. To back up his claim that the Fourth Gospel hews "pretty close up to the facts," Lewis bids us to read its dialogues. He mentions two, Jesus speaking with the Samaritan woman (John 4) and with the man born blind (John 9), but he never explains how they support his argument. He also tells us to "look at its pictures," and he focuses on one, Jesus doodling in the presence of the woman caught in adultery (John 8:6).[37] Based on his feel for literature developed over a lifetime of reading, Lewis claims that John 8:6 is not myth or legend. He is so sure of himself that he sets up what he considers to be two irreconcilable alternatives: Either it is "reportage—though it may no doubt contain errors—" or someone "without known predecessors or successors, suddenly anticipated the whole technique of modern, novelistic, realistic narrative."[38] Lewis is confident the dilemma will work in his favor. *Either* the Gospel is an eyewitness report, *or* it is something he considers impossible in the first century, a work of realistic fiction.

To examine his claim, we must first ask a question about the story of the adulterous woman that Lewis should have investigated before basing an argument on it: was it originally in John's Gospel at all? Such questions belong to the realm of textual criticism, formerly known as lower criticism. Given Lewis's respect for the method, it is ironic that, out of all the scenes he could have chosen to argue for the historicity of John, he chose this one, since textual critics

36. W. Norman Pittenger, "Apologist versus Apologist," *Christian Century*, Oct. 1, 1958, 1104–7. Lewis, "Rejoinder to Dr. Pittenger," in *God in the Dock: Essays on Theology and Ethics*, ed. Walter Hooper (Grand Rapids: Eerdmans, 1970), 179.

37. He also considers John 13:30, "and it was night," a "picture."

38. "MTBC," 155.

unanimously agree it was not original to the Gospel.[39] Therefore, it is unlikely that the author of the Gospel saw it. At some point Lewis knew this, because he marked the following in a book he owned: "The woman taken in adultery, . . . as is well known, forms no part of the true text of St. John's Gospel, though it is inserted by most manuscripts at the beginning of the eighth chapter." Lock's chapter on John also notes that it is "almost certainly not a part of the Gospel."[40] Even Lewis's "master," George MacDonald, acknowledged the textual issues, but he might also have inadvertently encouraged Lewis to ignore them. In MacDonald's novel *Thomas Wingfold, Curate,* the title character wonders how the story "got into that nook of the gospel of St. John, where it has no right place . . . just there, I mean, betwixt the seventh and eighth chapters. . . . There is no doubt of its being an interpolation." Wingfold notes that "the Alexandrian manuscript is the only one of the three oldest [copies of the Bible] that has it, and it is the last of the three." But he still thinks John witnessed the incident. "I wonder if St. John told the lovely tale as something he had forgotten, after he had finished dictating all the rest." That said, "it doesn't matter much: the tale must be a true one," and he compares it to a bird,

> floating about like a holy waif through the world of letters!—a sweet gray dove of promise that can find no rest for the sole of his foot! Just this one story of all stories a kind of outcast! and yet as a wanderer, oh, how welcome! Some manuscripts, I understand, have granted it a sort of outhouse-shelter at the end of the gospel of St. Luke. But it all matters nothing, so long as we can believe it; and true it must be, it is so like him all through. And if it does go wandering as a stray through the gospels, without place of its own, what matters it so long as it can find hearts enough to nestle in, and bring forth its young of comfort![41]

39. While the story is not original to the Gospels, it is ancient and even has "all the earmarks of historical veracity." But it is almost certain that John never saw it. Bruce Metzger, *A Textual Commentary on the Greek New Testament* (Stuttgart: Deutsche Bibelgesellschaft/German Bible Society, 1994), 187–89, and *The Text of the New Testament: Its Transmission, Corruption, and Restoration,* 3rd ed. (Oxford: Oxford University Press, 1992), 188, 223–24. See also Jennifer Knust and Tommy Wasserman, *To Cast the First Stone: The Transmission of a Gospel Story* (Princeton: Princeton University Press, 2018).

40. M. R. James, *The Apocryphal New Testament* (Oxford: Clarendon, 1924), 2; Lock, "Gospel according to St. John," 257.

41. Lewis, *George MacDonald: An Anthology* (1946; repr., New York: HarperCollins,

MacDonald's curate waxes poetic as he insists on the truth of the tale, and as long as one reads it devotionally, all is well: the textual problems don't matter. But Lewis doesn't have that luxury. He isn't leaning on the story for spiritual comfort but claiming it as a historical linchpin—weight it cannot bear.

Lewis deals his argument another blow when he contends that realistic fiction didn't exist in the ancient world. He says no more about it in "Modern Theology and Biblical Criticism," but he does discuss it in an earlier essay, "What Are We to Make of Jesus Christ?" (1950), also in the context of rejecting the idea that the Gospels are legends. The only definition of "legend" he offers here is negative: the Gospels aren't "artistic enough" to be legends. They're "clumsy," and they leave out large portions of Jesus's life. Then he moves to the dialogues in John. Other than bits of Plato, Lewis knows of nothing else like them in ancient literature. This is more information than "Modern Theology and Biblical Criticism" offers, but it's still insufficient, because he never explains why he thinks they are almost unique. What do Johannine dialogues and (unidentified) bits of Plato share that set them apart from all other ancient literature? Does Lewis think John's dialogues are special even in contrast to the Synoptics? If so, how? We ask these questions in vain. The answers may be clear to him, but he doesn't share them. He only asserts that there is nothing like John's dialogues until the advent of the nineteenth-century European novel.

Without further ado, Lewis launches into Jesus scribbling on the ground in John 8:6, asserting, "Nothing comes of this. No one has ever based any doctrine on it. And the art of *inventing* little irrelevant details to make an imaginary scene more convincing is a purely modern art. Surely the only explanation of this passage is that the thing really happened? The author put it in simply because he had *seen* it."[42]

Reading "Modern Theology and Biblical Criticism" with "What Are We to Make of Jesus Christ?" reveals two assumptions Lewis applies to the Gospel of John: (1) The presence of "pictures"—that is, vivid irrelevant details in an ancient text—indicates eyewitness testimony (2) because ancient writers had not yet developed the technique of inventing such details to make fiction more realistic. In fact, both assumptions are wrong.

2001), xxxvii; *Thomas Wingfold, Curate*, vol. 3 (London: Hurst and Blackett, 1876), ch. 82.

42. Lewis, "What Are We to Make of Jesus Christ?," in *Essay Collection*, 40 (emphasis in original). See also "MTBC," 155; "Christian Apologetics," in *Essay Collection*, 157. Biblical scholar Richard Bauckham also finds this part of Lewis's argument weak in "Are We Still Missing the Elephant?"

Lewis wasn't the first to argue that John's details prove the Gospel must have been written by an eyewitness. A commentary on John by Frédéric Godet (English trans. 1876) also sets up a dilemma, but not the same one Lewis does. "In the presence of details like these," Godet writes, either we have "a daring charlatan" or "we here possess the narrative of one of the nearest eyewitnesses." Godet's dilemma is liar or eyewitness rather than Lewis's eyewitness or impossibility. To support his claim, Godet cites the famous biblical scholar Ernest Renan, who sees a "multitude of little details which imprint on [John] the inimitable stamp of reality." If these details are not historical fact, Godet continues, they "inspire disgust," because John must have "intended to conceal the figure of the novel-writer under the mask of the historian."[43] Archbishop of Canterbury William Temple (d. 1944) makes a similar comment, minus Godet's visceral vehemence. To Temple, the Gospel of John has so much "the 'feel' of exact memory that I am uneasy about an interpretation which involves a view of it as pervasively influenced by an imagination stimulated by later beliefs."[44] By 1950, however, dissenting voices had arisen. C. J. Wright observes, "Those who point to the 'vividness' of the narrative, in proof of its 'actuality,' forget that this dramatic vividness pervades the Gospel: it is evidence of the character of the author's mind, and not of the precise historicity of his narrative."[45]

Godet, Renan, and Temple, like Lewis, think John's vivid detail proves the Gospel is an eyewitness account, but none of them hints at Lewis's reason for saying so: that ancient authors never invented such detail to make fiction more realistic.[46] On this, Lewis is wrong, and he should have known better, having taken a first in "Greats," the study of ancient Greco-Roman literature. In the first century CE when John was written, the art of adding vivid detail to narratives to make them appear realistic was widespread. It was called *enargeia,*

43. Frédéric Louis Godet, *Commentary on the Gospel of St. John,* vol. 1., trans. Frances Crombie and M. D. Cusin (Edinburgh: T&T Clark, 1876), 255–56.

44. William Temple, *Readings in St. John's Gospel,* series 1 and 2 (London: Macmillan, 1947), 32.

45. Wright, *Jesus the Revelation of God,* 145.

46. I have not discovered anyone prior to Lewis who argues that ancient authors did not use irrelevant details in their fictional works. One author postdates Lewis: Leon Morris, *Studies in the Fourth Gospel* (Grand Rapids: Eerdmans, 1969), 142, who makes the same argument but cites no sources to support it. R. Alan Culpepper, *Anatomy of the Fourth Gospel* (Philadelphia: Fortress, 1983), 314, calls Morris's claims "indefensible" for the same reason I do—the historical record proves him wrong.

and it was "central to all ancient theory on pictorial vividness in literature."[47] A foundational text on the topic appears in Dionysius of Halicarnassus. *Enargeia* is produced by descriptions that appeal to the senses, he writes, and it comes from "grasp of circumstantial detail."[48] The first-century rhetorician Quintilian notes that *enargeia* must be included in a list of ways to create rhetorical ornamentation and embellishment, and it can be produced "from the description of attendant circumstances." Instructing his readers on how to create it, he advises, "We shall succeed in making the facts evident, if they are plausible; it will even be legitimate to invent things of the kind that usually occur" by including *circumstantiae,* irrelevant details. In other words, Quintilian tells his students to invent plausible facts and irrelevant details to make their writing more vivid and thus more realistic.[49]

The invention of irrelevant fictional detail was regularly employed by Greco-Roman historians. As Andrew Walker observes, "fact and fiction seem to coexist without contradiction" in ancient historiography. *Enargeia* "was never regarded as an alternative to the truth," he explains. "As fiction, ancient historiography frequently sets as its goal verisimilitude—understood as a likeness to reality, and not as a fidelity to 'the facts'—and its success was often measured, by ancient critics and historians alike, by the degree to which the representation is 'visually perceived' by the reader."[50] Ancient Christian authors were aware of the implications of such techniques. Origen observed that it is very difficult, and sometimes impossible, "to substantiate almost any story as historical fact, even if it is true." No one should approach the Gospels with "unreasoning faith," he continues; they must apply their intelligence to decide what is factual in them and what isn't.[51] These very lines were selected by church fathers of unimpeachable orthodoxy, Basil of Caesarea and Gregory of Nazianzus, for their *Philocalia* of Origen. Knowing all of this, we see

47. G. Zanker, "Enargeia in the Ancient Criticism of Poetry," *Rheinisches Museum für Philologie* 124, no. 3/4 (1981): 304.

48. Dionysius of Halicarnassus, *Lysias* 7, in *The Critical Essays,* vol. 1, trans. Stephen Usher (Cambridge, MA: Harvard University Press, 1974), 32–33.

49. Quintilian, *Inst. Or.* 8.3.70, 8.6.67–68; Zanker, "Enargeia," 299; F. Heinrich Plett, *Enargeia in Classical Antiquity and the Early Modern Age: The Aesthetics of Evidence* (Leiden: Brill, 2012), 9, 11.

50. Andrew D. Walker, "*Enargeia* and the Spectator in Greek Historiography," *Transactions of the American Philological Association (1974–2014)* 123 (1993): 374.

51. Origen, *Contra Celsum* 1.42, trans. Henry Chadwick (Cambridge: Cambridge University Press, 1953), 39; see also *The Philocalia of Origen,* ed. George Lewis (Edinburgh: T&T Clark, 1911), 73–74.

that Lewis's dilemma fails. Ancient authors did invent vivid, irrelevant fictional detail to make their work seem more realistic long before the advent of nineteenth-century novels.

Oblivious to his predicament,[52] Lewis rather rudely states that anyone who doesn't agree with him has "not learned to read" and should consult Auerbach: that is, Erich Auerbach's book *Mimesis*.[53] So I did, and I discovered that Auerbach doesn't support him either. In fact, Lewis misread Auerbach exactly as he did Lock, pulling the opposite of what he said from his work. Since Lewis never explains how his argument intersects with Auerbach's, one must winkle it out. I see it centering on the two topics he highlights, dialogues in ancient literature and the presence of "pictures" that are irrelevant to the story.

Lewis, Auerbach, and the Historicity of Biblical Narrative

Mimesis was published in German in 1946 and English in 1953. Subtitled "The Representation of Reality in Western Literature," the book opens with the chapter "Odysseus' Scar," which launches immediately into book 19 of Homer's *Odyssey*, where Odysseus comes home to Ithaca incognito. He wants to hide his identity, but his old nurse, Euryclea, recognizes him as she washes his feet and sees the distinctive scar on his thigh. Throughout book 19 there is "copious direct discourse," dialogue in the same mode as the Gospel of John.

52. Philip Ryken is the only one I know who gives any indication of recognizing the absurdity of Lewis's argument, and the only thing he says about it is "here Lewis is writing entirely tongue-in-cheek." Ryken, "Inerrancy and the Patron Saint of Evangelicalism: C. S. Lewis on Holy Scripture," in *The Romantic Rationalist*, ed. John Piper and David Mathis (Wheaton, IL: Crossway, 2014), 61. But how can Lewis be anything but serious when he immediately writes that those who don't agree with him don't know how to read and urges them to consult Auerbach?

53. "MTBC," 155. Erich Auerbach, *Mimesis: The Representation of Reality in Western Literature* (Princeton: Princeton University Press, 2003). Auerbach was a colleague of Bultmann when both were at Marburg. Auerbach writes, "I have been in contact with Bultmann for over two decades—contact that was interrupted only by the war; I owe much to his counsel" (*Mimesis*, 567). Bultmann may have influenced *Mimesis* in general and Auerbach's work on ch. 2 in particular. See Jane O. Newman, "The Gospel according to Auerbach," *Publications of the Modern Language Association* 135, no. 3 (2020): 455–73; Martin Vialon, "Erich Auerbach und Rudolf Bultmann: Probleme abendländischer Geschichtsdeutung," in *Marburger Hermeneutik zwischen Tradition und Krise*, ed. Matthias Bormuth and Ulrich von Bulow (Göttingen: Wallstein Verlag, 2008), 176–206.

Furthermore, Auerbach writes, "Homer does not omit to tell the reader that it is with his right hand that Odysseus takes the old woman by the throat to keep her from speaking, at the same time that he draws her closer to him with his left. Clearly outlined, brightly and uniformly illuminated, men and things stand out in a realm where everything is visible."[54] Here, in the second paragraph of *Mimesis,* we learn that Western fiction has included both dialogue and novelistic detail from the beginning. But what Auerbach introduces next is even more pertinent: the large middle section of the foot-washing scene, a flashback detailing how Odysseus got his scar, which Auerbach highlights as a digression that does nothing to further the narrative (p. 4).

Auerbach contrasts the abundance of irrelevant visual detail in Homer to its utter absence in the story of the binding of Isaac in Genesis 22. In Homer there is "never a gap" for a reader to puzzle over (p. 7), but the biblical story is full of them, from the question of why God would order Abraham to sacrifice his son in the first place, to the indeterminacy of Abraham's physical location, to a dearth of description of people or things. There is no visual detail in the story. "It is unthinkable that an implement, a landscape through which the travelers passed, the serving men, or an ass should be described," Auerbach observes (p. 9). In contrast, Homer's works "delight in physical existence . . . , and their highest aim is to make that delight perceptible to us" through description and the "copious direct discourse" that structures the Homeric foot-washing scene through the conversations of Odysseus, his nurse, and his wife (p. 13; cf. p. 3). However,

> it is all very different in the Biblical stories. Their aim is not to bewitch the senses, and if nevertheless they produce lively sensory effects, it is only because the moral, religious, and psychological phenomena which are their sole concern are made concrete in the sensible matter of life. But their religious intent involves an absolute *claim* to historical truth. The story of Abraham and Isaac is not better established than the story of Odysseus, Penelope, and Euryclea; *both are legendary. But the Biblical narrator . . . had to believe in the objective truth of the story* of Abraham's sacrifice—the existence of the sacred ordinances of life rested upon the truth of this and similar stories. He *had to believe in it* passionately; *or else (as many rationalistic interpreters believed and*

54. *Mimesis,* 3. Hereafter, page references to this book will be given in parentheses in the text. Like Lewis, Auerbach "gave no preliminary definition of either reality or representation." Jacques Rancière, "Auerbach and the Contradictions of Realism," *Critical Inquiry* 44 (2018): 227.

> *perhaps still believe) he had to be a conscious liar*—no harmless liar like Homer, who lied to give pleasure, but a political liar with a definite end in view, lying in the interest of a claim to absolute authority. (p. 14, emphasis mine)

Just as Lewis misread Lock on John and pulled the opposite of what Lock said from his work, so he does to Auerbach, perhaps after reading this paragraph. It is not the Homeric tale rife with "lively sensory effects" that makes "an absolute *claim* to historical truth" but the biblical narrative that lacks them. I emphasize "claim" because Auerbach believes both accounts are "legendary." Neither the biblical nor the Homeric tale is more likely to be historically true because it does or does not reflect the "sensible matter of life," that is, include concrete details. This is the first point to emphasize in contrast to Lewis, and the second is Auerbach's argument that whoever wrote Genesis 22 had to *believe* it was true, or else "he had to be a conscious liar." Auerbach has almost no interest in applying his work on literary realism to the question of historicity defined as "it actually happened." But Lewis is intensely interested in the question. Could a misreading of this paragraph in *Mimesis* have influenced his either-or dilemma in "Modern Theology and Biblical Criticism"?

"Odysseus' Scar" touches upon the historicity of other stories in the Hebrew Scriptures, but Auerbach's observations on them, too, serve only to underscore Lewis's mistake. Although Auerbach never implies that irrelevant details or direct discourse make a text more likely to be historical—the opposite is true—he sets out two criteria that might. First, he believes that showing the personal development of human figures through their story arc "gives the Old Testament stories a historical character, even when the subject is purely legendary and traditional" (p. 18). Second, characters who wrestle with dilemmas and contradictions also give a story the appearance of historicity. To Auerbach, the saga of King David exemplifies both criteria. Thus he concludes, "it is clear that a large part of the life of David as given in the Bible contains history and not legend." He adds, "Abraham, Jacob, or even Moses produces a more concrete, direct, and historical impression than the figures of the Homeric world—not because they are better described in terms of sense (*the contrary is the case*) but because the confused, contradictory multiplicity of events, the psychological and factual cross-purposes, which true history reveals, have not disappeared in the representation" (p. 20; emphasis mine).

I don't agree with the criteria Auerbach proposes to distinguish legend from "true history," but my opinion is irrelevant. Auerbach clearly states why he thinks a story is more likely to reflect real events, and it is not through direct dialogue and details "described in terms of sense" that serve no purpose in furthering the narrative. Instead, it is through character development and a "confused, contradictory multiplicity of events" and motives. Both criteria are dead on arrival for Lewis's argument on the historicity of John because (1) Jesus shows no character development whatsoever in any of the Gospels, and (2) the only place he struggles with a dilemma is in Gethsemane in the Synoptics.[55] Unfortunately for Lewis, Jesus's anguished prayer to God, "Take this cup away from me; but not what I want, but what you want" (Mark 14:36), does not appear in John.

In his first chapter, Auerbach analyzes passages from the Hebrew Scriptures. In the second, he turns to the New Testament, and to one Gospel dialogue in particular. His work on this dialogue doesn't help Lewis either, even though he does note a few things that look like they might. But they don't, because Auerbach uses them to introduce a major argument for his book as a whole that contradicts what Lewis asserts about the historicity of John.

Auerbach begins with the *Satyricon* of Petronius, an author whose "literary ambition, like those of the realists of modern times, is to imitate a random, everyday, contemporary milieu." He thinks Petronius succeeded because he wrote a satire, and from this point follows the first part of his argument, what he calls the "separation of styles." After Homer and until modern times, ancient authors did indeed "imitate everyday life," but primarily in comic texts (pp. 30–31).

There is a major exception to Auerbach's rule of separation of styles that leads directly to an important argument in his book, and when Auerbach responded to critics of *Mimesis,* he singled it out as the thing that gave "unmistakable, even overpowering clarity" to his thesis about "stylistic differentiation" (pp. 561–62). The major exception is the Christian Gospels. Auerbach supports and illustrates his argument with a close reading of Peter's dialogue with the enslaved woman in Mark 14. The rule of separation of styles—a high literary style for serious matters that has little use for realism versus a low style full of realism in comedy—"cannot possibly apply in this case," he writes. Peter's denial of Jesus in Mark, "entirely realistic both in regard to locale and *dramatis personae*—note particularly their low social station—is replete with problem and tragedy" (p. 41). Note well what Auerbach has argued thus far. Homer's *Odyssey,* clearly fictional and written to entertain, is full of realistic details, but Genesis 22 is not. After Homer and until modern times, the rule of separation of styles holds true with one exception: the Gospels, which are at the same time highly serious and "entirely realistic." They combine both styles.

55. Luke 2:52, where the child Jesus "increased in wisdom," hardly ranks as narrative character development.

According to Auerbach, the Gospels break the rule because they uphold belief in the incarnation of Jesus. He explains, "The mingling of styles . . . was rooted from the beginning in the character of Jewish-Christian literature; it was graphically and harshly dramatized through God's incarnation in a human being of the humblest social station, through his existence on earth amid humble everyday people and conditions" (pp. 41, 65). In Jesus, God made flesh, "high" and "low" unite even when it comes to literary style.

As we focus on the few slim elements of Lewis's essay that intersect, however slightly, with Auerbach, we are forced to ignore the bulk of Auerbach's argument in his first two chapters; instead, we must highlight what he does not say. Auerbach never says what Lewis suggests he does in "Modern Theology and Biblical Criticism." Lewis argues that, because the Gospel of John contains dialogues and realistic "pictures," it is *either* "reportage" *or* its author, "without predecessors or successors," has "anticipated the whole technique of modern, realistic, narrative." If you don't believe him, read Auerbach. However, Auerbach says the opposite. There are many ancient predecessors of and successors to John who wrote in the realistic mode. The *Odyssey* and comedies like the *Satyricon* are full of dialogue and "pictures," and the presence of realistic dialogue and irrelevant detail in a text has no bearing whatsoever on how likely it is to be historically true.

Mimesis makes two points that might appear to support Lewis. The first is an aside, and Auerbach never mentions it again: "Peter, whose personal account may be assumed to have been the basis of the story, was a fisherman from Galilee of humblest background and humblest education" (p. 41). Auerbach doesn't back up the assumption with evidence, much less cite anything from his own work on realism to argue that it "really happened," because he isn't interested in the historicity of Peter's story but in his humble social location. Unlike literature narrated in the "high style," Peter's denial of Jesus when the woman questions him is "insignificant" except to those personally involved (p. 42).

The second is the only place where Lewis and Auerbach even begin to mesh. Auerbach writes, "A scene like Peter's denial fits into no antique genre. It is too serious for comedy, too contemporary and everyday for tragedy, politically too insignificant for history—and the form which was given is one of such immediacy that its like does not exist in the literature of antiquity. This can be judged by a symptom which at first glance may seem insignificant: the use of direct discourse" (p. 45). The conversation between Peter and the woman is notable, he continues, because "brief, direct dialogue" with only a few participants is rare in ancient literature, and direct discourse in ancient histories usually concerns lofty matters (p. 46).

Once again we must focus on what Auerbach doesn't say. He never implies that the uniqueness of Mark's dialogue makes it more likely to be "reportage." Although this passage is where Auerbach and Lewis draw most closely together, they are still miles apart. Both claim that the sort of dialogue that appears in the Gospels—Auerbach highlighting Mark, and Lewis John—is unique. Lewis never explains why, but Auerbach does: "In the last analysis the differences in style between the writings of antiquity and early Christianity are conditioned by the fact that they were composed from a different point of view and for different people." The pagan stories were written "from above," and the Christian "directly for the everyman" (pp. 46–47). To Auerbach, Mark's dialogue is rare because it was written for a non-elite audience.

Although Auerbach never says the presence of realistic detail makes a story more likely to be an eyewitness account, two works of biblical scholarship Lewis owned do. The first is the chapter on the Synoptic problem in his Gore commentary, which Lewis marked up liberally, including the following sentence: "Vivid, realistic touches in Mark suggesting the reminiscences of an eye-witness do not reappear in the other two [Synoptic Gospels]."[56] He read a similar sentence in Rudolf Otto's *The Kingdom of God and the Son of Man*. Regarding Luke 11:15–23 (Jesus and Beelzebul), Otto claims, "Its realism shows it to be no invention."[57] Could these words equating literary realism and historical truth have influenced what Lewis wrote in "Modern Theology and Biblical Criticism" and "What Are We to Make of Jesus Christ?"—ideas he then misattributed to Auerbach?

Lewis's invocation of Auerbach as deus ex machina doesn't save him in "Modern Theology and Biblical Criticism," but he cites him more appropriately in *The Discarded Image* (1964). After he delivered the lecture in 1959, Lewis might have realized that his claim that there was no vivid, irrelevant detail in fiction until the nineteenth-century novel was wrong. Perhaps someone in the audience spoke to him privately or sent him a letter urging him to rethink the matter, for in *The Discarded Image* Lewis highlights medieval literature's "realising imagination," its "sheer foreground fact, the 'close-up,'" concepts he summarizes as "vividness."[58] But, he notes, "the medievals had hardly any models for it." In other words, he has gone from claiming in his essays that,

56. F. D. V. Narborough, "The Synoptic Problem," in *NCHS*, part 3, 35.

57. Rudolf Otto, *The Kingdom of God and the Son of Man* (London: Lutterworth, 1938), 90.

58. It may be objected that the book compiles a series of lectures Lewis had given in some form beginning in 1932 (Walter Hooper, *C. S. Lewis: A Companion and Guide*

until the nineteenth century, there was no narrative with vivid details unless it was an eyewitness report to implying that "vividness" began to flourish in the Middle Ages. Lewis cites Auerbach here, but he doesn't as he continues: while medievals had few predecessors that employed the "realizing imagination," they did have Homer. Lewis gives two examples of vividness from the *Iliad*—Hector's baby being afraid of his father's helmet and the tears of Hector's wife—but he thinks that Homer's concrete details are limited to these. Even when he mentions Euryclea recognizing Odysseus, he ignores Auerbach's chapter "Odysseus' Scar," a bewildering omission I can't begin to explain.[59]

Stranger still is the fact that Lewis devotes a chapter of *Experiment in Criticism* (1961) to "realisms" without mentioning Auerbach at all. Lewis defines "realism of presentation" quite like he did in his essays: it makes something "palpable and vivid, by sharply observed or sharply imagined detail," and his treatment of it here is better than it was before. He gives many examples of "realism of presentation," which he differentiates from "realism of content," his term for fiction that is "probable or true to life." The two sorts of realism may combine variously: a piece of fiction may have one or the other or neither or both. In contrast to "Modern Theology and Biblical Criticism" and "What Are We to Say about Jesus Christ?" Lewis doesn't write about when realism developed or how it may indicate the historicity of a narrative. The closest he comes to what he wrote in those essays is his statement that "the great achievements of the nineteenth-century novel" have led modern readers to expect realism of content in their fiction.[60] The differences on the topic between "Modern Theology and Biblical Criticism" (1959) and the two later books, *An Experiment in Criticism*(1961) and *The Discarded Image* (1964), make me think someone challenged Lewis on his use of Auerbach in the lecture, motivating him to restate his concept of vividness in the later publications. Because he didn't publish the lecture in his lifetime, there was no need to revise it.

Lewis vs. Bultmann Redux

After the name Auerbach abruptly concludes this section of the first bleat, Lewis pivots to a different subject, a single sentence in Bultmann's book *The-*

[London: HarperCollins, 1996], 524), but authors revise their work according to their current thinking, and Lewis may have done so here.

59. *The Discarded Image* (Cambridge: Cambridge University Press, 1964), 206–7.

60. *An Experiment in Criticism* (Cambridge: Cambridge University Press, 1961), 57–60.

ology of the New Testament: "Observe in what unassimilated fashion the prediction of the parousia (Mark viii, 38) follows upon the prediction of the passion (viii, 31)."[61] Lewis's disagreement with Bultmann hinges on the word "unassimilated," since Lewis believes that the prediction of the parousia—Jesus's return in glory—follows the first passion prediction quite well. This belief might have been influenced by his reading a passage in von Hügel's *Essays and Addresses* that integrates "the Suffering of the Messiah, and the Return of this same Messiah in Power and Majesty," noting that "they first appear at Caesarea Philippi [Mark 8:31, 38] in close interconnection."[62] These words may have rooted Lewis's certainty that Mark's "sequence is perfect. Only a Bultmann could think otherwise."[63]

Lewis does not misread Bultmann here, but their views on Mark 8:31–38 differ because they approach it with different methods and mind-sets. Bultmann is a form critic, someone who thinks the Synoptic Gospels are "composed of a series of layers which can on the whole be clearly distinguished," and his application of form criticism convinces him the text is not unified.[64] We will look at this method more in the fourth bleat. Bultmann doesn't think Jesus predicted his death; rather, early Christians constructed Mark 8:31 as prophecy after the fact. Without telling his readers why, he has decided that Jesus could not have predicted his own passion, and he interprets Mark accordingly. This sort of skepticism is what Lewis criticized in *Miracles* regarding Lock's treatment of Jesus's prediction of Peter's death in John 21. When Bultmann approaches Mark with this mind-set, he separates the two predictions. When Lewis reads the passage as a literary whole, he makes an excellent case for how one flows from the other.

Turning over a few more pages in Bultmann's book, Lewis reads what he says about the "personality" of Jesus:

61. Bultmann, *Theology of the New Testament*, vol. 1 (New York: Charles Scribner's Sons, 1951), 30.

62. Von Hügel, *Essays and Addresses on the Philosophy of Religion*, series 1 (London: J. M. Dent and Sons, 1928), 129; see also Hans Rollmann, "Baron Friedrich von Hügel and the Conveyance of German Protestant Biblical Criticism in Roman Catholic Modernism," in *Biblical Studies and the Shifting of Paradigms, 1850–1914*, ed. Henning Graf Reventlow and William Farmer (Sheffield: Sheffield Academic Press, 1995), 197–222, esp. 210.

63. "MTBC," 155–56.

64. Bultmann, *Jesus and the Word*, trans. Louise Pettibone Smith and Erminie Huntress Lantero (1934; repr., New York: Charles Scribner's Sons, 1958), 12.

> The personality of Jesus has no importance for the kerygma either of Paul or of John or for the New Testament in general. Indeed the tradition of the earliest Church did not even unconsciously preserve a picture of his personality. Every attempt to reconstruct one remains a play of subjective imagination.[65]

Lewis disagrees. It is Bultmann against the world, he retorts, because Lewis is certain that anyone can see Jesus's personality in the Gospels. He is not alone in holding this opinion. The British biblical scholar E. Basil Redlich, for example, called Bultmann's work on the Gospels "subjective" because he deems them unreliable. Therefore, Redlich wrote, "it is not surprising that to him the figure and Personality of Jesus are very faint and unsubstantial."[66] This is not to say that Lewis's critique is correct. He pours out a flood of objections against Bultmann, but most of them miss the mark because Lewis never investigates what Bultmann meant by "personality." Lewis makes assumptions that hobble his response, preventing him from noticing how much he actually agrees with the German scholar.

Both men discuss the term "personality" repeatedly in their work. In "Modern Theology and Biblical Criticism" Lewis implies that personality indicates a recognizable human being, claiming that there are only three people in all of Western literature who simultaneously possess "historical reality" and whom we know as "real people." With a self-confidence that may have stupefied his audience in 1959 as much it does me today, he asserts that everyone knows who they are: "Plato's Socrates, the Jesus of the Gospels, and Boswell's Johnson."[67] This isn't the first time Lewis names these three men to illustrate his understanding of personality. He highlighted them in *The Personal Heresy* (1939) and mentioned them when he described his turn to Christ in *Surprised by Joy*.[68] They are more significant in his thought than one might guess.

Bultmann, too, had a decades-long history of working with the concept of personality before *Theology of the New Testament* appeared in English in 1951.

65. Bultmann, *Theology of the New Testament*, 1:35.

66. E. Basil Redlich, *Form Criticism* (London: Duckworth, 1939), 181f., quoted in Robert W. Funk, introduction to *Faith and Understanding I*, by Rudolf Bultmann, ed. Robert W. Funk, trans. Louise Pettibone Smith (London: SCM, 1969), 11 n. 4.

67. "MTBC," 156.

68. C. S. Lewis and E. M. W. Tillyard, *The Personal Heresy: A Controversy* (1939; repr., New York: HarperOne, 2017), 66–67; *Surprised by Joy* (San Diego: Harcourt Brace Jovanovich, 1955), 236.

Much of this work would have been difficult for Lewis to access because it was either unpublished or untranslated, and Lewis's German was "wretched."[69] That said, he could have consulted Bultmann's *Jesus and the Word,* which was published in English in 1934. Reading even the first few pages would have helped him understand Bultmann's treatment of the concept, and he may have been surprised by what he found there: evidence that he and Bultmann advocated for many of the same things about personality in general and Jesus's personality in particular.

In *Jesus and the Word,* Bultmann notes that a historian investigates

> only phenomena and incidents determinable in time—"what happened" . . . ; for the essential of history is in reality nothing super-historical, but is event in time. Accordingly this book lacks all the phraseology which speaks of Jesus as great man, genius, or hero. . . . There is also no consideration of the eternal values of his message, of his discovery of the infinite depths of the human soul, or the like. . . .
>
> For the same reason, *interest in the personality of Jesus* is excluded. . . . I do think that we can now know almost nothing concerning the life and personality of Jesus, since the early Christian sources show no interest in either, are moreover fragmentary and often legendary; and other sources about Jesus do not exist. Except for the purely critical research, what has been written in the last hundred and fifty years on the life of Jesus, his personality and the development of his inner life, is fantastic and romantic.[70]

In the last sentence we learn that Bultmann's antipathy to what might be called the "cult of personality" of Jesus did not stem from obtuseness on his part, as Lewis implies, but from an allergic reaction to how German scholars had discussed it for the previous hundred and fifty years. As Louise Pettibone Smith and Erminie Lantero explain in their translator's preface, Bultmann's view on the personality of Jesus "differs radically from that popularized by liberal scholars of pre-World War One days."[71] For example, he disagrees with their emphasis on the effect of Jesus's personality as a "great man," the like of which

69. Lewis to Helmut Kuhn, March 11, 1954, *CL,* 3:439.

70. *Jesus and the Word,* 7–8 (emphasis in original).

71. Smith and Lantero, "Translators' Preface to the New Edition," *Jesus and the Word,* vi. Bultmann is reacting most strongly against Wilhelm Herrmann and Ernst Troeltsch. See Brent W. Sockness, *Against False Apologetics: Wilhelm Herrmann and Ernst Troeltsch in Conflict* (Tübingen: Mohr Siebeck, 1998).

the world had never seen. Believe it or not, Bultmann and Lewis agree wholeheartedly on this point, as letter 23 of *The Screwtape Letters* on the "historical Jesus" demonstrates.

Screwtape, "Personality," and the Historical Jesus

Lewis never defines the term "historical Jesus," although it isn't self-explanatory even to Christians. Therefore, one can't help but wonder how well *Screwtape*'s first readers understood letter 23, which focuses on it. If my experience discussing the letter with groups ranging from university undergraduates to octogenarian churchgoers is representative, they didn't understand it at all.

The "historical Jesus" refers to the human Jesus during his lifetime on earth—or, more exactly, to what one can plausibly reconstruct about him, a figure scholars distinguish from the "Christ of faith." The historical Jesus was born a baby and crucified under Pontius Pilate. The Christ of faith was born of the virgin Mary and raised from the dead. As the last few sentences imply, the "quest of the historical Jesus" limits itself to what human arts and sciences can verify about him, and it brackets out the supernatural.[72]

Lewis so dislikes the quest that he hands it over to Screwtape to skewer. The demonic payoff in promoting it is substantial: "For the real presence of [God], . . . we substitute a merely probable, remote, shadowy, and uncouth figure, one who spoke a strange language and died a long time ago. Such an object cannot be worshipped," Screwtape writes. Whether he knew it or not, when Lewis demonized the quest, he was affiliating more with the German scholars of the first half of the twentieth century than with their British counterparts. A lasting effect of Gore's focus on the incarnation in *Lux Mundi* was to prevent British scholarship from joining the "sudden, and for the most part destructive, retreat from the historical Jesus which was . . . typical of German theology in the twentieth century."[73]

72. See Sarah Tanzer, "The Historical Jesus," in *The Jewish Annotated New Testament*, ed. Amy-Jill Levine and Marc Zvi Brettler, 2nd ed. (Oxford: Oxford University Press, 2017), 628–33.

73. John Muddiman, "The Holy Spirit and Inspiration," in *The Religion of the Incarnation: Anglican Essays in Commemoration of Lux Mundi*, ed. Robert Morgan (Bristol: Bristol Classical Press, 1989), 121. After the publication of Albert Schweitzer's *Quest of the Historical Jesus* in 1906, and influenced in no small part by Bultmann's rejection of the quest, German scholarship on the historical Jesus receded until Ernst Käsemann revived it in 1953. See Käsemann, "The Problem of the Historical Jesus," in *Essays on New Testament Themes*, trans. W. J. Montague (Naperville, IL: Alec R. Allenson, 1964), 15–47.

When Screwtape advises his "nephew" Wormwood to encourage the pursuit of the historical Jesus, he uses the same words Bultmann rejects in the passage from *Jesus and the Word* quoted above: Wormwood should make people think about Jesus as "a 'great man' in the modern sense of the word." Screwtape, speaking for the upside-down world of hell, advocates thinking about Jesus in this way. Both Lewis and Bultmann reject this portrayal of Jesus, and they agree with each other against Screwtape and the scholars Screwtape is trying to promote.

But didn't Lewis think Jesus was a great man? What is the "modern sense" of the phrase that prevents him from applying it to Jesus?[74] Lewis seems to have only a superficial notion of how the word "personality" was applied to Jesus in biblical scholarship. He knew enough to associate it with the previous generation but not enough to grasp how crucial it was to Bultmann's ideas on Jesus's "personality." However, there is one place where Lewis did read about the concept: his Gore commentary, where the English scholars contributing to the volume employed the word just as their German counterparts had. The author of the essay on the Synoptic problem writes, "Any one who follows up the lines of study here laid down will discover in the Synoptic Gospels different varieties of apprehension of the many-sided Truth which is in Jesus, representing the reactions of various types of people to that all-embracing Personality which showed itself through His Life and Teaching."[75] Lock's article on John observes, "The book will show that the impression of the Lord's Personality was so great both in His lifetime and in His subsequent effect upon the Church that it could only be represented by striking miraculous incidents."[76] A 1929 review of Gore's commentary nods approvingly, "The great fundamental truths of the Incarnation, the Virgin Birth, the Physical Resurrection, as also the Personality of our Lord . . . under the scrutiny of the best modern scholarship, emerge even more clearly defined and more firmly established than ever."[77]

English biblical scholars adopted this understanding of Jesus's personality from the generation of German scholars prior to Bultmann, including Adolf von Harnack and Johannes Weiss, who believed Jesus made a huge impact on

74. Lewis speaks well of the term "great men" in a letter to Owen Barfield, July 23, 1939, *CL*, 2:260, also in the context of discussing the personal heresy.

75. Narborough, "Synoptic Problem," 42.

76. Lock, "The Gospel according to St. John," 241. See also C. H. Turner, "The Gospel according to St. Mark," in *NCHS*, part 3, 55.

77. Arnold Pinchard, *Church Times*, Feb. 1, 1929, as quoted by F. Hugh Pope, "Dr. Gore's Bible Commentary," *Blackfriars* 10, no. 11 (1929): 1078.

the history of the world through his "insight, courage, conviction, and inspiration, all of which derive from personality."[78] According to Harnack, these qualities are "the real levers of history."[79] To Weiss, Christ's impact on the world flowed more from his force of personality than from his resurrection.[80] For Harnack, Weiss, and other German liberals like them, the more Christians imitated Jesus's extraordinary life as a "great man," the more his personality lived on, and the better the world became. Of course, such optimism died a grisly death in the trenches of World War I. In 1938 Bultmann could look back and reflect, "Thus people speak of the influence of Christ on the course of world history, of the effects which His spirit has had on human manners and morals, of its uplifting and civilizing influence on nations. The world war showed little of all this . . . a war between nominally Christian peoples."[81] The force of Jesus's "incomparable personality" as expressed in his followers did nothing to stop the civilizational wreckage of the First World War, and therefore, Bultmann thought, the whole concept must be reevaluated.

Bultmann voices other objections to an emphasis on Jesus's personality. First, the human Jesus is dead, and, he says, a dead man can influence no one: "As a *Thou*, in the sense of a fellow man, he has vanished." Bultmann claims that his contemporaries who died in the Great War "actually mean more to us [in terms of encounter with a 'personality'] . . . because we were associated with them as with a living *Thou*. To try to create such experiences of encounter with a person of the past seems to me to be artificial and to lead to sentimentality."[82]

Lewis agrees with Bultmann to some extent even here. In the same part of *The Personal Heresy* where he talks about Socrates, Jesus, and Johnson, Lewis discusses the sort of attention he thinks the living should devote to the personalities of almost all the dead—exempting Christ and Johnson from the great mass of the dead whom we cannot know because both of them "exist for us as a man." He can imagine having a conversation with Johnson, but there are limits as to how one might imagine Johnson responding, since his personality

78. James F. Kay, *Christus Praesens: A Reconsideration of Rudolf Bultmann's Christology* (Grand Rapids: Eerdmans, 1994), 15.

79. Harnack, quoted in Kay, *Christus Praesens*, 16.

80. Kay, *Christus Praesens*, 12, 18.

81. Bultmann, *This World and Beyond: Marburg Sermons* (New York: Scribner's Sons, 1960), 68.

82. Kay, *Christus Praesens*, 34–35; Bultmann, "On the Question of Christology," in *Faith and Understanding I*, 127–28, 137.

"is obstinate and resistant." One can't make him say anything one would like in an imaginary conversation.[83]

Then Lewis shifts gears. It might be more socially acceptable for someone to devote herself to the memory of a dead poet than to the presence of a live Pekinese. But "you can do something for the Peke," he notes, and it can respond to you, neither of which holds true for the dead poet. The sort of people who dwell on the personalities of the dead, Lewis claims, "are cosseting with substitutes an emotion whose true object is our neighbor." He continues, "For the sake of personality, therefore, we must reject the personal heresy. . . . For the proper pleasure of personality, that is, for love, we must go where it can be found—to our homes or our common rooms."[84] The only difference between Bultmann and Lewis in discussing how one can or should interact with a deceased personality lies in their stance on Jesus—a huge difference to be sure, but one that must not blind us to what they hold in common.

Bultmann also argues that no one needs the example of Jesus's personality to make moral progress, because other people can inspire it just as well: "Along with such statements often appears . . . the attempt to prove that some ideas or impulses entered history for the first time in Christianity. . . . [But] *newness* is not a category which is determinative for the divine. . . . Newness can be claimed equally for this or that imbecility. Newness is never a guarantee of the *value* of what claims to be new."[85]

Lewis agrees wholeheartedly with Bultmann on all of these points, which are interconnected. In letter 23, Screwtape says that calling the historical Jesus a great man "conceal[s] the very substantial agreement between His teachings and those of all other great moral teachers." The fact that Jesus does not teach a new or unique system of ethics is a commonplace for Lewis, a point he hammers home especially in the appendix to *The Abolition of Man*. Like Lewis, Bultmann argues against the tendency to make an idol of the new just because it is new. Part and parcel of the nineteenth-century emphasis on Jesus's personality was the claim that it was incomparable; no one in history had ever seen the like. The appeal to Jesus's uniqueness was an attempt to honor him, but a false accolade is worthless, and both its logic and substance are wrong. "New" does not equal better, and Jesus's moral teaching wasn't even new. Lewis

83. Lewis, *Personal Heresy*, 66–67.

84. Lewis, *Personal Heresy*, 68–69.

85. Bultmann, "Liberal Theology and the Latest Movement," in *Faith and Understanding I*, 38, 35.

and Bultmann understood that Jesus's moral teaching was not unique and that this was a good thing.

Neither Lewis nor Bultmann devised these ideas on the uniqueness of Jesus's teaching; they go back to Origen of Alexandria (d. 254). Origen wrote a book of Christian apologetics against Celsus, who criticized Jesus's ethical teaching "on the grounds that it is commonplace, and in comparison with other philosophers contains no teaching that is impressive or new." Origen rebuts Celsus: God did so on purpose. All humanity holds the same "sound conception of moral principles. There is nothing amazing about it if the same God has implanted in the souls of all men the truth which He taught through the prophets and the Saviour." Lewis agreed, and he marked this passage in his copy of Origen.[86]

There is yet another connection between Lewis's views on the historical Jesus as they appear in letter 23 and Bultmann's argument with his liberal predecessors on personality. Bultmann asks an important question: what did liberal theology actually accomplish? German scholars hoped it would "lead to a comprehension of the real figure of Jesus on which faith could be based," but Bultmann calls this hope "delusional." It can't "serve as a basis for faith, for *all its results have only relative validity*. How widely the pictures of Jesus presented by liberal theologians differ from one another! How uncertain is all knowledge of 'the historical Jesus'! Is he really within the scope of our knowledge? Here research ends with a large question mark—and here it *ought* to end."[87]

Screwtape says almost exactly the same thing. Every generation produces a new and different historical Jesus, and these ever-changing Jesuses prove how arbitrary the quest really is. It is chasing a phantom. In fact, Screwtape observes, "materials for a full biography [of Jesus] have been withheld," a statement both Lewis and Bultmann endorse.[88]

Although the two men agree on many fronts, the German makes observations about Jesus's personality that Lewis can legitimately dispute—if by "legitimately" one means engaging what Bultmann actually said. For example, when liberals prior to Bultmann thought about Jesus's personality, they

86. Origen, *Contra Celsum* 1.4, pp. 8–9. Lewis also would have seen it in Tyrrell, *Christianity at the Cross-Roads* (London: Longmans, Green, 1910), 51.

87. Bultmann, "Liberal Theology and the Latest Theological Movement," in *Faith and Understanding I*, 30 (emphasis in original).

88. *The Screwtape Letters* (London: Geoffrey Bles, 1942), letter 23, p. 119. See also Patrick Gray, "Screwtape and the Historical Jesus," *CSL: The Bulletin of the New York C. S. Lewis Society* 34, no. 6 (2003): 1–7.

speculated on his messianic self-consciousness. On that definition, Bultmann thinks the attempt to understand his personality is doomed because scholars can't agree on whether Jesus thought he was the messiah. In *Jesus and the Word,* he writes, "Considering that it was really no trifle to believe oneself Messiah, that, further, whoever so believed must have regulated his whole life in accordance with this belief, we must admit that if this point is obscure we can, strictly speaking, know nothing of the personality of Jesus. I am personally of the opinion that Jesus did not believe himself to be the Messiah, but I do not imagine that this opinion gives me a clearer picture of his personality."[89]

If Lewis had read this passage, he would have disagreed, but at least he would have grappled with something substantive. Bultmann did not think Jesus believed himself messiah, but from the time Lewis read Moffatt's *Theology of the Gospels,* he was convinced that Jesus did, to the point that Lewis based his most famous argument, the "liar, lunatic, or Lord" trilemma, on the conviction that Jesus thought of himself not only as messiah but even as God. This argument is the subject of the next chapter.

There is one more place Bultmann and Lewis agree. After the passage quoted above, Bultmann concedes that there are good reasons "for being interested in the personalities of significant historical figures, Plato or Jesus, Dante or Luther, Napoleon or Goethe, [but] it still remains true that this interest does not touch that which such men had at heart; for *their* interest was not in their personality but in their *work.* And their work was to them not the expression of their personality . . . but the cause to which they surrendered their lives. . . . The 'work' from *their* standpoint is the end they really sought."[90] Here Lewis would have found a soulmate, for Bultmann has repeated a key point of Lewis's argument against the "personal heresy": great human beings are concerned not with themselves but with their work, and those who love them will follow their lead.

Lewis reacts caustically to Bultmann in this section of "Modern Theology and Biblical Criticism," but for the most part it is Lewis who emerges the loser. His faults are legion. He assumes that Bultmann's concept of personality matches his own, but he hasn't consulted *Jesus and the Word* to put what Bultmann wrote in *Theology of the New Testament* into a more generous context, and he lacks sufficient knowledge of how nineteenth- and early twentieth-century biblical scholars wrote about Jesus's personality to ascertain why Bultmann opposes them. If Lewis had remedied these faults, he still would have

89. *Jesus and the Word,* 9.
90. *Jesus and the Word,* 9–10 (emphasis in original).

disagreed with Bultmann about the messianic consciousness of Jesus and how Jesus's personality shines through the Gospels, but there, at least, he would have engaged a solid argument rather than a straw man. Instead, he has fallen victim to a problem he cautioned others about: "If you join at eleven o'clock a conversation which began at eight you will often not see the real bearing of what is said."[91]

The Second Bleat

The second and third bleats are the shortest and least problematic. The second begins with an attack on liberal theology, which Lewis doesn't define. Without prelude, he dives in. According to Lewis, "all theology of the liberal type" claims that (1) Jesus's first followers departed from what Jesus said and did, misrepresenting his teaching, and (2) only now have clever scholars been able to recover and rightly interpret it.

Lewis had put both points into the mouth of Screwtape in the early 1940s. Liberals claim "Christianity began going wrong, departing from the doctrine of its Founder, at a very early stage," and Screwtape advises Wormwood to capitalize on the idea to encourage the quest of the historical Jesus, who may be unearthed by "clearing away later 'accretions and perversions'" that allegedly distort Christianity.[92]

Contrary to Lewis's opening salvo, "theology of the liberal type" is not monolithic. To be sure, some German Protestant liberals like Harnack did think early Christians soon deviated from the teaching of Jesus.[93] But English Roman Catholic liberalism is not the same as its German Protestant cousin. When George Tyrrell explains how the English Catholic differs from the German Protestant variety, he mocks the assertion that Christian thought went off the rails after Jesus was crucified:

> No sooner was the Light of the World kindled than it was put under a bushel. The Pearl of Great Price fell into the dustheap of Catholicism, not without the wise permission of Providence, desirous to preserve it till the

91. Lewis, introduction to *On the Incarnation*, by Athanasius, ed. and trans. A religious of C.S.M.V. [Sister Penelope Lawson] (1944; repr., Crestwood, NY: St. Vladimir's Seminary Press, 1996), 4.

92. *Screwtape*, letter 23, 117.

93. See Adolf von Harnack, *What Is Christianity?*, trans. Thomas Bailey Saunders (1901; repr., Philadelphia: Fortress, 1986), 13–14, and throughout.

> day when Germany should rediscover it and separate it from its useful but deplorable accretions. Thus between Christ and early Catholicism there is not a bridge but a chasm. Christianity did not cross the bridge; it fell into the chasm and remained there, stunned, for nineteen centuries. The explanation of this sudden fall . . . is the crux of Liberal Protestant critics.[94]

Against the Protestant liberals he satirizes, Tyrrell thinks Catholic liberals preserve Christ's teaching. In a sentence Screwtape probably read, Tyrrell insists, "With all its *accretions and perversions* Catholicism is, for the Modernist, the only authentic Christianity."[95] Lewis wouldn't agree with Tyrrell about Catholicism, but both men, the liberal and nonliberal alike, reject the idea that early Christians abandoned Jesus's teaching.

Lewis devotes the bulk of this bleat to the second claim, that only now have modern scholars been able to recover the teaching of Jesus. This is absurd, he says, because an author's contemporaries are more likely to understand him than readers millennia later. This is true up to a point—there are good and bad readers at any given time—and it is one reason why biblical scholars strive to put Scripture into historical context, a practice Lewis seems to condemn in the fourth bleat. Here Lewis writes, "I feel it in my bones—I know it beyond argument" that liberal reconstructions are impossible.[96] Such epistemology might fly unquestioned in a lecture, but if he had revised "Modern Theology and Biblical Criticism" for publication, one hopes he would have supported his feelings with arguments and supplied even one example from biblical scholarship, rather than from the fields of literature and philosophy, to illustrate his point.

The Third Bleat

The third bleat, short and sweet, almost succeeds. Lewis states that liberal theologians assume miracles are impossible, and whether he is thinking of nineteenth-century German liberals or the mid-twentieth-century British as characterized by Glasson, he is correct. They have no more insight into the question than anyone else does. Even Bart Ehrman—perhaps the best-known agnostic biblical scholar of the early twenty-first century, who would not agree with Lewis about much—concurs. Proclamations on the possibility of miracles

94. Tyrrell, *Christianity at the Cross-Roads*, 40–41.
95. Tyrrell, *Christianity at the Cross-Roads*, xx–xxi (emphasis mine).
96. "MTBC," 158.

lie outside a biblical critic's realm of expertise.[97] However, when Lewis brings up Scripture that predicts the future, he moves from the theoretical to the specific, and other factors enter the equation. Biblical scholars who accept the possibility of miracles in general may also argue that certain predictions can be interpreted very well without recourse to them, as Lock does with John 21:20–23.

The Fourth Bleat

The fourth bleat, Lewis's "loudest and longest," is the most challenging to work with from its first sentence, which lays out a hodgepodge of biblical-critical methods: "All this sort of criticism attempts to reconstruct the genesis of the texts it studies; what vanished documents each author used, when and where he wrote, with what purposes, under what influences—the whole *Sitz im Leben* of the text."[98]

The moment a student of the Bible lays eyes on the words *Sitz im Leben,* one thing, and one thing alone, comes to mind: form criticism, a method of analyzing the Bible that was born, thrived, and fell into senescence over the course of the twentieth century. The term *Sitz im Leben,* coined by Hermann Gunkel in 1906, means "setting in life"—that is, the settings in which the words that would eventually become Scripture were told before they were written down. Gunkel pioneered the method, and Lewis relies on his form-critical work with the Psalms down to the bones of *Reflections on the Psalms,* as demonstrated by its chapters on praising and royal psalms, categories Gunkel developed. Form criticism was also applied to the New Testament. Bultmann and his colleague Martin Dibelius isolated sections of the Gospels and tried to place them in their ancient oral contexts, speculating on how sayings of Jesus and stories about him may have functioned in their life settings as they were passed along by word of mouth.[99]

British scholars of the New Testament were not uniformly enthusiastic about form criticism. In 1959, Vincent Taylor notes that Bultmann's application

97. Bart D. Ehrman, *The New Testament: A Historical Introduction to the Early Christian Writings,* 7th ed. (New York: Oxford University Press, 2020), 255–59. Liberals themselves argue that their reasons for rejecting the supernatural are more sophisticated than this, and Lewis addresses some of those reasons in *Miracles.*

98. "MTBC," 158.

99. David R. Law, *The Historical-Critical Method: A Guide for the Perplexed* (New York: T&T Clark, 2012), 140–80, esp. 142, 150. Gunkel, *Introduction to Psalms: The Genres of the Religious Lyric of Israel* (Macon, GA: Mercer University Press, 1998).

of form criticism to the Gospels is "acute and suggestive, but the tendency of his criticism is radical in the extreme." However, it is also valuable because "it has pressed home the necessity of tracing the *Sitz im Leben* of the Gospel tradition to the life and needs of the primitive communities."[100] Taylor's publications helped British New Testament scholars warm somewhat to the method.[101]

When Lewis highlights the technical term most indelibly associated with form criticism at the beginning of his bleat, a biblical scholar can't help but think he is going to criticize Bultmann again. But with two exceptions, what follows has nothing to do either with Bultmann or with form criticism. Instead, Lewis appears to understand the "*Sitz im Leben* of the text" as everything he had listed in the first sentence: "what vanished documents each author used, when and where he wrote, with what purposes, under what influences." Biblical scholars do care about these things, but they have little to do with *Sitz im Leben* as form critics define it. Gore's biblical commentary identifies what Lewis is actually talking about: the rather confusingly named "literary criticism."

> *Literary criticism* investigates the date and authorship of a text, the circumstances under which it was composed, the scope and purpose and nature of the work. It asks such questions as whether it is the production of one author or more than one; whether it is based on or embodies earlier writings: and if so, what is their date and character, and have they been altered by the editor? This kind of criticism is sometimes known as "higher" criticism, not from any claim to superiority on the part of those who exercise it, but in contrast to "lower" or "textual" criticism which only aims at ascertaining the actual words that the author wrote. It is higher because it builds upon and assumes the work of the lower criticism.[102]

Lewis was not the only one evaluating the impact of "literary criticism" on biblical interpretation in 1959. His Oxford colleague Helen Gardner, also a scholar of English literature, published her own lecture series on the topic that year, and it discusses many of the same things Lewis does in "Modern Theology and Biblical Criticism," including Gore's commentary, higher criticism of the Gospels, source and form criticism, and the Bible's use of language, myth,

100. Vincent Taylor, *The Gospel according to St. Mark* (London: Macmillan, 1959), 19–20. See also Funk, *Faith and Understanding I*, 11, and Vincent Taylor, *The Formation of the Gospel Tradition* (London: Macmillan, 1933).

101. Law, *Historical-Critical Method*, 158.

102. E. J. Bicknell, "The Function of Literary and Historical Criticism," *NCHS*, 18.

and history. But Gardner, in contrast to Lewis, exhibits a near-perfect grasp of contemporary biblical scholarship, making her careful and sophisticated lectures thoroughly superior to his.[103] One need not be a professional biblical scholar to get it right, but at the very least one must have an adequate working knowledge of the field. As Richard Cunningham put it, Lewis's "ignorance of some elementary critical problems" in biblical scholarship can mislead him, and his "refusal to acquaint himself with responsible Biblical criticism is almost inexcusable."[104]

Today, the German word scholars use for all but the first item in Lewis's list is *Einleitung* (introduction). Such introductions are indispensable. They attempt to answer the "when, where, and why" questions everyone asks when reading an unfamiliar text. Since Lewis wrote his own *Einleitung* of sorts on medieval literature, *The Discarded Image*, one might wonder if he is playing the hypocrite here, but I don't think he is. As the bleat continues, he does not cavil so much against putting a text in its historical context as he objects to those who profess to know the unknowable while doing so.

Source vs. Influence

The first item in the list, the "vanished documents each author used," is Lewis's roundabout way of referring to source criticism, the "higher criticism" that reigned supreme at the end of the nineteenth century. Source criticism developed in Germany, and Lewis employs its German name, *Quellenforschung*, in a letter he wrote to the *Times Literary Supplement*. His letter is cited by the *Oxford English Dictionary* to illustrate usage of the word, which the *OED* defines as "The study of the sources of, or influences upon, a literary work."[105] However, this is not quite how biblical scholars define it. Sources, yes; influences, no.

In the *TLS* letter, Lewis implies that source criticism traces how one author's work influences another's. As an example, he discusses a review of Roger Lancelyn Green's book *Land of the Lord High Tiger*. The reviewer thought that Lewis's lion Aslan had influenced the creation of Green's tiger, but Lewis corrects him. It had not, and he would know, because he and Green were friends.[106]

103. Helen Gardner, *The Business of Criticism* (Oxford: Clarendon, 1959), 76–157.

104. Richard B. Cunningham, *C. S. Lewis: Defender of the Faith* (Philadelphia: Westminster, 1967), 84, 94.

105. *Oxford English Dictionary*, s.v. "Quellenforschung (*n.*)," July 2023, https://tinyurl.com/ycbk7ywb.

106. "MTBC," 160.

Almost every time Lewis brings up source criticism, he disparages it, and he is no outlier among his peers. Source criticism, like its younger sibling form criticism, met with a mixed reception in Great Britain across academic disciplines. The classicist A. D. Nock, writing in 1932, notes that "*Quellenforschung* has not always had a good press in England. . . . But there is good *Quellenforschung* as well as bad." C. H. Herford, a literary scholar, calls *Quellenforschung* "a pre-eminently German study" that had borne fruit in some ways but not others. "In England," he observes, "the German doctrine of 'sources' . . . has never struck deep root."[107]

Lewis's best-known comment on source criticism is his mistake about the number 73 bus in *Screwtape*, which, many correspondents informed him, did not pass by the British Museum. He responded ruefully that "higher critics" of the future would seize upon the error to argue that *Screwtape* wasn't written in the twentieth century, but centuries later "by five different 'Hands.'" After the death of his friend Charles Williams, Lewis told the author of an obituary that she had highlighted important aspects of Williams's personality that his own tribute had missed. A "higher critic," he said, would deduce from the discrepancies either that Williams "had never existed" or that one of them had misrepresented him.[108]

But Lewis gave credit where it was due when he received a gift copy of the book *St. Paul: The Apostle* from its translator, K. C. Thompson. Thompson told him that his work "involved not only abbreviation, but considerable recasting, with a new beginning and end, as well as a rewriting of many passages." In his thank-you note to Thompson, Lewis wrote that he was intrigued to "meet a real 'recension'" that had undergone the changes that "'higher critics' attribute to nearly all ancient texts. I didn't believe it ever happened in real life."[109]

A letter to Charles Brady further illustrates Lewis's understanding of source criticism as tracing influence. Brady, an American professor of literature, wrote two articles in which he tried to identify authors who had influenced Lewis. Lewis responded by telling Brady that his "*Quellenforschung* is good," confirming several influences Brady had posited, rejecting others, and informing him of some he had missed.[110]

107. A. D. Nock, review of *Die Kosmologie des Plinius*, by Wilhelm Kroll, *Classical Review* 46, no. 4 (1932): 186; C. H. Herford, "The Elizabethan Age in Recent Literary History," *Quarterly Review* 431 (April 1912): 359.

108. *Screwtape*, letter 1, p. 13; Lewis to Thomas Wilkinson Riddle, May 17, 1944, *CL*, 2:614; to Anne Ridler, June 3, 1945, *CL*, 2:658–59.

109. Lewis to K. C. Thompson, Jan. 5, 1961, *CL*, 3:1222.

110. Charles A. Brady, "Introduction to Lewis," *America*, May 27, 1944, 213–14; "C. S. Lewis: II," *America*, June 10, 1944, 269–70; Lewis to Brady, Oct. 29, 1944, *CL*, 2:629–31.

Drawing from what Lewis writes on source criticism, we see that he is at some definitional cross-purposes with biblical scholars, who do not think it has anything to do with influence. Source critics of the Bible hypothesize how an author took a text and reused it in a new work. Lewis does refer to source criticism as biblical scholars define it when he drops the following sentence in "Modern Theology and Biblical Criticism" without comment: "And of course we agree that passages almost verbally identical cannot be independent."[111]

Lewis distinguishes between source and influence in his pamphlet *The Literary Impact of the Authorized Version,* but still not as biblical scholars do. There are various ways to describe how an earlier book may influence the author of a later one, he observes. The first is as a source. An author's "immediate source" of information on the gods Mars and Venus might be Boccaccio, but the "ultimate source is Homer." Someone might say the author was influenced by Homer, but most would not. He writes, "If anyone wishes to call a source an influence, let him do so, but let him recognize a source as a very special kind of influence. Most of us, I expect, would prefer to distinguish source from influence altogether. A source gives us things to write about; an influence prompts us to write in a certain way."[112] Distinguishing source from influence is better than not, but biblical scholars don't think about either term as Lewis does here.

After he considers and rejects several examples of scholarly reconstruction in "Modern Theology and Biblical Criticism," Lewis reports, "Our faith in the method wavers; and our faith in Christianity is proportionately corroborated."[113] His choice of words reveals how much is at stake for him in refuting higher critics: faith in Christianity itself. But this is a false dichotomy, as innumerable Christians who practice "the method" have kept their faith. In the first part of the fourth bleat, Lewis doesn't address form and source criticism as biblical scholars understand them, but something else, what he calls "imaginary histories." Since the phrase appears three times in three consecutive paragraphs, I will take it as his preferred designation for the object of his attack.[114]

111. "MTBC," 163.

112. Lewis, *The Literary Impact of the Authorized Version,* Facet Books Biblical Series (1950; repr., Philadelphia: Fortress, 1963), 14–15. He uses the same language at the end of his appended note to *Till We Have Faces* (Orlando, FL: Harcourt, 1956), where he says that Apuleius is the source of the book but didn't influence him (313).

113. "MTBC," 163.

114. "MTBC," 159. He uses the same phrase and argument in a letter to Francis Anderson, Sept. 23, 1963, *CL,* 3:1459.

Imaginary Histories

Lewis builds his case against biblical scholars' construction of imaginary histories by recounting his experience with reviewers of his own books, some of whom professed knowledge about how he felt while he was writing them. I am not aware of any modern scholar who has attempted this feat regarding the author of a biblical book, and Lewis provides no example here. There is an example in a book Lewis reviewed, *Principles and Problems of Biblical Translation* (1955), but he doesn't mention it in "Modern Theology and Biblical Criticism." The book's author, Werner Schwarz, quotes a passage written by Wessel Ganfort (d. 1489). Schwarz reflects, "One sees Wessel, good-natured, smiling, while he is writing these words."[115] In his copy, Lewis underlines the imagined emotions ("good-natured, smiling") and writes a question mark in the margin as if to say, "How do you know?" In "Modern Theology and Biblical Criticism," his critique doesn't seem to stem from any malpractice in biblical scholarship but rather from his battle against the "personal heresy," which among many other things includes trying to reconstruct how authors felt, what their intentions were, and how their lives affected what they wrote. As the essay continues, Lewis condemns scholars who try to learn what influenced authors, what they intended, who their audience was, and when and why they wrote.

When Lewis read the Bible, he was always more interested in content than context, and he could be rather harsh toward those who weren't, mixing legitimate criticism with polemic. Trying to guess how biblical authors felt as they wrote is indeed futile, but it is a different thing entirely than investigating when and why they wrote. Most readers want to know these things, even if it is impossible to get them right. Lewis correctly observes that all modern biblical scholars, no matter how brilliant, are so far removed from the ancient world that they are bound to get things wrong, and he justly disapproves of scholars like Bultmann who express certainty about things they can never know. It is the last point that seems to be the key to Lewis's frustration with some biblical scholarship: its unwarranted certainty.

No scholarship lasts forever, and Bultmann's heyday has passed, just as Lewis predicted it would. Bultmann's mode of form criticism is no longer practiced, and some of his work has been discredited.[116] Intellectual fashions,

115. Werner Schwarz, *Principles and Problems of Biblical Translation: Some Reformation Controversies and Their Background* (Cambridge: Cambridge University Press, 1955), 57.

116. See Richard Bauckham, "Are We Still Missing the Elephant?," 427–29; Bruce W.

like all fashions, change, and the oracular pronouncements some biblical scholars intoned in the first half of the twentieth century look as silly to us now as old hairstyles. Many critical biblical scholars today exhibit more intellectual humility than did certain of their predecessors, but the field has advanced in part because they ask unanswerable questions about historical contexts irretrievably lost. When Lewis reads the Bible, he sometimes tries to put it in historical context, but he doesn't do so often enough. Context defines content, and when Lewis ignores context, he misinterprets Scripture. The next chapter on the "liar, lunatic, or Lord" argument will offer specific examples, shining a painfully bright spotlight on the problem.

Lewis vs. Tyrrell

At the end of the fourth bleat, Lewis turns a supercilious gaze on the Jesuit priest George Tyrrell (1861–1909), a prominent figure in the Roman Catholic modernist movement. Like Lewis, Tyrrell was an Irishman who spent most of his career in England. Like the French Catholic modernist Loisy, Tyrrell was excommunicated for his pains. But that is not the end of the story. In 1943, Pope Pius XII, who had studied liberal German scriptural scholarship with Tyrrell's close friend Baron von Hügel, issued a letter allowing Roman Catholic exegetes more latitude than they had enjoyed in the past,[117] and in 1963, as Vatican II was in session and Lewis died, Tyrrell's *Christianity at the Cross-Roads* (1910) was republished with a foreword by Alec Vidler.[118] In 1971 Norman Pittenger, reviewing another book by Vidler on Catholic modernists, concludes, "It is a tragedy that the earlier Modernists . . . (Tyrrell especially) . . . had to fail—perhaps to fail in order that a half-century later they might succeed."[119] On the 100th anniversary of Tyrrell's death in 2009, his fellow Jesuits described him as a "religious genius."[120]

Longenecker and Mikeal C. Parsons, eds., *Beyond Bultmann: Reckoning a New Testament Theology* (Waco, TX: Baylor University Press, 2014).

117. Pius XII, *Divino Afflante Spiritu*; Rollmann, "Baron Friedrich von Hügel," 215.

118. George Tyrrell, *Christianity at the Cross-Roads* (London: Allen & Unwin, 1963).

119. Norman Pittenger, "The Continuity of Catholic Modernism," *Journal of Religion* 51, no. 2 (1971): 144.

120. "George Tyrrell Revisited," Jesuits in Ireland (website), Feb. 3, 2009, https://tinyurl.com/25d24tee.

In the second bleat, we saw Screwtape quote Tyrrell without mentioning him. In the fourth bleat, Lewis calls him by name, penning a farrago of his work that brings "Modern Theology and Biblical Criticism" to a close.

Lewis begins with a quote from *Christianity at the Cross-Roads*. He tears it apart, but once again he misreads his source, which prevents him from noticing the many substantial convictions he and Tyrrell share.

Skepticism about the New Testament, Lewis observes,

> might, I think, begin at the very beginning with the thought which underlies the whole *demythology* of our time. It was put long ago by Tyrrell. As man progresses he revolts against "*earlier and inadequate expressions of the religious idea. . . . Taken literally, and not symbolically,* they do not meet his need. And as long as he demands to picture to himself distinctly the term and satisfaction of that need he is doomed to doubt, for his picturings will necessarily be drawn from the world of his present experience."
>
> In one way of course Tyrrell was saying nothing new. [Older theology] had said as much, but it drew no such conclusions as Tyrrell. Perhaps this is because the older tradition found our conceptions inadequate to God whereas Tyrrell finds it inadequate to "the religious idea." He doesn't say whose idea. But I am afraid he means Man's idea.[121]

As he is wont to do throughout the essay, Lewis dips a finger into an ongoing conversation, pulls out a few drops, and disregards the pool from which he drew. Quoting Tyrrell, he focuses on the phrase "inadequate expressions of the religious idea" and how that religious idea should be understood, "literally" or "symbolically." Lewis claims that Tyrrell doesn't specify whose religious idea he is talking about, so Lewis fills in the blank: "I am afraid he means Man's idea." I am afraid he is incorrect, and from the moment he sets his foot wrong here, he stumbles to the end of the essay.

One must plunge into the larger context of Tyrrell's book to understand what he does say. We have already seen that he rejects the German liberal Protestant stance that early Christians departed from the teaching of Jesus. Tyrrell believes the Roman Catholic Church has preserved Jesus's teaching, despite inevitable "accretions and perversions," and he builds on this point as the book progresses. Like Bultmann

121. "MTBC," 164–65, quoting Tyrrell, *Christianity at the Cross-Roads*, 125 (emphasis mine). In the remainder of this section, pages from Tyrrell's book will be given in parentheses in the text.

and Lewis, Tyrrell disdains the liberal Protestant portrayal of Jesus as a "great moral teacher" whose example, if followed by enough people, will change the world. But Tyrrell takes his argument in a different direction. In order to follow it, we turn to Lewis's characterization of Tyrrell's thought as "demythology." This word, forever associated with Bultmann's demythologizing, never appears in Tyrrell's book, but Lewis is quite right to apply it to him. Tyrrell anticipates exactly what Bultmann will say decades later about the impossibility of "modern men" accepting the world-picture of Jesus, the three-tiered cosmos of the first century. He writes:

> For Jesus, what we call His apocalyptic "imagery" was no mere imagery but literal fact. But for us it can be so no longer. We can no longer believe in the little local Heaven above the flat earth, from which Jesus is to appear in the clouds; nor in all the details of the vision governed by this conception. To do so would be to reduce our minds to chaos and scepticism and make us incapable of faith of any sort. Criticism, on the other hand, forbids us to believe that He was making mysteries and puzzles of plain moral truths that He elsewhere expressed plainly, or to deny that He was giving a revelation of the transcendental world of religion. He belonged to the apocalyptics in His religious conceptions, as He did to the prophets in His ethical. (p. 95)

Tyrrell faces a problem. It is one thing, he says, "to recognise that . . . the doctrine of Catholicism is the same as that of Jesus; it is another to contend that . . . it can be accepted by the modern mind. If, against Liberal Protestantism, we can vindicate Catholicism as the true Christianity of Christ, do we not seem to bring the Christianity of Christ into peril, and to render the task of the apologist well-nigh impossible?" (p. 91).

According to Tyrrell, the source of, and solution to, the problems he outlines in the first half of his book—his conviction that Catholicism preserves the teaching of Jesus but nineteenth-century liberal Protestantism does not; the difficulty that Jesus's belief in a literal three-tiered cosmos poses for the modern apologist—rest on understanding what "apocalyptic" means to Jesus. This is the "religious idea" that Tyrrell, *contra* Lewis's remark, clearly defines.[122] Tyrrell writes, "We must now try to get hold of the 'idea' embodied in the

122. Tyrrell's definition of the "religious idea" can be fluid, but it centers on Jesus and the transcendent. See p. 99, where "the 'religious idea'" governs the human "need to adjust . . . to the invisible world"; p. 100, "Religion deals entirely with the transcendent. Its 'idea' unfolds itself and comes into clearer consciousness in an infinity of directions and degrees, dependent on its mental, moral and social environment";

apocalypticism of the Gospel." Its "three organic constituents" in Jesus's life are "the Kingdom of Heaven; His own Christhood; the temporal immediacy of the End" (p. 171). These three work together for Tyrrell. Jesus emphasized "the other-worldly, supernatural life of the coming Kingdom," he notes, "and this excessive transcendentalism is the great reproach made against Catholicism by the Liberal Protestant" (p. 66).

Here lies the crux of Tyrrell's argument against liberal German Protestants: they deny Jesus's apocalypticism as Tyrrell defines it—an otherworldly event—and substitute a "great moral teacher" whose ethics, if practiced, will bring about the kingdom of God on earth. He thinks this idea is unjust because "the mere fact that he expected the Kingdom tomorrow proves that the faith and hope of Jesus was not in progress or evolution. What sort of Gospel had it been for the poor, the sorrowful, the persecuted, the oppressed, to know that, not they, but their class, would be relieved in some remote age by the advance of civilisation and morality?" (p. 119).

Herein also lies the problem for "modern man." Jesus believed in a literal three-tiered cosmos and the imminent end of the world (p. 101). According to Tyrrell—as to Bultmann—the former is now impossible to accept, and the latter just didn't happen. So what are modern Christians to do? Tyrrell thinks they should

> abandon the apocalyptic form and retain what it stands for. This would be easy if it stood for ethical principles [as the German liberals thought]. . . . *But the transcendental can never be expressed properly. Translated into the terms of our present philosophy, the "idea" of Jesus remains symbolic.* To whatever degree we dematerialise our symbols of the spiritual, material they must remain. Our own symbolism would be as unacceptable for a later age as the apocalyptic symbolism is for us. The only remedy lies in a frank admission of the principle of symbolism. With this admission we have no need to abolish the Apocalypse, which, as the form in which Jesus embodied His religious "idea," is classical and normative for all subsequent interpretations of the same. In the long series of translations the original sense may be easily perverted if the original text be lost. What each age has to do is to interpret the apocalyptic symbolism into terms of its own symbolism. (pp. 102–3; emphasis mine)

---

p. 109, "The need of harmony between himself and the transcendent is, as we have said, the essence of the religious 'idea.'"

To revisit what Lewis quoted from Tyrrell at the beginning of the bleat, "As man progresses he revolts against '*earlier and inadequate expressions of the religious idea. . . . Taken literally, and not symbolically,* they do not meet his need.'" After putting these words in context, we can understand what Tyrrell said and how Lewis misinterprets it. For Tyrrell, the "religious idea" is not "Man's idea," as Lewis conjectured, but Jesus's apocalyptic world-picture, the cosmology of his time that is "inadequate" in ours. But even if the picture were adequate, Jesus couldn't express it adequately because human language isn't up to the task. The nature of language itself leaves no remedy for it except symbolism.

And Lewis agrees. Not here, because he is caught up in refuting Tyrrell, but in another essay, "Is Theology Poetry?" (1945), where he writes, "We are invited to restate our belief in a form free from metaphor and symbol. The reason why we don't is that we can't."[123] This is a fiendishly difficult topic for anyone to tackle, and as Lewis tries to explain how early Christians attempted to put the transcendent into words, he offers historically dubious claims.

Is Theology Poetry?

He begins strong: Theology uses symbolic language. God is not a biological father, and Jesus "did not come 'down' to earth in the same sense as a parachutist."[124] Why did early Christians use such language, then? Did they believe it? Did they take it "literally"? Lewis conjectures that they didn't think about it at first, but when they did, he knows what they decided. Without saying what that was, he moves to a slightly different idea, divine anthropomorphism, the belief that God has a body.[125] When anthropomorphism came up "explicitly before the Church," it was condemned. He guesses this took place in the second century, but he isn't correct; the "Church" with a capital C never condemned it, and intra-Christian disputes on the topic continued long after the second century. The first sentence in Origen's *On First Principles* reports that "some will try to say that even according to our Scriptures God is a body." Origen disagrees, but he takes the argument seriously enough to address it at length, demonstrating that it is still a live issue in the third century.[126] Lewis

123. "Is Theology Poetry?," in *Essay Collection*, 18.

124. "Is Theology Poetry?," 17.

125. See Francesca Stavrakopoulou, *God: An Anatomy* (New York: Alfred A. Knopf, 2022).

126. "Is Theology Poetry?," 17. Origen, *On First Principles* 1.1.1, ed. and trans. John Behr, vol. 1 (Oxford: Oxford University Press, 2017).

does better in *Miracles* when he sets a controversy on anthropomorphism in its proper timeframe, the late fourth to early fifth century, but even in *Miracles* he gets it wrong.[127]

The major source for the controversy is the fifth-century monk John Cassian. Cassian writes that the bishop of Alexandria in Egypt wrote a letter condemning anthropomorphism in 399. This letter was ill-received by Egyptian monks, especially one Serapion, whom his fellow monks held in high esteem because of his perfect discipline of prayer. When the powers that be realize that Serapion must be persuaded to abandon his image of an embodied God before his monastic brothers will follow suit, they break him down, and he finally accepts the bishop's letter. But when everyone gathers to thank God for their hard-won unity, Serapion finds himself unable to pray. He bursts into tears, throws himself on the ground, and wails, "They have taken my God from me, and now I have no one to lay hold of, and I do not know whom to adore!"[128]

As Lewis retells the story in *Miracles,* the letter from one bishop in 399 transmogrifies into "Christianity" as a whole condemning the anthropomorphic monks and anthropomorphism in general, which "the Church" did not do and has never done. Lewis belittles the story of Serapion's fall from prayer warrior to man bereft of the divine as "the desert monk who felt he had lost something . . . is recognized as 'muddle-headed.'"[129] His judgment of Serapion probably stems from the fact that he doesn't cite Cassian; rather, he cites Gibbon's *History of the Decline and Fall of the Roman Empire* citing Cassian. Lewis almost certainly didn't read Cassian, much less any of the scholarship putting the long, fierce, theologically complex fights on divine anthropomorphism in context, at any point in his life, and it shows.[130] Cassian—who does condemn anthropomorphism, so much so that he blames it on demons—doesn't say Serapion was "recognized as 'muddle-headed'" for clinging to the idea of an embodied God. Instead, he writes that Serapion himself felt muddled (*senex mente confusus*) when he tried to pray and could not—a very different thing.

127. "Is Theology Poetry?" appears to be a draft of *Miracles* ch. 10. Lewis also discusses the topic in "Must Our Image of God Go?," in *Essay Collection,* 66–67.

128. Cassian, *Collectiones* 10.2–3.

129. *Miracles,* 76.

130. See Elizabeth A. Clark, *The Origenist Controversy: The Cultural Construction of an Early Christian Debate* (Princeton: Princeton University Press, 1992); Mark DelCogliano, "Situating Sarapion's Sorrow: The Anthropomorphite Controversy as the Historical and Theological Context of Cassian's Tenth Conference on Pure Prayer," *Cistercian Studies Quarterly* 38, no. 4 (2003): 377–421.

At the end of his life, Lewis summarizes his earlier words on divine anthropomorphism in a response to John A. T. Robinson's book *Honest to God*, the religious publishing phenomenon of 1963. Robinson wanted to restate traditional language about God in new ways, but Lewis drily remarks that Robinson is behind the times: no one believes in a God who sits on a throne anymore. "We call that belief anthropomorphism, and it was officially condemned before our time. There is something about this in Gibbon."[131] After reading what Lewis wrote on anthropomorphism in "Is Theology Poetry?," *Miracles*, and his response to Robinson, from the outside it looks like "something in Gibbon" sums up Lewis's knowledge of the matter. Although there is no evidence of him expanding his knowledge, he does soften to the topic in *Letters to Malcolm* (1964), conceding that the major problem with belief in divine anthropomorphism is that it might prevent someone from becoming a Christian.[132] But "even at its crudest," it doesn't harm Christians themselves. No one, he says, is damned for picturing God with a beard.[133]

Back in "Is Theology Poetry?" Lewis continues, "But till the question [of anthropomorphism] was raised . . . people believed neither the one answer nor the other." Here he falls prey to the same error for which he rightly condemns biblical scholars on miracles: he cannot know this. Then he does answer the question: he thinks most, but not all, "first generation Christians" thought of God anthropomorphically. "But this doesn't mean . . . that the essence of their belief was concerned with details about a celestial throne room," he clarifies.[134] To some extent he's right, because the "essence" of the faith in the first century probably did not consist of speculation on the interior design of God's house. Nonetheless, based on the amount of apocalyptic literature produced by early Christians, at least some writers found such things fascinating, and it may have formed the center of *their* spiritual lives.

Tyrrell and Lewis agree that human language must use symbols to express transcendent ideas, but they differ on Tyrrell's last point in the paragraph quoted above: "What each age has to do is to interpret the apocalyptic symbolism into terms of its own symbolism." Tyrrell thinks moderns are in revolt

131. Lewis, "Must Our Image of God Go?," 66.

132. In a letter to Bede Griffiths, April 24, 1936, *CL*, 2:189, Lewis states that "anthropomorphism" had that effect on him.

133. *Letters to Malcolm: Chiefly on Prayer* (New York: Harcourt, Brace & World, 1964), 22. Here he differs from Cassian, who writes that Serapion's error has negated all of his spiritual progress and imperiled his immortal soul. *Collectiones* 10.4.

134. "Is Theology Poetry?," 17.

against biblical apocalyptic language, and they should translate it into more adequate terms, which will also be symbolic. The "original text," Scripture, should be retained as a corrective, lest these new terms wander too far from the "classical and normative" ideas of Jesus. Lewis, too, had personal experience with wanting to revolt against scriptural language, but rather than archiving Scripture to consult as needed, he insisted on keeping it front and center. He explains why in another essay, "The Weight of Glory."

The Bric-à-Brac of Heaven

The idea of glory is "associated with palms, crowns, white robes, thrones, and splendour like the sun and stars," Lewis writes.[135] In other words, with images called "apocalyptic" because they come straight from John's Apocalypse. But, he continues, they don't appeal to him, "and in that respect I fancy I am a typical modern." In fact, the modernist Tyrrell agrees; they don't appeal to him either: "Is it in physical radiance . . . that our spiritual nature will find its explanation and satisfaction? Is it in the bric-à-brac, rococo Heaven of the Apocalypse . . . that our souls are to find rest?"[136]

Lewis finds symbolic language about transcendent things in Scripture inadequate, but when he forces himself to examine it, he uncovers treasure that he would not have discovered had he jettisoned the unappealing language:

> If I had rejected the authoritative and scriptural image of glory and stuck obstinately to the vague desire which was, at the outset, my only pointer to heaven, I could see no connection at all between that desire and the Christian promise. But now, having followed up what seemed puzzling and repellent in the sacred books, I find, to my great surprise . . . that the connection is perfectly clear. Glory, as Christianity teaches me to hope for it, turns out to satisfy my original desire.[137]

He uses the word "desire" here because "The Weight of Glory" was a sermon preached to a congregation that would have been puzzled by his preferred term, "Joy," the longing that cannot be fully satisfied in this age but only in the next. By working through Scripture's inadequate symbolic language—neither

135. "The Weight of Glory," in *Essay Collection*, 101.
136. Tyrrell, *Christianity at the Cross-Roads*, 150.
137. "Weight of Glory," 102.

taking it "literally" nor rejecting it—Lewis finds that it points to the fulfillment of his desire for God.

The same thing happens to Tyrrell. Immediately after the line Lewis quoted at the beginning of this section, "As man progresses he revolts against 'earlier and inadequate expressions of the religious idea. . . . Taken literally, and not symbolically, they do not meet his need,'" Tyrrell writes:

> And as long as he demands to picture to himself distinctly the term and satisfaction of that need he is doomed to doubt. . . . Not till he resigns *the desire to see what is hopelessly beyond the range of his present vision*, is his faith pure and unshaken. Faith believes that this need relates to another order of experience; that *the present order serves only to evoke, exercise and strengthen it, but can never satisfy it*. This implies that, in his deepest being, man belongs already to that other order. He has a power, whose meaning and purpose are hid from him through lack of a proper object for their exercise. A cage-born bird, he wonders what his wings are for. He tries to make a heaven out of earth, as it were ropes out of sand. *He was made for something else—he does not know what.*[138]

Lewis could have written this entire paragraph, because it perfectly encapsulates his concept of Joy. In *Surprised by Joy*, he had to figure out the hard way that, to use Tyrrell's words, "the present order serves only to evoke" but never to "satisfy it." Lewis also knew that he wanted to reach "that other order." Much of *Surprised by Joy* is dominated by his quest for Joy, but only after Lewis "resigned the desire to see what was hopelessly beyond his present vision" did he have a hope of reaching it. As he puts it in *Mere Christianity*, "Creatures are not born with desires unless satisfaction for those desires exists. A baby feels hunger: well, there is such a thing as food. A duckling wants to swim: well, there is such a thing as water."[139] Or, to paraphrase Tyrrell, a bird has wings because it is born to fly.

It would be lovely to conclude the chapter on this glorious note of concord between Lewis and Tyrrell. But Lewis isn't finished, so neither are we.

A Dog, a Mouse, and the Ascension of Jesus

Back in "Modern Theology and Biblical Criticism," Lewis names the resurrection, ascension, and second coming of Jesus as doctrines we might find

138. Tyrrell, *Christianity at the Cross-Roads*, 125 (emphasis mine).
139. *Mere Christianity* (1952; repr., San Francisco: HarperSanFrancisco, 2001), 136.

"inadequate to our thoughts" if taken literally. But what, he asks, if they are "expressions of God's thought"? Even so, "It might still be true that 'taken literally and not symbolically' they are inadequate. From which the conclusion commonly drawn is that they must be taken symbolically, not literally; that is, wholly symbolically. All the details are equally symbolical and analogical." He continues, "But suppose a dog were trying to form a conception of human life."[140]

What follows is one of my favorite Lewisian analogies. A dog can picture life only in doggy terms. Human experience would be as incomprehensible to a dog as God's life is to us, and just as likely to be correct. Lewis even manages to get in a snap at a "modernist dog" who would ask to be taken to the vet. The analogy looks like Lewis at his best, but it is not original to him, for Tyrrell writes something similar for the same purpose. Because humans must form their pictures of other worlds from their experience of this one, Tyrrell notes, the embodiment of the religious idea "can never be more than symbolic." But it isn't *wholly* symbolic. If it were, we would have no way to access it: "It could not touch us, nor we it." The part of the transcendent we are able to grasp, he says, "can never be more than a symbol of the totality of possible experience that lies beyond. A man is not absolutely unknowable for a mouse, but the mouse's knowledge of him can only be in terms of mouse-life."[141]

Same argument, different animal. Tyrrell and Lewis end up in the same place, but Lewis didn't borrow the analogy from him. Instead, he took it from Friedrich von Hügel, a close friend of Tyrrell, who may himself have been inspired by Tyrrell's mouse. Von Hügel imagines that our dogs "know us only vividly, not clearly; we evidently strain their minds after a while—they then like to get away amongst servants." Lewis wrote "Delicious!!" next to this sentence, and he marked von Hügel's next passage, too: "And yet, how wonderful! dogs thus require their fellow-dogs, the shallow and clear, but they also require us, the deep and dim; they require indeed what they can grasp; but they as really require what they can but reach out to, more or less—what exceeds, protects, envelopes, directs them. And, after a short relaxation in the dog-world, they return to the bracing of the man-world." Von Hügel continues:

> The source and object of religion, if religion be true and its object be real, *cannot*, indeed, *by any possibility, be as clear to me even as I am to my dog* [emphasis in original]. For the cases we have considered deal with realities inferior to

140. "MTBC," 165.
141. Tyrrell, *Christianity at the Cross-Roads*, 100.

> our own reality (material objects, or animals), or with realities level to our own reality (fellow human beings), or with realities no higher above ourselves than are we, finite human beings, to our very finite dogs. Whereas, in the case of religion—if religion be right—we apprehend and affirm realities indefinitely superior in quality and amount of reality to ourselves, and which, nevertheless (or rather, just because of this), anticipate, penetrate and sustain us with a quite unpicturable intimacy. The obscurity of my life to my dog, must thus be greatly exceeded by the obscurity of the life of God to me.[142]

To rephrase what von Hügel, Tyrrell, and Lewis share in the less appealing language of abstraction, human beings have only a partial grasp of the transcendent because, by definition, it is beyond us. Our knowledge and our language fall short because both are unavoidably imperfect. The only things we can grasp are symbols, but there is more—the reality they attempt to communicate.

As he concludes the fourth bleat, Lewis applies his mischaracterizations of Tyrrell to the ascension of Jesus, and his argument descends into chaos. First, he criticizes Tyrrell by extending the canine analogy. Lewis's hypothetical dog might realize that its ideas of human life are symbolic, but the dog doesn't know enough to determine which details are "entirely symbolic." Tyrrell, through his mouse, agrees. Tyrrell never uses the words "entirely" symbolic, but Lewis, impervious to his errors, builds upon them. "Dr Tyrrell can tell that the story of the Ascension is inadequate to his religious idea, because he knows his own idea and can compare it to the story." But, Lewis says, he really can't, because the story is transcendent, and thus unknowable—an idea Tyrrell actually endorses.

Then Lewis observes that in a purely physical sense, "Motion away from the earth—which is what Ascension means—would not in itself be an event of *spiritual significance*" (emphasis mine). As we will see in a moment, Tyrrell makes the same point in the same words. Lewis continues, "Therefore, you argue, the spiritual reality can have nothing but an analogical connection with the story of an ascent. For the union of God with God and of Man with God-man can have nothing to do with space. Who told you this?" We can ask the same of Lewis: Who told you this? Because Tyrrell doesn't say it. In fact, Tyrrell says almost nothing about the ascension. The words "ascension" and "ascend" appear once each in his book, both on the same page, where he discusses resurrection in the context of "the apocalyptic vision of Christ":

142. Von Hügel, *Essays and Addresses*, 102–3. Because Lewis writes the Greek of John 13:10 on p. 47, and because of his handwriting style, I estimate he read the book ca. 1930–1931, when he was reading John in Greek.

> Those who accept [the resurrection] as a purely physical event . . . must, in consistency, accept the rest of the apocalyptic vision in the same sense. . . . What [the apostles] actually saw could only confirm them in their literalism—they saw Jesus risen in physical form; they saw Him ascend to the physical heavens; they saw those heavens opened. . . .
>
> Now we may ask ourselves what *spiritual significance* and value could these phenomenal happenings possibly have for faith? Apart from some truly transcendental reality which they figure, and which alone is the object that explains and satisfies our spiritual unrest, what interest can physical phenomena and marvels have for religion? The physical resurrection and ascension could, at most, be signs and symbols of Christ's spiritual transformation, of the fulness of His eternal and transcendent life; they could never be its substance. Is it in physical radiance and power and subtlety and swiftness that our spiritual nature will find its explanation and satisfaction? Is it in the bric-à-brac, rococo Heaven of the Apocalypse of S. John that our souls are to find rest?[143]

Tyrrell's final sentence takes us back to Lewis's "Weight of Glory": human language can never capture the transcendent. But if the resurrection were a "purely physical event," what could it mean? What kind of "spiritual significance" could it have? Not much, chime Lewis and Tyrrell in unison.

One may agree or disagree with Tyrrell, but one must read him in context. He thinks Jesus's "religious idea" was otherworldly, arguing against German Protestant liberals who envisioned the kingdom of heaven as a march to utopia on earth. So, as he summarizes his thoughts on resurrection, Tyrrell claims, "To thrust immortality into the background, . . . to make the reign of morality on earth, in ourselves and in society, the whole meaning of the kingdom of God" is to abandon Christianity itself.[144] With this he seems to veer from one extreme, earthly utopia, to the other, complete transcendence. Lewis may have disagreed with him on this point, had he considered it. I disagree with him because, like Lewis, I think Christian hope looks to a physical resurrection from the dead on a renewed earth, the reality of which Tyrrell understates at best.

As he concludes the lecture, Lewis writes, "When I know as I am known I shall be able to tell which parts of the story were purely symbolical and which, if any, were not." The first part of the sentence quotes the second half of 1 Corinthians 13:12, "Then I will know, even as I am known." Such blessedness is not for here and now, but for later. Lewis, like Paul, must wait.

143. Tyrrell, *Christianity at the Cross-Roads*, 149–50, emphasis mine.
144. Tyrrell, *Christianity at the Cross-Roads*, 154.

Lewis's statement seems to pack a powerful punch against Tyrrell—if one doesn't read Tyrrell. For at the end of his chapter "The Apocalyptic Vision of Christ," he writes, "The Messiahship of Jesus is, then, the symbolic expression in terms of apocalyptic imagery, of certain transcendent realities. . . . It is a visionary presentment of a transcendental truth, which we can present to ourselves in no other way; which we see *per speculum et in aenigmate,* but not *facie ad faciem.*"[145] Tyrrell is quoting the Latin translation of the first half of 1 Corinthians 13:12, "For now we see in a mirror and in riddles, but then we will see face to face." Like Lewis, Tyrrell realizes that, in order to know what is symbolic and what is not, one must wait. The two men agree, forming a perfect whole as they complete each other's quotations of 1 Corinthians 13:12.[146]

Tyrrell died in 1909, and Lewis in 1963. I hope that both of them now know and are known, and that they gaze upon the truth, whatever it may be, face-to-face, in happy conversation with each other.

Conclusion

If he had read his sources more carefully and generously, Lewis might have felt sheepish when he realized how much he agreed with the scholars he bleated against. From start to finish, he would have found common ground with them. Walter Lock didn't think the Gospel of John was a romance or allegory; it was ancient history. Bultmann, with a few significant exceptions, expounds the same ideas on personality Lewis does, and the modernist Tyrrell turns out to be a kindred spirit haunted by Joy. How good, true, and beautiful it would have been for Lewis to help bridge the gap between his readers and the higher critics by recognizing the many important things he and they shared!

"If we are to be critics," Lewis once said, "we must condemn as well as praise; we must sometimes condemn totally and severely, though only with fear and trembling."[147] I have condemned almost all of "Modern Theology and Biblical Criticism" while suffering both emotions, and I must conclude that the essay largely fails, not because Lewis wasn't a higher critic, but because in this instance, at least, he wasn't a good reader, the very thing he threw against his opponents. He misread almost every text he touched in "Modern Theology and Biblical Criticism." He didn't have to be a biblical scholar to get them right; the one

145. Tyrrell, *Christianity at the Cross-Roads,* 184.

146. Lewis and Tyrrell genuinely disagreed about many things, but since Lewis didn't address them in "MTBC," I don't address them here.

147. *Studies in Words,* 2nd ed. (Cambridge: Cambridge University Press, 1967), 330.

thing needful was to pay attention to what they actually said. And as his appeal to Auerbach demonstrates, the problem was not limited to texts outside his area of expertise. Dame Helen Gardner, Lewis's Oxford colleague who refused the chair in Medieval and Renaissance English at Cambridge specifically so he could take it, didn't hesitate to mention the problem in her 1966 commemoration of his life and work. Lewis, she observes, could sometimes exhibit "an almost wilful refusal to recognize what the work he is discussing is about."[148] Concerning Scripture, nowhere is this more evident than in "Modern Theology and Biblical Criticism," where the unwarranted confidence of his rhetoric is borne aloft by the vigor of its expression. Atop a mountain of misreadings, he thunders, and anyone who disagrees with a theory shot through with more holes than St. Sebastian simply can't read. Carried away by his own truculence, he rarely explains how his examples serve his argument, and he sometimes offers no relevant examples at all. His prose may dazzle, but the gorgeous writing and sparkling analogies often amount to no more than a gilded façade, fool's gold on clay.

We don't know why "Modern Theology and Biblical Criticism" wasn't published in Lewis's lifetime, and perhaps it should never have been published at all. The material in the unpublished *Letters to Malcolm* chapter critiquing academic biblical scholarship draws from the lecture, and the fact that neither piece made it into print before his death could indicate Lewis's misgivings. But because the lecture was published in 1967, and because it has been cited widely and almost entirely positively since that time, it is legitimate and necessary to subject it to scrutiny so that Lewis's readers can understand the New Testament, and especially the Gospel of John, better.

The lecture was prompted by Lewis reading Vidler reading John, which led to the first bleat, where Lewis misread Lock reading John. The Gospel of John, so important to Lewis from the beginning of his adult Christian life, often sits at the center of his most problematic work on Scripture. His rejection of good scholarship on the Gospel began when he disregarded Gore's wiser work in the 1930s, and from that point forward, misreading John is the cardinal sin of Lewis's biblical interpretation, the hinge on which his least successful efforts turn. We have seen how it affects "Modern Theology and Biblical Criticism," and it also disrupts the integrity of his "liar, lunatic, or Lord" argument.

148. Helen Gardner, "Clive Staples Lewis 1898–1963," *Proceedings of the British Academy* 51 (1966): 418.

8. LIAR, LUNATIC, OR LORD?

Lewis's Use of Scripture in His Argument for the Divinity of Christ

> *Look, the secular response to the Christ story always goes like this: he was a great prophet, obviously a very interesting guy, had a lot to say along the lines of other great prophets. . . .*
>
> *But actually Christ doesn't allow you that. He doesn't let you off that hook. Christ says: No. I'm not saying I'm a teacher, don't call me teacher. I'm not saying I'm a prophet.*
>
> *I'm saying: "I'm the Messiah." I'm saying: "I am God incarnate."*
>
> —Bono

C. S. Lewis's version of the "liar, lunatic, or Lord" argument propelled him to rock-star status among Christian apologists, and it is so well known that even real rock stars have used it. As U2's Bono phrases it, Jesus continues: "I know you're expecting me to come back with an army, . . . but actually I am the Messiah. At this point, everyone starts staring at their shoes, and says: Oh, my God, he's gonna keep saying this. So what you're left with is: either Christ was who He said He was, the Messiah, or a complete nutcase."[1]

The "liar, lunatic, or Lord" argument was so important to Lewis that he recycled it over and over.[2] It appears in his first work of apologetics, *The Problem of Pain*; in his first fairy tale for children, *The Lion, the Witch and the Wardrobe*;

1. Michka Assayas, *Bono: In Conversation with Michka Assayas* (New York: Riverhead Books, 2005), 204–5.

2. Lewis did not invent the argument but rather restated it in his own inimitable way. P. H. Brazier outlines its history prior to Lewis in "'God . . . or a Bad, or Mad,

and even in his retelling of the myth of Psyche and Cupid, *Till We Have Faces*; but the most famous version appears in *Mere Christianity*.

The Problem of Pain presents it as a dilemma, a choice between two alternatives, just as Bono does:

> There was a man born among [the] Jews who claimed to be, or to be the son of, or to be "one with," the Something which is at once the awful haunter of nature and the giver of the moral law. The claim is so shocking . . . that only two views of this man are possible. Either he was a raving lunatic of an unusually abominable type, or else He was, and is, precisely what He said. There is no middle way. If the records make the first hypothesis unacceptable, you must submit to the second.[3]

Lewis treats several phrases—to be (God), to be the son of (God), and to be one with (God)—as synonyms. In his opinion, whoever claims to be Son of God, or one with God, is claiming to be the one true God.

In *The Lion, the Witch and the Wardrobe* Lewis applies the argument to the character of Lucy, but he adds a third alternative, creating a trilemma. When Lucy insists that she really was in Narnia, Professor Kirke tells her worried siblings that she's either crazy, or lying, or telling the truth. These are the only options. "Logic! Why don't they teach logic at these schools?" he exclaims in exasperation.[4]

The argument also appears in *Till We Have Faces* when the main character, Orual, struggles to make sense of her sister Psyche's description of her new life on the divine mountain. Orual knows that Psyche is scrupulously honest, and Orual's companion Bardia convinces her that she has not gone mad, but it takes Orual the whole book to accept the fact that Psyche had told her the truth.

The best-known form of the "liar, lunatic, or Lord" argument appears in *Mere Christianity*, which also lays out a trilemma. Lewis builds it like this: Among the Jews "there suddenly turns up a man who goes about talking as if He was God. He claims to forgive sins. He says He has always existed." Lewis asserts that such ideas are especially problematic for Jews, who believe in only one God. Therefore, Jesus must be (1) silly or conceited to the point of being

---

Man': C. S. Lewis's Argument for Christ—a Systematic Theological, Historical and Philosophical Analysis of *Aut Deus aut Malus Homo*," *Heythrop Journal* 51 (2010): 1–30.

3. *The Problem of Pain* (1940; repr., New York: Macmillan, 1944), 11–12.

4. Lewis, *The Lion, the Witch and the Wardrobe* (London: Geoffrey Bles, 1950), ch. 5.

a lunatic, (2) a devil, or (3) who he says he is, the Son of God. In other words, he is either mad, bad, or God.[5]

Despite the philosopher Peter Kreeft's claim that the argument is so "logically tight" that it's irrefutable, some have critiqued its logic.[6] My focus here, however, is not the trilemma's formal logic but its use of Scripture. An argument is only as strong as its premises, and this argument's premises come from Lewis's interpretation of the Gospels. Because he was a longtime student of Greek, he could and did read the New Testament in that language, a skill that anyone who wants to make serious scriptural arguments about Jesus must acquire.[7] Even so, his scholarly expertise lay neither in theology nor in biblical studies, and his frequent wading into these areas could get him into trouble. Like many who venture into waters beyond their native shore, he sometimes underestimates and other times is simply unaware of the dangers outside his ken. There be dragons in those waters, eager to swallow the unwary, and Lewis falls prey to them time and again through his simplistic use of the Gospels.

All hands on deck potentially go down with him. N. T. Wright, a biblical scholar who appreciates Lewis, notes that those who rely on his argument, but "who never moved on or grew up theologically or historically, would be in a dangerous position when faced even with proper, non-skeptical historical investigation, let alone the regular improper, skeptical sort," because "Lewis

5. *Mere Christianity* (1952; repr., San Francisco: HarperSanFrancisco, 2001), 51–52. For Lewis, the argument doesn't stop here: if Jesus isn't "Lord" but is a liar or lunatic, then one can't accept him as a good moral teacher. That assertion too has been challenged, but it is beyond the scope of this chapter.

6. Peter Kreeft, *Fundamentals of the Faith: Essays in Christian Apologetics* (San Francisco: Ignatius, 1988), 59. Perhaps the best-known philosophical challenge to Lewis's argument is John Beversluis, *C. S. Lewis and the Search for Rational Religion*, rev. and updated ed. (Amherst, NY: Prometheus, 2007), rebutted by David A. Horner, "*Aut Deus aut Malus Homo*: A Defense of C. S. Lewis's 'Shocking Alternative,'" in *C. S. Lewis as Philosopher: Truth, Goodness, and Beauty*, ed. David Baggett, Gary R. Habermas, and Jerry L. Walls (Downers Grove, IL: IVP Academic, 2008), 68–84. Others who have critiqued or defended Lewis's trilemma include Daniel Howard-Snyder, "Was Jesus Mad, Bad, or God . . . or Merely Mistaken?," *Faith and Philosophy* 21, no. 4 (2004): 456–79, and Stephen T. Davis, "The Mad/Bad/God Trilemma: A Reply to Daniel Howard-Snyder," *Faith and Philosophy* 21 (2004): 480–91.

7. David Lyle Jeffrey writes that after his conversion, Lewis read Scripture in Greek every day. "C. S. Lewis, the Bible, and Its Literary Critics," *Christianity and Literature* 50, no. 1 (2000): 99.

didn't give such a person sufficient grounding in who Jesus really was."[8] What is at stake, then? Nothing less than the haplessness of Lewis's readers who, thinking that they can rely on a watertight argument, discover instead that they are listing.

Before we look at Lewis's use of the Gospels in the "liar, lunatic, or Lord" argument, we need to touch upon his views of skepticism, especially regarding the Bible. Chapter 5 has shown that Lewis could be too critical for some of his readers. At the same time, his work also shows that he valued a certain sort of skepticism. One of the biggest influences on his intellectual development, his tutor William Kirkpatrick, was a relentlessly logical atheist who questioned everything. One might think that after Lewis turned to Christ, he would repudiate his old teacher, but instead Lewis eulogized him with high praise: "My debt to him is very great, my reverence to this day undiminished."[9] A Kirkpatrick-esque character lives on not only in the Chronicles of Narnia, thinly veiled as Professor Kirke, but also in the novel *That Hideous Strength* as MacPhee. Even after personally participating in marvelous supernatural wonders, MacPhee accepts none of them, but he still enjoys the love and respect of the novel's Christian community. Ransom, the leader of the community, remarks, "He is our skeptic; a very important office."[10]

On one hand, Lewis's treatment of real people and fictional characters alike demonstrates his respect for skepticism, even if it excludes the divine. On the other, the last two chapters of this book have examined his reactions to the skepticism some New Testament scholars have leveled upon the Gospels. Since turnabout is fair play, some of those scholars—and their successors—have had small regard for him, in part because he read the Gospels as straightforward history. A sort of amphibian in reverse, Lewis was at home neither on the hard dry land of fundamentalism nor in navigating the ever-shifting currents of biblical scholarship.

The lack of a worthy sparring partner in the arena of biblical scholarship did Lewis no favors. He was willing to change his mind when he was wrong, as he did after a debate with the philosopher Elizabeth Anscombe, and he was pleased to befriend someone who criticized his work.[11] Several letters from

8. N. T. Wright, "Simply Lewis: Reflections on a Master Apologist after 60 Years," *Touchstone*, March 2007, https://tinyurl.com/3srpehen.

9. *Surprised by Joy* (San Diego: Harcourt Brace Jovanovich, 1955), 148.

10. *That Hideous Strength* (1946; repr., New York: Macmillan, 1965), 184.

11. *Journal of Inklings Studies* 1, no. 2 (Oct. 2011) is devoted to the controversy on *Miracles*.

Nan Dunbar, a young classics scholar, persuaded him that his interpretation of a certain Latin concept was incorrect.[12] Through their epistolary exchange, Lewis and Dunbar became great friends, and he liked her so much that he feted her in a serio-comic poem (in Latin!), writing, "Nan is more learned than all the girls, / . . . She does not allow you to be careless."[13]

If Lewis had entertained a critique of his use of Scripture from a sort of biblical equivalent to Anscombe or Dunbar, this chapter could have been very different. We might imagine Austin Farrer filling the gap, but to the best I can tell, he did not. I would like to think Lewis would appreciate how this chapter engages his ideas. He relished a good argument—Farrer called him "a bonny fighter"—and remarked, "to find an opponent is almost to find a friend."[14] Lewis challenged his own friends' work incessantly, scholar and nonscholar alike, and he pulled no punches. If he were to read this, I hope he would find a friend here, even though I can turn what he wrote to his pen pal Vera Mathews back on him: "I will pay you the compliment (for it is one: the naked truth is not for fools) of giving you a perfectly honest criticism. I don't think the story, as it stands, will do."[15]

Liar, Lunatic, Lord, or Legend?

Lewis once observed, "If the first step in an argument is wrong, everything that follows will be wrong." The first step in the "mad, bad, or God" argument is the claim that Jesus said he was God, or Son of God, or had always existed.[16] It is an argument from history, not faith. But did Jesus really say these things? And if he did, what did they mean in the first century? Do we understand now what those words meant then?

It's important to emphasize at the outset that Jesus calling himself by what looks like a divine title is a different thing entirely from other people doing so. His followers call him Son of God in the Gospels, and the evangelist John says he was preexistent, but none of that matters here. Lewis's argument requires

12. Lewis to Nan Dunbar, Oct. 24, 1955, *CL*, 3:665.

13. Lewis to Nan Dunbar, April 20, 1956, *CL*, 3:740.

14. Austin Farrer, "The Christian Apologist," in *Light on C. S. Lewis*, ed. Jocelyn Gibb and Owen Barfield (London: Geoffrey Bles, 1965), 25. Lewis, *The Personal Heresy* (1939; repr., New York: HarperOne, 2017), 49.

15. Lewis to Vera Mathews, Feb. 17, 1952, *CL*, 3:166.

16. Lewis, *Problem of Pain*, 104. Lewis defines the Jewish God, the one he argues that Jesus claimed to be, as "the Being outside the world, who had made it and was infinitely different from anything else." *Mere Christianity*, 51.

Jesus to say it himself. *Jesus* is the potential liar or lunatic, not his followers. We will also disregard Jesus's actions unless Lewis brings them up, because he highlights what Jesus says, not what he does. Lewis defines his argument narrowly, and we will analyze it as such. It is also important to emphasize that the goal of this chapter is not to try to disprove that Jesus was God. It is simply to evaluate how Lewis employed Scripture in trying to prove that he was.

Some biblical scholars have approached the question "Did Jesus say he was God?" with what Lewis regards as unacceptable skepticism. They find a fourth alternative to the "liar, lunatic, or Lord" trilemma: legend. Lewis does not mention legend in *The Problem of Pain* or *Mere Christianity*, but he does in the essay "What Are We to Make of Jesus Christ?"[17] There he writes that his opponents argue that "the Man did not really say these things, but . . . His followers exaggerated the story, and so the legend grew up that he had said them."[18] Variations on this theme were and still are standard among academic biblical scholars, although they require much more careful critique than Lewis offers.[19] He doesn't explain the "legend" argument fully or fairly, and his refutations of it are inadequate for three reasons.

First, he believes an appeal to legend is an illegitimate way out of the problem because the Jews are the last people on earth to turn a man into God.[20] He is wrong on this point, to which we shall return shortly. His second refutation concerns literary genre. As a scholar of English literature and a voracious reader, Lewis insists that the Gospels are not legends. The tricky part for us in grasping his argument lies in discerning his definition of legend, because he doesn't define it here. Lewis seems to think his opponents define legend as "falsehood." We must read between the lines to see that Lewis rejects that understanding, but he fails to clarify his own; he only says what legends are not: the Gospels can't be legends in a literary sense because they are too clumsy, and a real legend would say more about Jesus's life before he began his public ministry.[21] His remarks on legend here seem to be based on "feel," demonstrating no engagement even with other literary scholars.

17. Lewis, "What Are We to Make of Jesus Christ?," in *Essay Collection*, 38–41. The article was published in 1950, after the BBC broadcasts but before their publication *in toto* as *Mere Christianity*.

18. "What Are We to Make of Jesus Christ?," 40.

19. See Bart D. Ehrman, "Liar, Lunatic, or Lord? Finding the Historical Jesus," in *Jesus, Interrupted* (New York: HarperCollins, 2009).

20. "What Are We to Make of Jesus Christ?," 40.

21. "What Are We to Make of Jesus Christ?," 40. Cf. "MTBC," 155. In arguments with Owen Barfield circa 1927–1928, Lewis defines "legend" immediately after defining

Lewis never asks how biblical scholars define legend. Some of them would equate it to falsehood, but he could have turned to Rudolf Bultmann's friend Martin Dibelius, whose scholarship was influential in the mid-twentieth century when Lewis was writing. Dibelius defines legend as "A narrative about some sainted person. The term 'legend' does not in itself raise the question of historicity."[22] It seems Lewis is attacking at least a partial straw man in attempting to refute opponents of his trilemma. If he had engaged what biblical scholars actually wrote about legend instead of what he imagined they did, he might have done better. As we observed regarding the conflicts between Lewis and Bultmann in the last two chapters, definitions are helpful if one has any hope for a fruitful conversation. He understood this fact well enough in his own field, once writing a fellow literary scholar, "You come to the subject, obviously, from a whole literature on the novel, . . . of which I know hardly anything. It is therefore v. possible that many words . . . have overtones for you which they lack for me."[23]

His third refutation of the legend argument is another false dilemma that crumbles to dust when we touch it. He observes that the Gospels contain random visual details like Jesus doodling on the ground in John 8:6, and these "pictures" must come from eyewitness testimony. This argument was decisively dispatched in chapter 7.

Since Lewis never explains why biblical scholars don't take every bit of the Gospels as history, he can't refute them. As Alasdair I. C. Heron rightly notes, "Lewis's strictures upon the historical-critical study of biblical material do less than justice . . . to the integrity of the enterprise as seriously undertaken."[24]

If I were to insist that the Gospels are complete fiction, this chapter would slam to a halt, because Lewis held the opposite view, and we would share no common ground. However, almost all biblical scholars think the Gospels contain some historically accurate material about Jesus; they just argue about what, exactly, that is. From this point forward, then, for the sake of a more interesting conversation, let us concede to Lewis that the Gospels aren't legends, however one may define the term, and accept what they say about Jesus at face value, as many readers do. In other words, we'll work under the assumption that Jesus is reliably represented in all four canonical Gospels.

---

myth. He notes that those who recount a legend think it is true, and when they depart from the truth, they do so unconsciously, carried away by their topic. *CL*, 3:1619.

22. Martin Dibelius, *From Tradition to Gospel* (Cambridge: James Clarke, 1971), xv.

23. Lewis to Eugène Vinaver, Aug. 26, 1959, *CL*, 3:1083.

24. Alasdair I. C. Heron, "What Is Wrong with Biblical Exegesis? Reflections upon C. S. Lewis' Criticisms," in *Betraying the Gospel: Modern Theologies and Christian Orthodoxy*, ed. Andrew Walker (Wilmore, KY: Bristol Books, 1990), 151–52.

Define "Divine"

Even when we interpret the Gospels as reliably representing the words of Jesus, Lewis's arguments about "Son of God" run headlong into a wall of difficulties. The first problem is that Lewis retrojects fourth-century concepts of Jesus into first-century documents. To understand what he does, we must take a quick trip back in time to the fourth-century Christological councils, the church gatherings that addressed the person of Christ.

The Council of Nicaea (325 CE) and the First Council of Constantinople (381 CE) tried to articulate the relationship of Jesus to God, a topic that had been disputed for centuries, in part because the Scriptures aren't at all clear about it. These disputes are known as the Christological controversies. Creeds that emerged from the councils, written in Greek, defined Jesus as the "only" (*monogenēs*) Son of God, "begotten" (*gennēthenta*) by and "one in being" (*homoousios*) with the Father. We will have more to say on "only" and "begotten" below. These words appear in the New Testament, but *homoousios*, "one in being," does not, and applying it to Jesus was highly controversial at first, especially among those Christians now deemed orthodox.

Lewis reads these later concepts from fourth-century creeds back into the New Testament, most of which was written in the first century, seemingly unaware that he is doing so. For example, when he talks about Jesus forgiving sins, he writes: "This makes sense only if He really was the God whose laws are broken and whose love is wounded in every sin. In the mouth of any speaker who is not God, these words would imply what I can only regard as a silliness and conceit unrivalled by any other character in history."[25]

We will examine Lewis's assertion on Jesus forgiving sins at the end of this chapter, focusing here on broader aspects of Christology. To Lewis, Jesus is God with a capital *G*, the one God, beside whom there is no other, fully God in his human life on earth.[26] If Jesus were not fully God during his incarnation, Lewis wrote in 1939, "the universe w[ould] have disappeared."[27] He is not unique in entertaining this thought, which was also held by Archbishop of Canterbury Wil-

25. *Mere Christianity*, 52.

26. Compare Lewis to Greeves, Dec. 11, 1944, *CL*, 3:1555, where Lewis tries to convince him of the full divinity of Christ. He cites Matt. 28:19, John 15:26, Col. 1:12, Matt. 23:34, and Mark 2:18–19 and mentions that John's Prologue goes without saying. Lewis may have drawn some of his ideas about John's Prologue from E. L. Mascall's *The God-Man* (Westminster: Dacre, 1940), which he recommended to correspondents throughout the 1940s.

27. Lewis to Barfield, Aug. ? [*sic*], 1939, *CL*, 2:268.

liam Temple, who reacted against Charles Gore's interpretation of the kenosis of Jesus in *Lux Mundi* (see chapter 2). If the human Jesus had emptied himself of divine knowledge, Temple asks Gore, "What happened to the rest of the universe during the period of our Lord's earthly life?" Jesus could not rule as God when he was an infant, but if one follows Gore's interpretation, Temple argues, "for a certain period the world was let loose from the control of the creative Word."[28] Later, Austin Farrer will come to the rescue, writing, "None of us would suppose that the infant Jesus in the cradle had yet unfolded or expressed the union of God and man in Christ"; he went through "several phases of his development."[29] By 1941, Lewis can admit to the Regius Professor of Divinity at Oxford, "I am pretty ignorant of the theology of the Incarnation."[30] As time passes, he gets a firmer grasp on the topic, but many Christians can sympathize with what he exclaims near the end of his life, reporting what a Roman Catholic friend had told him: "This is a subject on which nearly every statement anyone can make always turns out to be heretical and 'the only safe thing is not to think about it at all'!"[31]

Lewis read books on how the concepts of God, Son of God, and related terms like Son of Man and Wisdom were understood in their first-century

28. William Temple, *Christus Veritas* (London: Macmillan, 1924), 142–43, as quoted by Ramsey, *An Era in Anglican Theology: From Gore to Temple; The Development of Anglican Theology between "Lux Mundi" and the Second World War, 1889–1939* (New York: Scribner, 1960; repr., Eugene, OR: Wipf & Stock, 2009), 41.

29. Farrer, "Bultmann and All That," in *Austin Farrer: Oxford Warden, Scholar, Preacher*, ed. Markus Bockmuehl, Stephen Platten, and Nevsky Everett (London: SCM, 2020), 148–49.

30. Lewis to Canon Oliver Chase Quick, Jan. 18, 1941, *CL*, 2:462.

31. Lewis to K. C. Thompson, Feb. 11, 1962, *CL*, 3:1316–17, where he also discusses Apollinarianism without naming it. Compare his letter to Sister Penelope, July 29, 1942, *CL*, 2:526–27, and "The World's Last Night," in *Essay Collection*, 45–46, where his treatment of the infant Jesus's state of knowledge is more sophisticated. Writing to Peter Bide, June 14, 1960, *CL*, 3:1161, Lewis mentions the pitfalls of Patripassianism. He was aware of the concept of development of doctrine as early as 1929, as demonstrated by his notes on Matthew Arnold's *St. Paul and Protestantism*, which, according to Charlie Starr, he made between January 1929 and July 1930. Arnold paraphrases John Henry Cardinal Newman, a section Lewis underlines (indicated here by italics): "[Newman] says . . . to Protestants: The doctrines you receive are no more on the face of the Bible, or in the plain teaching of the ante-Nicene Church, which alone you consider pure, than the doctrines you reject. *The doctrine of the Trinity is a development, as much as the doctrine of Purgatory*. Both of them are developments made by the Church, by the post-Nicene Church." Arnold, *St. Paul and Protestantism* (London: Smith, Elder, 1892), 100.

context, but sometimes he misunderstood them, sometimes he seems to have abandoned them before reaching the more nuanced sections, and other times they themselves misled him. He marked an example of the last in his Gore commentary, where H. L. Goudge claims Jews never "think of men as made divine by the gift of immortality." For Greeks, "with their gods of like passions with ourselves, the thought of deification presented no difficulty; to the Hebrews it was impossible."[32] Goudge was wrong; as we will see, Jews could and did think of human beings as divine. But Lewis evidently took him at his word.

Another factor that may have affected Lewis's interpretation was his disdain for the *koinē* ("common") Greek in which the New Testament was composed, which he considered a degraded form of the language used only by non-native speakers.[33] This judgment was widespread from Erasmus to the Victorians, but it was overturned in the late nineteenth century by the discovery of a huge cache of ancient documents, the Oxyrhynchus Papyri. Already in 1908, when Lewis was nine years old, scholars can report that "it is needless to describe" how the papyri prove that *koinē* was "in reality normal first-century spoken Greek."[34] In 1927, an introductory Greek textbook calls the idea that New Testament Greek is "the ordinary colloquial tongue of the day, spoken throughout the Graeco-Roman world" axiomatic.[35] Lewis never took these scholarly advances into account, as he writes in 1961, "The *koine*, I take it, was a language in which no one prayed, joked, made love, or thought—a neutralised, internationalised language for business and government: cut off equally from the fireside and the library."[36]

Even among orthodox Christians, Lewis's confusion about first-century Christology is not unique. Regarding the phrase "Son of God," Michael Peppard observes, "We all think we know what it means, and indeed, we do know what it meant for the theologians gathered at the Council of Nicaea."[37] Rendel

32. H. L. Goudge, "The Theology of St. Paul," in *NCHS*, part 3, 407. On p. 414, another passage Lewis marked, Goudge notes that "Son of God" in Paul and "perhaps elsewhere" refers to the pre-incarnate Word.

33. Lewis, introduction to *Letters to Young Churches: A Translation of the New Testament Epistles*, by J. B. Phillips (New York: Macmillan, 1947), vii.

34. Adam Nicolson, *God's Secretaries: The Making of the King James Bible* (New York: HarperCollins, 2003), 82; James Hope Moulton, *A Grammar of New Testament Greek*, vol. 1, *Prolegomena*, 3rd ed. (Edinburgh: T&T Clark, 1908), 4.

35. H. E. Dana and Julius R. Mantey, *A Manual Grammar of the Greek New Testament* (Toronto: Macmillan, 1927), iv–v.

36. Lewis to Eric Routley, Feb. 17, 1961, *CL*, 3:1240.

37. Michael Peppard, *The Son of God in the Roman World: Divine Sonship in Its Social*

Harris, a Cambridge biblical scholar of the generation just prior to Lewis, could write of British theologians in particular, "They are always more at home in the fourth century than in the first!"[38] Once again, however, Austin Farrer is an exception to the rule. "It may be true that Christ did not talk about himself with the absolute language of Deity," he wrote, and it was "certainly true that he did not express himself in the sort of language used by the Fathers by the time the Nicene creed was formulated."[39]

Lewis was more aware than most that words change over time. In one of his popular works, *Mere Christianity,* he discusses the evolution of the word "gentleman."[40] In one of his scholarly books, *The Discarded Image,* he looks at the word "fairy," writing that someone might "read the old texts" with "some ready-made, modern concept" of it, but "naturally, the proper method is the reverse; we must go to the texts with an open mind and learn from them what the word *fairy* meant to our ancestors."[41] He wrote an entire book on how meanings change, *Studies in Words.* The first page tells us that "in older books one knows what one does not understand but in the later [books] one discovers, often after years of contented misreading, that one has been interpolating senses later than those the author intended."[42] Lewis never seems to have treated Gospel language about Jesus with caution. Instead, he approached phrases like "Son of God" with "years of contented misreading" to the end of his life.

He knew better. Some readers, he said, don't pay attention to what words meant in their historical context and so condemn themselves to a "lifetime of persistent and carefully guarded delusion." But "if we read with insufficient regard for change in the overtones, and even the dictionary meanings, of words . . . content with whatever effect the words accidentally produce in our modern minds," we won't understand what the author wrote. "The dominant sense of any word lies uppermost in our minds. Wherever we meet the word, our

---

and Political Context (Oxford: Oxford University Press, 2011), 9. See also James D. G. Dunn, *Christology in the Making: A New Testament Inquiry into the Origins of the Doctrine of the Incarnation* (Philadelphia: Westminster, 1980), 12–13.

38. Rendel Harris, *The Origin of the Prologue to St John's Gospel* (Cambridge: Cambridge University Press, 1917), v.

39. Farrer, "How Far Is Christian Doctrine Reformable?," in Bockmuehl, Platten, and Everett, *Austin Farrer,* 120.

40. Lewis, *Mere Christianity,* xiii–xiv; see also Lewis, *Studies in Words,* 2nd ed. (Cambridge: Cambridge University Press, 1967), and "The Death of Words," in *On Stories, and Other Essays on Literature,* ed. Walter Hooper (New York: Harcourt, 1982), 105–7.

41. *The Discarded Image* (Cambridge: Cambridge University Press, 1964), 123.

42. Lewis, *Studies in Words,* 1.

natural impulse will be to give it that sense." But, he continues: "We are often deceived. In an old author the word may mean something different." He calls the modern meanings that people unconsciously read into familiar words "dangerous senses because they lure us into misreadings."[43] Lewis never realized that his own words indict his understanding of Christological terms like "Son of God" in the Gospels.

Since he was exquisitely attuned to the fact that meanings change over time, Lewis should have investigated what "Son of God" meant to first-century Jews, but there is no evidence he did. In his own scholarly field, English literature, he realized that "you must, in so far as in you lies, become an Achaean chief while reading Homer, a medieval knight while reading Malory, and an eighteenth-century Londoner while reading Johnson. Only thus will you be able to judge the work 'in the same spirit that its author writ' and to avoid chimerical criticism."[44] This plea reflects the German philosopher and literary critic Johann Gottfried von Herder (d. 1803), who writes, "Become with shepherds a shepherd, with a people of the sod a man of the land, with the ancients of the Orient an Easterner, if you wish to relish these writings in the atmosphere of their origin." For Herder as for Lewis, the use of language was an intrinsic part of the spirit of an age and an expression of how its people understood themselves.[45] But when it came to reading the Gospels, Lewis was blind to the need to take his own advice and become a first-century Jew, and so he produced "chimerical criticism" himself. He fell into the same trap even when he discussed more recent forms of Christianity within his purview. A scholarly note criticizing his book *Preface to Paradise Lost* points out that Lewis "seems to have taken little pains to discover the actual content of Christian theology as taught in Milton's time—and this on his own showing is vital to his theme." Poor Lewis was mortified.[46]

Another problem with his Christology is that he harmonizes the diverse ways the Gospels portray Jesus. That is, instead of reading each Gospel as its own

43. *Studies in Words*, 3, 12–13.

44. Lewis, *A Preface to Paradise Lost* (1942; repr., London: Oxford University Press, 1961), 64; cf. his letter to Greeves, Nov. 1, 1916, *CL*, 1:244. "In the same spirit that its author writ" quotes Alexander Pope, "An Essay on Criticism," part 2, though Pope's line begins "With."

45. Quoted in Hans W. Frei, *The Eclipse of Biblical Narrative: A Study in Eighteenth and Nineteenth Century Hermeneutics* (New Haven: Yale University Press, 1974), 185. Compare Lewis, *The Discarded Image*, 6.

46. Charles Earle Raven, *Cambridge Review* 64 (May 15, 1943): 315, as quoted in *CL*, 2:574; Lewis to Barfield, May 17? [*sic*], 1943, *CL*, 2:574.

story, he blends them together, so the divergent Scriptures that fueled debates about Jesus in the early church disappear from view. In chapter 2 I noted how his reading Moffatt's *Theology of the Gospels* at the beginning of his adult Christian life encouraged such blending. When readers harmonize, they often interpret the first three Gospels through the lens of the fourth, John, just as Moffatt did. Lewis is no exception, although, as we will see, he does it more creatively than most.

Since Lewis relies on the Gospels for his biblical "proofs" of the "liar, lunatic, or Lord" argument, we will begin there too. The three Synoptic Gospels—Matthew, Mark, and Luke—are often studied together because they are so similar. For compelling reasons, the vast majority of biblical scholars agree that Mark was written first, around the year 70.[47] Most scholars also believe that Matthew and Luke used Mark to write their own Gospels. Analyzing the ways in which Matthew and Luke edited Mark and hypothesizing about why they did so is called redaction criticism. Redaction criticism is a valuable antidote to harmonization, and I will use it extensively in this chapter. Although the term "redaction criticism" first appeared around 1954–1956, rather late in Lewis's career, similar methods had been employed much earlier—even in the first centuries of the church.[48] In fact, Lewis himself gives as good an explanation of it as anyone might to a general audience, though we must keep in mind that he is not talking about redaction criticism but the creation accounts in Genesis:

> Stories do not reproduce their species like mice. They are told by men. Each re-teller either repeats exactly what his predecessor had told him or else changes it. He may change it unknowingly or deliberately. If he changes it deliberately, his invention, his sense of form, his ethics, his ideas of what is fit, or edifying, or merely interesting, all come in. If unknowingly, then his unconscious (which is so largely responsible for our forgettings) has been at work. Thus at every step in what is called—a little misleadingly—the "evolution" of a story, a man, all he is and all his attitudes, are involved.[49]

47. Those reasons are too voluminous to outline here. See E. P. Sanders and Margaret Davies, *Studying the Synoptic Gospels* (Philadelphia: Trinity Press International, 1989).

48. In his homilies on Matthew, Chrysostom compares and contrasts the same stories in Matthew and Luke. Discrepancies between them do not alter the "truth" of the narrative, he writes, but simply demonstrate that the two evangelists told their stories differently because they had different aims. See Jerome D. Quinn, "Saint John Chrysostom on History in the Synoptics," *Catholic Biblical Quarterly* 24, no. 2 (1962): 140–47. See also J. G. Herder (1744–1803), who urged readers not to harmonize the Gospels but rather to look at how each evangelist portrayed Jesus's story. David R. Law, *The Historical-Critical Method: A Guide for the Perplexed* (London: Continuum, 2012), 121, 185–88.

49. *Reflections on the Psalms* (New York: Harcourt, Brace & World, 1958), 110.

These words will resonate in surprising ways later in this chapter when we apply them to how Lewis himself retells Scripture. For now, we'll conclude this section with a procedural point: when Lewis cites a passage from the Synoptic Gospels without giving a reference, I will begin by looking at its Markan form. I will note any relevant parallels in Matthew and Luke, and then move to John, which is not a Synoptic Gospel because it differs so much from the other three.

Jesus's (Lack of) Divine Disclosure in the Synoptic Gospels

Does Jesus "go about talking as if He was God" in the Gospel of Mark? Even taking everything in that Gospel as the actual words of Jesus, the answer is an unambiguous no. He doesn't say much about himself at all in the Synoptics, as Charles Gore explains in *Jesus of Nazareth*, the book Lewis read and praised so extravagantly at the beginning of his Christian life in 1933.[50] Moffatt, too, observes that Jesus never uses "Son of God" in the Synoptics "to denote his own person."[51] That said, the author of Mark clearly intends to portray him as Son of God.[52] God calls Jesus his son twice, at the baptism and the transfiguration (Mark 1:11; 9:7), and demons recognize his sonship (3:11; 5:7). The only time Jesus comes close to applying the term to himself, however, is during his trial before the Sanhedrin. The high priest asks him if he is "the Son of the Blessed One," and Jesus agrees, but this conversation takes place on the last day of his life, in a small group in the middle of the night. It is hardly public proclamation.[53] The only human being to confess Jesus as "Son of God" in Mark is the Roman centurion at the foot of the cross after Jesus dies (15:39).

50. *Jesus of Nazareth* (1929; repr., Oxford: Oxford University Press, 1950), 34.

51. James Moffatt, *The Theology of the Gospels* (London: Duckworth, 1912), 132–33.

52. Christians writing in English will often denote Jesus *the* Son of God with the definite article and divine capitalization. The situation is different in ancient Greek, both because there was no use of capital letters for emphasis and because there are times when Jesus is called "Son" in the Gospels without the definite article in Greek, but English translations add it anyway. Because there are permutations of the presence and absence of the definite article "the" modifying "Son" in regard to Jesus in both Greek and English, the complexities of which far exceed the scope of this chapter, I refer to Jesus as "Son of God" without the article unless context demands otherwise.

53. A hastily convened event (Mark 14:2), the trial takes place only in front of the Sanhedrin in the middle of the night on a major Jewish feast. From a historical standpoint, the Markan trial is so problematic that rivers of scholarly ink have been devoted to examining it. See, e.g., Raymond E. Brown, *The Death of the Messiah*, 2 vols. (New York: Doubleday, 1994).

A curious thing in Mark's Gospel that the other two Synoptics adopt is how Jesus silences both humans and demons who recognize his special status. Readers see this in the first Markan miracle, an exorcism at Capernaum (1:21–25). The theme is so pervasive that it has acquired a name, the messianic secret.[54] Far from talking about himself as if he were divine, Jesus does the opposite in Mark: he never calls himself Son of God or God, and when others do, he almost always tells them to be quiet.[55] The same holds true in Matthew and Luke.

This fact should not be news to anyone, since Christians have recognized it from the beginning. In a homily on Matthew 5, Chrysostom states matter-of-factly that Jesus never speaks clearly about his divinity anywhere in the Gospel because he doesn't want to alarm people. If the crowds listening to Jesus's sermon on the mount were puzzled when he expanded upon the Jewish law ("You have heard it said, but I say to you . . ."), how much more confounded would they be if he called himself God![56] Chrysostom's words exude complete comfort both with the fact that Jesus doesn't use divine language about himself in what we now call the Synoptic Gospels and, by extension, with the idea that Christology may change and develop over time.

Chrysostom's thinking is not unique. His contemporary Augustine (d. 430) states without apology that we are indebted to "John alone" for the idea that Jesus is equal to God the Father. The other three Gospels, he writes, concern themselves with Jesus the man.[57] Centuries later, Thomas Aquinas says the same thing. "The others show him as a man. . . . John only says that he is God."[58]

Jesus accepts another title, messiah, in the context of small, private groups before his grand entrance into Jerusalem at the end of his life. The word "messiah" does not indicate equality with God, and it often doesn't include any notion of divinity. Unlike Bono as quoted at the beginning of the chapter, Lewis knew this, and that's why he doesn't use the term in his argument.

"Messiah" is a Hebrew word that means "anointed with oil." Any person or thing could be anointed and thus become a messiah, but as the word changed meaning over time, kings and priests in particular were identified as messiahs

54. Wilhelm Wrede, *The Messianic Secret*, trans. J. C. G. Greig (Greenwood, SC: Attic Press, 1971). First published in German in 1901, the book continues to be influential (though not unchallenged) in biblical studies to this day. Gore, *Jesus of Nazareth*, 59, brings up the messianic secret, but the concept must not have stuck with Lewis.

55. Two exceptions to this aspect of the messianic secret are Mark 14:61–62 and 5:19.

56. Chrysostom, *Homilies on Matthew* 16.

57. Augustine, *On the Harmony of the Gospels* 1.4.7.

58. Thomas Aquinas, *Commentary on John* 1.67.

because they were anointed when they were crowned or ordained (to apply anachronistic terms). As late as the fourth century CE, educated Greek-speaking Christians like Eusebius of Caesarea were well aware of this ancient usage.[59] After the destruction of Jerusalem in 586 BCE, when the Jews no longer ruled their own sovereign nation, the word took on additional meaning: a hoped-for military leader who would overthrow oppressive powers. God would send this leader as his instrument, so a messiah was always subordinate—never equal—to God the Father.

Jesus calls God "father" twice in Mark (8:38; 14:36), but his father is also the father of his disciples (11:25) and therefore not uniquely paternal to Jesus in the Synoptics (this will change in John). As Raymond Brown asks, why must anyone assume that "'my Father' implies a more intimate relationship to God than 'your Father'?"[60] Nonetheless, from everything we can see, the author of Mark firmly believes Jesus is God's son, a person of great authority, and he wants his readers to believe it too. But the "lunatic" of Lewis's argument, the megalomaniac who proclaims himself the preexistent equal of God, is not present there.[61] Even more, in every Gospel—including John, where Jesus is the most divine of all—Jesus differentiates himself from God.

He does so at least twice in Mark. First, a man approaches Jesus and asks, "Good teacher, what must I do to inherit eternal life?" Jesus responds, "Why do you call me good? No one is good but God alone" (Mark 10:17–18). Matthew, evidently struck by the implications of this response, revises both the question and the answer, as we can see via redaction criticism: "What good *deed* must I do to have eternal life?" the man asks, and Jesus responds, "Why do you ask me about *what is good*?" (Matt. 19:16–17). Thus Matthew retains the Markan vocabulary "good" but removes any perceived separation between Jesus and God.

Second, when Jesus predicts the coming of the Son of Man, he says, "But of that day or hour no one knows, not even the angels in heaven, nor the Son, but only the Father" (Mark 13:32). Once again Matthew may have had a problem with this, since many ancient manuscripts of Matthew omit "nor the Son," removing with that phrase the possibility of Jesus's ignorance.[62] It's important

59. Eusebius, *Ecclesiastical History* 1.3.3–7.

60. Raymond E. Brown, *An Introduction to New Testament Christology* (New York: Paulist, 1994), 85.

61. See Lewis, *Miracles* (1947; repr., New York: Macmillan, 1960), 109, for another form of the "liar, lunatic, or Lord" argument using the term "megalomania."

62. Bruce Metzger, *A Textual Commentary on the Greek New Testament* (Stuttgart: Deutsche Bibelgesellschaft/German Bible Society, 1994), 51–52.

to recognize that the Christologies of Mark and Matthew sometimes differ; they do not always speak with one voice. Readers who confine themselves to Lewis's work would never know this.

Lewis was aware of passages in which Jesus differentiates himself from God, but to the best of my knowledge he never grappled with them in a way that would reveal an inkling of the complexities of first-century Christology.[63] In this he might be more Catholic than the pope—a cliché Lewis the Belfast Protestant would not appreciate—since pre- and post-Nicene fathers like Chrysostom and Augustine readily acknowledged them. The fathers were fully aware of biblical ambiguities about the person of Christ, and they had to treat them in detail in order to make their case among competing views.

I'm convinced Lewis never intended to suppress scriptural evidence or to deceive anyone through his "liar, lunatic, or Lord" argument. Instead, I think that, like many other Christians before and since, he read the Gospels through an obscuring post-Nicene lens. As Albert Schweitzer once observed, the Jesus we see in the Gospels is more a reflection of us than him.[64] No one is exempt from reading their own bias into Scripture.

Jesus doesn't call himself "Son of God" in Matthew or Luke, either, although in Matthew, as opposed to Mark, several human beings do hail him as such in his earthly life: his disciples in Matthew 14:33 and Peter in Matthew 16:16. Satan does, too, in the temptation scene before the public ministry begins. Nonetheless, Jesus's divine sonship in Matthew and Luke "is everywhere presupposed."[65] Presupposed, but not exposed, to borrow John A. T. Robinson's felicitous phrase, since Matthew and Luke mimic their predecessor Mark in keeping Jesus quiet about his divine nature before he rises from the dead.[66]

There is one exception to this silence in Matthew and Luke, however—the "thunderbolt fallen from the Johannine sky,"[67] Matthew 11:27 and its parallel

63. Lewis to Marg-Riette Montgomery, Dec. 16, 1952, *CL*, 3:266, briefly notes, "Our Lord said 'He that hath seen Me hath seen the Father', but also 'My Father is greater than I'" (John 14:9, 28).

64. Schweitzer, *The Quest of the Historical Jesus*, trans. W. Montgomery (London: Adam and Charles Black, 1910), 4.

65. John A. T. Robinson, "The Last Tabu? The Self-Consciousness of Jesus," in *The Historical Jesus in Recent Research*, ed. James D. G. Dunn and Scot McKnight (Winona Lake, IN: Eisenbrauns, 2005), 558.

66. Robinson, "The Last Tabu?," 559.

67. Robinson, "The Last Tabu?," 559.

passage Luke 10:22: "All things have been delivered to me by my Father; and no one knows the Son except the Father, and no one knows the Father except the Son and anyone to whom the Son chooses to reveal him." With this example my own readers may accuse me of being Jesuitical, and they may be right: I say that Jesus never calls himself the "Son of God" in Matthew and Luke, but here he calls himself the Son, and this clearly in close relation to God the Father. Isn't that putting too fine a point on it? Since it's the only place in the Synoptics where Jesus uses such language, I think it safe to say that Jesus does not "go about" talking of himself as Son of God in the Synoptics. One swallow does not make a summer. It does, however, fly us with some velocity to the shore of deep Johannine waters, where our lightly laden swallow will join a flock.

Levels of Divinity in the Judaism of Jesus

Before diving into the Gospel of John, we must try to understand what "Son of God" might have meant to Jews in the first century. In the modern Western world, calling someone "Son of God" would be shocking, just as Lewis said it was regarding Jesus. Such is the long reach of the Christological councils, which extends even to those who have never heard of them. But it's exaggerating only a little to say that, in Jesus's world, calling someone "Son of God" was dull as ditchwater, and most of the time it would attract just about as much attention. Nevertheless, as G. K. Chesterton quipped, those who trouble themselves to examine it under a microscope will find that even ditchwater teems with quiet fun.[68] We'll see the same hold true for the phrase "Son of God" when we analyze it in its ancient context.

"It is well to remind ourselves that calling someone 'son' in relation to God is ambiguous," writes Raymond Brown. "It need not mean . . . that one has God's own nature, but may connote only a special relationship to God."[69] Jewish texts offer multiple examples of how any good person could be a son of God. In Wisdom 2:18, being righteous pairs with being God's son. In Sirach 4:10, someone who takes care of widows and orphans "will be like a son of the Most High."[70] Philo of Alexandria, the great Jewish philosopher and

68. Maisie Ward, *Gilbert Keith Chesterton* (1942; repr., Lanham, MD: Sheed & Ward, 2005), 546.

69. Brown, *Introduction to New Testament Christology*, 80.

70. Lewis knew the so-called Apocrypha and Pseudepigrapha (even 1 Enoch), as evidenced in his essay "The World's Last Night," 43. I use these books to illustrate the concept "Son of God," first because they represent the same Second Temple Judaism

contemporary of Jesus, writes, "those who do what is virtuous and pleasing to nature are sons of God."[71] Philo uses the Hebrew Scriptures to support his point. Those who "live in knowledge of the One [God] are rightly called sons of God, as even Moses acknowledges when he says, 'You are sons of the Lord God' [Deut. 14:1] and 'God who begat you' [Deut. 32:18] and 'Isn't he himself your father?' [Deut. 32:6]." Furthermore, Philo says, those who aren't yet fit to be called a son of God may be brought into that state under the wings of God's first-born, the Logos—on whom more shortly.[72]

Whole groups of ordinary people, including the nation of Israel, as Philo saw in Deuteronomy 14:1, may also be called sons and daughters of God (Wisd. of Sol. 9:7, with daughters explicitly stated in the Greek), and most particularly the nation's kings (see Pss. 2, 89, and 110 in the Greek).[73] Adela Yarbro Collins explains, "In Jewish tradition . . . the two ideas, king of Israel and Son of God, are equivalent."[74] Jews shared this idea in common with their pagan neighbors, but for Jews the royal Son of God was not himself divine. By far the most famous Son of God in Jesus's lifetime was the Roman emperor Augustus. Surprisingly, Philo does not dispute his right to the title, perhaps because both Jews and Greeks could call any good person a son of God.[75] Therefore, as James D. G. Dunn sums it up, "In the first century AD 'Son of God' and 'God' were used much more widely in reference to particular individuals than is the case today."[76]

Luke also uses "Son of God" in a flexible way, as seen in his version of a dispute between Jesus and some Sadducees. The Sadducees challenge Jesus with a question about a hypothetical woman who marries seven brothers in

---

as the Gospels, and second because some of them are part of the Septuagint (LXX), the Greek Bible that was the Scripture of the early church, including the authors of the Gospels. See Timothy Michael Law, *When God Spoke Greek: The Septuagint and the Making of the Christian Bible* (Oxford: Oxford University Press, 2013).

71. *On the Special Laws* 1.318.

72. *On the Confusion of Tongues* 145–146.

73. Adela Yarbro Collins and John J. Collins, "King as Son of God," in *King and Messiah as Son of God: Divine, Human, and Angelic Messianic Figures in Biblical and Related Literature* (Grand Rapids: Eerdmans, 2008), 1–24, 55–58.

74. Adela Yarbro Collins, "Mark and His Readers: The Son of God among Jews," *Harvard Theological Review* 92 (1999): 406.

75. Adela Yarbro Collins, "Mark and His Readers: The Son of God among Greeks and Romans," *Harvard Theological Review* 93 (2000): 99. Philo, *On the Embassy to Gaius* 143–151.

76. Dunn, *Christology*, 18.

turn. Whose wife will she be in the resurrection? Jesus calls the question moot because "the sons of this age" marry, but the ones deemed worthy of that age do not. They are equal to angels, and "they are sons of God, being sons of the resurrection" (20:27–36). That is, Luke's Jesus implies that all resurrected humans will be "sons of God." And they are not the only ones who become sons of God by virtue of their resurrected status. Paul says the same thing about Jesus. The beginning of Paul's letter to the Romans announces that Jesus descended from David according to the flesh but was "determined Son of God in power according to the spirit of holiness by resurrection from the dead" (1:3–4). Paul never mentions Jesus's conception by the Holy Spirit or birth to a virgin anywhere in his work. In Romans, he is determined Son of God when he is resurrected.[77]

We haven't yet examined the application of the word "God" to Jesus, but we must do so as we approach the Gospel of John. Lewis wrote that Jesus went about "talking as if He was God." Again, this would be eccentric in our time, but it was less so at the time of Jesus, even when we confine ourselves to Jewish texts. There were levels of divinity in the ancient world rather than the stark dualism Lewis assumes, not only among the Greeks but also among the Jews. In a passage broadcast in the BBC radio talks but not included in the booklets that became *Mere Christianity*, Lewis notes that someone might say Jesus didn't go about saying he was God, but his followers did. "But that's only shifting the difficulty. They were Jews too: the last people who would invent such a thing, the people who had never said anything of the sort about Moses or Elijah." Later he writes that Jews, in contrast to pagans, set an "absolute chasm" between God and humanity, and only Jews could have "told the stories they told about Moses & Elijah and yet left these persons absolutely, sheerly human."[78]

Lewis did well to omit these words from his book, because some Jews did not leave Moses "sheerly human." Philo bristles at the claims of the Roman emperor Gaius Caligula to divinity, writing, "Sooner could God change into a man than a man into God," but when Philo reads Exodus 7:1, he comments,

77. Here, too, there is no definite article; Jesus is "Son of God," not "the Son of God." The translation and interpretation of this verse is disputed. Martin Hengel could write, "More has been written about [Rom. 1:3–4] than about any other New Testament text." Hengel, *The Son of God: The Origins of Christology and the History of Jewish-Hellenistic Religion* (Philadelphia: Fortress, 1976), 59. See also Farrer, who compares the Christology of Rom. 1:4 and Phil. 2 in "Bultmann and All That," 147–49.

78. Walter Hooper, *C. S. Lewis: A Companion and Guide* (London: HarperCollins, 1996), 308; Lewis to Mr. Yoxall, Dec. 28, 1949, *CL*, 2:1013.

"The Lord said to Moses, 'See, I have made you like God to Pharaoh.'"[79] Philo expands upon Moses's divinity, adding that he was called "God and king of the whole nation."[80] Nor does Philo reserve the designation "God" for Moses. It could apply to anyone. Moses was bold enough to say that "the man who is wholly possessed with the love of God and who serves the living God alone is no longer man, but God." Granted, Philo qualifies what this godhood means: "That said, he is the God of people, not of nature, so that he may leave to the father of all to be the king and God of gods."[81] The superior person is to humanity what God is to the cosmos, just as Moses is God of his own body and the passions of his soul, all of which he subjects to himself. Moses does not truly become God any more than a counterfeit coin is genuine.[82] Nonetheless, Philo does what Lewis claims no Jew ever did or could do: he calls Moses and other human beings God.

Philo propounds various levels of divinity for many people. Abraham becomes "one with the angels."[83] Both Abraham and Moses become immortal, and Moses's soul becomes divine. Moses's brother, the high priest Aaron, is exalted in a complicated exegesis of Scripture. Philo reads Greek Leviticus 16:17 as "every man will not be (a man) in the tent of meeting."[84] If the high priest is not a man in the tent of meeting, Philo notes, neither is he God, because he serves God. Therefore, he is neither God nor man but something else entirely, hovering in the rarified space between. Nor is this lofty status unique to Aaron the high priest. Any refined person is neither God nor human because of their great virtue.[85] Anyone who is filled with God "is said to come

79. The difference between Philo's treatment of Augustus's and Caligula's divine claims seems to be that Philo considered the former a great benefactor, while the latter was quite the opposite.

80. See *Embassy to Gaius* 118; *On the Sacrifices of Cain and Abel* 9; *On the Life of Moses* 1.158.

81. *That Every Good Person Is Free* 43.

82. *Sacrifices* 9; *That the Worse Attacks the Better* 160–162.

83. *Sacrifices* 5.

84. *On Dreams* 2.230–234. Philo and the early Christians shared the same Scriptures, the Greek Septuagint, which sometimes differs significantly from the Hebrew.

85. Interpretation of Philo on this subject is disputed. An excellent treatment of the topic in general is Richard Bauckham, "Moses as 'God' in Philo of Alexandria: A Precedent for Christology?," in *The Spirit and Christ in the New Testament and Christian Theology*, ed. I. Howard Marshall, Volker Rabens, and Cornelius Bennema (Grand Rapids: Eerdmans, 2012), 246–65.

near God in a kind of family relation, for having given up and left behind all mortal kinds, he is changed into the divine, so that such men become kin to God and truly divine."[86]

Philo was not the first Jew to identify Moses with God; the second-century BCE playwright Ezekiel the Tragedian beat him to it. In one of Ezekiel's plays, Moses dreams that he is on Mt. Sinai. God on his throne beckons him, hands Moses his scepter and crown, and exits the scene. The stars fall on their knees before the enthroned Moses, and he wakes up.[87] In this vision, Moses has taken the place of God. He holds all power, and the heavens worship him. In other words, in the dream, at least, he is God. Neither is Philo the only Jew to confer the title "God" on a living human being, as the prophet Isaiah calls a newborn baby *El gibbor*, "mighty God" (Isa. 9:6). Within Isaiah's original context, the baby may have been Hezekiah. Christians have claimed it was Jesus, and as much as that may be so in later Christological interpretation, Isaiah surely had someone in mind when he wrote it.

What we have seen so far demonstrates several important truths. First, devout Jews could conceive of various levels of divinity. Second, any human might attain one of those levels and be called God—even though Philo thought that few in fact would. Third, such beliefs were compatible with what Lewis called "monotheism." Today it is better known that ancient Jews were not monotheistic in the way Lewis understood the word,[88] but he held that conviction honestly, as we can see from a page he marked in his copy of Frederic Kenyon's *The Bible and Modern Scholarship* (1948). Kenyon explains the significance of the Ras Shamra discoveries, which include stories about the Canaanite gods El, Asherah, and Baal. He notes that Canaanite mythology "offers some parallels with Hebrew beliefs, but the differences are more marked. Its polytheism . . . contrasts strongly with the Hebrew monotheism of the worship of Jehovah. So far from providing an origin for Hebrew religion, it brings out

86. Philo, *Questions on Exodus* 2.29. This work is extant only in Armenian. *Questions and Answers on Exodus*, trans. Ralph Marcus, Loeb Classical Library 401 (Cambridge, MA: Harvard University Press, 1953), 70. I am indebted to David Runia for this reference and much else on the topic. See D. T. Runia, "God and Man in Philo of Alexandria," *Journal of Theological Studies* 39 (1988): 48–75, esp. 69–70.

87. "Ezekiel the Tragedian," in Carl R. Holladay, *Fragments from Hellenistic Jewish Authors*, vol. 2: *Poets* (Atlanta: Scholars Press, 1989), 363–67.

88. Paula Fredriksen, "Mandatory Retirement: Ideas in the Study of Christian Origins Whose Time Has Come to Go," *Studies in Religion* 35, no. 2 (2006): 231–46.

the superiority of the latter even before the period of the great prophets."[89] Such statements, which divide polytheism from monotheism with a guillotine flash, to the unquestioned superiority of the latter, issuing from the likes of Sir Frederic Kenyon, who was director and principal librarian of the British Museum, president of the British Academy, a classicist and a papyrologist, would have been hard for Lewis to resist, even if he had wanted to.

Jesus's Claims to Divinity in the Gospel of John

We have seen ancient Jews apply the word "God" to people other than God. What about the idea of preexistence—that is, existing before the creation of the cosmos? In *Mere Christianity,* Lewis understands preexistence as a condition limited to the one God of Israel,[90] but at least some Jews prior to and contemporary with Jesus did not. To them, preexistence is not limited to God, and possessing it does not make one identical to God.

Someone may ask, "What about John 1:1?" But this verse, simple as it appears in English, is almost impossible to translate from Greek, and summoning it produces more heat than light.[91] Lewis never cites it to support his version of the trilemma, most certainly because it is in third-person narration, and the rules of the game require Jesus to say it himself. However, it is the first thing Lewis brings up when a correspondent asks him about the deity of Jesus.[92] Because it is an important verse in Christological controversies, and because Jesus does claim preexistence in first-person narration in John 8:58, we will look at it briefly now.

Logos, Wisdom, and Preexistence

Many English translations of John 1:1 read, "In the beginning was the Word, and the Word was with God and the Word was God." The verse looks clear, but nothing could be further from the truth. It bristles with thorny problems, and we must grasp one of the prickliest, the use of the Greek word here translated "Word," which is *logos.*

89. Frederic G. Kenyon, *The Bible and Modern Scholarship* (London: John Murray, 1948), 12–13.

90. Lewis, *Mere Christianity,* 51.

91. See David Bentley Hart, *The New Testament: A Translation,* 2nd ed. (New Haven: Yale University Press, 2023), 533–36, 550–52.

92. Lewis to Mr. Searles, May 7, 1960, *CL,* 3:1149.

Logos may be translated "word," which is acceptable but inadequate, because it holds a much broader range of meaning, beginning with the straightforward "spoken word," and then the more heady "reason or rationality" (compare: "*log*ic"), before launching into full philosophical flight in authors like Philo, who writes:

> To [God's] Logos, his chief messenger [Greek *archangelos*], highest in age and honor, the father of all has given the privilege to stand on the border and separate the creature from the creator. He [the Logos] pleads with the immortal as suppliant for afflicted mortality and acts as ambassador of the ruler to the subject. He rejoices in this privilege and affirms, "I stood between the Lord and you" [Deut. 5:5], neither unbegotten/uncreated [*agennētos*] as God, nor begotten/created [*gennētos*] as you are [plural], but midway between the two extremes, a pledge to both.[93]

To Philo, the Logos is God's oldest and most honorable figure, the chief messenger who mediates between the immortal, uncreated deity and mortal, created humanity, happily serving both like an ambassador between a ruler and his subjects. The Logos stands midway between God and humanity, paradoxically neither uncreated like God nor created like humanity. Philo characterizes the Logos as preexistent here and elsewhere. He writes, "God's firstborn, the Logos, . . . the beginning. . . . The Logos is the oldest/most important image of God."[94]

Philo also calls Wisdom "the first-born mother of all things" and explicitly identifies her with the Logos, saying, "Wisdom is the Logos of God."[95] It is important to look at these two figures in tandem.

Proverbs personifies Wisdom as a woman who is preexistent with God, and this is what she says about herself:

> The Lord created me at the beginning of his work,
> the first of his acts of long ago. Ages ago I was set up,
> at the first, before the beginning of the earth. (Prov. 8:22–23)

93. *Who Is the Heir* 205–206. Unless otherwise noted, translations are my own.

94. *On the Confusion of Tongues* 146–147; cf. *Conf.* 63; *On Agriculture* 51; *On Dreams* 1.215.

95. *Questions on Genesis* 4.97; *On Drunkenness* 30; *Allegorical Interpretation* 1.65. Cf. *On Dreams* 2.242–245.

In Proverbs 8:35, Wisdom says, "whoever finds me finds life," a clear parallel to John 1:4, "in him [the Logos] was life." The book of Sirach also has Wisdom present herself as preexistent and immortal: "Before the ages, in the beginning, he created me, and for all the ages I shall not cease to be" (24:9). In the Jewish book of Wisdom, the title character is not only preexistent but even *monogenēs*, or "unique" (7:22; 9:9), just like the Logos in John's Prologue (1:14).

The first verses of the Gospel of John imply that Jesus is the Logos, but decades before John was written, Paul had already identified Jesus with Wisdom, calling him "Christ the power of God and the Wisdom of God. . . . From [God] you are in Christ Jesus, who became Wisdom for us from God" (1 Cor. 1:24, 30). In other words, the preexistent Logos and preexistent Wisdom are identified with each other, and some Jews who followed Jesus, like Paul and John, identified Jesus with them. Jesus may be God, but that claim cannot rest on his preexistence, since preexistence doesn't make the Logos and Wisdom God.

Lewis should have been aware of the Jewish material behind John's Prologue. He learned about Philo's Logos as "Son of God" in Baron von Hügel's *Essays and Addresses on the Philosophy of Religion*, which he read and marked throughout by the early 1930s.[96] Rendel Harris had laid out the interconnections among Logos, Wisdom, and Jesus early in the twentieth century in a book that would have been easily accessible to him.[97] Lewis almost taps into Wisdom/Logos Christology in the essay "What Are We to Make of Jesus Christ?" where he cites Matthew 23:34 as an example of Jesus taking over the prerogatives of God: "This Man is sitting looking down on Jerusalem . . . and suddenly comes an extraordinary remark—'I keep on sending you prophets and wise men.' Nobody comments on it. And yet, quite suddenly, almost incidentally, He is claiming to be the power that all through the centuries is sending wise men . . . into the world."[98]

If Lewis had engaged in a little redaction criticism at this juncture and looked up the Lukan parallel to the verse, it might have transformed his thinking, for in Luke 11:49 Wisdom sends prophets and wise men into the world (see Wisd. of Sol. 7:27). Rendel Harris pointed this out in 1917, and so did Moffatt's *Theology of the Gospels*.[99] A British scholar of our day, James Dunn,

96. Friedrich von Hügel, *Essays and Addresses on the Philosophy of Religion*, series 1 (London: J. M. Dent and Sons, 1928), 80.

97. Harris, *Origin of the Prologue*.

98. Lewis, "What Are We to Make of Jesus Christ?," 38.

99. James Moffatt, *Theology of the Gospels*, 166–67. The next page discusses Philo, the Logos, and the Parables of Enoch. Lewis's annotations on the book stop on p. 144.

notes: "What pre-Christian Judaism said of Wisdom and Philo also of the Logos, Paul and others say of Jesus. The role that Proverbs, ben Sira [= Sirach], etc. ascribe to Wisdom, these earliest Christians ascribe to Jesus. That is to say . . . *Jesus was being identified as Wisdom*."[100] An action that Lewis thought must make Jesus equal to God, sending the wise into the world, does not. It makes him equal to Wisdom. Lewis didn't have to read Dunn, who wrote decades after his death, to make these connections. All of the primary texts were available to him, as well as experts like von Hügel, Moffatt, and Harris to interpret them.

Scholars have long wondered and argued about exactly what Wisdom and the Logos are.[101] Whatever else they may be, they aren't human beings, but Jewish literature contemporary with Jesus did identify at least two people, and another who may be some sort of person, as preexistent.

The first appears in the Testament of Moses, where Moses says about himself, "He designed and devised me, and he prepared me from the foundation of the world that I should be the mediator of his covenant" (1:14). The second, in Psalm 109:3 (in the Greek Septuagint), is a royal figure whom God brought forth "before the morning star." The third preexistent figure appears in the Book of Parables in 1 Enoch, probably dated to around the turn of the Common Era, just prior to the advent of Christianity.[102] This is the mysterious Son of Man. "In that hour that Son of Man was named in the presence of the Lord of Spirits, and his name, before the Head of Days. Even before the sun and the constellations were made, his name was named before the Lord of Spirits. . . . He was chosen and hidden in his presence before the world was created and forever" (1 En. 48:2–3, 6).[103] We will return to the phrase "Son of Man," a most important one to Jesus, and a most vexed one in biblical scholarship, at the end of this chapter.

100. Dunn, *Christology*, 167.

101. Thomas Tobin, "Logos," in *The Anchor Bible Dictionary*, ed. David Noel Freedman (New York: Doubleday, 1992), 4:351; cf. Daniel Boyarin, *Border Lines: The Partition of Judaeo-Christianity* (Philadelphia: University of Pennsylvania Press, 2004), 114.

102. See Paolo Sacchi, "The 2005 Camaldoli Seminar on the Parables of Enoch: Summary and Prospects for Future Research," in *Enoch and the Messiah Son of Man: Revisiting the Book of Parables*, ed. Gabriele Boccaccini (Grand Rapids: Eerdmans, 2007), 499–512, esp. 511.

103. Translation of George W. E. Nickelsburg and James C. VanderKam, *1 Enoch: A New Translation* (Minneapolis: Fortress, 2004), 62.

Inventing Scripture

The strongest scriptural support for the "liar, lunatic, or Lord" argument doesn't appear in Lewis's books but rather in his essay "What Are We to Make of Jesus Christ?" Ironically, he tethers it to the strangest thing he ever wrote on the topic. "[Jesus] says again, 'I am the begotten of the One God; before Abraham was, I am,' and remember what the words 'I am' were in Hebrew. They were the name of God, which must not be spoken by any human being."[104] The second half of Jesus's alleged statement, "before Abraham was, I am," comes from John 8:58. This verse is Lewis's strong suit, to which we shall return shortly. But the first half, "I am the begotten of the One God," presents an enigma. Jesus never says anything like it, either before John 8:58 or elsewhere in the Gospel of John or in the entire New Testament. Jesus uses a form of the Greek verb "begotten" about himself only once in all four Gospels (John 18:37), and when he does, it has nothing to do with his conception.

Astute readers of the King James Version may protest, but their concerns can be mollified by a quick detour on the translation of the Greek word *monogenēs*. *Monogenēs* means "unique" or "only," even though the KJV occasionally adds "begotten" to it. Why would the KJV do this? It goes back to Jerome's translation of *monogenēs*, "only," as the Latin *unigenitus*, "only begotten." His word choice was probably influenced by the fourth-century Christological controversies discussed above.[105] Jerome's usage made its way into the KJV in verses like John 1:14, 1:18, 3:16, 3:18, the only places in the Gospels where *monogenēs* refers to Jesus. But even they don't support Lewis.

I am not saying that Lewis made up words of Jesus to pass off as Holy Writ. But there is only one book from which orthodox Christians may legitimately draw to quote Jesus, and that is the New Testament. Lewis doesn't offer these words as his own paraphrase, but very clearly as "Jesus says," and the only record of the historical Jesus saying anything is the Gospels. When Lewis quotes the words of Jesus to make a historical argument about the person of Jesus, the Gospels are the only source to which he can appeal, and that is why I describe him as "inventing Scripture." Of course, Lewis is far from the first person to

104. Lewis, "What Are We to Make of Jesus Christ?," 39.

105. Dale Moody, "God's Only Son: The Translation of John 3:16 in the Revised Standard Version," *Journal of Biblical Literature* 72, no. 4 (1953): 213–19.

believe the Bible contains something it doesn't. To take a well-known example, many people think the dictum "God helps those who help themselves" appears in Scripture, but it does not.[106]

Lewis knew that even the best books contain misquotations, and readers should not accept a quotation without question; they should look it up and confirm it for themselves.[107] After taking his advice, I find that Lewis's phantom verse amplifies an important point. The heart of his "liar, lunatic, or Lord" argument is that Jesus "goes about" talking as if he were God. As we've seen so far, he does not. But Lewis may be convinced that he does this more than Scripture indicates because he has unwittingly concocted material that he then attributes to Jesus. Again, he is not alone in doing so. We haven't engaged Bono's claim in the epigraph to this chapter that Jesus said "I am God incarnate" for the excellent reason that Jesus never said any such thing. Lewis and Bono are very different people, but they have at least two things in common: both possess a superb creative imagination, and both have a sometimes questionable grasp of biblical Christology.

Lewis invents more Scripture in "What Are We to Make of Jesus Christ?" when he claims the following as an example of Jesus calling himself Son of God: "The moment at which the High Priest said to Him, 'Who are you?' 'I am the Anointed, the Son of the uncreated God, and you shall see Me at the end of all history as the judge of the universe.'"[108] Although certain elements of this statement do appear in his trial, Jesus never says any of it in the Gospels. The conversations—plural—differ from what Lewis said and from each another. Anyone can see this by employing a Gospel synopsis, a tool that was readily available in Lewis's day, but one he doesn't appear to have used. He marked up the article "The Synoptic Problem" in his Gore biblical commentary heavily, but he did not underline this sentence: "Even the most elementary student of the Synoptic Gospels should possess a 'synopsis' in which the text is arranged in parallel columns."[109] If he had acted on that directive and taken his own advice to hunt up quotations and read them in context, he would have found this:

106. https://tinyurl.com/2ahaw5ps.

107. Lewis to Sister Madeleva, June 7, 1934, *CL*, 2:142.

108. Lewis, "What Are We to Make of Jesus Christ?," 38.

109. F. D. V. Narborough, "The Synoptic Problem," in NCHS, part 3, 33.

Matt. 26:63–64
And the high priest said to him, "I exhort you by the living God, tell us if you are the Christ, the Son of God." Jesus said to him, "**You say so**. But I tell you, from now on you will see the Son of Man sitting at the right hand of the power and coming on the clouds of heaven!"

Mark 14:61–62
The high priest asked him and said, "Are you the Christ, the son of the Blessed?"

Jesus said, "**I am**, and you will see the Son of Man sitting at the right hand of the power and coming with the clouds of heaven!"

Luke 22:67–70
[They said] "If you are the Christ, tell us." He said to them, "**If I tell you, you won't believe, and if I ask, you won't answer**. But from now on the Son of Man will be sitting at the right hand of the power of God." All of them said, "Are you then the Son of God?" He threw back at them, "**You say that I am**."

John 18:19–21
Then the high priest questioned Jesus about his disciples and his teaching. Jesus answered him, "**I have spoken openly to the world. I have always taught in the synagogue and the temple where all the Jews gather. I have said nothing in secret.**[110] **Why do you question me?** Question the ones who heard what I said to them. They know what I said."

Only in Mark does Jesus affirm that he is Christ and Son of God, with a simple "I am," and not with the words Lewis puts into his mouth. But even if Jesus did say what Lewis said he did, the titles "the Anointed" (Christ/messiah) and "Son of . . . God" don't make him God, and they don't constitute blasphemy. What is the "blasphemy" that the high priest accuses him of, then? As Jesus continues (in the Synoptics but not in John), he alludes to "one like a Son of Man" (Dan. 7:13). This allusion is so important that I will look at it in detail at the end of the chapter.

Lewis puts more words into Jesus's mouth in "What Are We to Make of Jesus Christ?" He writes, "[Jesus] says, 'If you are ashamed of Me, if, when you hear this call, you turn the other way, I also will look the other way when

110. One of the many differences between John and the Synoptics is that John doesn't include the messianic secret. Here he seems purposely to refute it.

I come again *as God without disguise*'" (compare Mark 8:38; Luke 9:26). And another: "If anything whatever is keeping you from God *and from Me*, whatever it is, throw it away" (compare Matt. 5:29 and parallels).[111] Lewis probably knew he was paraphrasing the Gospels, but the italicized sections are supposals; Jesus never said anything like them, and nothing resembling them appears anywhere in the Bible. One might try to defend him by noting that the original audience of the essay was a Boys' Club.[112] Perhaps he was embellishing a bit for the young people? But that doesn't reflect the Lewis we know, the last person who would condescend even to children when he wrote about Jesus.

Another example of imaginary Scripture appears in *Reflections on the Psalms*, where Lewis claims that Jesus "denied all sin of Himself. (That, indeed, is no small argument of His Deity . . .)." Unless Jesus were God, Lewis continues, this "would be the arrogance of a paranoiac."[113] He cites no verse here because he can't; Jesus doesn't say that he is sinless. New Testament authors outside the Gospels do, including Paul, who writes, "He made the one who didn't know sin to be sin for us" (2 Cor. 5:21).

The bottom line is that Lewis has misled himself about what Jesus says. This is not an inconsequential error, as with his slight misquotation of von Hügel in *The Problem of Pain* (chapter 3). Instead, Lewis puts words into Jesus's mouth and lays them down as the precarious cornerstone of his "liar, lunatic, or Lord" argument.

Now is the time to remember what Lewis wrote about stories not reproducing themselves like mice. Sincerely believing that he recalls what Jesus said in the Gospels, Lewis's unconscious has been busy at work, and we, outside his mind at some critical distance, recognize how the words he attributes to Jesus mix up post-Nicene Christology with his own insistence that Jesus talks about himself as if he were God, even in the Synoptics. Discarding the new "Scripture" Lewis creates does not by itself invalidate his argument, but it does eliminate many of the biblical "proofs" to which he appeals.

"I Am"

Happily for Lewis, the second half of his quotation, "before Abraham was, I am" (John 8:58), supports his argument better than any other Scripture he

111. "What Are We to Make of Jesus Christ?," 41 (emphasis mine).

112. Ronald Selby Wright, ed., *Asking Them Questions: A Selection from the Three Series* (London: Oxford University Press, 1953), 8–9.

113. *Reflections on the Psalms*, 135–36.

submits as evidence, but even it is not as clear as he might think. "I am" has multiple meanings in the Gospels, and since Lewis read Greek, he must have known this.[114] In John 9:9 the man born blind uses it in its most simple form as the affirmative "It is I." In Mark 14:62, Jesus's response to the high priest in the trial scene above, it probably means no more than "yes." In John 18:5, with classic Johannine double entendre, Jesus employs it both in this way and with divine implications, simultaneously affirming his identity as Jesus of Nazareth and proclaiming the sacred name of God in its Greek form, *egō eimi* ("I am"), as the soldiers' involuntary prostration at the power of the name indicates. He may or may not be using it in both senses in John 8:58. Within the context of the passage Jesus claims preexistence, but as we've seen, being preexistent doesn't make anyone God with a capital *G*. However, since Jesus's foes pick up rocks to stone him, John almost certainly wants to portray Jesus as applying the name of God to himself, and his audience as hearing it that way. If this is true, and I think it is, Jesus does claim divinity here, and Lewis has a legitimate verse to support his argument.

He alludes to another verse in John that initially appears to make a stronger case than it actually might, John 10:30, "The Father and I are one."[115] Read through a post-Nicene lens, the verse seems unambiguous. Nevertheless, ancient Christians later deemed heretical were able to put it to good use, some arguing for the unity of Jesus's will and others for the unity of his person.[116] The verse is not self-interpreting—but nothing in the Bible or any other text is. John 10:30 does associate Jesus very closely with God, but at the same time it leaves some latitude for determining how that might work.

The larger context of John 10:30 underscores what this chapter has argued about ancient definitions of "Son of God" and "God." When "the Jews" say they want to stone Jesus because he is making himself a god (10:33), Jesus quotes Psalm 82:6: "Is it not written in your law, 'I said, you are gods'? If those to whom the word of God came were called gods—and Scripture cannot be annulled—can you say that the one whom the Father has sanctified and sent into

114. Philip B. Harner, *The "I Am" of the Fourth Gospel: A Study in Johannine Usage and Thought* (Philadelphia: Fortress, 1970); David Mark Ball, *"I Am" in John's Gospel: Literary Function, Background, and Theological Implications* (Sheffield: Sheffield Academic Press, 1996). Lewis overinterprets it in a letter to Rhona Bodle, Feb. 10, 1949, *CL*, 2:915–16, where he equates the "I am" of John 8:58 with the "I am" of Mark 14:62.

115. *Problem of Pain*, 11.

116. Raymond E. Brown, *The Gospel according to John I–XII* (Garden City, NY: Doubleday, 1966), 403 n. 30.

the world is blaspheming because I said, 'I am a Son of God'?" (10:34–36).[117] John's Jesus knew that human beings were called sons of God, and sometimes even gods, in the Hebrew Scriptures.[118]

Jesus calling himself Son of God, even if this title doesn't mean "God," brings up another question: How kosher was it to apply such titles to yourself? In the ancient world, the answer was "not very." Just as it would be today, exalting oneself was a faux pas at best; better to wait for someone else to do it for you. But even though Jesus does say these things about himself in John, he also insists that he doesn't: "If I testify about myself, my testimony is not true. There is another who testifies on my behalf, and I know that his testimony to me is true" (5:31–32). Entities who testify on his behalf include John the Baptist, the works God has given Jesus to do, the Scriptures, and God. In a conflict with his fellow Jews, Jesus notes: "If I glorify myself, my glory is nothing. It is my Father who glorifies me, he of whom you say, 'He is our God'" (8:54–55).[119]

In sum, we have seen that an ancient Jew could be called preexistent and not be God, Son of God and not be God, and even God and not be God. That is not to say that those words *can't* indicate divinity in first-century Judaism but only that they don't *have* to. In the first century, they may indicate a level of divinity but not union with God per later Christian creedal definitions. Any righteous person may be a son of God. Some righteous people may be called God, and a few share preexistent status with the Jesus of John, if not the Jesus of the Synoptics. But none of these things makes the person so designated *homoousios*, "one in being with the Father," equal to God in the post-Nicene sense that Lewis implies. Even without deeming the Gospels "legend," there are legitimate alternatives outside the box that Lewis tried to build around his trilemma.

The most convincing verse Lewis cites is John 8:58, "before Abraham was, I am." If the Gospel of John accurately reports the words of Jesus, and if we understand "I am" as Jesus claiming to be equal with God, then Jesus does claim to be God. But this still doesn't confirm the "liar, lunatic, or Lord" argument, because Jesus also distinguishes himself from God in John, most famously in 14:28, where he says that "the father is greater than I." Trying to square this

117. John 10:33 is translated "a god," since the Greek does not have the definite article. The same is true of 10:36, "a Son of God."

118. As we have seen above regarding Isa. 9:6's *El gibbor*. See also 1 Sam. 28:13, where the shade of Samuel is described as god (*elohim*).

119. See M. David Litwa, *Desiring Divinity: Self-Deification in Early Jewish and Christian Mythmaking* (Oxford: Oxford University Press, 2016).

circle has defeated great minds for millennia.[120] Furthermore, Jesus's divine self-disclosure in John differs drastically from what he says in the Synoptics. Jesus just doesn't talk about himself like that there, and Lewis rarely recognizes and never acknowledges the importance of the difference. As chapter 2 of this book explains, this propensity may stem at least in part from his reading Moffatt's *Theology of the Gospels* early in his adult Christian life.

If Lewis wants to read the Gospel of John as historical "reportage," as he notes in "Modern Theology and Biblical Criticism," he must also grapple with how it differs from the Synoptics. Even amateur historians must acknowledge where their sources don't cohere with each another. As a nineteenth-century scholar of John wrote, "When two different accounts having to do with the same thing are, in their different elements, so mutually related that both of them cannot be historically true in the same respect, we can only accept the one that has the preponderance of historical probability on its side."[121] Ignoring this rule is a major flaw in Lewis's apologetics with serious implications that he can disregard for only so long. Like a man who denies the existence of gravity as he falls through the air, he is headed for the inevitable crash at the bottom. Even if Jesus does claim divine status in John 8:58, Lewis must deal with the competing—and sometimes opposing—words of Jesus in the other Gospels, which he never does. He either ignores or harmonizes them.

Harmonizing in Gethsemane

His harmonizing blind spot is unmistakable in a letter to a Mrs. Jones about the relationship between Jesus and God. Lewis reflects on Jesus's prayer in

120. Cf. Theodore of Mopsuestia: "If one attentively considers the words of our Lord, he will find that many of them are varied in their meaning. Some show his greatness, others his weakness and evidently, after a thorough examination, cannot be suitable to him." *Commentary on the Gospel of John*, ed. Joel C. Elowsky, Thomas C. Oden, and Gerald L. Bray, trans. Marco Conti, Ancient Christian Texts (Downers Grove, IL: IVP Academic, 2010), 5. Augustine, *Treatise on Faith and the Creed* 9.18, writes, "And, indeed, on this subject of the Father and the Son, learned and spiritual men have conducted discussions in many books, in which, so far as men could do with men, they have endeavored to introduce an intelligible account as to how the Father was not one personally with the Son."

121. F. C. Baur ("Über die Composition und den Charakter des johanneïschen Evangeliums," *Theologische Jahrbücher* 3 [1844], 398–99), quoted in Jörg Frey, "Ferdinand Christian Baur and the Interpretation of John," in *Ferdinand Christian Baur and the History of Early Christianity*, ed. Martin Bauspiess, Christof Landmesser, and David Lincicum (Oxford: Oxford University Press, 2017), 215.

the garden the night before his crucifixion, noting that, even though Jesus was one with God, he experienced the same human feelings as anyone else would under the circumstances. These feelings prompt Jesus to ask God, "Let this cup pass from me." At the same time, because his humanity and divinity were unified, his soul could answer, "Not my will but yours." Lewis continues: "The Matthew passage and the John passage both make clear this unity of will. The Matthew one gives in addition the human feelings."[122]

Here Lewis makes a mistake: he implies that Jesus prays for the removal of the cup (which signifies his torture and death) in John. However, this prayer never occurs in the Gospel. Lest anyone think that John didn't know about the prayer, internal evidence speaks loudly to the contrary. Before the Johannine Jesus enters the garden, he muses: "Now is my soul troubled. And what shall I say? Father, save me from this hour? No, for this purpose I have come to this hour" (12:27). In the garden itself, he asks Peter, "Am I not to drink the cup that the Father has given me?" (18:11). John's Jesus appears purposely to refute the Synoptic "let this cup pass from me." Once again, Lewis "remembers" Scripture that does not exist, and he doesn't register Scripture that does.

It may be churlish to fault the beleaguered man for his confusion, staggering as he was under a heavy weight of daily correspondence, all of which he answered. If Lewis were a Roman Catholic under consideration for sainthood, his martyrdom-by-letters might be a significant item in the pro-canonization column. But it is a telling mistake nonetheless, and it helps explain why he constructed the trilemma the way he did.

He continues: "God c[ould], had He pleased, have been incarnate in a man of iron nerves, the Stoic sort who lets no sigh escape Him. Of His great humility He chose to be incarnate in a man of delicate sensibilities who wept at the grave of Lazarus . . . sweated blood at Gethsemane. . . . If He had been incarnate in a man of immense natural courage, that w[ould] have been for many of us almost the same as His not being incarnate at all."[123] A piece of writing may do good in one context even if it fails in another. As spiritual counsel, one hopes it helped Mrs. Jones. But as an exposition of Scripture, it is deficient. First, Lewis makes the mistake about Jesus asking for the cup to be taken away in John. Then he imagines what he considers to be an off-putting Jesus, a "Stoic sort" who would bear up bravely under the prospect of crucifixion, an ideal figure no one could relate to. In contrast to this savior, Lewis quotes Luke 22:44, Jesus sweating blood. Now he has bottled himself up in an unfortunate exegetical

122. Lewis to Mrs. Frank L. Jones, Feb. 23, 1947, *CL*, 2:764. What Lewis says in this letter about the "will" and "feelings" of Jesus also echoes Gore, *Jesus of Nazareth*, 54.

123. Lewis to Mrs. Frank L. Jones, Feb. 23, 1947, *CL*, 2:764–65.

pickle. Jesus's prayer to the Father to remove the cup appears in all three Synoptic Gospels, but Luke removes the agonized emotion Jesus feels in Mark. For this reason and others, textual critics think the mention of Jesus's sweat like blood is not original to the Gospel.[124]

More important than the textual issue is the fact that the Jesus whom Lewis imagines and rejects actually *is* the Jesus of John's passion narrative, precisely the figure Lewis hypothesized, someone who never prays that the cup be taken away. Jesus hoots at the very thought of it in John 18:11. Lewis does see that "the human feelings" Jesus suffers in Matthew are not present in John, but (1) he doesn't recognize that John's Jesus actively rejects the cup prayer, and (2) he doesn't apply his insight to the big picture. Jesus's stoic control of himself in John's passion narrative is evident and widely acknowledged, and not just by modern scholars. John Chrysostom noticed that Jesus suffers mightily at Gethsemane in Matthew, but he doesn't suffer in the garden at all in John. Therefore, Chrysostom observes, Jesus appears less human in John's passion narrative than in Matthew's. But, he continues, John corrects this impression by having Jesus weep at the tomb of Lazarus, a passage that doesn't appear in Matthew. Jesus's tears over Lazarus in John prove that he really does share our human nature.[125]

That Lewis missed the stoic characterization of Jesus in John is astounding, especially given his reputation for sensitive reading as a literary scholar. It is a revealing moment. The differences between the Synoptics and John are clear, and he doesn't see them. There are two possible reasons why.

The first may go back to his reading Gore's *Jesus of Nazareth*. Gore, usually an astute observer of the differences between John and the Synoptics, drops the ball here. He waxes eloquent on Jesus's agony in the garden, "one of the most moving pictures of human history," quoting Hebrews 5:7, where Jesus prays with loud cries and tears to the one who can save him from death, but he never mentions the fact that the scene plays out quite differently in John.[126]

The second and more probable reason lies in Lewis's deep emotional attachment to Jesus's suffering in Gethsemane. In 1939, as he watched the inexorable approach of World War II, he told his friend Bede Griffiths that he would rather die than go through another war, but he took solace in thinking about Gethsemane, thankful every day that this scene, out of everything in the life of

124. Metzger, *Textual Commentary*, 51. See also Claire Clivaz, *L'ange et la sueur de sang (Lc 22,43–44) ou comment on pourrait bien encore écrire l'histoire* (Leuven: Peeters, 2010).

125. Chrysostom, *Homilies in John* 63.2.

126. *Jesus of Nazareth*, 109–10.

Jesus, had been preserved. Sixteen years later, Lewis tries to help a correspondent by reminding her of the passage: "Our Lord was afraid (dreadfully so) in Gethsemane. I always cling to that as a very comforting fact."[127] Matthew and Mark's picture of Jesus in Gethsemane comforted Lewis for decades, and his lived experience meditating on it may have led him to read it into John.

I am not the first to notice Lewis's harmonizing blind spot. In 1958 the Christian apologist Norman Pittenger took him to task for conflating the Synoptics and John to support the "liar, lunatic, or Lord" argument. I agree with Pittenger on this point, though not on the others he levels against Lewis. Like Chrysostom, Aquinas, Gore, Moffatt, Farrer, and—as one born out of due time—me, Pittenger knows that Jesus doesn't claim to be God in the Synoptics.[128] In his "Rejoinder to Dr Pittenger," Lewis remarks, "I could never see how one escaped the dilemma of [either God or a bad man] by confining oneself to the synoptics." He supports his statement with two examples. First, he writes, "of course all three synoptics" have Jesus calling himself Son of God in his trial.[129] We have seen that they do not. The second is the audacity of Jesus in forgiving sins not against himself, but against others, an argument he also uses in *Mere Christianity* and "What Are We to Make of Jesus Christ?"[130] A discussion of that passage will bring this chapter to a close.

"Your Sins Are Forgiven": Jesus as Son of Man

We begin with Mark 2, where Jesus heals a paralytic and tells him his sins "are forgiven." It is important to note the passive voice. He doesn't use the active voice, "I forgive your sins," but the passive, "Your sins *are forgiven*" (2:5), which distances the action from Jesus. As E. P. Sanders observes, "[Jesus] was

127. Lewis to Bede Griffiths, May 8, 1939, *CL*, 2:258; to Mary Willis Shelburne, April 2, 1955, *CL*, 3:590.

128. Norman Pittenger, "Apologist versus Apologist: A Critique of C. S. Lewis as 'Defender of the Faith,'" *Christian Century*, Oct. 1, 1958, 1105–6. Moffatt, *Theology of the Gospels*, 132–33. I read Brant Pitre's treatment of the "Liar, Lunatic, or Lord" argument in his book *The Case for Jesus: The Biblical and Historical Evidence for Christ* (New York: Image, 2016) long after I published the first version of this chapter. While he and I agree on some things, we disagree about Jesus calling himself God/divine in the Synoptics. Detailing our disagreement on this topic could easily fill another book.

129. "Rejoinder to Dr Pittenger," in *God in the Dock: Essays on Theology and Ethics*, ed. Walter Hooper (Grand Rapids: Eerdmans, 1970), 180.

130. "Rejoinder to Dr Pittenger," 179–80.

presumably speaking for God (note the passive), not claiming to be God."[131] Lewis overlooks the passive voice, as we can see most clearly in "What Are We to Make of Jesus Christ?" Here he insists that Jesus calls himself God in the Gospels not just a few times but "throughout the whole thing. For instance, He went about saying to people, 'I forgive your sins.'"[132] However, Jesus doesn't say this, so Lewis has once again misremembered Scripture, putting words into his mouth that Jesus never said. This is no small thing.

Lewis's thoughts on the passage, to borrow the phrasing of Nicholas Perrin, run as follows: "Jesus forgives, no one can forgive but God alone, therefore Jesus must be God."[133] But the second premise, "no one can forgive but God alone," may not be correct when put in its first-century context. Redaction criticism is useful to help sort it out.

When Matthew retells Mark's story, he omits the words "Who can forgive sins but God alone?" perhaps because he realized they were incorrect. In Mark and Matthew, another person had been forgiving sins energetically before Jesus appeared on the scene: John the Baptist, whose baptism served precisely that purpose (Mark 1:4; Matt. 3:11). Matthew also makes an important addition to Mark: he writes that the crowds "glorified God, who had given such authority to *human beings*" (Matt. 9:8). Thomas Aquinas highlights these very words as an example of how the Synoptic Gospels portray Jesus as human, not divine.[134] Even in John, Jesus's disciples receive the power to forgive the sins of those who haven't sinned against them:

Matthew 9:2–3, 8
When Jesus saw their faith, he said to the paralytic, "Take heart, child, your sins are forgiven." And behold, some of the scribes said among themselves, "He blasphemes."

They glorified God, **who had given such authority to human beings.**

Mark 2:5–7, 12
When Jesus saw their faith, he said to the paralytic, "Child, your sins are forgiven."

There were some scribes sitting there, questioning in their hearts, "Why does he speak like this? He blasphemes. **Who can forgive sins except God alone?" . . .**

131. E. P. Sanders, *Jesus and Judaism* (Philadelphia: Fortress, 1985), 273–74.
132. "What Are We to Make of Jesus Christ?," 38–39.
133. Nicholas Perrin, *Jesus the Temple* (Grand Rapids: Baker Academic, 2010), 140.
134. Thomas Aquinas, *Commentary on John* 1.67.

Everyone was amazed and glorified God, saying, "We've never seen anything like this!"

John 20:22–23

He breathed (on them) and said to them, "Receive the holy spirit. Those whose sins you forgive are forgiven them; those you retain, are retained."

John the Baptist and Jesus's disciples weren't the only ones who acted as human conduits of God's forgiveness; so did the Jewish priests. Leviticus describes what God told them to do in language similar to Mark 2:5: "The priest will make atonement for you, for the sin you committed, *and you will be forgiven*" (Lev. 4:35). The passive voice—the same one Jesus uses in the Gospels—is repeated to the same purpose throughout Leviticus 4–5. The fact that it is priests who parley God's forgiveness may be the impulse behind the scribes' dismay in Mark and Matthew: Jesus was taking for himself the role of a priest, even though he wasn't one.[135] The scribes may have been upset because Jesus was usurping not the power of God but the power of the priests in the Jerusalem temple, making himself what N. T. Wright calls "a one-person Temple substitute."[136]

In response to his critics, Jesus doesn't say he has authority to forgive sins because he is Son of God, but because he is Son of Man: "So that you may know that the Son of Man has authority on earth to forgive sins . . ." (Mark 2:10). Son of Man is Jesus's favorite self-designation, leading Lewis to say that it was the "description of Himself which He delighted in" most.[137]

Generations of scholars have debated whether or not Jesus actually called himself Son of Man, but we may ignore them, since the self-imposed parameters of this chapter limit us to taking the Gospels at face value. Over time the phrase developed different meanings, and sometimes it can be hard to tell which one is intended. The most common meaning of "Son of Man" in the Hebrew Scriptures is "human being," as occurs often in Ezekiel. Jesus probably uses the phrase in this sense in Mark 2:10 and Matthew's parallel,

135. James D. G. Dunn, *The Partings of the Ways: Between Christianity and Judaism and Their Significance for the Character of Christianity* (London: SCM, 1991), 59–61.

136. N. T. Wright, "Jesus' Self-Understanding," in *The Incarnation: An Interdisciplinary Symposium on the Incarnation of the Son of God*, ed. Stephen T. Davis, Daniel Kendall, and Gerald O'Collins (Oxford: Oxford University Press, 2002), 57. Cf. Sanders, *Jesus and Judaism*, 273–74.

137. *Reflections on the Psalms*, 134.

especially in light of Matthew's comment about God giving such authority to human beings.

It took on additional meaning before the time of Jesus, particularly in Daniel 7 and the Parables of Enoch. In Daniel "one like a Son of Man" appears with the clouds as an exalted figure who receives dominion and power from God. He represents the entire nation of Israel, perhaps as its "prince," the archangel Michael.[138] He is "like a Son of Man" in Daniel because he looks like a human being in the vision, but in the Parables of Enoch he becomes a divine figure. Here (but not in Daniel) the Son of Man is preexistent.

Jesus uses "Son of Man" in its Danielic sense at least twice. The first is Mark 13:26, when he speaks to four disciples privately with an allusion to Daniel 7:13: "Then they will see the Son of Man coming on clouds with great power and glory." If Jesus is referring to himself, he lays claim to some sort of exalted status, though not equality with God, since the Son of Man in Daniel 7:13 seems to be subordinate to God.

Jesus also uses "Son of Man" in an exalted sense in his trial before the Sanhedrin (Mark 14:61–64). The high priest asks him, "Are you the Christ, the son of the Blessed?" Jesus responds, "I am, and you will see the Son of Man sitting at the right hand of the power and coming with the clouds of heaven!" Then the high priest, like the scribes in Mark 2, accuses Jesus of blasphemy. But the high priest, unlike the scribes, may have a point. Not because Jesus agrees he is messiah, which didn't constitute blasphemy at the time, though it could and did get you killed for insurrection.[139] Nor because he agrees he is son of the Blessed, because any good person can be a son of God. Nor because he uses the words "I am," which here mean only "yes." Rather, the blasphemy may be applying "Son of Man" to himself in its Danielic or even Enochic sense.[140] Lewis comes very close to recognizing this in "The World's Last Night" when he quotes Matthew 26:64 (KJV), "Hereafter shall ye see the Son of Man sitting on the right hand of power, and coming in the clouds of heaven." Lewis writes that "by these words" Jesus was "inviting crucifixion." However, Lewis

138. Dan. 7:13; 7:27; 10:21; 12:1.

139. See Adela Yarbro Collins, "The Charge of Blasphemy in Mark 14.64," *Journal for the Study of the New Testament* 26, no. 4 (2004): 379–401; and Darrell L. Bock, *Blasphemy and Exaltation in Judaism: The Charge against Jesus in Mark 14:53–65* (Grand Rapids: Baker Books, 1998).

140. Yarbro Collins, "Charge of Blasphemy," 399–400. The Enochic sense may underlie Jesus's words, but this possibility is speculative, whereas the allusion to Daniel is certain.

directs this remark not to Jesus calling himself "Son of Man" but to the idea of his return in glory.[141]

"Son of Man" sometimes indicates a higher Christology than "Son of God," even in John. Nathaniel lauds Jesus with titles that build to a crescendo: "Rabbi, you are the Son of God! You are the King of Israel!" But Jesus crowns the apex of the series himself: "You will see heaven opened and the angels of God ascending and descending upon the Son of Man!" (John 1:49–51). The titles progress from lesser to greater: Son of God, king of Israel (who is also a son of God, but one with a higher rank than the average son), and Son of Man.[142]

Jews at the time of Jesus held multiple levels of divinity, and it is important to understand that "Son of Man" never rose to the level of equality with God. Nonetheless, it could indicate a higher level of divinity than "Son of God," with the added bonus that Jesus actually did call himself "Son of Man" in all of the Gospels—even the Synoptics. If Lewis had said, "Jesus went about talking as if he were Son of Man," he would be asserting something much more likely to be true than "Jesus went about talking as if he were God." If he then explained why the phrase "Son of Man" could sometimes be so potent, he would have made a stronger case for his argument, though he still would not have proven it. But he did not, probably because its meaning continued to evolve over time. In the second century, "Son of Man" began a downward trajectory to indicate Jesus's humanity, while "Son of God" crisscrossed it on its way up to indicate Jesus's divinity.[143] Lewis's argument reflects these later meanings, what he calls the "dangerous sense" in *Studies in Words,* and thus he was lured into misreading the Gospels.[144]

We do know that Lewis read several books, scholarly and otherwise, that discussed the term. We also know how much he valued at least one of them. His good friend Sister Penelope, a prolific author on Scripture, sent him a copy of her new book *Windows on Jerusalem* in 1941, and his thank-you note high-

141. "The World's Last Night," 42.

142. Thanks to Pheme Perkins for her insights on this passage. See Daniel Boyarin, *The Jewish Gospels* (New York: New Press, 2012), 25–26, and Benjamin E. Reynolds, "The Use of the Son of Man Idiom in the Gospel of John," in *Who Is This Son of Man? The Latest Scholarship on a Puzzling Expression of the Historical Jesus,* ed. Larry W. Hurtado and Paul L. Owen (London: T&T Clark, 2011), 101–29. For an opposing view, see Larry Hurtado's summary essay in *Who Is This Son of Man?,* esp. 170.

143. Collins and Collins, "Jesus as Son of Man," in *King and Messiah,* 150–51.

144. *Studies in Words,* 13.

lights her treatment of "Son (p. 9)" as something that "particularly pleased" him.[145]

Sister Penelope writes that the phrase "sounds queer to our ears and queerer still in Greek, for there it is literally 'the son of the man,' which really means nothing. But in Semitic parlance the phrase was as clear as day: 'son of' conveys the idea of unity of nature rather than of derived existence, and the one-like-to-a-son-of-man in Daniel's vision meant simply The Man, the being pre-eminently human, who, as contrasted with the inferior beasts, stands for faithful Israel."[146] The passage begins well with the observation on how odd the phrase "son of the man" would sound to a Greek audience. But what follows is problematic. She does not explain what she means by "unity of nature" as opposed to "derived existence." It is true that the Semitic phrase "son of x" could name a member of a category. For example, "sons of the prophets" are "prophets" (2 Kings 6:1). But are they prophets through their "unity of nature" or their "derived existence"? More importantly, the figure in Daniel 7:13 is not "simply The Man, the being pre-eminently human"; he is "one *like* a Son of Man." Jewish apocalyptic literature uses this language to describe angels, whose phantasmagorical appearance stymies the visionary's ability to put it into words. The same language, "one like a Son of Man," introduces the exalted heavenly Jesus in Revelation 1:13, whose eyes were like a flame of fire, and whose face shone like the sun.

Lewis said that he got more out of *Windows on Jerusalem* than from "a good many Gifford Lectures," so it is not surprising if he unquestioningly accepted its definition of "Son of Man."[147] But he also read other books on the topic that should have alerted him to disputes about the phrase. Lewis underlined part of a sentence in Moffatt's *Theology of the Gospels* that could well have influenced Sister Penelope: "Thus the term *Son of Man*, in its messianic sense, is not wholly due to the pious reverence of the early Christians, who were

145. A Religious of the Community of St. Mary the Virgin, Wantage [Sister Penelope Lawson], *Windows on Jerusalem: A Study in the Mystery of Redemption* (London: Pax House, 1941). Lewis to Sister Penelope, April 10, 1941, *CL*, 2:479.

146. *Windows on Jerusalem*, 9. Sister Penelope correctly notes that Dan. 7–12 was written under the persecution of Antiochus IV Epiphanes, but she overinterprets the passage when she compares the Danielic Son of Man to the suffering servant of Isaiah, both of whom in her opinion experienced the "rhythm" of "mission-humiliation-exaltation." There is no suffering Son of Man in Dan. 7:13–14. She is right to compare this passage to the Parables of Enoch but wrong in claiming that the Son of Man figure there also suffered. *Windows on Jerusalem*, 10.

147. Lewis to Sister Penelope, April 10, 1941, *CL*, 2:479.

responsible for attaching divine significance to a name which in the original Aramaic upon the lips of Jesus meant no more than 'man' or 'some one,' or a self-designation. This we shall see later on."[148]

Unfortunately, Lewis may never have gotten "later on" in the book, since his annotations stop well before Moffatt returns to the topic and expands upon the meaning of the term in Daniel 7:13 and Enoch much as I did above. Moffatt even works through Matthew 9:2–3, 8 about the Son of Man forgiving sins almost exactly as I did, although he arrives at different conclusions.[149] But it is the simpler meaning of "Son of Man," the one Lewis underlined in Moffatt, that may have stuck with him and affected his perception of the phrase ever after.[150] He exhibits the influence of both Moffatt and Sister Penelope when he writes in *Reflections on the Psalms* that "'Son of Man' means Man, the Man, the archetypal Man."[151]

The same thing happened when he read a book by another one of his favorite authors, Rudolf Otto. Lewis counted Otto's *The Idea of the Holy* in his list of ten books that "did the most to shape [his] vocational attitude and [his] philosophy of life."[152] However, Otto's later work, *The Kingdom of God and the Son of Man* (1938), didn't seem to affect him much. Lewis marked the beginning and the end of it, but he left the large middle section on the Son of Man blank. Like Sister Penelope, James Moffatt, and me, Otto begins his discussion by noting that Son of Man can mean "human being." Then he investigates the phrase in the Parables of Enoch and later in relation to Jesus and his self-understanding. Otto describes Enoch's Son of Man as "not merely a strange, but a quite wonderful figure that arises, that of deity, highly exalted . . . therefore untouchable, unapproachable, far from the sinful world; foreseeing from eternity and revealing in his own time the mediating figure of the Son." The Son of Man in Enoch is among "the most lofty conceptions that have ever

148. *Theology of the Gospels*, 20. Lewis found much the same idea in his Gore commentary, although he did not mark this line: "Since in Aramaic 'Son of Man means simply 'man.'" P. Levertoff, "Special Introduction to the Gospel according to Matthew," in *NCHS*, part 3, 147.

149. *Theology of the Gospels*, 151–59.

150. What Lewis marks later in Moffatt's book is telling, as it emphasizes Jesus's "consciousness of divine sonship," e.g., 88, 130–31, 144 (see chapter 2 of this book). Lewis doesn't write anything in the book after p. 144.

151. *Reflections on the Psalms*, 133–34.

152. "Ex Libris," *Christian Century*, June 6, 1962, 719. See Adam Barkman, "Rudolf Otto, *The Idea of the Holy*," in *C. S. Lewis's List: The Ten Books That Influenced Him Most*, ed. David Werther and Susan Werther (London: Bloomsbury Academic, 2015), 113–34.

appeared in the realm of religion."[153] Otto argues that Jesus thought of himself as Son of Man in the Enochic sense but did not want anyone to know it. He doesn't use the term "messianic secret," but he does compare Jesus's reticence about his exalted identity in the Synoptics to the fact that the Son of Man in the Parables of Enoch was "hidden" with God until the time came to reveal him.[154] Only at the end of his life does Jesus reveal who he is to those outside his inner circle. Otto continues:

> But before the Sanhedrin, he confessed his Messianic rank in the form of the conception of the Son of Man as that was the familiar form in this case. He was the Christ, in so far as he was the one who would be the Son of Man:
>
> > ye shall see the Son of Man sitting at the right hand of the divine Power, and coming with the clouds of heaven.
>
> He was the Christ, i.e. the Elect of God, as the one destined to be the Son of Man. Enoch also would have had to answer in this way if the same question had been put to him in a similar situation.[155]

Lewis may not have read Moffatt and Otto's more considered thoughts on the Son of Man, but he did mark two sections on the term in his Gore commentary. L. Elliott Binns sees the Son of Man as a "personal being" and a preexistent judge in the Parables of Enoch. Lewis marks the next line: "Thus some features of the New Testament conception of the 'Son of Man' are foreshadowed in Enoch, which cannot be read back into Daniel."[156] W. O. E. Oesterley compares and contrasts the Son of Man figure in Daniel 7:13–14 with the one in the Parables of Enoch. He believes Daniel uses the phrase simply to say the figure looks like a man, but the Parables insist upon the figure's "transcendent character." Lewis underlines Oesterley's next sentence: "So that the use of the title 'the Son of Man' in the Synoptic Gospels is based on its use in the Book

153. Otto, *Kingdom of God*, 194, 212.

154. Otto, *Kingdom of God*, 219–25.

155. Otto, *Kingdom of God*, 225. Lewis read another scholarly book (or at least a section of it) by Otto's Marburg colleague Rudolf Bultmann, who understood the Son of Man in much the same way as Otto did. See Bultmann, *Theology of the New Testament*, vol. 1 (New York: Charles Scribner's Sons, 1951), 30. Lewis quotes and criticizes the section directly before Bultmann's remarks on the apocalyptic Son of Man, "MTBC," 155 (see chapter 7 of this book).

156. L. Elliott Binns, "Daniel," in *NCHS*, part 1, 551.

of Enoch, not on that in Daniel."[157] That is, the Synoptic Gospels use "Son of Man" to express some level of divinity.

Lewis's decision not to include such challenging material in his radio broadcasts is understandable, but he might have been more nuanced in print. In this critique, too, I was anticipated by Pittenger and rebutted by Lewis, who says such a tactic would be counterproductive, as it would confuse his readers.[158] One can acknowledge some wisdom in this response. A nonspecialist audience can take only so much detail. At the same time, apologists must transmit fundamental data as accurately as they can within such constraints. As Bultmann wrote, "no end is gained by making the matter seem easier than it really is." For better or worse, Bultmann would "rather frighten a reader away than attract one who wants something for nothing."[159]

Lewis's response to Pittenger was not the only time he sacrificed accuracy for a misguided attempt to help his audience navigate rough waters. We may remember his debate with Elizabeth Anscombe. By all accounts—including Lewis's own—Anscombe won. Describing it the next day in a letter to Wittgenstein, Anscombe writes that the moderator of the debate "started going for Lewis, who had said something about having written [*Miracles*] 'at a fairly popular level'—he reproached him almost in moral terms, that one should not, for the sake of popularizing, put up a bad argument."[160] Everything I've written here demonstrates how much I agree with that moderator. Wearing his apologist hat, Lewis calls himself a "translator" of Christianity.[161] He wants to speak to his audience in their own language, but he does not always interpret his base text correctly. Therefore, his translation sometimes falters.

157. W. O. E. Oesterley, "The Religious Background of the New Testament in Jewish Thought," in *NCHS*, part 3, 13.

158. Lewis, "Rejoinder to Dr Pittenger," 183.

159. Rudolf Bultmann, "View-Point and Method," in Dunn and McKnight, *Historical Jesus in Recent Research*, 55.

160. Anscombe to Ludwig Wittgenstein, Feb. 2, 1948, Collegium Institute Anscombe Archive at the University of Pennsylvania, Kislak Center for Special Collections, Rare Books and Manuscripts, box 13, file 2. Quoted in John Schwenkler, "Untempted by the Consequences: G. E. M. Anscombe's Life of 'Doing the Truth,'" *Commonweal*, Dec. 2, 2019. I appreciate Dr. Schwenkler's help with this reference. See also Jim Stockton and Benjamin J. B. Lipscomb, "The Anscombe-Lewis Debate: New Archival Sources Considered," *Journal of Inklings Studies* 11, no. 1 (2021): 35–57, and Lipscomb, *The Women Are Up to Something* (Oxford: Oxford University Press, 2022), 147–48.

161. Lewis, "Rejoinder to Dr Pittenger," 183.

Conclusion

Lewis's apologetics delight many readers. They are classics in the genre, and they have changed people's lives. But his most famous argument falls short, leaving itself open to legitimate criticism. Let me be clear: I have not been trying to challenge, much less reject, Nicene and Chalcedonian definitions of Jesus. Neither have I argued that the Gospels don't present Jesus as Son of God, or even God, because they do, even in the Synoptics.[162] The point under scrutiny here is whether or not the Gospels present Jesus *saying such things himself*, and if he does, asking what they mean in their first-century context. We have found that Jesus almost never self-identifies as divine in three out of four Gospels, something recognized long ago by such luminaries as Chrysostom, Augustine, and Aquinas. This fact says nothing one way or the other about the truth of Christ's divine nature. I may be a good cook, but my failure to go about publicly proclaiming it does not negate the reality of my culinary expertise.

All I have tried to do is show that Lewis's case from Scripture is not the proof of Jesus's divinity he thought it was. The biblical arguments supporting my thesis are not new, but the chapter does break new ground in studies of Lewis. It examines how he has used—and especially how he has misused—Scripture, particularly when he claims Jesus said something he is never recorded to have said and employs it as the foundation for an argument on the Jesus of history. But even if one overlooks the composition of these new words Lewis puts into the mouth of Jesus, he still ignores too many of the disconcerting realities of the Gospels, which are the only significant records of Jesus's earthly life we possess. He doesn't interpret Scripture in its historical context, so when Jesus actually does call himself "son" or imply he is God or preexistent, Lewis assumes anachronistic definitions of the terms. If the Gospels had articulated Jesus's relationship to God as clearly as Lewis thought they did, the Christological controversies in the first few centuries of the church need never have taken place. Therefore, the "liar, lunatic, or Lord" argument should trouble even Christians who accept the creeds, because it oversimplifies history and Scripture, the multifaceted Jewish realities of the first century, and the variant Christologies of the Gospels, especially the differences between the Synoptics and John regarding Jesus's divine self-disclosure. The argument's rickety foundations collapse in conversation with knowledgeable people. I hope this

162. For example, when Jesus calms the storm (Mark 4:35–41 and parallels), he does what only God can do: control the elements (see Job 26:12).

chapter will help remedy the problem, even though it too falls short of a full treatment of very complex material.

Lewis insisted to the end of his life that the "liar, lunatic, or Lord" argument was sound, but he didn't think it encompassed a full understanding of the divinity of Jesus. If Christianity were true, he said, it could never be "fully comprehensible."[163] On this point, Lewis and academic biblical scholars agree. No "proof" can ever settle the question. Like Bultmann, Lewis knew that relying on anything other than God for his "security" would make that thing an idol—a conviction poignantly expressed in his poem "The Apologist's Evening Prayer":

> From all my lame defeats and oh! much more
> From all the victories that I seemed to score;
> From cleverness shot forth on Thy behalf,
> At which, while angels weep, the audience laugh;
> From all my proofs of Thy divinity,
> Thou, who wouldst give no sign, deliver me.
> Thoughts are but coins. Let me not trust, instead
> Of Thee, the thumb-worn image of Thy head;
> From every thought, even from my thoughts of Thee,
> Oh thou fair Silence! fall and set me free.[164]

163. Lewis to Mary Neylan, Oct. 28, 1962, *CL*, 3:375.

164. *Collected Poems*, 328. He sent the poem to Sister Penelope in 1942 in response to her offer to pray for any "special needs" he might have.

3

BEYOND ALLEGORY

The Subtle Use of Scripture in the Chronicles of Narnia

9. ALLEGORY OR OTHERWISE?

Find out what the author actually wrote and what the hard words meant and what the allusions were to, and you have done far more for me than a hundred new interpretations or assessments could ever do.

—C. S. Lewis, *An Experiment in Criticism*[1]

Although Lewis's use of Scripture in the "liar, lunatic, or Lord" argument is questionable, he redeems it in the Chronicles of Narnia, where he does the best work of his life with the Bible. But not everyone agrees with me. An analogy from the first book in the series, *The Lion, the Witch and the Wardrobe,* can help explain why.

When the White Witch meets Edmund for the first time, she recognizes the danger he poses, especially when she learns that he is one of four siblings. Ancient lore had it that four "Sons of Adam and Daughters of Eve" would bring her reign to an end, so she acts quickly to cement her hold on Edmund, and Narnia, by plying him with enchanted Turkish delight, concealing her dark magic in the sticky sweet.[2]

Some people think of the Narniad itself as Turkish delight—a sort of literary sugar pill that entices unsuspecting children with fantasy but then delivers

1. C. S. Lewis, *An Experiment in Criticism* (Cambridge: Cambridge University Press, 1961), 121.

2. The White Witch acts the part of what Lewis calls "Venus infernal" (see his poems "Thou Only Art Alternative to God" and "Infatuation," in *Collected Poems,* 227, 411). Venus was associated with stickiness and gumminess, and this may be why Lewis has Edmund request, and the Witch provide, Turkish delight. The same witch tempts Digory to take an apple for himself in the western garden in *The Magician's Nephew*. In the poem "To G.M.," he writes about a garden with golden apples and "med'cinable gums." *Collected Poems,* 329. For how Lewis uses Venus in his work, see ch. 8 of Michael Ward, *Planet Narnia* (Oxford: Oxford University Press, 2008), 164–89.

a whopping dose of Christianity. Like Edmund when he finally realizes what the White Witch is up to, they feel shocked, used, and betrayed when they discover the heretofore hidden "biblical allegory." Several authors have played with this idea in their own books. Laura Miller offers a memoir-critique of the Chronicles in *The Magician's Book: A Skeptic's Adventure in Narnia*. Lev Grossman's trilogy *The Magicians,* written in part to poke fun at Narnia lovers, combines genuine homage with no small amount of amused disdain. Another trilogy, Philip Pullman's *His Dark Materials,* is perhaps the best-known and certainly the most anti-Christian jeremiad against the Narnia series.[3]

My own experience with the Chronicles is the opposite of theirs, and it probably speaks for more readers. Even as a child who knew almost nothing about the Bible, I recognized the major biblical references right away, and as I studied Scripture and reread the Chronicles, I delighted in finding richer meaning in the books every time I picked them up. Like Edmund's sister Lucy in *Prince Caspian,* I saw Aslan get bigger every time I returned to Narnia. Later still, after I read Lewis's *Experiment in Criticism,* I learned that this experience is one of the markers of a classic: it is capacious enough to grow with you, rewarding every rereading.[4]

What makes uncovering layers of meaning such a delight? To answer that question with another, who doesn't love the joy of discovery, of finding hidden treasure and making it one's own? As we do this, we enter more fully into the imaginative world of the author, and when that author is Lewis, the literary layers are no accident. He constructed them meticulously from his knowledge of over two thousand years of Western culture, so another benefit of uncovering deeper meaning in his books is the chance to enter into conversations that are so engrossing that they have continued for millennia.

Lewis was a master of ceremonies of such conversations, no less in the Chronicles of Narnia than in his books for adults. He incorporated an audacious variety of sophisticated material into his children's books, including the Jewish and Christian Scriptures, Greco-Roman and Norse mythology, ancient and medieval philosophy, astronomy, poetry, and drama, to name just a few.[5]

3. Laura Miller, *The Magician's Book: A Skeptic's Adventures in Narnia* (New York: Little, Brown, 2008); Lev Grossman, *The Magicians: A Novel* (New York: Viking, 2009); Philip Pullman, *His Dark Materials: The Golden Compass, The Subtle Knife, The Amber Spyglass* (New York: Everyman's Library, 2011).

4. Lewis expresses this realization to Greeves, Dec. 7, 1935, *CL,* 2:170.

5. In a talk entitled "What Did Tolkien Really Think about *Narnia*?" delivered Sept. 7, 2024, at the Undiscovered C. S. Lewis Conference at George Fox University

Part 3 of this book focuses on one literary layer of the Chronicles, its biblical references, but discussing this element by itself is a little dangerous, as it may perpetuate a misunderstanding that Lewis himself fought: the notion that the series is "biblical allegory." It is not, and to counter the claim we must first address four terms: *quotation, allusion, echo,* and *allegory*.

A quotation replicates a text word for word outside its original setting. Sometimes writers point it out with quotation marks, and sometimes they don't. Lewis calls the former a "flagrant quotation" and the latter an "embedded quotation." He quotes Scripture seven times in the Chronicles: once in *The Voyage of the "Dawn Treader,"* twice in *The Magician's Nephew,* and four times in *The Last Battle,* and all of these are embedded; they are not identified with quotation marks. In theory, one might think that even embedded quotations of Scripture would be easy to see, but in practice they are not. What if the quoted words, in addition to being biblical, are also very common? Is there a minimum number of words that must appear in order for them to count as a quotation? Can just one word count?[6] If so, how can we tell that it really is a quotation? Lewis amplifies the problem when he writes that embedded quotations may be "sentences or phrases . . . artfully worked into an author's own language so that an ignorant reader might not recognize them," which is exactly what he does in the Chronicles.[7] The seven biblical quotations are embedded to such an extent that, to my knowledge, only one of them has been identified before the publication of this book.[8]

Lewis alludes to Scripture much more often than he quotes it. An allusion is more or less recognizable depending on its strength, with a strong allusion

---

in Portland, Oregon, Holly Ordway demonstrated that J. R. R. Tolkien's critique of Lewis's riotous medley of sources differs from what many writers and readers have thought about it for decades. Although he personally did not like the Chronicles, he ultimately recognized their value, even providing copies to his grandchildren, and his lack of enthusiasm did not affect his friendship with Lewis. An earlier form of the argument appears in Ordway, *Tolkien's Modern Reading: Middle-earth beyond the Middle Ages* (Park Ridge, IL: Word on Fire Academic, 2021), 75–81, and the later version will be published in the journal *Sehnsucht*.

6. See Beate Kowalski, "Selective versus Contextual Allusions: Reconsidering Technical Terms of Intertextuality," in *Methodology in the Use of the Old Testament in the New: Context and Criteria,* ed. David Allen and Steve Smith (New York: T&T Clark, 2019), 95–97. My use of these terms is not highly technical here.

7. *The Literary Impact of the Authorized Version,* Facet Books Biblical Series 4 (1950; repr., Philadelphia: Fortress, 1963), 17.

8. Lewis to Patricia Mackey, June 8, 1960, *CL,* 3:1158.

resembling its source more closely than a weak one does. An allusion may be harder to identify than a quotation, because by definition an allusion does not replicate its source verbatim. People of good will may disagree about whether an allusion is present or not and, if it is present, whether it is intentional or not. That said, an allusion is easier to catch than an echo. An echo is the hardest intertextual note to hear since it bears only a slight resemblance to its source. More so than with quotations and allusions, picking up an echo depends on the ear of the hearer.[9]

Allegory or Fairy Tale?

Quotations, allusions, and echoes may adorn any genre of literature, but some readers have surmised that, because the Chronicles contain so much biblical symbolism, they must be allegorical. In theory and in practice, symbolism and allegory do overlap, but the Chronicles, which are bursting with symbolism, were not composed as allegory. The first book Lewis published after his conversion, *The Pilgrim's Regress,* was an allegory, and his first major book of literary criticism, *The Allegory of Love,* remains a respected scholarly treatment of the genre.[10] When Lewis insists that he did not write the Chronicles as allegory, he knows what he's talking about. But many people, from readers in the 1950s to more recent commentators, have assumed that they are. Journalist Polly Toynbee, for example, writing in 2005 when Disney's first Narnia movie appeared, claims that the series is "a strange blend of magic, myth and Christianity, some of it brilliantly fantastical and richly imaginative, some (the clunking allegory) toe-curlingly, cringingly awful."[11] Narnia critics like Toynbee aren't the only ones who call it allegory; Narnia lovers do, too. Lewis received letters from fans he had to disabuse of the notion, and sometimes even personal tutelage didn't do the trick. Thirteen-year-old Patricia Mackey received a letter from Lewis explaining why the Chronicles were not allegory,

9. See Richard Hays, *Echoes of Scripture in the Letters of Paul* (New Haven: Yale University Press, 1989); Brenton D. G. Dickieson, "Mixed Metaphors and Hyperlinked Worlds: A Study of Intertextuality in C. S. Lewis's Ransom Cycle," in *The Inklings and King Arthur: J. R. R. Tolkien, Charles Williams, C. S. Lewis, and Owen Barfield on the Matter of Britain,* ed. Sørina Higgins (Berkeley, CA: Apocryphile Press, 2018), 81–113.

10. Richard Angelo Bergen, "*The Lion, the Witch and the Wardrobe*: Mere Allegory or More Allegory?," *Journal of Inklings Studies* 9, no. 1 (2019): 46.

11. Polly Toynbee, "Narnia Represents Everything That Is Most Hateful about Religion," *Guardian,* Dec. 5, 2005, https://tinyurl.com/yf82yp73.

but that didn't stop her from writing as an adult and an English teacher that "reading through the entire series built my understanding of allegory as a literary technique."[12] Of course, most people who read the Chronicles aren't literary scholars, and making a mistake about genre isn't illegal or immoral, so if someone wants to call them an allegory, what's the problem? We may begin to answer that question by looking at Lewis's understanding of the concept.

He published his first scholarly definition of allegory early in his career, and little did he know that he would be restating it in some form or other for the rest of his life:

> Allegory, in some sense, belongs not to medieval man but to man, or even to mind, in general. It is of the very nature of thought and language to represent what is immaterial in picturable terms. . . . On the one hand you can start with an immaterial fact, such as the passions which you actually experience, and can then invent *visibilia* to express them. If you are hesitating between an angry retort and a soft answer, you can express your state of mind by inventing a person called *Ira* [Anger] with a torch and letting her contend with another invented person called *Patientia* [Patience]. This is allegory.[13]

By 1958, his definition is simpler but essentially the same. "By an allegory I mean a composition (whether pictorial or literary) in which immaterial realities are represented by feigned physical objects, e.g. a pictured Cupid allegorically represents erotic love . . . or, in Bunyan, a giant represents Despair."[14]

According to Lewis, an allegory "is like a puzzle with a solution," and an author writes it deliberately. He contrasts it to myth, which he calls "higher" than allegory because "into an allegory a man can put only what he already knows: in a myth he puts what he does not yet know and c[ould] not come to know in any other way."[15] An allegory is a created thing—what the ancient Greeks called a *poiema*, a conscious literary production. Famous modern examples include John Bunyan's *Pilgrim's Progress* and George Orwell's *Animal Farm*.[16] An author plans an allegory, and every item in it stands for something

12. Note from Patricia Mackey, *CL*, 3:1158.

13. *The Allegory of Love: A Study in Medieval Tradition* (Oxford: Clarendon, 1936), 44–45.

14. Lewis to Mrs. Hook, Dec. 29, 1958, *CL*, 3:1004.

15. Lewis to Lucy Matthews, Sept. 11, 1958, *CL*, 3:971; to Peter Milward, Sept. 22, 1956, *CL*, 3:789–90.

16. Lewis considered *Animal Farm* a nearly perfect book but not an allegory. He

else.[17] Myth, on the other hand, can be a vehicle of unforeseen discovery, even for its author. Both allegory and myth contain symbolism, but just because something has symbols in it doesn't make it an allegory.

Lewis gives different accounts of the genesis of the Chronicles of Narnia as he retells it to curious correspondents. According to one version, he didn't know exactly what he was doing. He explains that from about the age of sixteen, he had a picture in his head of a faun with an umbrella in the woods. When he was about forty, he decided to make a story out of it. He didn't know what to do at first, but "suddenly Aslan came bounding" in, and his presence brought everything together.[18]

In another account, he seems to have worked more purposely, but still not to write an allegory: "If Aslan represented the immaterial Deity in the same way in which Giant Despair represents Despair [in Bunyan's *Pilgrim's Progress*], he would be an allegorical figure. In reality however he is an invention giving an imaginary answer to the question, 'What might Christ become like if there really were a world like Narnia and He chose to be incarnate and die and rise again in that world as He actually has done in ours?' This is not an allegory at all."[19]

If the Chronicles were not composed as allegories, what are they? Lewis answers the question in two ways: they are fairy tales, and they are "supposals."

In 1956, Lewis published "Sometimes Fairy Stories May Say Best What's to Be Said" in the *New York Times*, and it is an oddly defensive piece for such a venue. He writes:

> Let me now apply this to my own fairy tales. Some people seem to think that I began by asking myself how I could say something about Christianity to children; then fixed on the fairy tale as an instrument; . . . then drew up a list of basic Christian "truths" and hammered out "allegories" to embody them. This is all pure moonshine. I couldn't write that way at all. Everything began with images; a faun carrying an umbrella, a queen on a sledge, a magnificent lion. At first there wasn't anything Christian about them; that element pushed itself in of its own accord.[20]

---

called it a "beast-fable," a dystopia, and a myth. Lewis, "George Orwell," in *On Stories, and Other Essays on Literature,* ed. Walter Hooper (1966; repr., Orlando: Harcourt, 1982), 103–4.

17. Lewis to Eliza Marian Butler, Aug. 18, 1940, *CL,* 2:438.

18. "It All Began with a Picture," in *On Stories,* 53.

19. Lewis to Mrs. Hook, Dec. 29, 1958, *CL,* 3:1004.

20. "Sometimes Fairy Stories May Say Best What's to Be Said," *New York Times,* Nov. 18, 1956, 310.

Lewis can barely contain his irritation with those who think he wrote the series as allegory; it pops off the page like hot oil sputtering from a pan. Instead, he calls his books fairy tales.

After the section quoted above, he discusses genre, using its German name, *Form*, as he explains how he "fell in love" with fairy tale as the Form best suited to tell his story. To emphasize the point, he concludes this section of the article by setting the following sentence apart as its own paragraph:

> I wrote fairy tales because the Fairy Tale seemed the ideal Form for the stuff I had to say.[21]

It must have been frustrating for Lewis to read the editor's remarks at the end of the piece, which note that he had "recently completed . . . his 'Narnia' series of seven allegorical tales for children."

Lewis calls the Chronicles fairy tales many times in many other places, including his essays, letters, and the dedication of the first book in the series, *The Lion, the Witch and the Wardrobe.*[22] Both it and the second book, *Prince Caspian,* open with the same words, a variation on the standard "Once upon a time": "Once there were four children." The first chapter of *The Silver Chair* likens Narnia to a real-life fairy tale, and Lewis concludes *The Last Battle* with the classic fairy tale ending, "they lived happily ever after," framing the series with the unmistakable markers of the genre.[23]

In addition to calling them fairy tales, Lewis also calls the Chronicles "supposals."[24] When he uses the word, he says he didn't begin with the idea of writing a Christian story. Instead, he *supposed* a land like Narnia and imagined what would happen if Jesus were incarnated as a lion there, explaining that "allegory and such supposals differ because they mix the real and the unreal in different ways."[25]

Why should we care that Lewis didn't want his readers to think he wrote

21. He writes a similar sentence in a letter to the Milton Society of America, Oct. 25, 1954, using the word "genre" instead of "Form" (*CL,* 3:517).

22. "On Three Ways of Writing for Children," in *On Stories,* 37; Lewis to Mary Nelan, July 30, 1949, *CL,* 2:961; to Sister Penelope, Jan. 10, 1952, *CL,* 3:158, to Mary Willis Shelburne, April 17, 1953, *CL,* 3:323.

23. For more technical definitions, see Jack Zipes, ed., *The Oxford Companion to Fairy Tales,* 2nd ed. (Oxford: Oxford University Press, 2015).

24. He uses the word "supposal" as early as 1936 in *Allegory of Love,* 115.

25. Lewis to a fifth-grade class in Maryland, May 24, 1954, *CL,* 3:479–80; to Mrs. Hook, Dec. 29, 1958, *CL,* 3:1004.

the Chronicles as allegories? There are at least three reasons, and the first is because he did. As their author and an expert on the genre, he wanted people to use the term as he understood it. The second is because genre awareness helps anyone read any text better. This book has shown how important that idea was to Lewis, and he was especially sensitive about the genre allegory. His colleagues "most often go wrong," he complained, "in the hasty assumption of an allegorical sense," noting that "the mere fact that you *can* allegorise the work before you" doesn't mean it *is* an allegory, since anyone can allegorize anything.[26]

Lewis didn't compose the Chronicles as allegories, and he didn't want people to think he had, but he was sometimes willing to accept allegorical interpretation of his work because an author's intention for a text and a reader's reception of it may diverge. In such a conflict, he sides with the reader, at least in one letter he wrote about his Ransom trilogy. "When I've said that there is no allegory in [the trilogy], you may well reply 'Well, that is what the books mean to an intelligent reader and what does it matter what *you* meant them to mean?'—a point of view I wholly agree with."[27] That said, we would do well to disregard this statement when it comes to the Chronicles. Ironically, approaching them as biblical allegory can prevent us from seeing how subtly Lewis does use the Bible in the series. This is the third and most important reason we should care, as I hope the following chapters will demonstrate.

On Ordering

Gregory the Great described the Bible as "a river broad and deep, shallow enough here for a lamb to go wading, but deep enough there for an elephant to swim."[28] The same might be said of Lewis's use of the Bible in the Chronicles of Narnia. A few of his biblical references appear on the surface of the story, visible to anyone who is barely acquainted with Scripture, but most of them emerge only as subtle allusions and echoes that one must dive deep to recover.

Scripture-loving lambs wading into the Chronicles will find their attention drawn first to *The Magician's Nephew* and *The Lion, the Witch and the Wardrobe.* Just by listing them in this order, however, I am poking a monster of a debate

26. Lewis, "On Criticism," in *On Stories,* 140–41.

27. Lewis to Wayland Hilton Young, Jan. 31, 1952, *CL,* 3:162. Compare Lewis to Eliza Marian Butler, Aug. 18, 1940, *CL,* 2:438–39; Peter Milward, "C. S. Lewis on Allegory," *Rising Generation* 114, no. 4 (1968): 227–32.

28. Gregory the Great, *Commentary on Job* 4.

that has roiled students of the Narnian canon for decades—though others will see it as a tempest in a teacup. Should one read *The Magician's Nephew* first, because it tells the story of the creation of Narnia, or hold to the order of publication and start with *The Lion, the Witch and the Wardrobe*?[29] I have always championed the latter, but here (and only here) I will make an exception, because *The Magician's Nephew* is the Narnian counterpart to Genesis 1–3, the first chapters of the first book of the Bible. Our focus on Scripture makes this a logical place to start. I will then move to *The Lion, the Witch and the Wardrobe, The Horse and His Boy, Prince Caspian, The Voyage of the "Dawn Treader," The Silver Chair,* and *The Last Battle.*

I have written what follows with the understanding that readers are familiar with the Chronicles, which I summarize only enough to put biblical references into their Narnian context. But that means many delightful and important parts of the series—some of my favorite parts—won't come up at all. This affects us from the very beginning, as we skip blithely over the first half of *The Magician's Nephew.*

29. See Peter Schakel, "'It Does Not Matter Very Much'—or Does It? The 'Correct' Order for Reading the Chronicles," in *Imagination and the Arts in C. S. Lewis: Journeying to Narnia and Other Worlds* (Columbia: University of Missouri Press, 2002), 40–52.

10. THE MAGICIAN'S NEPHEW

In the beginning . . .

—John 1:1

Lewis loved the stories of E. Nesbit, whose children's books were popular in the early twentieth century when he was a boy. He did not forget about them as he grew up. In 1927, when he was twenty-eight, he wrote his father a letter mentioning Nesbit's "fairy tales."[1] The first half of *The Magician's Nephew* reads much like her books, with children in Edwardian England having magical adventures. Lewis even names her best-known characters, the Bastable children, on the first page of his book, proving that the resemblance is no accident.[2] Nesbit's influence helps explain why there are no biblical allusions in *The Magician's Nephew* until the second half of the book, when Aslan creates Narnia. Because the biblical allusions begin there, so will we.

Aslan sings his world into being roughly on the model of God in Genesis 1. The first thing God creates is light. Aslan does the same in Narnia, but Lewis wields his authorial power to answer a question that has bedeviled readers of Genesis at least since Philo of Alexandria, the great first-century Jewish contemporary of Jesus: how can there be "evening and morning" on day one without the sun, moon, and stars, which God makes on day four?[3] Address-

1. Lewis to his father, March 30, 1927, *CL*, 1:680.

2. In 1948 Lewis told Chad Walsh that he was working on a children's book "in the style of E. Nesbit." Walsh, *C. S. Lewis: Apostle to the Skeptics* (New York: Macmillan, 1949), 10. In an unpublished letter of May 22, 1952, Lewis notes, "E. Nesbitt's [*sic*] works are splendid, I think: especially *The Phoenix and the Wishing Carpet* and *The Amulet*." Both titles are slightly incorrect; they should be *The Phoenix and the Carpet* and *The Story of the Amulet*. "C. S. Lewis Letter to Schoolchildren Discussing Narnia Up for Auction," *Daily Mail*, Sept. 7, 2018, https://tinyurl.com/2c5khmax. See also Mervyn Nicholson, "What C. S. Lewis Took from E. Nesbit," *Children's Literature Association Quarterly* 16 (1991): 16–22.

3. Philo, *On the Creation of the World* 31 (VIII) and 55 (XVIII).

ing this ancient conundrum explains why Aslan, unlike God, creates heavenly bodies like the stars and sun first.

When Aslan's newborn stars appear, they sing. The stars in Genesis don't, but we may remember an allusion to the creation story in the book of Job. God asks Job, "Where were you when I laid the foundation of the earth? Tell me, if you have understanding. . . . Who laid its cornerstone when the morning stars sang together and the sons of God shouted for joy?" (38:4–7). Lewis echoes it again to describe the sun rising on Narnia's first morning: "You could imagine that it laughed for joy."[4] Even as a teenaged atheist, Lewis found this passage "ineffably beautiful."[5]

After making light, God creates plants and animals, and so does Aslan, first bringing forth plants and then animals, some of which in Narnia burst out of the earth. Lewis mainly follows the chronology of Genesis 1 in this part of the book, but the animals that emerge from the earth are modeled on Genesis 2. To understand why it is important to distinguish between the two chapters, readers must know that Genesis 1:1–2:4a and 2:4b–25 tell two different creation stories with two different orders of creation (see chart on pp. 225–26 below). Genesis 1 proceeds like a campaign under an orderly general, with one or two major events scheduled per day. Most of the days are punctuated with the formula, "It was good." First, God separates light from darkness and water from dry land. Then plants, the sun, moon, and stars, sea creatures and birds, and mammals appear, in that order. Finally, humanity appears as the apex of creation, simultaneously male and female. When God looks at everything he has made in Genesis 1, he deems it "very good."

In Genesis 2, on the other hand, God creates humanity before he makes anything else, and the narrator says there were no plants in the world when he made the first human. This is the first indication of how different the two creation stories are, but more differences follow. For example, the narrator of Genesis 1 gives no details about how humanity is formed, but the narrator of Genesis 2 says God created them from the earth, a word that highlights a pun. Genesis was written in Hebrew, and Genesis 2 is full of Hebrew puns that cross uneasily, when they cross at all, into English. The Hebrew word for "human," *adam*, is one of these, because God makes the *adam* out of the dust of the *adamah* (earth). "Adam" with a capital *A*, a particular man named with a proper noun, does not yet exist. What we have instead is a common noun

4. *The Magician's Nephew* (1955; repr., New York: Scholastic, 1983), ch. 8. Lewis quotes part of Job 38:7, "when the morning stars sang together," at the end of *Perelandra*, ch. 8.

5. Lewis to Greeves, Aug. 4, 1917, *CL*, 1:333.

for humanity in general.[6] In a feeble attempt to replicate the pun in English, one might say that the "earthling" was created from the earth. Lewis, who wrote three books of interplanetary science fiction, might have enjoyed this wordplay, had he known it.

Aslan makes land animals come out of the earth.[7] And just as God breathes life into the human "earthling" in Genesis 2:7, so specially chosen Narnian animals become articulate beings when Aslan breathes on them. Lewis was far from the first person to imagine a pristine world full of talking beasts. Jewish tradition from the second century BCE includes a belief that all the animals, and not just the serpent, could speak in Eden. The Book of Jubilees, which tries to explain some of the many things that aren't clear in Genesis, notes that when the human couple left the garden, "the mouth of all the beasts and cattle and birds and whatever walked or moved was stopped from speaking because all of them used to speak with one another with one speech and one language." According to Jubilees, they must have spoken Hebrew, since it was "the tongue of creation."[8] In the first century CE, Philo also speculates that all the primeval beasts could speak.[9]

Aslan selects two from each species to become talking animals. Although the narrator doesn't say so explicitly, they seem to be male and female, just as Noah takes breeding pairs on his ark in one version of the flood story (Gen. 6:19–20).[10] The way Aslan chooses his talking beasts, whom he selects from a larger group of dumb animals, reflects a hypothesis Lewis held about the creation of humanity: he imagines the *adam* as a child of two anthropoids whom God called and then made human.[11] Aslan rephrases Genesis 3:19 when

6. See Phyllis Trible, "A Love Story Gone Awry," ch. 4 of *God and the Rhetoric of Sexuality* (Philadelphia: Fortress, 1978).

7. Ch. 9.

8. Jubilees 3:38 and 12:26–27. Even though Jubilees and other works we'll soon look at such as 1 Enoch are not in the Bible, they are based on it, and they are indispensable witnesses to ancient Jewish thought. Some of these extrabiblical books, like 1 Enoch, made an impact on early Jewish and Christian thought. Therefore they are important to take into account here. See Matthias Henze, *Mind the Gap: How the Jewish Writings between the Old and New Testament Help Us Understand Jesus* (Minneapolis: Fortress, 2017).

9. *Questions in Genesis* 32. The idea also appears in Werner Schwarz, *Principles and Problems of Biblical Translation: Some Reformation Controversies and Their Background* (Cambridge: Cambridge University Press, 1955), 83, which Lewis marked in his copy.

10. In Gen. 7:2–3, a different version of the flood story, God tells Noah to take seven pairs of each clean animal and one pair of each unclean creature.

11. Lewis to Sister Penelope, Jan. 10, 1952, *CL*, 3:157.

he warns the newly verbal animals not to act like the dumb beasts, "for out of them you were taken and into them you can return."[12]

Aslan doesn't create humanity in Narnia, since the humans who will live there immigrate from England, but after he forms animals, he does awaken other sentient beings (one can't call them "people"): fauns, satyrs, and dwarves, dryads and naiads. These are Aslan's final work, and he bids them and the talking animals, like the humans who are God's final creation in Genesis 1:28, to care for their new world.[13]

The last time Lewis uses the first chapter of Genesis in *The Magician's Nephew* is when Aslan transforms the London cab horse Strawberry into the winged horse Fledge. When Fledge tries out his new wings, the lion asks, "Is it good, Fledge?" and Fledge replies, "It is very good, Aslan" (cf. Gen. 1:31).[14]

The phrase "very good" is both very small and very common. People say "very good" all the time, and more likely than not, they aren't quoting Genesis. We can identify it as a biblical quotation only by comparing its context in *The Magician's Nephew* to the context of its source, Genesis 1:31. Since we know we're reading a creation story based on Genesis, when we see the phrase "very good," we can be sure it is quoting that book. As we will see, all of Lewis's biblical quotations in the Chronicles are like "very good": small, common phrases that one may identify as biblical quotations by comparing contexts.

Genesis 1:1–2:4a The first creation story	**Genesis 2:4b–25** The second creation story	***The Magician's Nephew*** Creation story
Day 1: God creates light and separates light from darkness. It was good.	God creates the *adam* ("earthling") from *adamah* (earth) when no vegetation yet exists.	Aslan creates stars and the sun; the stars sing.
Day 2: God creates the sky; God separates waters above from waters below.	God breathes into the *adam* to make it a living being.	

12. Ch. 10.
13. Ch. 10.
14. Ch. 12.

Day 3: God creates dry land and plants. It was good.	God plants a garden and sets the *adam* to tend it.	Aslan creates plants.
Day 4: God creates the sun, moon, and stars; God separates day from night. It was good.		
Day 5: God creates aquatic animals and birds. It was good.		
Day 6 part 1: God creates land animals. It was good.	God creates every "animal of the field and bird of the air" out of earth (*adamah*).	Aslan creates animals from the earth and breathes on them to make them talking beasts. The stars sing again.
Day 6 part 2: God creates human beings, male and female. Everything was very good.	God separates the *adam* into two people, male and female.	Aslan creates fauns, satyrs, dwarves, dryads, and naiads. Fledge judges his wings "very good."

While Aslan is busy creating Narnia, several human beings are standing close by: Digory Kirke, the titular nephew; his uncle Andrew, the titular magician; and Digory's friend Polly. Amazed by the fertility of a place that can grow a whole new lamp post from a discarded iron bar, Uncle Andrew calls Narnia "the land of youth."[15] This phrase awakens a great hope in the heart of his nephew. From the beginning of the book, Digory has been walking in the valley of the shadow of death. His mother is dying, and more than anything else he longs for her to be cured. Can the creator of the land of youth help? When Digory asks Aslan, tears fall from the lion's eyes, just as Jesus wept at the tomb of Lazarus (John 11:35).[16] Readers who miss the biblical parallel may think Aslan's tears mean "no," but those who do see it can put it in context. In John, after Jesus weeps, he raises Lazarus from the dead. The larger context of the scene bodes well for Digory and his mother.

15. Ch. 9.
16. Ch. 12.

But Aslan must attend to other things first. He had given Fledge wings to fly Digory west to a garden with silver apples that will protect Narnia from the witch Digory unwittingly brought into the world. Hearing the words "garden" and "apple" in close proximity to a creation story will make readers think of the garden of Eden, and there are unmistakable parallels to it. In Genesis 2, God plants his garden and fills it with trees, and the *adam* who tends the garden is allowed to eat fruit from all of them except the tree of knowledge of good and evil. If he eats from it, God tells him, he will die. In Genesis 3 there is a temptation scene.

There are also fundamental differences between the biblical and the Narnian gardens. The garden of Genesis 2–3 is in the east (Gen. 2:8), but its Narnian counterpart is in the west. In Lewis's thought, the western garden always represents the mythological garden of the Hesperides. The Hesperides are the three daughters of Hesperus, a Greek word meaning "west," and they guard a tree full of golden apples. Lewis's love of the place hearkens back to some of his earliest writing. In 1916, teenaged Lewis describes it as his "'dream garden' where 'the west winds blow.'"[17] That same year he writes his poem "Hesperus" about a "garden of delight" populated by the divinity and his daughters.[18] Lewis later wrote that the tale was one of the greatest of all the Greek myths, and he employs it in his work throughout his life.[19] Along with almost all of the main characters from the Chronicles, we will return to the western garden at the end of *The Last Battle*.

Fledge, Digory, and Polly cannot complete their journey to the garden in one day. They need to rest overnight, and they discover to their dismay that they forgot to bring food. Digory thinks Aslan should have thought of this for them, and Polly wonders if he would have if they didn't ask him. Fledge is sure he would have, but he speculates that Aslan "likes to be asked," an echo of the Lord's Prayer, which tells us to ask for "our daily bread."[20]

When they arrive at the garden, they find a wall around it with a sign that warns them to enter via the gates, not by climbing over the wall, and that they may take fruit only for others, not themselves. But the witch is not one to follow rules. Before the children arrived, she had bypassed the gates, climbed over the wall, and stolen fruit from the tree, thus exemplifying John 10:1: "Amen,

17. Lewis to Greeves, June 29, 1915, *CL*, 1:134, and July 11, 1916, *CL*, 1:209.

18. "Hesperus," in *Collected Poems*, 111–12.

19. See, e.g., *An Experiment in Criticism* (Cambridge: Cambridge University Press, 1961), 42–44.

20. Ch. 12. Cf. Matt. 6:9–13; Luke 11:2–4.

amen, I say to you, anyone who does not enter the sheepfold by the gate but climbs in by another way is a thief and a bandit."

The witch plays the role of Genesis 3's serpent, tempting Digory to defy the sign and take an apple for himself. She calls the fruit "the apple of life" and claims that anyone who eats it will not die.[21] Digory doesn't grasp the implications of her words at first, but she connects the dots for him: the fruit could save his mother's life. Its beauty had attracted him even before he realized what it could do, and now he faces dire temptation. Can he both obey the lion and take fruit home for his mother? He knows the answer, and he makes his choice. Unlike the first couple in Genesis 3, he emerges from the garden victorious.

When Digory presents the apple to Aslan, the lion praises him by saying "Well done!" a quotation of the words of the master to his servant in Matthew 25:21.[22] Like every other biblical quotation in the Chronicles, its subtlety makes it hard to catch, but we know Lewis placed it there on purpose, not only because the contexts of his book and the verse match, but also through what he writes in his sermon "The Weight of Glory." What is glory? Lewis asks. Could it indicate God's approval? And if it does, should one strive for it? Yes, he concludes: "I saw that this view was scriptural; nothing can eliminate from the parable the divine *accolade*, 'Well done, thou good and faithful servant.'" This accolade, he explains, brings about the "lawful pleasure of praise."[23] Observing how Lewis interprets Scripture elsewhere helps us recognize the same Scripture when he embeds it in the Chronicles.

Aslan bids Digory to plant the apple, and it grows overnight into a tree that will protect Narnia from the witch. But this isn't the end of the story, and Digory earns more than the lawful pleasure of praise for handing the apple to Aslan. His obedience allows the lion to give him a more tangible reward the next day, when he receives the first fruit the tree bears to take home to his mother. She will not die, but live, and the promise of Aslan's tears in the allusion to Lazarus is fulfilled.

More biblical references conclude the Narnian half of the book. Aslan asks Fledge's former owner, Frank the London cabby, to care for the land and raise food. Like the *adam* in Genesis 2, he will be a gardener, and the lion invites Frank and his wife, Helen, to reign as king and queen of Narnia. There is warrant to consider them "chosen before the world was founded" (Eph. 1:4), es-

21. Ch. 13.

22. Ch. 14.

23. "The Weight of Glory," in *Essay Collection*, 101; see also his letter to Mary Neylan, April 26, 1941, *CL*, 2:480–81.

pecially when we see that Lewis underlined that verse in his Moffatt New Testament. Like the couple in Genesis 3:21, Frank and Helen receive new clothes from the one who made their world—but here they are clothed with joy rather than in disgrace. The narrator reports that Frank and Helen's children will marry Narnia's indigenous nymphs, naiads, and dryads, which resolves the infamous conundrum of Genesis 4: whom did Cain marry?[24]

Aslan sends the children back to London, and the book wraps up with a glorious reversal of fortune worthy of E. Nesbit, who always restores absent parents and lost prosperity to her young characters in the end. For his part, Digory is sure they will all "live happily ever after," just as one should in a fairy tale.[25]

24. See Lewis to Sister Penelope, Jan. 10, 1952, *CL*, 3:157.
25. Ch. 15.

11. THE LION, THE WITCH AND THE WARDROBE

> *"Amen, amen, I say to you, that the hour is coming, and is now here, when the dead will hear the voice of the Son of God, and those who hear will live."*
>
> —John 5:25

The Lion, the Witch and the Wardrobe was the first Chronicle published and the best known, and its major biblical references may be the most easily recognized, as its overarching theological themes are the passion, death, and resurrection of Aslan the Christ figure.

Lucy is the first of four siblings to enter Narnia, where Mr. Tumnus the faun identifies her as a "Daughter of Eve," one of four "sons of Adam and daughters of Eve" prophesied to bring about the fall of the White Witch and to reign over Narnia. Before the prophecy is fulfilled, however, the children undergo trials brought about largely by Lucy's brother Edmund, who doesn't come to his senses until it is almost too late. In the same letter to Patricia Mackey that explains why the Chronicles are not allegory, Lewis writes: "Edmund is like Judas a sneak and traitor. But unlike Judas he repents and is forgiven (as Judas no doubt w[ould] have been if he'd repented)."[1] In *The Lion, the Witch and the Wardrobe*, the outcome is infinitely happier for Edmund than it was for Judas. It is a children's book, after all, and even though it's a fairy tale, it is not as dark as the original Brothers Grimm can be.

Other than the words "Adam" and "Eve," the first biblical allusion appears when Mr. Beaver mentions Aslan in chapter 7. "At the name of Aslan" (compare Phil. 2:10, "at the name of Jesus"), the children feel different. Edmund, who has already sided with the White Witch, is overcome with dread. But the other three, especially Lucy, experience a burst of joy. In chapter 8, when the beaver tells them more about Aslan, hearing his name affects them as if they had heard "good news." "Good news" is the literal meaning of the Greek *euangelion*, which is often translated into English as "gospel." Several times in the Chronicles

1. Lewis to Patricia Mackey, June 8, 1960, *CL*, 3:1158.

Lewis takes a traditional Christian term like "gospel," renders it back to its ancient Greek meaning, and hides it in plain sight. Our attention skips like a stone atop the surface of the word, but when the stone falls, we can plumb the deeper significance of the term. I don't know what to call this sort of wordplay, because I've never seen anything else like it. But I do know what it's not. It is not allegory, where a material object stands for an altogether different abstract concept. "Good news" and "gospel" are exactly the same thing, but the former is colloquial and thus unobtrusive.

Mr. Beaver explains that Aslan is "king" and "lord" and implies that he is savior when he tells the children that only Aslan can enter the witch's castle to rescue Mr. Tumnus. As he speaks, Edmund fidgets uncomfortably. He hadn't set out to be on the wrong side of Narnian history, but he had eaten the witch's food, and there he was. Like Mr. Tumnus, Edmund can't save himself. In a difficult period of Lewis's life with his own brother, who struggled with alcoholism, he wrote that it is a "rule of the universe that others can do for us what we cannot do for ourselves. . . . That is why Christ's suffering *for us* is not a mere theological dodge, but the supreme case of the law that governs the whole world . . . [and] the ultimate law of the spiritual world."[2]

The White Witch demands Edmund's life, appealing to Deep Magic from the dawn of time, which allows her to kill traitors. She must have "blood as the Law says," with "the Law" referring to the Jewish law with its divinely ordained system of animal sacrifice.[3] Lewis may also echo Hebrews 9:22, a verse he marked in his Moffatt New Testament. As Moffatt phrases it, "No blood shed, no remission of sins!" Aslan accepts her claim. There is no way around it, since the decree came from the lion's father himself. Unbeknownst to anyone else, however, Aslan offers his life for Edmund's, reflecting Romans 5:8: "But God showed his love for us, because when we were still sinners, Christ died for us."

Lewis had little interest in arguing about theories of the atonement. He believed that accepting Christ's act was more important than understanding how it worked. He put this plainly in *Mere Christianity* and under the guise of allegory in *The Pilgrim's Regress*. Early in that book, the main character, John, was subjected to a theological lecture, but he "could not understand a single syllable." Lewis later made a handwritten note on the passage to explain what he meant: "The doctrine of the Atonement, usually in what theologians call its

2. Lewis to Greeves, July 2, 1949, *CL*, 2:953.

3. When Lewis capitalizes "the Law," he is usually referring to the Jewish law, but all cultures of the ancient Near East prior to the advent of Christianity engaged in animal sacrifice.

Anselmic form, is explained to us in youth and we do not understand it." He then suggests the "Christus Victor" model—Christ the victor over death—as an alternative.[4] One ancient expression of this model is worth following up for the light it shines on *The Lion, the Witch and the Wardrobe.*

The germ of the idea comes from Origen as he reflects on Matthew 17:22, Jesus's prediction that the Son of Man will be betrayed into human hands. Origen then jumps to John 13:27, where Satan enters into Judas right before he betrays Jesus. Now Origen's inventive mind recalls how God also gave the Old Testament character Job into the power of Satan, and he gets to the point: Just as God allowed Job to be tormented by Satan, so God allowed Jesus to fall into the hands of the devil and his unholy hordes to be tortured and killed. But those evil powers had no idea what they had let themselves in for, "since none of them knew the wisdom of God which was hidden in a mystery. . . . Contrary to their expectation, it was to the destruction of their own kingdom and power" to receive the Son. Jesus destroys Satan, the ruler of death, by his own death.[5] In the same way, the White Witch believes that Aslan's death will ensure her triumph, but she is ignorant of the Deeper Magic, the mystery from before the dawn of time, when "Death itself would start working backward." She thinks killing Aslan will secure her rule, unaware that it is the very thing that will destroy her. The fact that Aslan knows about the Deeper Magic implies that he, like the Logos of John 1:1, was preexistent, present with his father before time began.[6]

Origen's ideas enjoy a thriving afterlife as later thinkers revive them. Gregory of Nyssa writes: "It was not in the nature of [the devil] to come in contact

4. *Mere Christianity* (1952; repr., San Francisco: HarperSanFrancisco, 2001), 181–82; *The Pilgrim's Regress,* Wade Annotated Edition, ed. David C. Downing (Grand Rapids: Eerdmans, 2014), 9. Compare letters to Bede Griffiths Dec. 21, 1941, *CL,* 2:502, and Oct. 13, 1942, *CL,* 2:531. Lewis writes in the latter that he had thought the Anselmic form was not present in the New Testament or in most of the early church fathers. Writing Mr. Young, Oct. 31, 1963, *CL,* 3:1476, Lewis mentions the Christus Victor model, but he favors it neither more nor less than other models, noting that trying to pin such things down is a mistake. Lewis's attitude to the doctrine of the atonement is yet another way he was influenced by the general tendency of Gore's *Lux Mundi.* As Michael Ramsey notes, it was "commonplace to say that in the Anglican theology characteristic of our period the Atonement was very far from the centre." *An Era in Anglican Theology: From Gore to Temple; The Development of Anglican Theology between "Lux Mundi" and the Second World War, 1889–1939* (New York: Scribner, 1960; repr., Eugene, OR: Wipf & Stock, 2009), 44.

5. Origen, *Homilies on Matthew* 13:8–9.

6. See chapter 8 for more on the Logos and preexistence.

with the undiluted presence of God. . . . Therefore, in order to ensure that the ransom on our behalf might be easily accepted [by Satan], the Deity was hidden under the veil of our nature, so that, as with ravenous fish, the hook of the Deity might be gulped down along with the bait of flesh, and thus, life was introduced into the house of death."[7] For Gregory, Satan is like a hungry fish that jumps at the chance to snap at Jesus. If he had known that he was attempting to imbibe divinity, he would never have dared. Satan could kill Jesus's human nature, but he didn't reckon with the power of his divine nature, which he couldn't swallow.

Another Gregory, Gregory the Great, identifies Gregory of Nyssa's fish with Leviathan, the sea monster in Job 41, which Gregory the Great calls the devil. God baits his hook with Jesus's humanity, which hides the sharpness of the hook, Jesus's divinity. The weakness of the human nature gives Leviathan confidence to bite, but he is pierced through by the divine nature.[8] This, Gregory says, is the mystery of the incarnation that saves the world. It is also a stellar example of allegory as Lewis defines it, a conscious construction wherein every concrete object (the fish, the hook) stands for an abstract concept (Satan, Jesus's divinity).

All of the above is not just an edifying digression into the church fathers. It is almost certainly what Lewis had in mind when he wrote about the death and resurrection of Aslan, as we can see from a letter he sent to his friend Sister Penelope. In 1941 she gave him a copy of her book *Windows on Jerusalem*, and his thank-you note highlights her "really splendid account of *how* God can't help deceiving the devil" (56). On page 56 the good sister urges her audience to read Gregory of Nyssa, and she quotes "an old Easter carol" that puts Gregory the Great's allegory to verse:

> Hook that His Manhood hid awhile
> Hath caught Leviathan by guile,

7. Gregory of Nyssa, *Catechetical Institutes* 24.4, in *Nicene and Post-Nicene Fathers*, series 2, vol. 5, *Gregory of Nyssa: Dogmatic Treaties, Etc.*, trans. William Moore and Henry Austin Wilson (Oxford: Parker, 1893). For a more recent translation with an introduction, see *Saint Gregory of Nyssa: Catechetical Discourse: A Handbook for Catechists*, trans. Ignatius Green (Yonkers, NY: St. Vladimir's Seminary Press, 2019). Long after writing this section, I discovered I was not the first to link Gregory with Aslan's conquering death. See Andrew Walker, "Under the Russian Cross: A Research Note on C. S. Lewis and the Eastern Orthodox Church," in *A Christian for All Christians*, ed. Andrew Walker and James Patrick (Washington, DC: Regnery Gateway, 1992), 63–67.

8. Gregory the Great, homily 25, in *Reading the Gospels with Gregory the Great: Homilies on the Gospels, 21–26*, trans. Santha Bhattacharji (Petersham, MA: St. Bede's, 2001), 84–85.

> That monster vile;
> Christ upon the rood doth quell
> Our ancient foe, the prince of hell.[9]

And so, it seems, it made its way into Lewis's fairy tale.

Lewis devotes great care to portraying the Passion of the Lion. Susan and Lucy play the roles of Peter, James, and John, the disciples Jesus chose to stay close to him as he prayed in the garden of Gethsemane in the Synoptic Gospels (Mark 13:32–42), and the Witch and her minions taunt and torment Aslan just as the Romans did Jesus (Mark 15:16–20), but Aslan "made no resistance at all." His passivity echoes that of the suffering servant in Isaiah 53:7:

> He was oppressed, and he was afflicted,
> yet he did not open his mouth;
> like a lamb that is led to slaughter,
> and like a sheep that before its shearers is silent,
> so he did not open his mouth.

Aslan is the servant's antitype, or counterpart, just as the New Testament book of Acts says Jesus is (8:32–33).[10] In fact, Aslan embodies the verse in Isaiah even more than Christians believe Jesus did, since the lion, unlike the Christ, was literally shorn and muzzled before he was executed on the stone table.

After Aslan dies, Susan and Lucy stand in for the myrrh-bearing women, as the Eastern Orthodox Church calls them, Jesus's disciples who come to the tomb to anoint his body. When the girls have done everything for him that they can, they turn away, so they don't see the Stone Table break in two. Lewis writes that this is "a glance at the stone tables of the Mosaic Law and its breaking to our liberation from the curse of the law at the crucifixion," referring to both Exodus 32:19 and Galatians 3:13.[11]

The girls do not witness the moment of resurrection but wake up to find the table empty. Like Mary Magdalene at Jesus's tomb in the Gospel of John,

9. A Religious of the Community of St. Mary the Virgin, Wantage [Sister Penelope Lawson], *Windows on Jerusalem: A Study in the Mystery of Redemption* (London: Pax House, 1941), 55. Sister Penelope identifies the song as "*Cowley Carol* 54, taken from *Piae Cantiones*, by Peter of Nyland." See Lewis to Sister Penelope, April 10, 1941, *CL*, 2:479.

10. Lewis discusses the "second meaning" of Isaiah's suffering servant as Christ in *Reflections on the Psalms* (New York: Harcourt, Brace & World, 1958), 118.

11. Lewis to William L. Kinter, July 30, 1954, *CL*, 3:497.

Lucy fears that "they"—a pronoun that refers to the enemy both in John and in Narnia—have taken the body, only to turn around and recognize the resurrected one (John 20:1–2).[12] Then, in one of the best-loved scenes in all of the Chronicles, Aslan invites the girls to ride on his back to the witch's castle so he can revive the Narnians whom the witch has turned to stone. When he jumps over the castle wall like a champion steeplechase horse, Lewis may echo 2 Samuel 22:30 (see also Ps. 18:29), "by my God I can leap a wall." At the same time, he was probably thinking of a scene from his beloved Norse mythology. After "Balder the beautiful" dies, Balder's brother Hermodr rides Sleipnir the eight-legged horse to try to free Balder from Hel, the land of the dead. Hermodr and his mount face the tall iron gate of Hel, but they clear it at a single bound.[13]

Once inside the castle, the lion breathes on the statues just as God bade Ezekiel to pray for breath to animate the dry bones of Israel (Ezek. 37).[14] Aslan, having defeated death, now has the power to give life to others. The scene as a whole reflects the ancient Christian belief that Jesus descended to save the dead, the "harrowing of hell," a concept Lewis knew and loved. In 1936 he marked a passage in Gustav Aulén's *Christus Victor* that compares Jesus's descent to storming "hell's castle," and Aulén's image could have influenced the construction of this scene in *The Lion, the Witch and the Wardrobe.*[15]

The Eastern Orthodox icon of the resurrection on the next page illustrates the tradition, which Lewis saw reflected in 1 Peter 3:18–20 and 4:6.[16] Like *The Lion, the Witch and the Wardrobe* and the Gospels, the icon doesn't picture the moment of resurrection, since no one but Jesus witnessed it. Instead, it illuminates its deeper significance, Christ's victory over death. Jesus breaks through Death's door to release those whom Death had im-

12. Ch. 15.

13. Gylfaginning 49, in *The Prose Edda*, trans. Arthur Gilchrist Brodeur (New York: American Scandinavian Foundation, 1916), 74. For other similarities between Balder and Aslan, see Salwa Khoddam, "Balder the Beautiful: Aslan's Norse Ancestor in the Chronicles of Narnia," *Mythlore* 22, no. 3 (1999): 66–76.

14. Thanks to the students of Fr. Isaac Morales for this allusion.

15. Lewis to Mary Van Deusen, Jan. 31, 1952, *CL*, 3:163, and Audrey Sutherland, April 28, 1960, 3:1148; Gustaf Aulén, *Christus Victor: An Historical Study of the Three Main Types of the Idea of the Atonement* (London: SPCK, 1931), 125. See also Lewis's glorious poem "Lords Coëval with Creation," *Collected Poems*, 393–94. Chapter 13 of *The Great Divorce* expresses the idea through the character of George MacDonald.

16. Eastern Orthodox iconography of the resurrection varies, but this icon by Ivan Rumiantsev is typical. It is reproduced with the kind permission of All Saints Orthodox Church, Olyphant, Pennsylvania.

Resurrection of Our Lord and Savior Jesus Christ. All Saints Orthodox Church, Olyphant, Pennsylvania. Ivan Rumiantsev, 2008. Photo by Carol M. Highsmith. Library of Congress.

prisoned, represented in the icon by famous figures from salvation history like King David and King Solomon. He grasps the wrist of Adam with his right hand and Eve with his left to pull them from the tomb. Beneath his feet are the padlocks he opened to free his people, as well as personified Death itself, conquered and bound.[17] Jesus stands atop the flattened gates

17. Leonid Ouspensky and Vladimir Lossky, *The Meaning of Icons*, trans. G. E. H. Palmer and E. Kadloubovsky, 2nd ed. (Crestwood, NY: St. Vladimir's Seminary Press,

of "hell," a word that does derive from the Hel of Norse mythology. Both there and here, hell has nothing to do with eternal torment, as Lewis knew; it means only "the dead."[18] In the New Testament, the English word "hell" often translates the Greek word "Hades," the realm of the dead where everyone found themselves when they died. In the Hebrew Scriptures, the same concept is called "Sheol."

The Eastern Orthodox Church also commemorates the "harrowing of hell" through music in a hymn for Good Friday that personifies Hades:

> Hades, made ridiculous at seeing thee, O Deliverer of all,
> placed in a new tomb for the sake of all, trembled with fear.
> Its locks were shattered; its doors broken;
> The tombs were opened; and the dead awoke.
> Then Adam cried to thee with joy and gratitude.

The largest creature Aslan brings back from the dead, a giant, has the heft to demolish the locked gates of the castle so the revived statues can come out. As Matthew notes, the "gates of hell do not prevail against it" (Matt. 16:18). In Matthew "it" is the church, and in Narnia "it" is Giant Rumblebuffin. It is easy to forget that in Matthew 16:18 the church actively assaults the infernal gates.

Among the throng of resurrected statues are unicorns, and they carry with them an echo from the Psalms. The Coverdale Psalter was familiar to English churchgoers when Lewis wrote because it served as the text for the Anglican Book of Common Prayer. Coverdale's translation of Psalm 22:21 reads, "Save me from the lion's mouth: thou hast heard me also from among the horns of the unicorns." Unicorns are mentioned several times in *The Lion, the Witch and the Wardrobe*, but the biblical echo sounds when Aslan, the girls, and the newly resurrected statues rush from the castle toward the battle against the White Witch. When they arrive, the lion roars and attacks the witch, while "unicorns with their horns" make short work of her army. Lewis marked this verse in his copy of Coverdale's Psalter.[19]

In all four Gospels, women are the first to learn of the resurrection. Lewis follows the Gospels on this point, but the girls' presence first at Aslan's resur-

---

1982), 185–88; Michel Quenot, *The Resurrection and the Icon*, trans. Michael Breck (Crestwood, NY: St. Vladimir's Seminary Press, 1997).

18. Lewis to Mary Van Deusen, Jan. 31, 1952, *CL*, 3:163.

19. Ernest Clapton, ed., *Our Prayer Book Psalter* (London: SPCK, 1934), 46. *The Lion, the Witch and the Wardrobe*, ch. 16.

rection and then at the castle also serves a nonbiblical purpose: it keeps them away from most of the battle against the witch. Lewis's views on women have been analyzed and criticized at length, and we will return to them soon. Suffice it to say here that Aslan, like Father Christmas earlier in the book, disapproves of girls in combat, and they arrive too late to fight.[20] But Aslan does play a martial role: he kills the White Witch.

Chapter 8 of this book touched upon ancient understandings of the word "messiah," which included among them a military leader who will overthrow oppressive political powers in battle. When some first-century Jews anticipated a messiah, they thought he would overthrow the Romans who ruled their land. Jesus in his earthly incarnation did not do this, but in Narnia Aslan defeats the White Witch bodily. While many moderns have forgotten this definition of "messiah," Lewis had not, and he did not disdain the use of force in fighting evil. He wrote an essay entitled "Why I Am Not a Pacifist," an attitude that carried over to his children's books. When all other options failed, he believed physical force may have to play a decisive role.[21] Some readers will disagree with him, but they might keep in mind the historical context in which he wrote.[22] He arrived at the front lines to fight in the Great War on his nine-

20. Extended treatments of Lewis's views on women include Mary Stewart van Leeuwen, *A Sword between the Sexes? C. S. Lewis and the Gender Debates* (Grand Rapids: Brazos, 2010); Monika B. Hilder, *The Feminine Ethos in C. S. Lewis's Chronicles of Narnia* (New York: Peter Lang, 2012); and Edith Humphrey, *Further Up and Further In: Orthodox Conversations with C. S. Lewis on Scripture and Theology* (Yonkers, NY: St. Vladimir's Seminary Press, 2017), 243–75. Although the child Lucy avoids military action in *The Lion, the Witch and the Wardrobe,* the adult Queen Lucy fights in battle as an archer in *The Horse and His Boy*. Hence Lewis is more of a feminist in this matter, at least, than many of his contemporaries in the 1950s, when the book was published. Lewis may be amenable to Lucy's active role as an archer because of his knowledge of the ancient Amazons, warrior women who fought with bows and arrows against men.

21. Lewis, "Why I Am Not a Pacifist," in *Essay Collection,* 281–93. Writing to Bede Griffiths, Oct. 5, 1938, *CL,* 2:233–34, he outlines biblical reasons to support his position. See also Lewis to Mrs. Johnson, Nov. 8, 1952, *CL,* 3:246–47, and *Perelandra,* where Ransom agonizes over the fact that the only way to defeat the villain is to kill him.

22. Stanley Hauerwas, who argues that Lewis *should* have been a pacifist, does allow for Lewis's historical context in "On Violence," in *The Cambridge Companion to C. S. Lewis,* ed. Robert MacSwain and Michael Ward (Cambridge: Cambridge University Press, 2010), 189–202.

teenth birthday, and he did everything he could to support his nation's cause in World War II.[23]

Aslan is victorious through dying in Edmund's place, the shedding of his blood, his resurrection from the dead that made death work backward, and his physical attack on the witch, all of which were necessary to accomplish the task. The New Testament also discusses Jesus's victory in multiple ways. In the first two chapters of Hebrews alone, Jesus "made purification for sins" (1:3), propitiated the sins of the people as high priest (2:17), and destroyed death by death (2:14–15). Lewis agreed with the author of Hebrews that there was no reason to pit these ideas against each another.[24]

The militant deeds of the resurrected Aslan in *The Lion, the Witch and the Wardrobe* depart from the peaceful portrait of the resurrected Jesus in the Gospels and Acts and look forward to his second coming, especially as imagined in the book of Revelation, where Jesus is both a slain lamb and a victorious warrior who battles evil to replace the satanic "kingdom of this world" with himself and his followers (11:15; 1:5–6). In the same way, Aslan first dies and then fights to overthrow the dominion of the White Witch and install his chosen four as the new rulers of Narnia.

After the battle, but before the coronation, the narrator muses, "How Aslan provided food for them all I don't know; but somehow or other they found themselves all sitting down on the grass to a fine high tea."[25] A surprisingly fine meal appearing out of nowhere to feed a crowd sitting on a green alludes to Jesus's multiplication of loaves in Mark 6:39, but underneath the allusion lies something more: the messianic banquet.[26] Jesus predicted that when God reigned on earth—that is, in the kingdom of God—everyone on God's side

23. Lewis, *Surprised by Joy* (San Diego: Harcourt Brace Jovanovich, 1955), 188. In World War II, Lewis hosted children fleeing the Blitz, delivered the BBC radio talks that became *Mere Christianity*, and traveled the island speaking to troops. See also *Reflections on the Psalms*, 124–25, where Lewis expresses the belief that Jesus thought of himself as a spiritual militant who conquered death. For more on Lewis's war experience and how it may or may not have affected his writing, see Brian Melton, "The Great War and Narnia: C. S. Lewis as Soldier and Creator," *Mythlore* 30, no. 1/2 (Fall/Winter 2011): 123–42.

24. Lewis to Mr. Young, Oct. 31, 1963, *CL*, 3:1476.

25. Ch. 17.

26. Matthew also has them sit on grass; in Luke they simply sit down. John 6:10 notes that there was "a great deal of grass," so Lewis might have been thinking of John rather than Mark. Probably he wasn't thinking of any one Gospel but harmonized them, as he was wont to do.

would feast together (Matt. 8:11). This wasn't a new idea even at the time of Jesus, and there are many examples of it in Jewish literature. The most famous might be Psalm 23 ("You prepare a table before me in the presence of my enemies"), but the most extended are in Isaiah (see especially 25:6–10). The large middle section of 1 Enoch, called the Parables of Enoch, portrays the banquet with a messianic twist. In the Parables of Enoch 62–63, oppressive rulers persecute God's people and refuse to acknowledge God and his messiah, who eventually judge and destroy the oppressors. Then everyone who had remained faithful to God eats and rejoices with the messiah. The multiplication stories in the Gospels are a foretaste of this messianic banquet, but the one in Narnia is the real thing.

Lewis alludes to the messianic banquet so often in the Chronicles that I won't take the time to highlight all of the instances. He also brings it up constantly in his other work. "The Weight of Glory" counts five promises of Scripture, and the fourth is that we shall be "fed or feasted." In a letter to Mrs. Johnson, "a dinner party" heads the list of ways that he believes heaven is symbolized for us.[27] But—and this is very important—we must be careful not to read meaning into the words "heaven" and "symbol" that Lewis didn't intend. Neither is abstract to him. This is clear in Lewis's body of work as a whole, and an interview he gave to *Time* magazine nicely summarizes his thinking on the matter. The journalist writes:

> Lewis' idea of Heaven is not the 20th Century's watered-down version of ineffable, gaseous ecstasy, but a state as real as Sunday morning breakfast. It's right there in the New Testament, says Lewis, referring to the resurrected Christ taking food with His disciples: "If the truth is that after death there comes a negatively spiritual life, an eternity of mystical experience, what more misleading way of communicating it could possibly be found than the appearance of a human form which eats boiled fish?"[28]

The solidity of "heaven," emphasized especially through good eating, will become unmistakably clear in *The Last Battle*.

Aslan establishes his reign in Narnia by deputizing his chosen representatives, led by Peter Pevensie. In the Synoptic Gospels, another Peter is Jesus's

27. Lewis, "The Weight of Glory," in *Essay Collection*, 100; Lewis to Mrs. Johnson, Nov. 8, 1952, *CL*, 3:247.

28. "Religion: Don v. Devil," *Time*, Sept. 8, 1947, 66. In this interview, Lewis is referring to Luke 24:36–42.

right-hand man: "You are Peter, and upon this rock I will build my church" (Matt. 16:18).[29] When Jesus ascends, he leaves the apostles in charge with Peter at their head until he comes again in glory. Like the biblical apostle, the Narnian Peter is head of his congregation, and he is crowned high king over his siblings. After the coronation, Aslan slips away, ceding rule in his name to the new kings and queens. Although he returns to Narnia in person throughout the series, Aslan, like Jesus, delegates authority to ordinary people in his absence.

The Lion, the Witch and the Wardrobe and *The Magician's Nephew* are modeled primarily on a single biblical narrative, and so is the next Chronicle. Many readers have recognized Lewis's major scriptural allusions in the first two books, but what he does in the third might not be so obvious.

29. Peter's special status among the twelve is well known, and Lewis didn't need any book to tell him so. Nonetheless, it might be worth noting that he highlighted the entire section on Matt. 16:18 in his Gore commentary, a passage arguing that the person of Peter himself is the "rock" on which Jesus will build his church. P. P. Levertoff, "Special Introduction to the Gospel according to Matthew," in *NCHS*, part 3, 168.

12. THE HORSE AND HIS BOY

"If the Son sets you free, you will be free indeed."

—John 8:36

This book tells the story of Shasta, an enslaved boy who runs away in the company of two talking horses, Bree and Hwin, and Aravis, an aristocratic girl fleeing a forced marriage. At the beginning of the tale all four live in Calormen, a country Lewis envisions on the models of the *Arabian Nights*, the histories of Herodotus, and the "orient" of the Hebrew Scriptures.[1] Lewis's depiction of the Calormenes has met stiff criticism, and some readers find it impossible to move past his "othering" of the dark-skinned polytheists.[2] But the truth of the matter is more complex than one might think. As early as 1931, Lewis voiced his distaste for the "Oriental," a term he later links to the literary style of the book of Proverbs.[3] His bias against "Oriental" style is written into the pompous rhetoric of elite Calormene speakers in *The Horse and His Boy*, language that mimics Proverbs. Orientalism is a form of racism, but Lewis didn't recognize it as such. He condemns racism, locating it on the "lunatic fringe," as he puts it, and insists that both science and Christianity forbid it.[4] In the same essay where he characterizes Proverbs as "bearded Orientals uttering endless platitudes," he stands up for the "red, black, yellow, and brown" people whom white Europeans have oppressed through massacre, broken treaties, theft, enslavement, lynchings, rape, and more, rounding off his list of atrocities with the insult to the injuries, "odious hypocrisy."[5] In his copy of Charles

1. Lewis to Geoffrey Bles, April 13, 1953, *CL*, 3:322.

2. See Laura Miller, *The Magician's Book: A Skeptic's Adventures in Narnia* (New York: Little, Brown, 2008), 119–28.

3. "'Early Prose Joy': C. S. Lewis's Early Draft of an Autobiographical Manuscript," ed. Andrew Lazo, *VII: Journal of the Marion E. Wade Center* 30 (2013): 28.

4. Lewis, *The Four Loves* (London: Geoffrey Bles, 1960), 36–37.

5. Lewis, "The Psalms," in *Essay Collection*, 223; cf. "The Seeing Eye," in *Essay Collection*, 63.

Gore's *Philosophy of the Good Life* (which, Lewis said, "taught [him] a lot"), he underlines Gore's indictment of British Christian racism,[6] and Lewis predicts continued oppression when "needy and greedy" technocrats colonize space: "What they will be if they meet things weaker than themselves, the black man and the red man can tell," he writes.[7] Although his wording does not pass muster today, his point is clear: he deplores racism where he recognizes it. Supplying this context doesn't excuse his portrayal of the Calormenes, but it does allow Lewis to defend himself in his own words.

The four main characters of *The Horse and His Boy* hope to escape Calormen and reach Narnia and freedom. They do, and when they meet King Lune of Archenland at the end of the book, he calls Calormen "the land of slaves." Given these themes of slavery and escape, it is not surprising to find many allusions to Moses and the flight from Egypt in *The Horse and His Boy* and then to see that its biblical foundation is Exodus.

These allusions pervade the book. Before the story begins, baby Shasta was saved from death when he was put into a small boat and picked up by a Calormene, just as the infant Moses was put into a basket in the water to save his life and picked up by Pharaoh's daughter (Exod. 2:1–10). Both Shasta and Moses grow up with foster parents whom they reject to save their own people—although Shasta is unaware that they are his own people until after he saves them.

When he and Bree leave the fisherman's hut where Shasta was raised, they steal saddlebags that belong to Bree's Calormene, along with the money in them. Shasta feels guilty, but the horse reasons: "I think it's all right. We're prisoners and captives in enemy country. That money is booty, spoil."[8] Lewis borrows the word "spoil" from Exodus 12:35–36, the divinely sanctioned plundering of the Egyptians as the Hebrews flee slavery. The KJV reads, "And they spoiled the Egyptians." We know Lewis uses it purposely here from his allegorical interpretation of the parable of the unjust steward (Luke 16:1–13), where the master in the parable is "*The World*," and "the moral is 'Cheat your master.' If he gives us wealth, talent, beauty, power etc. use them for your own (eternal) purposes—spoil the Egyptian!"[9]

6. Lewis to Mary Neylan, March 26, 1940, *CL*, 2:375. Gore, *Philosophy of the Good Life* (1923; repr. London: J. M. Dent and Sons, 1938), 97.

7. Lewis, "Religion and Rocketry," in *Essay Collection*, 235.

8. Ch. 2.

9. Lewis to Bede Griffiths, June 4, 1959, *CL*, 3:1043 (emphasis in original), and Dec. 20, 1961, *CL*, 3:1304.

The children and horses must cross a great desert between Calormen and Narnia. Their trek doesn't last forty years like the Jews' wilderness wanderings between Egypt and the promised land, but it's still a long, hard journey. Little do they know that the times they think they are in the greatest peril are the times when Aslan is closest to them. At the end of the book, they realize he allowed and even precipitated their trials to guide and save them, and in retrospect they see their struggles in a new light. Biblical Jews likewise reinterpreted their own miserable wilderness wanderings, regarding them in hindsight as a sort of honeymoon period when they were alone with God like a new bride and groom. As Hosea writes: "Therefore, I will allure her, and bring her into the wilderness, and speak tenderly to her. . . . There she shall respond as in the days of her youth, as at the time when she came out of the land of Egypt" (Hosea 2:14–15). The last reference to Exodus in *The Horse and His Boy* returns to the theme of young love and marriage when we learn that Shasta marries Aravis, the girl he met on his wanderings, just as Moses met and married his wife Zipporah (Exod. 2:15–22).

Aravis's story also dips into Scripture. As part of her plan to escape a forced marriage, she sings and dances for her father like Herod's stepdaughter did for him (Mark 6:17–29) and feigns going out with her maid just as Jephthah's daughter actually did go out with her women to bewail her virginity before she was executed (Judg. 11:30–40). Jephthah's daughter knew she was going to die as a result of her father's terrible vow to kill the first person he saw walk out his door. When Aravis learns that her father had promised her in marriage, she plans to kill herself, but the mare Hwin intervenes, persuading her to run away instead. In order to safeguard her escape, Aravis drugs her maid. When Shasta hears this part of the story, he wonders aloud what happened to the girl, and Aravis replies nonchalantly that she must have been beaten, an act and attitude Aravis will pay for.

Near the end of the book, when the four main characters have almost arrived at the Hermit's house, a lion chases them and attacks Aravis on her horse, ripping her back with its claws. The lion is Aslan, and he later tells Aravis that the wounds replicate the punishment her drugged maid received. This story may echo one of the most bizarre passages in the Bible, Exodus 4:24–26.[10] Moses is traveling with his wife Zipporah when God attacks him. Zipporah quickly circumcises one of their sons, laying the foreskin on "his [Moses's?] feet" and proclaiming, "You are a bridegroom of blood to me!" Thus she wards off the violent deity. In *The Horse and His Boy,* Aravis is attacked rather than Shasta-the-Moses-figure, but the fact that Aravis resembles Zipporah in other

10. I am indebted to my student Caleb Skocy for suggesting this parallel.

ways (she is riding on a journey with "Moses," and she marries him) and that Aslan targets one of his friends could be enough to claim a scriptural echo. Lewis knew the passage, underlining it in his 1839 Bible.[11]

The "bridegroom" language of Exodus 4:25–26 may also have caught Lewis's eye. *The Horse and His Boy* talks about marriage far more than the other Chronicles, which almost never mention it. Weddings abound in this book, with two nuptials proposed but reviled (Aravis to Ahoshta and Susan to Rabadash) and three welcomed and accomplished (Aravis to Cor, and both horses to unnamed others).

Lewis alludes to Genesis 12:1 and Psalm 45:10 throughout the arc of Aravis's story. The allusions snap into focus when we compare their use in *Reflections on the Psalms,* where Lewis embeds Genesis 12:1 in a discussion of Psalm 45, "a laureate ode on a royal wedding."[12] The historical context of the psalm makes him think of "Oriental" weddings where a miserable girl is forced to leave home against her will (a scenario Lewis fictionalizes with tragic results for the bride, Psyche's mother, at the end of the first chapter of *Till We Have Faces*). The loss is painful, Lewis says, "but to be called up higher still costs more." Then he quotes Genesis 12:1, where God tells Abraham, "Get thee out of thy country, and from thy kindred, and from thy father's house." Lewis continues, "It is a terrible command; turn your back on all you know." But the reward in Genesis and Psalm 45 is the same: "'I will make of thee a great nation.'" Like Abraham in Genesis 12 and the bride in Psalm 45, Aravis is called to "forget her people and her father's house" (Ps. 45:10) in response to a God she does not know.[13] When King Lune expresses his sorrow that Aravis was driven from her "father's house," the biblical allusions are confirmed. But Aravis enjoys a happy ending: she is free, and her descendants help build a great nation, carrying on the royal line of Archenland in service to Aslan rather than to Tash.

The villain of *The Horse and His Boy,* the Calormene Prince Rabadash, invades Archenland as he attempts to seize another runaway would-be bride, Queen Susan. During the battle, he leaps from a wall but is caught on the way down by a hook that "had had a ring in it" to tie horses "ages ago." The hook with

11. C. S. Lewis personal library, Marion E. Wade Center, Wheaton College, Wheaton, IL.

12. *Reflections on the Psalms* (New York: Harcourt, Brace & World, 1958), 128.

13. Lewis underlines the second half of Ps. 45:10, "forget also thine own people, and thy father's house," in his 1839 Bible, and he weaves the words into *That Hideous Strength* as Jane Studdock meets the Pendragon (ch. 7). Lewis emphasizes the word "king," mentions marriage, and writes that he made Jane forget "her father's house."

the ring is reminiscent of a ring that hangs on a wall in the Temple Mount complex (Haram al-Sharif) in Jerusalem. Muslim lore has it that Muhammad's horse was tied there before they made their night journey through the seven heavens.[14] In the Hadith, Muhammad says: "I was brought al-Buraq who is an animal white and long, larger than a donkey but smaller than a mule, who would place his hoof a distance equal to the range of vision. I mounted it and came to the Temple (Bait Maqdis in Jerusalem), then tethered it to the ring used by the prophets."[15]

Lewis never visited Jerusalem, but he owned a book that told the story of the night journey, Washington Irving's *Life of Mahomet.* Irving writes, "Continuing their aerial course, they arrived at the gate of the holy temple at Jerusalem, where, alighting from Al Borak, Mahomet fastened her to the rings where the prophets before him had fastened her."[16]

Lewis may or may not have been thinking of al-Buraq's ring when he wrote about the hook in the wall in Archenland, but the possibility is worth considering in light of the fact that, among the Chronicles, the phrase "night journey" appears only in *The Horse and His Boy*. Even more, the first time it appears is the first time Shasta mounts the horse Bree in chapter 1, when Bree himself is tied to a ring.

If Lewis is echoing Muhammad's night journey, he flips the story on its head, because Rabadash, in contrast to Muhammad, isn't going anywhere. He is stuck, unable to move up or down, until his enemies pluck him off the wall. Once captured, he meets a fate similar to that of the Babylonian king Nebuchadnezzar in the book of Daniel. Nebuchadnezzar speaks arrogantly, so God makes him like a beast of the field who eats grass for seven years until he comes to himself, and his kingdom is restored (Dan. 4).[17] When Daniel retells the story later, he says that, because the king acted proudly, he dwelt with wild donkeys (Dan. 5:20–21). Rabadash speaks haughtily in front of Aslan, who turns him into a donkey. Shasta's people promise to feed him well until he may effect the cure Aslan prescribed and regain human form. When he does, a chastened Rabadash rules his kingdom peaceably ever after.

14. I am indebted to my student Katelyn Hageman for pointing out the parallel, which I would not have seen otherwise, and was inspired by her concerted work on it. For controversies about the ring, see Dore Gold, *The Fight for Jerusalem: Radical Islam, the West, and the Future of the Holy City* (Washington, DC: Regnery, 2007), 89; Hillel Cohen, *Year Zero of the Arab-Israeli Conflict 1929* (Waltham, MA: Brandeis University Press, 2015), 60–63.

15. Sahih Muslim 1:318.

16. Washington Irving, *Life of Mahomet*, Everyman's Library 513 (London: J. M. Dent and Sons, 1915), 78.

17. Lewis marks this passage in his 1839 Bible.

As he constructs this scene, Lewis may also be alluding to 2 Peter 2, especially as translated by James Moffatt, whose wording is reflected in *The Horse and His Boy*. Because Moffatt's work is often more an idiosyncratic paraphrase than it is a translation, we can trace how some of its eccentricities may have made their way into Rabadash's story.

Moffatt's version of 2 Peter 2, which Lewis marked up copiously, condemns those who "are not afraid to scoff at the angelic Glories" (2:11). Their "doom comes apace from of old, and destruction is awake upon their trail" (2:3). The KJV doesn't use the word "doom" in 2:3 ("whose judgment now of a long time lingereth not, and their damnation slumbereth not"), but Aslan uses it twice as he allows Rabadash to scoff and rant. First the lion tells him, "Your doom is very near," and then that it is "nearer."[18] Moffatt says of the arrogant, "like irrational animals . . . born for *capture* and corruption, they scoff at what they are ignorant of; and *like animals* they will suffer corruption and ruin, done out of the profits of their evil-doing" (2:12–13). The KJV doesn't include the word "capture," which is essential to the story of Rabadash, but all translations of 2 Peter do compare the scoffers to Balaam, "who liked the profits of evil-doing—but he got reproved for his malpractice: a dumb ass spoke with human voice" (2:15–16). Given the overlap between Moffatt's translation of 2 Peter 2 and Lewis's word choice in this section, it is likely that Moffatt influenced it.

The stallion Bree is also a prideful beast who gets his comeuppance from Aslan in a comic scene with serious theological underpinnings. Bree denies Aslan is a real lion, because then he must have paws, a tail, and even whiskers. Just as he says this, Aslan sneaks up behind him. He invites Bree: "Touch me. Smell me. Here are my paws, here is my tail, these are my whiskers. I am a true Beast."[19] This scene refutes Docetic thought, which asserted that Jesus was not a true human being with a real physical body. Instead, like a mirage, he *seemed* to have a body (the Greek root of the word "Docetic" means "to seem"). At the same time, it echoes the apostle Thomas, who doubted the reality of Jesus's bodily resurrection from the dead until Jesus told him to touch his wounds (John 20:24–29). By echoing Thomas, whose name means "twin," Lewis makes a sly addition to the theme of twins and doubles that permeates this book.[20]

18. Ch. 15.

19. Ch. 14.

20. For more on the theme of twins/doubling in *The Horse and His Boy*, see the chapter "Mercury" in Michael Ward, *Planet Narnia* (Oxford: Oxford University Press, 2008).

The mare Hwin, in contrast to Bree, is not only brave but humble. When she meets Aslan for the first time, she trots over to offer herself to him to eat because she would rather be "eaten by you than fed by anyone else." Thus she becomes the equine equivalent of Ignatius of Antioch (d. ca. 110), who wrote a letter expressing his eagerness to die for the Lord. En route to his martyrdom in Rome, he prays that he "may enjoy the wild beasts" who will devour him there. If they don't want to eat him, he will "compel them to do so," calling himself the "wheat of God, ground by the teeth of wild beasts, that I may be found the pure bread of Christ" (Letter to the Romans 4–5).

Then there is Lewis's echo of the Trinity. In chapter 11, "The Unwelcome Fellow Traveler," Shasta encounters an Aslan who walks incognito, shrouded in a fog so thick that the boy can't see him. At first, he can only hear him breathing. Breaking the silence, Shasta asks his companion if he is a ghost. The lion breathes on him and says, "That is not the breath of a ghost. Tell me your sorrows."

The use of the word "ghost" here was probably influenced by Moffatt's unique translation of Luke. Luke is the only Gospel where the resurrected Jesus appears to his disciples and scares them so much that they think he might be a *pneuma*, a Greek word that holds multiple meanings, but which only Moffatt, among all the English translations available to Lewis that I am aware of, renders as "ghost."[21] Like Aslan, the Lukan Jesus reassures his disciples by emphasizing the physicality of his body, saying, "A ghost has not flesh and bones as you see I have" (Luke 24:37–39, Moffatt). Lewis highlights this Lukan passage and uses Moffatt's word "ghost" in *Miracles* when he talks about the reality of Jesus's resurrection.[22]

This appearance of Jesus in Luke occurs while two disciples are telling their friends what had happened to them as they had walked to the village of Emmaus. A stranger had approached them, noticed that they looked sad, and asked them what they were talking about. After they told him, the stranger, "beginning with Moses and all the prophets . . . interpreted to them the things about himself in all the Scriptures" (Luke 24:27). Aslan does the same thing after Shasta pours out his sorrows, revealing that he was the lion they had met along the way. He was the one who had driven the four of them together; he was the comforting cat at the tombs, and he was the lion who forced them to a gallop so Shasta could head off the Calormene army. At the end of both scenes, the Lukan and the Narnian, the divine figure vanishes when the human characters realize who he is.

21. The Vulgate gives *spiritus*, and the KJV, Knox, and RSV "spirit."
22. *Miracles* (1947; repr., New York: Macmillan, 1960), 146.

Before Aslan disappears, Shasta asks, "Who *are* you?" He responds, "Myself" three times, with the third time "whispered so softly you could hardly hear it, and yet it seemed to come from all round you as if the leaves rustled with it." The third, almost inaudible "myself" alludes to the third person of the Trinity, the Holy Spirit, and with it Lewis has created a subtle effect indeed. Trinitarian theology is difficult to comprehend, so obscuring these words in literal fog and whispers is brilliantly appropriate. Even more, the word for "breath," which occurs so often in this scene, and the word for "spirit," as in the Holy Spirit, come from the same Greek word that Moffatt translated "ghost" in Luke 24:37–39: *pneuma*. Lewis is doing the same thing with breath/spirit/ghost/*pneuma* here as he did with good news/gospel/*euangelion* in *The Lion, the Witch and the Wardrobe*—turning a common English word into a Trojan horse that carries hidden theological firepower.[23]

Two more biblical verses are tucked into Lewis's tiny Trinitarian allusion. First, in Aslan's whisper Lewis may be echoing the "still, small voice" of God that the prophet Elijah hears in 1 Kings 19:12. The second verse is more significant and, fittingly, from Exodus. When Moses meets God for the first time, he doesn't see him face-to-face, but in the form of a burning bush, and without a formal introduction, so Moses must ask God who he is. God replies, "I am who I am" (3:14), a response very like Aslan's "Myself." Lewis himself repeats the biblical name "I am" three times in a row in the story of his conversion, *Surprised by Joy*. In the penultimate chapter he recounts how he felt the unwelcome Presence stalking him when he was alone in the dark, just as Aslan stalked Shasta as he walked alone through the night. Lewis writes, "My adversary . . . only said, 'I am the Lord'; 'I am that I am'; 'I am.'"[24] Three paragraphs later, he surrenders and admits "that God is God."

23. The word *pneuma* also means "wind," and Lewis may be thinking of the burst of wind that showered him with leaves on Addison's Walk Sept. 19, 1931 (see chapter 1 of this book). He confirms the echo of the Trinity in his letter to Sophia Storr, Dec. 24, 1959, *CL*, 3:1113.

24. *Surprised by Joy* (San Diego: Harcourt Brace Jovanovich, 1955), ch. 14, "Checkmate," 227–28.

13. PRINCE CASPIAN

"Do whatever he tells you."

—John 2:5

Prince Caspian contains the fewest biblical references of any of the Chronicles, and almost all of them appear late in the book, only when Aslan does. In their second visit to Narnia, the four Pevensie children discover that centuries have passed in its time after they returned to their own world at the end of *The Lion, the Witch and the Wardrobe.* Eventually they identify their mission: to restore the princeling Caspian to his rightful place as ruler of Narnia, a place that had been usurped by his wicked uncle Miraz.

Dwarves play a major role in the plot. Most are trustworthy, but a few are not. The dwarf Nikabrik loses faith in the old tales of Aslan and loses hope in Aslan's return, which leads him to foment revolt from within Caspian's inner circle of advisors. Nikabrik's attempt to summon the White Witch from the dead to "help" them may remind us of Saul, the first king of Israel, when he forces the so-called Witch of Endor to summon the ghost of the prophet Samuel from Sheol, the land of the dead (1 Sam. 28).[1] Then Saul, like Nikabrik, dies a violent death in battle within the day as a direct result of his action. Those who "consult the ghosts and the familiar spirits who chirp and mutter; . . . the dead on behalf of the living . . . will have no dawn," Isaiah warns (8:19–20). Both God and Aslan disapprove of necromancy, or illicit congress with the dead.

With everything against them militarily, the Narnians make a desperate bid to engage Miraz in single combat. High King Peter's letter of invitation opens in the same way as a Pauline letter: "Sender to recipient, greeting."[2] Here we may discern the tiniest tip of Lewis's hat to Paul, though the epistolary greeting was not unique to him.

1. Cf. Lewis, *Miracles* (1947; repr., New York: Macmillan, 1960), 145. I use "Witch of Endor" because it was Lewis's nickname for the housekeeper of his childhood home.

2. Ch. 13.

The bulk of the Scripture references in *Prince Caspian* are concentrated in the madcap procession that Aslan and Bacchus, the Greco-Roman god of wine, enjoy with the girls—and not just the human girls, Susan and Lucy, but also Bacchus's maenads, the women who travel with him. Like the "harrowing of hell" in *The Lion, the Witch and the Wardrobe,* the Bacchic procession serves to keep the girls away from battle. This long scene, in my opinion the best in the book, didn't make it into the 2008 film adaptation of *Prince Caspian,* perhaps for fear that its wine and pagan revelry would offend certain factions of its target audience. Never a teetotaler himself, and utterly dismissive of those who were (remember how he describes Scrubb's parents on the first page of *Voyage of the "Dawn Treader"*?), Lewis might appreciate the irony that the chapter with the most scriptural resonance in *Prince Caspian* may have been culled from the movie to protect the sensibilities of some of its most Bible-loving viewers. He objected "strongly" to Christians who forbade drinking wine, calling them "unscriptural," because wine is the "medium of the only rite [Jesus] imposed on all His followers," Holy Communion.[3] His wife, Joy Davidman, puts it more stridently: "He who turned water into wine to gladden a wedding is now accused by many of favoring that abominable fluid grape juice."[4]

In chapter 14, "How All Were Very Busy," the nasty schoolboys Aslan turns into pigs may remind readers of the legion of demons that Jesus throws out of the Gerasene demoniac and casts into swine in Mark 5:10–13. Lewis alludes to this porcine-themed exorcism in the second book of his science fiction trilogy, *Perelandra,* when the main character, Ransom, remembers that demons hate being cast into a void. But the boys in *Prince Caspian* aren't demonic, and the author doesn't kill them. Rather, in light of the overt references to Greek mythology in this part of the book, Lewis is probably alluding to Homer's *Odyssey,* where Circe turns men into pigs.[5]

The most intricate play of Scripture in the chapter occurs as the joyful troupe meets Caspian's old nurse, who is sick in bed. When Aslan heals her, we recall the miracle early in the Gospel of Mark where Jesus cures Simon Peter's bedridden mother-in-law (1:29–31). Shortly thereafter, a paralytic is lowered on a bed through a roof that his friends dismantle so he can reach Jesus (2:4). In like manner, the nurse's home in *Prince Caspian* is too small for Aslan to enter, so he lifts it up on his shoulders until it falls apart. Then Bacchus,

3. Lewis to Mrs. Johnson, March 16, 1955, *CL,* 3:580, and March 13, 1956, *CL,* 3:719.

4. Joy Davidman, *Smoke on the Mountain* (Philadelphia: Westminster, 1954), 46.

5. Charles A. Huttar, "'Let Grill Be Grill': The Metamorphoses of Rabadash and Others," *VII: Journal of the Marion E. Wade Center* 29 (2012): 28–29.

like Jesus at Cana in the Gospel of John, turns her water into excellent—and much-appreciated—wine (John 2:1–11). When Bacchus and Aslan join hands, such things are bound to happen. As he explains in *Miracles,* Lewis saw Bacchus/Dionysus as the mythical forerunner of Jesus the wine-giver, bringer of festivity and joy.[6] A dangerous figure indeed within his native Greco-Roman mythology, Bacchus becomes "safe" under the supervision of the lion, as Lucy and Susan realize at the end of chapter 11.

Bacchus was an important figure to Lewis from his earliest interest in myths as a teenager, especially through Euripides's play *Bacchae,* one of three books he liked best at school.[7] As a young adult on the cusp of conversion, Lewis even acted out Bacchic scenes. In 1930 he tells his "First Friend," Arthur Greeves, that his "Second Friend," Owen Barfield, was hosting a Bacchic festival to celebrate his homemade wine. Lewis writes, "The adopted baby is to be the infant Bacchus. Harwood with his fat shiny face, on the donkey, will be Silenus. [Barfield] and I Corybantes. [Mrs. Barfield] a Maenad. [Barfield] and I will write the poetry & she will compose a dance. You ought to come." Years later he reflects, "The man who rushed with the Maenads on the mountains to tear and eat the beast which also was the god" was closer to the spirit of Jews and Christians than the more "refined" Hindus and Stoics were.[8]

Lewis was far from the first Christian to identify Jesus with Bacchus, a connection that was not uncommon in early church literature, and which the Gospel of John itself may initiate.[9] He foreshadows the Bacchic scene in *Prince Caspian* in the second chapter of *The Lion, the Witch and the Wardrobe,* where Tumnus remembers glorious times past when Bacchus appeared and Narnian streams flowed with wine instead of water. This phenomenon alludes not just to Greco-Roman imagery but also to the Hebrew prophets, who announce that on the day of the Lord the mountains will drip with wine (Joel 3:18; Amos 9:13). The Hebrew word for wine in both verses is *'asis,* not the more common

6. *Miracles,* 114, 136.

7. *Surprised by Joy* (San Diego: Harcourt Brace Jovanovich, 1955), 113.

8. *Surprised by Joy,* 199–200; Lewis to Greeves, June 31 [*sic*], 1930, *CL,* 1:912–13; to Bede Griffiths, April 15, 1947, *CL,* 2:770.

9. For more on Bacchus and Jesus, see Dennis R. MacDonald, *The Dionysian Gospel: The Fourth Gospel and Euripides* (Minneapolis: Fortress, 2017), and Courtney J. P. Friesen, *Reading Dionysus: Euripides' Bacchae and the Cultural Contestations of Greeks, Jews, Romans, and Christians* (Tübingen: Mohr Siebeck, 2015). For more on Bacchus and *Prince Caspian,* see J. Patrick Pazdziora and Joshua C. Richards, "Balder, Adonis, Bacchus, Aslan: Frazer and Sacrament in *The Lion, the Witch and the Wardrobe* and *Prince Caspian,*" *VII: Journal of the Marion E. Wade Center* 34 (2017): 83–101.

yayin, so some teetotalling Christians have tried to argue that *'asis* is unfermented grape juice. However, other verses in Joel and Isaiah refute that claim. Joel 1:5 uses *'asis* as a synonym for *yayin,* and both drinks make one drunk. Isaiah 49:26 says the same. Lewis had no patience for anyone who claimed otherwise, writing, "Of course the wine of the Bible was real fermented wine and alcoholic," and he thought anyone who believed it wasn't must be "v[ery] ignorant." Lewis found it hard to excuse educated people who propagated "such lies about history." At the same time, the Bible condemned drunkenness, and so did he. Lewis's brother, Warren, was an active alcoholic, and he knew the ravages of alcoholism all too well.[10]

10. Lewis to Mrs. Johnson, May 14, 1955, *CL,* 3:608; to John M. Gordan, Jan. 26, 1960, *CL,* 3:1126.

14. THE VOYAGE OF THE "DAWN TREADER"

"I am the light of the world."

—John 8:12

Like *Prince Caspian*, the next two books in the series, *The Voyage of the "Dawn Treader"* and *The Silver Chair*, are not based on a single biblical narrative, but both are guided by an unspoken biblical motif, a theme that moves silently through the book. In *The Voyage of the "Dawn Treader"* it is "I am the light of the world" (John 8:12). Lewis, who read the Gospel of John in Greek just before his conversion in 1931, wrote soon after that "God 'is the Father of Lights and in Him is *no darkness at all*' [James 1:17; John 1:5]. . . . He is pure Light. . . . Go out on any perfect morning in early summer before the world is awake and see, not the thing itself, but the material symbol of it."[1]

John emphasizes light more than the other Gospels do, and it applies the image to Jesus differently. In Luke, Simeon compares the infant Jesus to light (2:32), and in Matthew, Jesus tells his followers "*You* are the light of the world" (5:14), but Jesus identifies himself as light only in John. It is the only Gospel that emphasizes the war between light and darkness, another major theme in *The Voyage of the "Dawn Treader,"* and it is the Gospel that has most visibly affected all of Lewis's writing on Scripture. He employs it in the other Chronicles, but it comes to the fore here.

That said, the book's first reference to the Gospel of John is oblique, if it is one at all. It concerns the boy everyone loves to hate, Eustace Clarence Scrubb, who turns into a dragon through his selfishness and greed. After Aslan grants Eustace the grace of penitential suffering in dragon form, he restores him to his human state, but first he tells him to undress. Dragon-Eustace is puzzled, but he soon realizes that, as a reptile, he can shed his skin. With Aslan's help, he scratches away many lizard layers, and he is thrown into a well, just as the invalid in John 5 longed to be lowered into the pool of Bethzatha to be healed. But in John, the man never touched the water; Jesus healed him without it. Therefore

1. Lewis to Greeves, Sept. 12, 1933, *CL*, 2:122 (emphasis in original).

the well in *The Voyage of the "Dawn Treader"* might not refer to Bethzatha but rather to the universal understanding of water as refreshment and renewal.

Because water is such an important symbol in the Chronicles, it is worth exploring in more depth. As an Irishman who grew up by the sea, Lewis considered "bathing" one of the great joys of life.[2] The Chronicles are full of water, from the pools in the Wood between the Worlds in *The Magician's Nephew*, to the children's initially delightful time at the seashore in *Prince Caspian*, to the Marshwiggles' fens in *The Silver Chair*, to the waterfall that opens *The Last Battle*. In the context of Eustace's altered physiology and other dragon-infested scenes in *The Voyage of the "Dawn Treader,"* it's worth noting that bodies of water from pools to oceans were associated with dragons everywhere in the ancient world—including Jewish and Christian thought.[3]

For Christians, water is the sine qua non of the sacrament of baptism, which marks both death and new life. That is exactly what it does for Eustace, who dies to some of the nastier aspects of his character and begins to build a better one. If Lewis is thinking of baptism here—and how could he not?—Eustace's "undragoning" before he hits the water might reflect the exorcisms performed before the sacrament in the Anglican rite.[4] But Eastern Orthodox tradition offers an even better crystallization of the images of water, dragons, and new birth. In their celebration of Theophany, the feast that commemorates Christ's baptism in the river Jordan, the Orthodox sing, "[He] is crushing the heads of the dragons on the waters [Ps. 74:13]. Let us therefore draw water with gladness. . . . For the grace of the Spirit is being given invisibly to those who draw with faith by Christ, God and the Savior of our souls."

Another Orthodox hymn on baptism speaks directly to Aslan dressing Eustace when he comes out of the pool. When Eustace tells his cousin the story, Edmund wonders how an animal with paws could dress anyone, and Eustace admits he doesn't remember how it was done. But the proof is that Eustace is wearing "new clothes."[5] Here Lewis is referring to the Greek of Galatians 3:27, "As many as have been baptized into Christ, have put on Christ." The Greek word underneath the English "put on," *enduō*, means "put on clothes." Eastern Ortho-

2. See his letters to his brother, Sept. 3, 1927, *CL*, 1:723; to Greeves, June 26, 1931, *CL*, 1:963–64; and to Belle Allen, Aug. 16, 1949, *CL*, 2:969, where Lewis closely connects water and light; *Surprised by Joy* (San Diego: Harcourt Brace Jovanovich, 1955), 178; and more.

3. Joseph Fontenrose, *Python: A Study of Delphic Myth and Its Origins* (1959; repr., Berkeley: University of California Press, 1980), 545–49.

4. This insight comes from Edith Humphrey via personal correspondence.

5. Ch. 7.

dox Christians chant Galatians 3:27 over and over at every baptism, and many Orthodox theologians have discussed its connection with the white garment that the newly baptized put on when they emerge from the water. Lewis might not have known the chant, but given his close connections to Orthodox circles in the 1950s (see chapter 1), it is very possible that he did. Even if he didn't, he read the New Testament in Greek and fully understood the implications of the verb *enduō*, as will be proven beyond a doubt at the end of *The Last Battle*.

Water, to mix metaphors, can be a two-edged sword. On one hand, it is required for life and desirable for cleanliness and comfort. On the other, out of proportion, or out of control, it kills. In *The Voyage of the "Dawn Treader,"* the destructive force of water is shown in a conventional way through a storm at sea, a must-have for any seafaring tale. Its terrible aspect also appears on Deathwater Island, which holds a lake that turns anything dipped in it to gold. The first danger the water poses is death by aurification, and the second is human violence goaded by greed. Aslan appears to a large group of people for the first time in the book to stop a fight over who owns the water, "shining as if he were in bright sunlight, though the sun had in fact gone." Then the narrator observes, "nobody dared to ask what it was. They knew it was Aslan."[6] This is one of the clearest allusions to Scripture in the Chronicles—almost but not quite a quotation of the second half of John 21:12: "None of the disciples dared to ask him, 'Who are you?' because they knew it was the Lord." Lewis reserves an exact quotation of the first half of the verse, "Come and have breakfast," for Aslan's final appearance at the end of the book, where he will shine even brighter.

Aslan's brilliance may remind readers of the only place in the Gospels where Jesus is explicitly compared to the sun, Matthew's version of the transfiguration: "He was transfigured before them, and his face shone like the sun" (17:2). Mark and Luke include the story but not Matthew's solar language, while the Gospel of John, otherwise so infused with light, doesn't include the scene at all.

The lion appears in a beam of light at another dangerous time for the seafarers, when the *Dawn Treader* is trapped in the darkness where nightmares come true. After Aslan helps them escape, everyone looks back, but they can't see it anymore, because "the Dark Island and the darkness had vanished forever." Aslan's light had "shone in the darkness, and the darkness did not overcome it," as John writes in the prologue to his Gospel (1:5). Both Jesus and Aslan have "come as light into the world" so their followers do not have to remain in the dark (John 12:46).

Light and dark, like water, are universal symbols. Untutored tots everywhere are afraid of the dark and long for light to come to vanquish the monsters under

6. Ch. 8.

their beds. John introduces the mortal combat between darkness and light in the prologue of his Gospel to set the stage for their standoff at the end of Jesus's life. It is no accident that after Satan enters into Judas at dinner, and Judas departs to betray Jesus, John concludes the scene with "And it was night" (John 13:30). To Lewis, this terse observation was "unforgettable."[7] An echo of the scene appears in Lewis's novel *Till We Have Faces*. The main character, Orual, has just performed the worst act of her life, forcing her sister Psyche to betray the trust of her lover the mountain god. As Orual departs, "the sun sets."

Before Johannine allusions crescendo at the end of *The Voyage of the "Dawn Treader,"* Lewis echoes other Scripture. The former star Coriakin, reluctant ruler of Dufflepud Island, eats only bread and wine, a quintessentially eucharistic repast. This does not read too much into a simple meal. "With things like Bread, Wine, Honey, Apples, there are all the echoes of myth, fairy-tale, poetry, & scripture," Lewis observes, a sentence that embodies the appeal of his writing better than anything anyone else could say.[8]

Coriakin is a grounded star. We saw that stars can be personified in the Bible when we looked at Job 38:7, "the morning stars sang together, and all the sons of God shouted for joy," in the chapter on *The Magician's Nephew*. Lewis echoes the first half of that verse in *The Voyage of the "Dawn Treader"* when the retired star Ramandu and his unnamed daughter greet the rising sun with their strange silver song. As they sing, thousands of white birds fly out of the sun, but only Lucy notices one of them placing something like a live coal in Ramandu's mouth. This alludes to Isaiah 6:1–7, where the prophet has a vision of God's heavenly throne room. Isaiah receives a burning coal in his mouth from a seraph, one of the six-winged creatures that guard the heavenly altar. In Hebrew *seraph* means "it burns." Although Lewis had no Hebrew, he knew that.[9] The seraph touches the fiery coal to Isaiah's mouth and proclaims, "Your guilt is departed and your sin is blotted out."

Ramandu explains that he is a "star at rest" who receives a fire-berry from the sun every morning, each one making him younger, until at last he will be young enough to dance again amid the heavenly host. Eustace, who doesn't understand, asks him if stars aren't just balls of flaming gas.[10] Ramandu replies, "Even in your world . . . that is not what a star is but only what it is made of." Then he informs them that they have already met a star—Coriakin—who

7. "MTBC," 155.

8. Lewis to Mary Van Deusen, March 19, 1955, *CL*, 3:583.

9. Lewis, *The Discarded Image* (Cambridge: Cambridge University Press, 1964), 71.

10. Tolkien represents Lewis thinking of stars in the same way in the poem "Mythopoeia" (lines 5–8).

lost his place in the heavens, sentenced to manage the Duffers as punishment. Ramandu refuses to tell them "what faults a star can commit."[11]

The belief that stars are sentient beings is not uncommon in ancient Jewish thought. Philo writes that God populates every bit of the cosmos with living things: land animals on earth, sea creatures in the water, and stars, which are said to be "mind of purest kind through and through," in the air.[12] As "minds," stars can sin. To explore this idea further, we turn again to Job 38:7:

> The morning stars sang together,
> and all the sons of God shouted for joy.

Job 38:7 is a glorious piece of Hebrew poetry. Every language has its favorite ways of writing poetry, and ancient Hebrew used what we now call poetic parallelism. One line expresses something, and the next line repeats a similar thought in different words. In Job 38:7, the stars sing, and the sons of God shout. Parallel subjects may be considered equivalent, so the "morning stars" are also "sons of God." In the context of Job, the "sons of God" are members of God's heavenly court, who are sometimes called angels. When Job 38:7 was translated from Hebrew into Greek, the Hebrew "sons of God" became "angels" (Greek *angeloi*), showing how fluid in kind these divine beings could be understood to be. To ancient Jews and Christians, "sons of God" and angels were closely aligned with stars, and as divine beings with free will, stars can sin. "How you are fallen from heaven, O Day Star, son of Dawn!" Isaiah exclaims. Although the star in Isaiah 14:12 refers to the king of Babylon, it later took on a legendary new life. Translated into Latin as "Lucifer," which means "light bearer," the Day Star was eventually identified with Satan.[13] The clearest Jewish text about stars sinning and punished appears in Enoch's Book of the Watchers, where there is "a prison for the stars and the hosts of heaven . . . because they did not come out at their appointed times" (18:14–15). Could Coriakin be one of these recalcitrant Enochic stars?

Ramandu's island marks "the beginning of the end of the world." In order to fulfill their quest to return the seven lost lords to Narnia, Ramandu tells the seafarers that they must leave one of their own company behind in the utter east.

11. Ch. 14.

12. Philo, *Dreams* 133. Lewis mentions Plato's view on "the true gods, deified stars" and its intersection with Scholastic ideas about angels in *The Discarded Image*, 41–42.

13. Jeffrey Burton Russell, *Satan: The Early Christian Tradition* (Ithaca, NY: Cornell University Press, 1981), 130–31.

Reepicheep the mouse, who has longed for exactly that his entire life, joyfully volunteers. As the *Dawn Treader* sails farther and farther east, the sun grows bigger and bigger, and the light grows more and more intense, but everyone thrives, developing eyes as strong as eagles, until the vessel almost runs aground.

The three children and the mouse disembark to wade through shallow water to the very end of the flat Narnian world, where Reepicheep leaves them to enter Aslan's country. He plunges over the edge of the world in his little coracle, to be seen no more until the end of the final book in the series, *The Last Battle*. The children will reunite with him there in the new Narnia, where the lion preserves all his saints.

Lewis was probably thinking of Enoch when he wrote about Reepicheep, too. In the Bible, Enoch "walked with God, and was no more, for God took him" (Gen. 5:21–24). The Hebrew Scriptures say nothing more on the topic, a silence that inspired many questions—Why did God take Enoch? Where? For how long?—which the authors of 1 Enoch attempted to answer. They believed the words "walked with God" meant that Enoch (like Reepicheep) enjoyed an especially close relationship with God, and that after God took him, Enoch lived with God to the end of the age. None of these speculations are in the Bible; they appear only in extrabiblical Enochic literature. Lewis points to this literature in his novel *That Hideous Strength* when he writes, "Arthur did not die; but Our Lord took him, to be in the body till the end of time . . . with Enoch and Elias and Moses and Melchisedec the King."[14]

After Reepicheep disappears, Lucy, Edmund, and Eustace meet a lamb. Portraying Aslan, the Christ figure of the Chronicles, as a lamb may seem like an obvious move to modern Christians, but in fact John is the only Gospel, and one of the few books in the entire New Testament, to symbolize Jesus as such.[15] In

14. *That Hideous Strength* (1946; repr., New York: Macmillan, 1965), ch. 13. On Lewis, Melchizedek, and the book of Hebrews, see also his letter to Mrs. Johnson, May 14, 1955, *CL*, 2:608.

15. Outside John and Revelation, the only verses in the New Testament that explicitly compare Jesus to a lamb are Acts 8:32 and 1 Pet. 1:19. Acts and 1 Peter use the Greek *amnos*, while Revelation uses only *arnion*, a word unique to Revelation in the New Testament with the exception of John 21:15, where it does not refer to Jesus. The NRSV translates 1 Cor. 5:7 to include the word "lamb," but it isn't present in the Greek, though it is implied in context. John 19:14 notes that Jesus was crucified at noon on the day of preparation for the Passover, which implies that Jesus is the paschal lamb, but the author allows his readers to make the connection themselves.

Depicting Jesus as a lamb has not been uncontroversial in Christian history. In the year 692, Eastern Christians at the Council in Trullo forbade it in visual art because

the first chapter of the Gospel, John the Baptist cries out, "Behold the lamb of God!" twice, the only explicit references the Gospel makes to Jesus as lamb. The book of Revelation also visualizes Jesus as a lamb. The last scene in *The Voyage of the "Dawn Treader"* is drawn mostly from John 21, the last chapter of the Gospel, which never refers to Jesus as a lamb, and from Revelation, which often does.

The children can barely look at the Lamb for its brightness, even with their eagles' eyes. This is the second time *The Voyage of the "Dawn Treader"* uses the aquiline image, and though it may seem unremarkable, or even clichéd, it's not. It draws first on Scripture and then on ancient Christian reflection on that Scripture. The Scripture is John and Revelation, both of which have long been symbolized in visual art by the figure of an eagle, most notably via Revelation 4. That chapter introduces four "living creatures," each with a different face: one a human, one an ox, one a lion, and one an eagle. They sing praise to God 24–7, every hour of every day. About a century after Revelation was written, Christians reflecting on it began to identify the four living creatures with the four canonical gospels. The eagle came to represent the Gospel of John because its high Christology "soars" above the other three. According to Augustine, the other three Gospels concern themselves with Christ's humanity, but the Gospel of John focuses on his divinity. Three of the living creatures are earthbound, and that is why they are attached to Gospels that focus on Jesus the man. But the eagle, which soars above the earth, represents Jesus the deity. Therefore, Augustine writes, the eagle can "gaze upon the light of the unchangeable truth with those keenest and steadiest eyes of the heart."[16]

The author of Revelation was named John, and since some early Christians believed he was the same man who wrote the Gospel of John, the eagle also came to represent the author of the Apocalypse. Today many academic biblical scholars (for excellent reasons) don't believe that the same person wrote both books, but because Revelation's author really was named John, and because the Gospel and the Apocalypse share some common features, almost everyone, academic scholar or not, includes Revelation in the category of "Johannine" literature.

Aslan, who glowed like the sun even though there was no sun on Deathwater Island, now shines even brighter on the edge of his world as Lamb. In

---

it might be interpreted as denying his humanity, and thus the incarnation. The Western church disagreed and continued to portray Christ as a lamb in its art, visual and otherwise. The Latin hymn *Agnus Dei*, "Lamb of God," which is sung at every Roman Catholic Mass before Communion, may have developed as a reaction against Eastern edicts forbidding lamb imagery. See Andrew Louth, *Greek East and Latin West: The Church, AD 681–1071* (Crestwood, NY: St. Vladimir's Seminary Press, 2007), 35.

16. *On the Harmony of the Gospels* 1.6.

Revelation 21 Jesus does exactly the same thing. At the end of Revelation, when the new Jerusalem descends from heaven to earth, John notes that the city has no need of a sun or a moon, "for the glory of God illuminates it, and its lamp is the Lamb." Having recognized this connection, we can look back at how Aslan appeared to Eustace on Dragon Island. There was no moon that night, Eustace told Edmund, but "there was moonlight where the lion was."[17]

The Lamb invites the children to "come and have breakfast."[18] This is an exact quote of the first half of John 21:12. Like "very good" and "well done" in *The Magician's Nephew,* it is not recognizable as a biblical quotation unless one reads it in context, although Lewis does confirm it in his letter to Patricia Mackey.[19]

In John 21, the disciples don't recognize Jesus at first, and then they do, and then they eat fish with him. In *The Voyage of the "Dawn Treader,"* the children don't recognize Aslan as the Lamb who asks them to eat fish with him until they've finished their meal, and he returns to his leonine form. Both of these meals, the Johannine and the Narnian, are messianic banquets, and both have eucharistic undertones. Lewis was well aware of this, once writing that "every meal can be a kind of lower sacrament."[20] How much more so a meal with Aslan on the border of Aslan's country!

A conflux of lion and lamb imagery also appears in the book of Revelation. At the beginning of Revelation 4, Jesus opens a door in heaven and invites John to go through it. After the vision of the four living creatures that follows, he sees God on his throne holding a scroll that no one in the universe can open except the "Lion of the Tribe of Judah." Lewis identified Aslan, whose name means "lion" in Turkish, with the Lion of Judah, a title that hearkens back to Genesis 49:9.[21] In Revelation 5, John waits anxiously, but no lion appears. Instead, a lamb steps forth. This is no ordinary animal but a lamb who is slain, bloody from his salvific death (Rev. 5:1–10). Lewis doesn't call Aslan a lamb when he is killed in *The Lion, the Witch and the Wardrobe,* but the echoes of Isaiah 53:7's "lamb led to slaughter" are audible to anyone who has an ear to hear.

At the very end of *The Voyage of the "Dawn Treader,"* Lewis leans heavily on the very end of the Gospel of John. Although Jesus is not portrayed as a lamb there, he does tell Peter to "feed my lambs" (John 21:15). Then he predicts how Peter will die. Peter's only response is to point to the Beloved Disciple and ask,

17. Ch. 7.

18. Ch. 16.

19. Lewis to Patricia Mackey, June 8, 1960, *CL,* 3:1158.

20. Lewis to Mary Van Deusen, March 19, 1955, *CL,* 3:583. He discussed this idea with his brother as early as Jan. 17, 1932, *CL,* 2:43.

21. Lewis to Carol Jenkins, Jan. 22, 1952, *CL,* 3:160.

"Lord, what about him?" Jesus answers, "If it is my will that he remain until I come, what is that to you? Follow me!" (21:21). Likewise, before Aslan sends the three children home, he gives Lucy and Edmund bad news: they will not return to Narnia. Lucy asks Aslan if Eustace will, and the lion tells her that it's none of her business; her job is to follow him in her own world. Then Aslan opens a door in the sky, and they go through it, just as John went through the door in the sky that Jesus opened for him in Revelation 4.

Writing to a young correspondent, Lewis said that Aslan becomes more like Christ on the edge of his world.[22] On the edge of his world in *The Voyage of the "Dawn Treader,"* Aslan takes Johannine form, even to the point of quoting Scripture verbatim from the Gospel of John. It is fitting that this book, the most mystical of the Chronicles, is densely interwoven with John's Gospel and Apocalypse, the most mystical books in the New Testament.

Jesus in Johannine literature	**Major allusions to Johannine literature in *The Voyage of the "Dawn Treader"***
Jesus is the lamb of God. (John 1:29, 1:36) Jesus is portrayed as a lamb throughout the book of Revelation.	Aslan appears in the form of a lamb.
The disciples don't recognize Jesus in his human form. (John 21:4)	The children don't recognize Aslan in his lamb form.
The Beloved Disciple and then Peter recognize Jesus. Jesus invites them to "come and have breakfast," and everyone eats fish together. (John 21:7–14)	The Lamb invites them to "come and have breakfast," and everyone eats fish together. Aslan transforms from lamb to lion, and the children recognize him.
Jesus tells Peter how he will die. (John 21:18–19)	Aslan tells Lucy and Edmund that they will not return to Narnia.
Peter asks Jesus what will happen to the Beloved Disciple. (John 21:21)	Lucy asks Aslan if Eustace will return to Narnia.

22. Lewis to Patricia Mackey, June 8, 1960, *CL*, 3:1158.

Jesus in Johannine literature	Major allusions to Johannine literature in *The Voyage of the "Dawn Treader"*
Jesus tells Peter that it's none of his business and to follow him. (John 21:22)	Aslan tells Lucy that it's none of her business and to follow him in her own world.
One of the four living creatures is an eagle, which later comes to symbolize the Gospel of John. (Rev. 4:7)	The children have "eagles' eyes" in the bright light.
The Lion of the tribe of Judah is in fact a lamb. (Rev. 5:5–6)	Aslan, usually a lion, takes the form of a lamb.
The new Jerusalem at the end of the world has no need of a sun or moon because God and the Lamb dwell there as its light. (Rev. 21:23)	Aslan glows like the sun on Deathwater Island, though there was no sun. Aslan emits moonlight on Dragon Island, though there was no moon. The Lamb at the end of the world on the border of his own country is so bright, the children can't look at it, even with their eagles' eyes.
John goes through a door Jesus opens in the sky. (Rev. 4:1)	The children go through a door Aslan opens in the sky.

15. THE SILVER CHAIR

"The truth will set you free."

—John 8:32

As with *The Voyage of the "Dawn Treader," The Silver Chair* has a silent biblical motif running through it like an underground river. In *The Silver Chair*, "the truth will set you free" (John 8:32). The central truth in the book is the identity of Prince Rilian, who has been stolen away from his father, King Caspian, and befuddled by a deceptive witch. The two children in the story, Eustace and Jill, discover more about who they truly are on their journey to liberate him.

Eustace and Jill have been thrown together in an uneasy partnership through their shared misery at school. "School," always a four-letter word to Lewis because of his own wretched childhood experience, is almost a character itself in *The Silver Chair*, which begins as a dystopian boarding school story. Experiment House, the object of Lewis's unrelenting ire and satire, is the location that frames the book. To escape it, Eustace suggests calling upon the name of Aslan to request passage into Narnia. He and Jill chant, "Aslan, Aslan, Aslan," but events overtake them in the form of the school bullies. As they flee through a door in a wall, they find themselves in Aslan's country, on the edge of a precipice of unthinkable height. Eustace looks down and blanches. Jill scoffs, but then, realizing the enormity of the drop, begins to faint. As Eustace tries to keep her from falling, he himself tumbles over the edge. Their separation creates a problem that reverberates throughout the book, since Jill is the only one left to speak to the lion who dashes over to cushion Eustace's descent with his breath.

After Eustace is safely on his way down, the lion departs without a word, but Jill encounters him again when she searches for water. She feels like she's dying of thirst, but access to the only stream in sight is blocked by the beast. After an anguished standoff, the lion tells her, "If you are thirsty, come and drink,"[1] which alludes to Isaiah 55:1's invitation, "Everyone who thirsts, come to the waters."

1. Ch. 2.

Since she doesn't know him, Jill doesn't trust in leonine beneficence. She voices her hope that there is another stream nearby, but the lion flatly states, "There is no other stream." Only he may grant access to the water that will quench her thirst, reminding readers of Jesus and the Samaritan woman at the well in the Gospel of John. The woman asks for the living water that only Jesus can give, the water that will quench her thirst forever. As they speak and she learns more about him, she calls Jesus "prophet" and "messiah," and he affirms, "I am" (4:26).

In her first conversation with Aslan, Jill doesn't recall the unfamiliar name she had chanted with Eustace at school, and she wonders aloud if the lion might be the "Somebody" they had invoked there. Like Jesus when he answers the Samaritan woman in John 4, Aslan confirms, "I am." As we saw in *The Horse and His Boy,* this is what God calls himself on Mount Sinai—which suggests another biblical connection. Although the mountain in *The Silver Chair* isn't named at the beginning of the book, it is at the end: "the Mountain of Aslan." Like God on Sinai or Zeus on Olympus, Aslan dwells on a mountain, as befits a divine being.

Once Jill drinks (the water quenches her thirst instantly), and the lion doesn't pounce, the two can talk, though not altogether comfortably, since he interrogates her about what happened to Eustace. When he asks Jill why she was so near the edge of the cliff, she replies, "I was showing off, Sir." The truth, offered without excuse, sets them free to speak more amiably with one another. The lion tells her that he called them to Narnia to complete a task. Jill, puzzled, replies that she thought that she and Eustace had called him. Aslan corrects her: "You would not have called to me unless I had been calling to you."[2] Lewis may be referring once again to Exodus, where God calls to Moses out of the burning bush, out of the blue (3:4). In addition, perhaps, are undertones of 1 John 4:10, "This is love, not that we loved God but that he loved us." Most especially, however, we hear John 6:44, "No one can come to me unless the father who sent me draws him."[3] He may also be touching upon the question of fate versus free will, a topic that comes up later in the book when Puddleglum the Marshwiggle blames fate after he eats a bit of a talking beast. That said, Lewis had no interest in the topic. "All that Calvinist question—Free-Will & Predestination, is to my mind undiscussable, insoluble," and in the end he calls it a "*meaningless*" debate.[4]

2. Ch. 2.

3. I am grateful to Anne Egbert for reminding me of this verse, which Lewis underlined in his Moffatt New Testament.

4. Lewis to Mary Van Deusen, Oct. 20, 1952, *CL*, 3:237, emphasis in original.

The source of the next biblical allusion in their conversation is obvious. Aslan gives Jill four signs by which she will recognize the lost prince. He makes her repeat them until she knows them by heart and tells her to keep on repeating them "when you wake in the morning and when you lie down at night, and when you wake in the middle of the night."[5] This alludes unmistakably to Deuteronomy 6:6–7, Moses's exhortation to the Israelites: "Keep these words that I am commanding you today in your heart. Recite them to your children and talk about them when you are at home and when you are away, when you lie down and when you rise."

Even as those words are coming out of Aslan's mouth, Jill realizes that she, like Eustace before her, is drifting off the mountain on the lion's breath. As the lion recedes from the story, so do overt biblical allusions, although there are subtle echoes. Before Prince Rilian was abducted, his mother was bitten and killed by a bright green snake. The woman-snake duo takes readers back to the garden of Eden, and especially Genesis 3:15, where God curses the snake: "I will put enmity between you and the woman, and between your offspring and hers; he will strike your head, and you will strike his heel." The children eventually realize that the green snake and the "Lady of the Green Kirtle" whom they meet on their journey are one and the same. In *The Silver Chair*, the Lady is a deceptively sweet figure. Is she a counterpart to the woman in Proverbs 7:23–27, who seduces a young man to follow her "like a bird rushing into a snare, not knowing that it will cost him his life," and whose house "is the way to Sheol," the underground realm of the dead? For that is how the Lady deceives Rilian, and that is where she leads him, to her underworldly kingdom.

It takes the children too long to find Rilian there. To push them along more quickly, Aslan appears to Jill in a dream as they tarry in the giants' castle. Dream visions sent by God to direct his people are not uncommon in the Scriptures, from Joseph's in Genesis to Joseph's in Matthew.[6] Jill's dream (not to mention the discovery that they're on the menu as the featured dish at the giants' Autumn Feast) propels the children and Puddleglum out of the castle and down to the ruined city below.

When they do locate the prince far beneath the ruins, they don't know who he is, and neither does he. He is a lunatic, befuddled by the green witch's spell and bound by her enchantment of lies. But for one hour every night he is lashed to the silver chair and comes to himself, and in that moment of truth

5. Ch. 2.

6. Gen. 37; 40–41; Matt. 1–2.

he asks the visitors to free him in the name of Aslan.[7] This is the last of the four signs Jill had received from the lion: the prince would be the first person they met who would ask them to do something in Aslan's name.

The Silver Chair highlights the name of Aslan, first when the children invoke it at the beginning of the book, and then as one of the signs. In the Bible, to request something in the name of the Lord is to ask the Lord himself; the name represents the deity. The phrase "name of the Lord" is so widespread in the Bible that it's impossible to pin down specific examples Lewis may have had in mind, but one that works especially well here is Joel 2:32, which Paul quotes in Romans 10:13: "Everyone who calls on the name of the Lord will be saved."

Now the prince knows himself, but he doesn't know who his rescuers are. Before Eustace gives him their names, he tells Rilian that they were "sent by Aslan." This isn't the first time Eustace has said that very thing. In his first conversation with a Narnian, he introduces himself and Jill to Glimfeather the owl, adding, "We were sent here by Aslan." Glimfeather repeats the phrase to Trumpkin, who emphasizes, "Sent by the Lion Himself, hey?" In the Parliament of Owls, Eustace notes that Aslan sent him, and Jill jumps in to correct him: "Sent both of us." Eustace says it again to Puddleglum in chapter 5. At the end of the book, right before the lion sends them back to his mountain with his breath, the word appears for the last time when Aslan confirms that they have accomplished the task "for which I sent you." Although the word "sent" appears throughout the Chronicles, in *The Silver Chair* it occurs with Aslan as its subject to an extent that dwarfs the uses in all the other Chronicles. Lewis knew that the Greek word for "one who is sent" is "apostle." He never uses "apostle" in the series, but he picks up its biblical resonance, performing the same sleight of hand with "sent" here as he did with "good news" in *The Lion, the Witch and the Wardrobe* and "breath" in *The Horse and His Boy*.

Finding the prince does not conclude their mission, however; far from it. The witch is not about to let the four of them go gently into the night, so she conjures up another spell on the spot to try to convince them that Narnia—or any world except her own—is an illusion. The "sun" they try to describe to her doesn't exist, she chides; it is simply a bigger and better lamp. Aslan—who, Eustace tells her, *sent* them to find Rilian—is a sweet storybook character and perfectly explainable as a bigger and better cat.[8] Her deception almost works.

7. Ch. 11.

8. See Alister McGrath, *The Intellectual World of C. S. Lewis* (Chichester, UK: Wiley-Blackwell, 2014), 140–42, for how Lewis uses the philosophy of Feuerbach in this scene.

But once again the truth, this time in the unlikely form of Puddleglum, sets them free when he stomps out the witch's drug-infused fire with his thick Marshwiggle feet and declares that he stands for Narnia, even if it is a figment of their imagination.

In short order the witch turns into a huge green snake, and they kill her. The moment she is dead, the narrator calls them "conquerors," an unsurprising word under the circumstances, since they had indeed conquered the witch.[9] But there is more to it than that. In choosing this word Lewis is echoing, alluding to, or, depending on one's definition, even quoting Scripture, because throughout the book of Revelation those who resist Satan—whom the author calls the ancient snake, the great dragon, and the deceiver (Rev. 12:9)—are "conquerors." All the words Revelation uses as synonyms for Satan apply to the witch, whom Rilian described as "the most devilish sorceress that ever planned the woe of men" when he was tied to the chair.

At first I thought Lewis echoed the biblical word "conquerors" unconsciously, but then I read a letter he sent to Alec Vidler that asked Vidler to publish a sermon Lewis had preached on Revelation 2:26–28, which Lewis entitles "The Weight of Glory."[10] Revelation 2:26–28 reads, "And the one who conquers and the one who keeps my works until the end, to him I will give authority over the nations, and he will rule them with an iron rod as ceramic jars are broken in pieces, even as I have received from my father, and I will give him the morning star."[11] The only part of the passage Lewis cites verbatim in "The Weight of Glory" is "morning star," but his letter to Vidler shows that he is contemplating the star in its biblical context—a context that begins with the words "the one who conquers." Elsewhere in the sermon he mentions the "pillars" of Revelation 3:12, a verse that begins with the same words: "The one who conquers I will make a pillar in the temple of my God."[12] Lewis's work with these verses, and the importance he gave them in characterizing his sermon to Vidler, lead me to think that the word "conquerors" in *The Silver Chair* is a purposeful echo of Revelation.

When Rilian retrieves his armor, he discovers that his shield has been transformed. It used to be black and unmarked, but now it is silver and emblazoned with a red lion. They kneel to kiss it before they leave the witch's lair. Westerners might not see it, but Eastern Christians will recognize this act as

9. Ch. 12.

10. Lewis to Alec Vidler, Aug. 17, 1941, *CL*, 2:490.

11. I have given my translation from the Greek since Lewis probably read it in Greek.

12. "The Weight of Glory," in *Essay Collection*, 100, 104.

the veneration of a holy icon. It is worth saying that neither in the Chronicles nor in Eastern Christian practice does anyone "worship an image." The honor directed to the icon belongs to the one behind it.

Meanwhile, the Underworld is engulfed in fire and water, time-honored biblical weapons of mass destruction (2 Pet. 3:5–7). Jill mentions the two elements in tandem as they begin to flee, and Lewis uses 2 Peter 3:5–7 in a similar context in his book *The Discarded Image.*[13] In *The Silver Chair,* our heroes successfully navigate all hazards, emerging with the prince just in time to reunite him with his father as Caspian breathes his last. Narnia's flag is lowered to half-mast, and the lion whisks the children back to his mountain with his breath.

Caspian's body floats there in a stream (perhaps the same one Aslan guarded at the beginning of the book, since the narrator likens both of them to glass), and once again Aslan weeps, implying by his tears that death is an unnatural foe, and grieving the dead is not ungodly. "The view that death is a hideous enemy is not unscriptural," Lewis wrote.[14] He insists that we must never "say that death doesn't matter. Nothing is less Christian than that," because Jesus himself wept over Lazarus.[15] We should keep in mind here, as we did with *The Magician's Nephew,* that the only time Jesus weeps over a friend, he raises him from the dead (John 11:35). Before Aslan raises Caspian, he tells Eustace to pluck a thorn from a thicket. Eustace plunges it into Aslan's paw, and a drop of his blood flows over the king, bringing him back to life.[16]

The word "thicket" reminds me of the story of the binding of Isaac, where Abraham pulls out a ram caught in a thicket "on the mount of the Lord" (Gen. 22:13–14). At first, I didn't think much of this possible echo of Scripture. But reading the book of Hebrews in Lewis's copy of Moffatt's New Testament made me change my mind. Moffatt's translation of Hebrews 11:17–19 reads: "It was by faith, when Abraham was put to the test, that he sacrificed Isaac; he was ready to sacrifice his only son, although he had received the promises and had been told that it is through Isaac that your offspring shall be reckoned—for he considered that God was able even to raise men from the dead. Hence he did get him back, <u>by what was a parable of the resurrection</u>" (Lewis's emphasis).

Moffatt's translation of the last clause, underlined by Lewis in his copy, is unique among the hundreds of English translations of it. No other English trans-

13. *The Discarded Image* (Cambridge: Cambridge University Press, 1964), 120–21.

14. Lewis to Edward T. Dell, March 5, 1961, *CL,* 3:1245.

15. "The Grand Miracle," in *Essay Collection,* 8–9; cf. *Miracles* (1947; repr., New York: Macmillan, 1960), 125.

16. Ch. 16.

lation includes the word "resurrection" because the Greek doesn't.[17] The NRSV, for example, differs so much from Moffatt that it's hard to believe it translates the same words: "and *figuratively speaking,* he did receive him back." Influenced by Moffatt, Lewis could even more efficiently connect the aborted sacrifice of Isaac with the idea of resurrection. In Genesis 22, Abraham sacrifices a ram caught in a thicket in place of Isaac, and in his translation of Hebrews 11:17–19, Moffatt compares Isaac's near-death experience to resurrection from the dead not just once, as in the Greek and every other English translation, but twice. Lewis moves from "thicket" to "thorn," a word that evokes Jesus's crown of thorns, which in the Gospels is followed by his blood, his death, and his resurrection from the dead.

Caspian's resurrection scene evokes speculative theological questions. Does Caspian need to be baptized in water? Even if he doesn't, does the archetypal importance of the sacrament demand some sort of water ritual no matter what world one lives and dies in? Lewis the medievalist might answer yes to these questions. In *The Allegory of Love,* he explains that, to Hugo of St. Victor, "Water . . . was an image of the grace of the Holy Ghost even before the sacrament of baptism was ordained."[18] There are other theological questions about Caspian we may also answer in the affirmative. Has he "washed his robes and made them white in the blood of the lamb" (Rev. 7:14)? Has the blood of Aslan justified him (Rom. 5:9) and cleansed him from all sin (1 John 1:7)? Whatever else the scene implies, Lewis's language echoes the water and the blood that pours from the side of the crucified Jesus in John 19:34.

Caspian has entered into eternal life in Aslan's Country, and the children must return to their own world. Aslan breaks precedent and accompanies them, although the people at Experiment House see only his back, an allusion to Moses seeing God's back in Exodus 33:23. Before he departs, Aslan breathes on Jill and Eustace (John 20:22).[19] He has breathed on other creatures in other Chronicles (e.g., the statues in the White Witch's castle), but his breath is especially active in this one, as it wafts the children from Aslan's mountain to Narnia at the beginning of the book, and from Narnia back to that mountain at its end.

17. The Greek is ὅθεν αὐτὸν καὶ ἐν παραβολῇ ἐκομίσατο.

18. Lewis, *The Allegory of Love: A Study in Medieval Tradition,* 2nd corrected ed. (Oxford: Clarendon, 1936), 46.

19. Ch. 16.

16. THE LAST BATTLE

If every one of them were written down, I suppose the world itself could not contain the books that would be written.

—John 21:25

The *Last Battle* is the Apocalypse of the Chronicles, its book of Revelation, and the seventh book that concludes the series. Its first line signals that this is the end: "In the last days of Narnia . . ."

The Devil Is an Ape

The story begins with an ape and an allusion to Revelation's beast from the sea, which itself alludes to the book of Daniel. There are no apes in Revelation or Daniel, the two biblical apocalypses, but we know that Lewis doesn't draw his images only from the Bible. As a scholar of medieval literature, he was well acquainted with the ancient bestiary tradition, a treasury of fanciful material about animals that was popular from late antiquity into early modern times. Lewis writes, "I should distrust the judgment of the critic who was unaware of their strange poetry, or who did not feel it to be wholly different in kind from that of the allegories."[1] In the bestiary tradition, the devil was thought to take the form of an ape.[2] The ape is a key player in *The Last Battle* because the devil is a key player in the book of Revelation.

Lewis worked with the equation devil = ape for years across several genres. In a letter, he mentions a concept familiar to the early church fathers: "The devil is the ape of God."[3] It appears in one of his poems: "Always evil was an

1. *The Allegory of Love,* 2nd corrected ed. (Oxford: Clarendon, 1938), 46; cf. *The Discarded Image* (Cambridge: Cambridge University Press, 1964), ch. 7, subheading "Beasts."

2. Janetta Rebold Benton, *The Medieval Menagerie: Animals in the Art of the Middle Ages* (New York: Abbeville, 1992), 89–90.

3. Lewis to Bede Griffiths, Jan. 17, 1940, *CL,* 2:327.

ape."[4] In both examples "ape" means "imitator." As he explains in *Reflections on the Psalms*, "We call [the devil] God's Ape; he is always imitating God."[5] According to the church fathers, evil is the privation of good because it lacks substance; by itself, it is nothing. Therefore it can do nothing but "ape," or try to imitate, the goodness it doesn't possess. In *Mere Christianity*, Lewis puts it memorably as "badness is only spoiled goodness," a phrase he had started to develop decades before: "The truth is that evil is not a real thing at all, like God. It is simply good *spoiled*. . . . Evil is a *parasite*. It is there only because good is there for it to spoil and confuse"—which is exactly what the ape does in *The Last Battle*.[6]

An ape looks like a human. Ancient Greeks and Romans considered the ape the ugliest beast "precisely because," out of all the animals, it looks the most like us.[7] Early Christians seized this idea and ran with it. They reasoned that, just as the devil wanted to be like God (as some have interpreted Isa. 14:13–14), apes want to be like people. Lewis incorporated all these ideas in *The Last Battle* through the figure of the ape Shift. Shift claims to be a man to comic effect, but in the end, it's not funny. His clumsy attempts to look like a person presage real problems. Mr. Beaver had cautioned the Pevensie children about just these dangers in *The Lion, the Witch and the Wardrobe* when he warned them against the White Witch, who looked human but wasn't. He told them that something that looks almost, but not quite, like something else can be dangerous. In a more abstract guise, this idea emerges in *The Last Battle* when the main characters discover that the most cunning lies are the ones closest to the truth.

In the first chapter of the book, Shift loiters by Caldron Pool, which bubbles and churns from a waterfall that pours into it with a roar like never-ending thunder. Any self-respecting waterfall produces this effect, so it usually wouldn't catch the attention of anyone—neither the reader of the book nor of any character in the scene. But viewed through the book's apocalyptic lens, both images, the roiling water and the thunderous din, appear to have been chosen quite carefully. We have already looked at the significance of water in the Chronicles and its archetypal qualities in human culture, but there is more to say about the role of water in Scripture. From the beginning of the Bible

4. "These Faint Wavering Far-travell'd Gleams," in *Collected Poems*, 419.

5. *Reflections on the Psalms* (New York: Harcourt, Brace & World, 1958), 106.

6. *Mere Christianity* (1952; repr., San Francisco: HarperSanFrancisco, 2001), bk. 2, ch. 2 ("The Invasion"), 44; Lewis to Greeves, Sept. 12, 1933, *CL*, 2:124, emphasis original.

7. H. W. Janson, *Apes and Ape Lore in the Middle Ages and the Renaissance* (London: Warburg Institute, 1952), 14.

to the end, water is a chaotic force that God can either control and subdue or let loose to wreak havoc. It is controlled in the creation story of Genesis 1, when God separates the waters above from the waters below and gathers the waters below to create hospitable dry land. God reverses the process in the uncreation of Genesis 7, when the waters merge together again to form the flood that destroys the world. These ideas recur in the Psalms, and the Gospels take them up when Jesus calms the storm and walks on water, demonstrating his mastery over it.

Even in the best of weather, large bodies of water intimidated people in the ancient world. Although one could bob along the surface cheerfully enough, there was no way to dive down deep for any length of time to see what lurked below. Therefore, when the biblical prophet Daniel has a vision that represents political turmoil, it's no surprise to see hostile nations symbolized by fearsome beasts that emerge from the depths of the sea (Dan. 7:1–8). Revelation 13 adapts Daniel's creatures into a single beast from the sea, and Lewis builds on both biblical texts with the appearance of the lion skin that bubbles up from Caldron Pool.

Chaotic water, thundery noise, and manifestations of the divine go together, also beginning in the Hebrew Bible. Thunder speaks for God throughout Scripture. The voice of God is often equated to thunder (e.g., Exod. 19:19; 2 Sam. 22:14; Job 37:5). Psalm 29:3 exalts, "The voice of the Lord over the waters; the God of glory thunders; the Lord over the mighty waters!" In Revelation, one like a son of man possesses "a voice like the sound of many waters" (1:15), and his followers roar like thunder and many waters (14:2; 19:6).

By delving beneath these two simple images of water and thunder, we see how subtly Lewis can deploy Scripture. Thundering water is literally white noise for the two characters in the first scene of *The Last Battle*, but it is also literary white noise that sets up an apocalyptic soundscape for its readers.

When Shift spots the lion skin, he makes his companion Puzzle the donkey jump into the water to pull it out. The medieval bestiary tradition links apes and donkeys, both of whom represent the devil.[8] The ape—old, ugly, and infinitely self-centered—manipulates the donkey with specious reasoning and emotional blackmail, forcing him to don the skin to "ape" Aslan. Shift will be the pseudo-Aslan's spokesman, while the donkey functions as the clumsy antichrist of the book.

Revelation never uses the word "antichrist," a term that appears in the New Testament only in First and Second John. Over time, however, Revelation's

8. Janson, *Apes and Ape Lore*, 16.

beast from the sea acquires that title, by which it is now commonly known, and Lewis uses it in a letter to describe Shift and Puzzle.[9]

An "antichrist" is someone set up in place of or in opposition to Christ, which is what happens in Revelation 12–13. The beast from the sea in Revelation receives his authority from a dragon identified as Satan, who is the deceiver of the world (12:9). The beast blasphemes God and wages war on God's people, but everyone else worships him. Then a second beast comes out of the earth to act as the first beast's spokesman (13:11–15). Later called the false prophet (19:20; 20:10), the second beast deceives the world, forcing everyone to worship the beast from the sea. In the last days of Narnia, Shift plays false prophet to Puzzle's unwilling anti-Aslan. Shift leads him about, speaks for him, and deceives the Narnians to make them worship him. Later in the book, a Calormene confirms the allusion to Revelation 13:11–15 when he calls Shift the "Mouthpiece of Aslan."[10]

Taking on the roles of the apocalyptic beast and its false prophet is a deadly serious matter, but Lewis lightens it up by giving the animals a more mundane task: Shift wants Puzzle to buy him oranges and bananas. Shift's love of fruit also comes from the bestiary tradition, which borrowed it from the ancient Greco-Roman world, and Christians who inherited the classical association of apes and fruit applied it to their interpretation of the Bible. Because the devil takes the form of an ape, and because they believed the devil tempted the human couple in the garden with a piece of fruit, some early Christians reasoned that apes too must be associated with fruit.[11] Like the roaring water of Caldron Pool, the ape's fruit doesn't look like much on the face of it. However, the image comes into its own at the end of the book, when it will be eaten rightly.

As the animals quarrel beside the pool, the donkey protesting Shift's plan, and the ape insisting on it, both are thrown off their feet by a small earthquake and a burst of thunder. Earthquakes, like thunder, are associated with the presence of God in the Scriptures. The primal scene is Exodus 19:18–19. When Moses approaches God on Mount Sinai, the earth shakes, and when Moses speaks, God answers him in thunder. This is a positive (if awe-ful) use of the image. In Revelation, earthquakes sometimes function in a positive way, as part of a theophany of God (8:5; 11:19), but more often they are used negatively, to mark his wrath and anticipate the coming collapse of the world that opposes him (6:12; 11:13; 16:18).[12] Lewis plays with this ambiguity in the first chapter

9. Lewis to Patricial Mackey, June 8, 1960, *CL*, 3:1158–59.

10. *The Last Battle* (New York: Macmillan, 1956), ch. 3.

11. Janson, *Apes and Ape Lore*, 43–44, 122–30.

12. Pontifical Biblical Commission, *The Inspiration and Truth of Sacred Scripture* (Collegeville, MN: Liturgical Press, 2014), 139–40.

of *The Last Battle*, where Puzzle, who is weak but fundamentally decent, sees the earthquake as a divine warning. Shift, who is clever but wicked, claims the opposite, that the earthquake is a sign of God's approval, and he bullies the donkey into agreement.

The ape's deception accelerates as he hoodwinks most of the citizens of Narnia. It seems that Aslan has returned! At first, King Tirian and his friend Jewel the unicorn are overjoyed by the good news. But their advisor Roonwit the centaur is not, informing them that the rumors are probably bad news. Roonwit's report is the first time the word "rumor" appears in the book, and the word "lie" follows it three times in quick succession.[13] Lewis is echoing Mark 13: "Beware that no one leads you astray. Many will come in my name and say, 'I am he!' . . . When you hear of wars and *rumors* of wars, do not be alarmed; this must take place, but the end is still to come. For nation will rise against nation, and kingdom against kingdom; there will be *earthquakes*" (13:5–8). Jesus continues: "And if anyone says to you at that time, 'Look! Here is the messiah!' or 'Look! There he is!'—do not believe it. *False* messiahs and *false* prophets will appear and produce signs and omens, to lead astray, if possible, the elect" (13:21–22).

Apocalyptic Numbers

As Roonwit is speaking to the king, a dryad staggers up to them, crying, "Woe, woe, woe!" because many Narnian trees, including her own, are being felled at that very moment. The dryad's cry is the fourth quotation from Scripture in the Chronicles. The word "woe" appears six times in *The Last Battle,* and only once anywhere else in the series, when Prince Rilian is bound to the silver chair for the last time. The triple "woe" in *The Last Battle* quotes Revelation 8:13, which occurs between the soundings of the fourth and fifth trumpets: "I heard an eagle crying with a loud voice as it flew in midheaven, 'Woe, woe, woe to the inhabitants of the earth, at the blasts of the other trumpets that the three angels are about to blow!'" In chapter 8 of *The Last Battle,* an eagle cries a single "woe" before he announces Roonwit's death to the king. The eagle tries to prepare the king by saying that his news will make him "sorrier of my coming than of the greatest woe that ever befell you." It may be a coincidence that the eagles both in Narnia and in Revelation utter "woe" in the eighth chapters of their respective books, but I prefer to think it is not. The reference itself, however, is undeniable.

Counting trumpets and woes introduces a related topic: the importance of numbers in Revelation and apocalyptic literature in general. As an apocalyptic novel rooted in the book of Revelation, the last Chronicle naturally conforms to

13. Ch. 2.

basic genre expectations. The word "woe" appears seven times in the Chronicles as a whole, with six of them in *The Last Battle*.[14] An eagle cries "woe" in the eighth chapters of both *The Last Battle* and Revelation. The genre apocalypse has a great affinity for numbers, and especially for the number seven, as we will soon see.

King Tirian and Jewel need to find out what's happening with the supposed return of Aslan. As they depart to investigate, a water rat tells them that Aslan himself had commanded the talking trees to be felled and literally sold down the river to the Calormenes. In fact, they learn that the Calormenes have begun to enslave Narnian citizens, allegedly on Aslan's orders. How could this be? The very thought is inconceivable to them, until Jewel, loath even to say the words, remembers that Aslan is "not a *tame* lion." But what does that mean? Can a good lion do bad things to his own people?

Not a Tame Lion

The notion that Aslan isn't "safe" appears in the first Chronicle, *The Lion, the Witch and the Wardrobe,* and pops up occasionally in others, but it takes on new shades of meaning in this one. While Aslan has allowed or even inflicted suffering for the greater good in earlier books (for example, letting Eustace turn into a dragon and then tearing his dragon scales off, or clawing Aravis to replicate the punishment her drugged maid received), there is no discernible reason for it here. Later in the book, several talking mice wonder what they've done to deserve such ill treatment. Surely they "might be told what it was!"[15]

The false Aslan won't tell them what they've done wrong, of course, but when the real Aslan appears, he doesn't either. In the same way, a fully satisfying answer to the question of why bad things happen to good people, at least from a human perspective, is not forthcoming in the Scriptures. The most profound treatment of the topic, the book of Job, takes great pains to emphasize that Job is blameless, but tragedy befalls him regardless. God's answer to Job at the end of the book is to stun him into silence with (poetically lovely) descriptions of his magnificence.

I can't solve the problem of evil here or anywhere else. Neither can I adequately address theodicy, the justification of the existence of a loving, powerful, all-knowing God with the existence of evil. But one thing I can do is (very)

14. In personal correspondence, Edith Humphrey suggests that "woe" may appear in *The Last Battle* six times to signify that "woe" is not the last word—it doesn't reach the perfect number seven.

15. Ch. 4.

briefly compare and contrast treatments of divine violence in *The Last Battle* and Revelation.[16]

In both books, the ruling deity allows disasters. In Narnia, Aslan lets his heroes die violent deaths, and God does the same in Revelation, most notably as described in the fifth seal, a vision of God's altar in heaven. Underneath the altar are those who gave their lives for God. They are not happy, so they shout to God, asking how long it will take to avenge their blood. They are told to rest a little longer, until their number is complete—the number of their fellows who are going to die as they had (Rev. 6:9–11). This passage is one example of God allowing his beloved ones to suffer. It also adds another disturbing element: God will actively inflict suffering, too. The souls under the altar rest assured that their persecutors will pay. From the perspective of Revelation's author, this is not a problem: the punishment is deserved; justice will be done (Rev. 16:5–7).[17]

Although *The Last Battle* never mentions retributive justice per se, it is nonetheless meted out. Note the passive voice of the verb that concludes the last sentence: "is meted out." Revelation makes regular use of the passive voice, often in what is called the divine passive, as we have already seen: the souls under the altar "are told" to rest a little longer. We can guess who is speaking, but the divine speaker is not identified.

The divine passive is implied regarding much of the violence in *The Last Battle*, even when it is not embedded in its verb forms. Shift the false prophet is apparently annihilated; we hear nothing about who smites him. Ginger the cat is stricken and ceases to be a talking beast. We know perfectly well who executes these judgments, but the agent is not named. The divine passive allows a deity to do what he must while absenting himself, if in name only, from the dirty work. One might think this appropriate for a children's book. Although some children relish graphically grisly ends (we might remember the original very grim fairy tales of the brothers Grimm, the aptly named Edward Gorey, and much of the oeuvre of Roald Dahl), others wouldn't appreciate a dramatization of Aslan killing his creatures, even the bad guys. But the fact that the

16. On Revelation's violence, see Leslie Baynes, "Revelation," in *The Cambridge Companion to the New Testament*, ed. Patrick Gray (Cambridge: Cambridge University Press, 2021), 313–30.

17. Writing to Mary Van Deusen, Jan. 31, 1952, Lewis discusses the problem of divine evil in Job and other Scripture, bringing up the question of God inflicting pain to achieve good. He notes that suffering may "*sometimes*" be "sent as a punishment" (using the divine passive), and this "is suggested by parts of the Old Testament and Revelation" (*CL*, 3:163).

Bible itself—definitely a book for grown-ups—uses the divine passive tells us that the urge to downplay the perception of gods gone wild runs deep.

Unlike God, King Tirian takes responsibility for his violent actions. He and Jewel find several Calormenes cutting down trees and whipping an enslaved Narnian horse as they force him to haul away the lumber. Horrified, they kill the Calormenes and flee, but they return to face justice. Here, as in *The Horse and His Boy,* the presence of Calormenes points to the book of Exodus and slavery. In Exodus 2:11–15, young Moses sees an Egyptian beating one of his own people, an enslaved Jew. Moses kills the oppressor, runs away, and is never held to account. In *The Last Battle,* Tirian and Jewel act more ethically than Moses.

The Calormenes detain them near the stable where Shift holds court, whence Puzzle the antichrist emerges to deceive Narnia. Tirian, watching all of this helplessly, prays to Aslan, offering himself up to be killed if that might save Narnia.[18] Since Tirian has already been associated with Moses, his self-offering probably echoes another passage in Exodus. After the golden calf incident, Moses tries to atone for his people. He asks God to forgive their sin—but if not, to blot him from the book God has written; that is, to kill him. God responds by telling Moses that he will blot from his book those who sin against him, and he leaves Moses alone (Exod. 32:30–34).[19] Lewis may also be thinking of Colossians 1:24, "I am now rejoicing in my sufferings for your sake, and in my flesh I am completing what is lacking in Christ's afflictions for the sake of his body, that is, the church." He interprets the verse in a letter: "When we willingly accept what we suffer for others and offer it to God on their behalf, then it may be united with His sufferings and, in Him, may help to their redemption or even that of others whom we do not dream of."[20]

Tirian hears nothing from Aslan, but he prays on, asking the lion to send help—perhaps even the children who had come to Narnia in troubled times past. Immediately he sees seven people as if in a dream. Only two of them, Jill and Eustace, come to Narnia at first, but the full panoply will arrive soon.

The Question of Susan

We have seen that numbers play a large role in apocalyptic literature. Of all the significant numbers in Revelation (3, 4, 7, 12, 666, 144,000, and more), seven is the most important. How could the same not hold true for the seventh

18. Ch. 4.

19. See Leslie Baynes, *The Heavenly Book Motif in Judeo-Christian Apocalypses 200 BCE–200 CE* (Leiden: Brill, 2012), ch. 2.

20. Lewis to Mary Van Deusen, Sept. 12, 1951, *CL,* 3:134–35.

book of the Chronicles of Narnia? The number appears in meaningful ways elsewhere in the series (for example, the seven lost lords in *The Voyage of the "Dawn Treader"*), but it holds a special place here. Tirian is the seventh in descent from King Rilian, and Emeth the Calormene is a seventh son.[21] At the beginning of chapter 9, the unicorn urges "us seven" (Tirian, Jewel, Eustace, Jill, Puzzle, Poggin, and the eagle) to approach Stable Hill. But the central seven in the book are the "seven friends of Narnia," often called simply "the seven": Digory, Polly, Peter, Edmund, Lucy, Eustace, and Jill, the main characters who have visited Narnia over the course of the series.

However, one person is missing: Susan. Her absence has elicited many questions, but I will ask a question I don't think anyone has asked about her before: Could the need for a significant seven in this book be one reason why Susan is "no longer a friend of Narnia"? Lewis modeled *The Last Battle* on Revelation, so the impulse to include a key set of seven in it must have been overwhelming. He had created eight main human characters in his earlier body of work. Did one of them now have to go?

If so, the next question might be, "Why Susan?" Philip Pullman, the loudest voice to condemn Lewis for writing Susan out of the new Narnia, focuses on the nylons-and-lipstick passage at the end of chapter 12, "Through the Stable Door." Pullman claims:

> The crux of it all comes, as many people have found, with the point near the end of the Last Battle (in the Narnia books) when Susan is excluded from the stable. The stable obviously represents salvation. They're going to heaven, they're going to be saved. But Susan isn't allowed into the stable, and the reason given is that she's growing up. She's become far too interested in lipstick, nylons and invitations.[22]

Every one of these points is specious. We will look at what the stable represents soon (it is not as simple as "heaven"), but first we turn to Susan.[23]

21. Eusebius of Caesarea found it worth mentioning that Moses was seventh in descent from Abraham (*Preparation for the Gospel* 9.29).

22. "A Dark Agenda?," Nov. 2002, SureFish.co.uk (defunct), https://tinyurl.com/yhtevsrk (archive). Now found at Bridge to the Stars.net, https://tinyurl.com/y567d2a4, which links to SureFish.

23. The word translated from Hebrew and Greek into English as "heaven" is hard for modern readers to grasp because it doesn't mean the same thing now as it did to ancient readers. Lewis was aware of the problem and explained it perfectly in *Miracles* (1947; repr., New York: Macmillan, 1960), 157–58.

Pullman presents her in the passive voice: "Susan *is excluded* from the stable" and "*isn't allowed* into the stable." If we change Pullman's verbs from passive to active, we must identify a subject. Pullman thinks the subject is Lewis, but in fact, it is Susan who has excluded herself from the stable. Lewis does not bar the door like some capricious authorial god. Rather, if we affirm her fictional character as a person with free will, we see that she refuses to enter. Susan is an apostate, someone who has abandoned her faith. As Kat Coffin writes, "To deny her that choice robs her of her own agency."[24]

Pullman ignores Eustace's statement right before Jill mentions the nylons and lipstick, when he tells the group that Susan has rejected Narnia as a make-believe game they played when they were children.[25] All four Pevensie siblings have grown up, but Susan, unlike the others, has not grown up in her faith. Reading this passage in context, one can see that enjoying nylons and lipstick does not keep her out of the stable. Lewis may not like them, and Jill dismisses them condescendingly at best, but Susan's interest in beauty products is not what prevents her from joining the others in Narnia. Her disbelief does.

Why might Lewis have made Susan the apostate? We can't be sure, but we can guess. Throughout the series, Lucy is the one closest to Aslan, the "Beloved Disciple" to his Johannine lion. She is always the first to believe, just like the Beloved Disciple is the first to believe in the resurrection in the Gospel of John (20:8). Lucy is the first of the four siblings to enter Narnia, and she maintains her faith under pressure in *The Lion, the Witch and the Wardrobe*. She is the first to see Aslan in *Prince Caspian*, and she sees esoteric things like Ramandu's fire-berry when no one else does. In *The Voyage of the "Dawn Treader,"* Edmund tells Eustace that Lucy "sees [Aslan] most often." In *Prince Caspian* she even sits "close to Aslan . . . divinely comfortable" at the last supper in the book, just like the Beloved Disciple reclines on the bosom of Jesus at his last meal in John (13:23). As for the other two children, Peter is the high king, and Aslan gave his life dramatically for Edmund. It would be harder to write them out than Susan.

Lewis may hint at Susan's apostasy in *Prince Caspian*, her last adventure in Narnia. In chapter 11, she snaps and sulks and insists that Aslan is not present long after Lucy knows he is. Susan does eventually see Aslan and apologize, telling her sister that she could have believed Aslan was there if she had let

24. "How Do You Solve a Problem Like Susan Pevensie? Narnia Guest Post by Kat Coffin," *A Pilgrim in Narnia* (blog), April 24, 2019, https://tinyurl.com/ycyh7mnx.

25. Ch. 12.

herself—an admission that may foreshadow her later refusal to believe.[26] But all is not lost. As Lewis wrote to a concerned child, there was still hope that Susan could enter Narnia later "in her own way."[27]

Through the Stable Door

In contrast to Susan the apostate, Eustace and Jill are once again apostles. Just as he does in *The Silver Chair*, Lewis implies they serve in this role when Jill says twice in chapter 7 of *The Last Battle* that Aslan *sent* them to help. Like Paul, who highlights Andronicus and Junia, a pair of male and female apostles in Romans 16:7, Lewis presents Jill as apostle without apology.

But even after she rescues Puzzle, and everyone tries to undo the donkey's deception, it's too late. They free a group of dwarves from a chain gang, and they reveal Puzzle as the false Aslan (he has repented and been forgiven), but the dwarves still refuse to join them. Eustace can't believe they don't even say thank you before they leave. However, a few minutes later, one of them, the dwarf Poggin, returns. This may be an echo of a story unique to Luke where Jesus heals ten lepers, but only one comes back to thank him (17:11–19).

Minus their antichrist, the triumvirate of Shift the ape, Rishda the chief Calormene, and Ginger the cat tell the assembled Narnians just enough of the truth to imperil Tirian's cause even more. There *was* a false Aslan, they say, but they claim that a real god, "Tashlan," waits in the stable to meet anyone who dares enter.[28] "Tashlan" is a portmanteau word, a combination of Aslan and Tash, the god of the Calormenes. Ginger the cat goes into the stable first to perpetuate the lie, but he receives the nastiest surprise of his life and as a result ceases to be a talking beast. When Shift is thrown through the door of the stable by Tirian, there is an earthquake, and the terrified Narnians cry out to be hidden from Tashlan. This probably refers to the sixth seal of Revelation, which begins with an earthquake and ends with everyone on earth calling for the mountains to fall on them to hide them from the wrath of God and the Lamb, "for the great day of their wrath has come" (Rev. 6:12–17).

A young Calormene officer, Emeth, who has devoted his life to serving Tash, volunteers to enter the stable.[29] If Susan is a believer-turned-apostate, Emeth is a pure-hearted seeker who will enjoy his reward. Anyone who knows Hebrew can

26. *Prince Caspian*, ch. 11.
27. Lewis to Martin Kilmer, Jan. 22, 1957, *CL*, 3:826.
28. Ch. 9.
29. Ch. 10.

predict this happy end from the moment they read his name, because it means "truth." Lewis provides an uncharacteristically long footnote on the word *emeth* in *The Abolition of Man*, citing Psalm 119:151, "You are near, Lord, and all your commandments are truth (*emeth*)," adding that the Hebrew word also means to be firm, reliable, or trustworthy.[30] In *The Last Battle*, Lewis plants hints about the meaning of the name for readers who don't know Hebrew throughout Emeth's dialogue with his commander Rishda. The first word out of Emeth's mouth after he addresses Rishda as "My Father" is "truly," and the next two times he speaks before he enters the stable, the words "true" or "truth" anchor his statements.

The entrance to the stable is usually called a "door," but when Emeth walks through it, the narrator calls it a "mouth." The word "mouth" alludes to another Hebrew image, the mouth of Sheol. In the chapters above on *The Lion, the Witch and the Wardrobe* and *The Silver Chair*, I mentioned that Sheol is the underground realm of the dead, called Hades in Greek and Hel in Norse mythology.[31] In the Hebrew Bible, Sheol is not a place of punishment but rather a dull, meaningless holding pen full of witless shades (Ps. 88:12). No one wants to go there. In Psalm 6, the psalmist tries to convince God to keep him alive, cannily implying that if he does, it is in God's own self-interest, for "in death there is no remembrance of you; in Sheol, who can praise you?" (Ps. 6:5; see also Ps. 88:10).[32] Sheol is often called a pit or a snare, but it's also personified as a mouth or throat: "Like a rock that one breaks apart and shatters on the land, so shall their bones be strewn at the mouth of Sheol" (Ps. 141:7). Isaiah writes, "Sheol has enlarged its appetite and opened its mouth beyond measure" (5:14). In Habakkuk, the arrogant "open their throats as wide as Sheol; like Death they never have enough" (2:5). In Numbers, when the earth opens its mouth, people go down to Sheol (16:30).

In their last battle, the characters' dread of the stable and its door grows, and one of their main objectives is to avoid being pushed up against it. Tirian calls it "the deadly door." The eagle calls it "accursed," and Eustace says he hates the very sight of it. Poggin explicitly compares the door to death. When Tirian and Jewel agree with Poggin, they confirm the instinct to identify the stable door with Sheol, since Tirian notes, "It is more like a mouth." Jewel predicts what will happen next when he wonders if it is "the door to Aslan's country" and if they will soon eat at Aslan's table.[33]

30. Lewis, *The Abolition of Man* (1943; repr., New York: Macmillan, 1947), 11–12.

31. Lewis makes this connection himself in *Miracles*, 145.

32. See Lewis, *Reflections on the Psalms*, 91.

33. Chs. 11–12.

Tirian's forces regroup next to a white rock, and a trickle of water from the rock refreshes and cheers them. Once again we may hear an echo of Exodus, particularly as it reverberates in the New Testament through Paul. When the Israelites wandering in the wilderness are thirsty, God makes water flow for them from a rock at Horeb (Exod. 17:5–7). In 1 Corinthians, Paul imbues the water with a Christological flavor. The Israelites "all drank the same spiritual drink. For they drank from the spiritual rock that followed them, and the rock was Christ" (1 Cor. 10:4).

When Tirian goes through the stable door, he is astonished to find himself not in a dark, cramped building but in sunny open air. Equally surprising, he is in the company of seven kings and queens, the seven friends of Narnia. He is especially amazed at Eustace and Jill. The last time he saw them, it looked like they had been through a war, because they had. But now they are *changed,* a word the narrator uses twice, once for each of the children, who are as clean and elegant as the other royals.[34] Tirian feels ashamed in their presence, assuming with good reason that he is gross with battle stains. But then he sees that he is not; he is dressed in new clothes, dewy fresh. The narrator emphasizes clothes throughout this section, noting that they are the sort people would wear for a royal feast. At the same time, they are supremely comfortable. Lewis detested uncomfortable clothing, describing his first school uniform in itchy detail at the beginning of *Surprised by Joy*.

Tirian, Jill, and Eustace don't realize it, but they are embodying Paul's words in 1 Corinthians 15:51–53: "Behold, I tell you a mystery. We will not all fall asleep, but we will all be *changed,* in a moment, in the twinkling of an eye, at the last trumpet. For the trumpet will sound, and the dead will be raised incorruptible, and we will be *changed*. For this corruptible body must *put on* incorruptibility, and this mortal body must *put on* immortality." Although the trumpet has not yet sounded in Narnia (it soon will), the dead have been raised, and they, too, have been changed. They have put on new, immortal bodies—an occasion for clean clothes if ever there was one. Lewis knew that under the words "put on," which occur twice in 1 Corinthians 15:53, is a Greek word that means "put on clothes" (*enduō*). We looked at this verb regarding Eustace in *The Voyage of the "Dawn Treader,"* where Lewis repeats "dressed" twice. He also plays with the idea in *Mere Christianity,* where he compares "putting on Christ" to "dressing up." He italicizes the verb to make sure we pay attention to it in "The Weight of Glory": we will "*put on* the splendour of the sun."[35]

34. Ch. 12.

35. *Mere Christianity,* 191, 195; "The Weight of Glory," in *Essay Collection,* 104. See

Tirian's clothes have changed "in a moment, in the twinkling of an eye." In other words (though not in a word this book employs), he has gone through purgatory. Lewis does use the word "purgatory" in two other books, *The Great Divorce* and *Letters to Malcolm*. A section of *Letters to Malcolm* chapter 20 retells the core of this Narnian scene in nonfantastical form. First Lewis acknowledges that his own Anglican tradition hasn't accepted the Roman Catholic doctrine of purgatory, and he outlines a form of the doctrine that, in his opinion, the Reformers rightly rejected. Then he turns to an early meaning of the word: "cleansing." Understood in this sense, purgatory isn't optional. "Our souls *demand* Purgatory, don't they?" he asks, and he describes a scenario just like the one Tirian has undergone: Would a soul want to enter eternal life smelly and grimy, even if God didn't care?[36] Lewis thinks not. This is not to say that he "believed" in purgatory. Even though he thought it "probable," he didn't see it affirmed in Scripture or at the early church councils, and he didn't think it should be imposed as doctrine, but he did enjoy contemplating it as "private speculation."[37]

The Eighth Day

Counting Tirian, there are eight kings and queens. But at this point in the story, the addition of an eighth doesn't subtract from the significance of the seven; to the contrary, it multiplies its meaning in a gloriously appropriate fashion. The monarchs don't realize it, but they have just entered into the fabled eighth day.

Once again we inhabit the realm of sacred numbers via early Christian interpretation of the numbers six, seven, and eight.[38] To understand the eighth day, we must remember the first days, the creation of the world in Genesis. Apocalypses that envision the end of the world often return to its beginning. In the beginning, God created the world in six days and rested on the seventh. But, early Jews and Christians wondered, what is a day to God, really? Psalm 90:4

---

also *Miracles*, 90, 162, and others, where, without citing particular verses, Lewis discusses Paul, "unclothing," and "re-clothing."

36. *Letters to Malcolm: Chiefly on Prayer* (New York: Harcourt, Brace & World, 1964), 107–9.

37. Lewis to Mr. Allcock, March 24, 1955, *CL*, 3:587–88.

38. For more on the importance of these numbers in the second century of the Christian church, see Joel Kalvesmaki, *The Theology of Arithmetic: Number Symbolism in Platonism and Early Christianity*, Hellenic Studies Series 59 (Washington, DC: Center for Hellenic Studies, 2013).

notes that to God a thousand years is like yesterday. Second Peter 3:8 reports that to God, a day is like a thousand years, and a thousand years like a day.

Sometime in the early second century CE, a Christian now known as Barnabas meditated upon the matter. He wrote that, since God created the world in six days, and a day to God is like a thousand years, the world as we know it will last for six thousand years. In the seventh millennium, Jesus will return, destroy the wicked, "change the sun and the moon and the stars," and rest, as befits the dignity of the seventh day. Then Barnabas puts new words into the mouth of God: "I will make a beginning of an eighth day, which is a beginning of another cosmos." Barnabas explains, "This is why we celebrate the eighth day with joy, the day on which Jesus rose from the dead."[39] Jesus was crucified on a Friday, the sixth day of the week, and in the tomb on Saturday, the seventh. He rose on Sunday, the first day, but early Christians loved to call Sunday the eighth day, a foretaste of the new world inaugurated by Jesus's resurrection, the new cosmos of life that would never end. An intriguing fact about the number eight also caught their attention. Arabic numerals were unknown in the ancient Mediterranean world. Instead, letters of the alphabet served double duty, with each letter also representing a number. Therefore, every word had a numerical value. The word "Jesus" in Greek adds up to 888.

The eighth day not only recapitulates the first day; it also redeems primal sin, so the sudden prominence of trees laden with luscious fruit at the end of chapter 12 and beginning of chapter 13 should come as no surprise. The presence of the fruit, its quality, and the characters' emotional reactions to it appear in a unified scene that alludes to so many disparate texts that it is a challenge to catch the allusions as they fly by, something like trying to focus on an individual fan blade while the fan whirs at full speed.

First, Lewis is contrasting the end-time fruit to the ape's fruit earlier in the book. The ape forced others to jump to his will and supply him with fruit as long as he had the power to make them. The kings and queens, on the other hand, hesitate before they eat. They wonder if they're allowed to pick it until Peter voices his intuition that yes, they are. Instead of being ruled by appetite, by simian greed and entitlement, they are humble. Their hesitation reminds us of the first woman's pondering whether she should eat from the tree God planted in the garden of Eden—which brings us full circle to *The Magician's Nephew* and how Lewis reimagined Genesis 3 there.

The book of Revelation also imagines redemption in a garden, so Lewis relies heavily on it, too. In Revelation 2:7, Jesus promises, "To the one who

39. Epistle of Barnabas 15.

conquers, I will give permission to eat from the tree of life that is in the paradise of God," a verse Lewis underlined in his Moffatt New Testament. The eight friends of Narnia have conquered, so they may eat from the tree at the end of their own book. The tree in the garden paradise in the last chapter of Revelation bears "twelve kinds of fruit, producing its fruit each month" (Rev. 22:2). The trees in Narnia also bear different varieties. Their flavor surpasses that of any other fruit they have ever tasted, and there are no annoying seeds or stinging insects buzzing about. In other words, it is ideal fruit—the Platonic idea of fruit. No one mentions Plato here, but Digory soon will. When he does, the narrator will refer to the fruit again to hammer the point home. Until then, suffice it to say that this Narnian fruit is a concrete and stealthy vehicle through which Lewis may introduce Platonic ideas to his young readers.

It is not only the fruit that is ideal. Their bodies are different, too, ideally suited to taste it as never before. Only human beings, Lewis writes, can enjoy God's physical creation through the senses. Animals experience the world, but they lack the capacity to appreciate it, and angels are "pure intelligences;" possessing no body to interact with material things. He continues: "I fancy the 'beauties of nature' are a secret God has shared with us alone. That may be one of the reasons why we were made—and why the resurrection of the body is an important doctrine."[40]

Bigger Than the Whole World

After they eat, they look around, marveling at the fact that the little hovel of a stable is much bigger on the inside than it appears to be on the outside. This prompts Lucy to speak for the first time in the book, and she makes the only reference to the nativity of Jesus in the Chronicles.[41] At the end of *The Voyage of the "Dawn Treader,"* Aslan told Lucy that she would not return to Narnia because she had to learn who he was in her world. She has clearly done so, for she is able to say that there, a stable once held something bigger than the whole world.[42]

Lucy is not an Eastern Orthodox Christian, but she echoes a line from the Orthodox hymn for December 20: "O manger of senseless beasts, receive him

40. *Letters to Malcolm*, 18.

41. Lewis does hide a reference to the birth of Jesus in *The Lion, the Witch and the Wardrobe*. On June 3, 1953, he replies to Hila Newman, a child who asked him what Aslan's "other name" was. He wants her to figure it out, so he feeds her clues, including the fact that Aslan "arrived at the same time as Father Christmas" (*CL*, 3:334).

42. Ch. 13, referring to Luke 2:16.

whom the heavens cannot contain!" Another Orthodox hymn that prepares for the feast of the nativity is worth contemplating here too, since its first three lines reflect what we have read in *The Last Battle* so far, and the last line foreshadows where the book is going.

> The tree of life blossoms forth from the virgin in the cave!
> Her womb is a spiritual paradise planted with the divine fruit.
> If we eat of it, we shall live forever and not die like Adam.
> Christ comes to restore the image which he made in the beginning.

The ungrateful dwarves who had refused to join Tirian sit near the royals, but they think they're crowded inside a pitch-black, stinking stable. Lucy tries to help them see the truth, that they're outdoors in the sunshine, to no avail. She brings them violets, but they can neither see nor smell them, and when she presses a little bouquet under a dwarf's nose, he tries to strike her, accusing her of assaulting him with manure. There is little doubt that Lewis is alluding to 2 Corinthians 2:15–16, a passage he marked in his Moffatt New Testament: "I live for God as the fragrance of Christ breathed alike on those who are being saved and on those who are perishing, to the one a deadly fragrance that makes for death, to the other a vital fragrance that makes for life."

He is also dramatizing Amos 5:18, a verse he knew well enough to quote in a letter to his brother: "Alas for you who desire the day of the Lord! Why do you want the day of the Lord? It is darkness, not light."[43] Early Christians identify the day of the Lord with the eighth day, and they warn anyone who isn't ready for it to take care. The fourth-century bishop Basil of Caesarea summarizes it perfectly, quoting Joel 2:11 and then Amos 5:18, almost as if he wrote it for this chapter:

> "The day of the Lord . . . is great and very terrible," and elsewhere, "Woe unto you that desire the day of the Lord: to what end is it for you? The day of the Lord is darkness and not light." A day of darkness for those who are worthy of darkness. . . . This day without evening, without succession and without end, is not unknown to scripture, and it is the day that the Psalmist calls the eighth day, because it is outside this time of weeks. Thus whether you call it day, or whether you call it eternity, you express the same idea.[44]

43. Lewis to his brother, Feb. 18, 1940, *CL*, 2:352.

44. Basil of Caesarea, *Hexaemeron* Homily 2, in *Nicene and Post-Nicene Fathers*, series 2, vol. 8, *St. Basil: Letters and Select Works*, trans. Blomfield Jackson (New York: Christian Literature Company, 1895), 64–65, slightly modified. For an explanation of

The dread day of the Lord, the eighth day, is a dark day for the dwarves because they are "worthy of darkness." They have made themselves into creatures who can perceive nothing but.

With these dwarves, Lewis recycles the main point of *The Great Divorce*: that a life built on the choice to turn away from God is a life that cuts itself off from reality, because there is no reality but God. Utter distortion is the inevitable result. Over and over again (in *The Great Divorce, Mere Christianity,* and most succinctly in "The Weight of Glory"), he returns to a concept he never names but that permeates his work: theosis, the process by which a creature of God is turned into a child of God, becoming a "little Christ," or, to use scriptural language, conformed to the image of God (Rom. 8:29). In 2 Peter 1:3–4, God promises that his people may share the divine nature, a verse Lewis underlines in his Moffatt New Testament. Lewis quotes another passage related to theosis, John 10:33 (cf. Ps. 82:6), at the end of *The Great Divorce.*[45] According to Lewis—who relies on age-old Christian teaching—every person ever born faces a choice: become more and more "real," which is to say more divine, or dwindle into nothing. The dwarves, embodying the opposite of theosis, have chosen nothing.

Calling Time

At this moment the true Aslan suddenly makes his first appearance in the book. First, he greets Tirian with "Well done," another reference to Matthew 25:23 (see chapter 10 of this book), and then he turns to the dwarves to try to reach them one last time. The book of Joel describes Aslan's efforts: "Even now, says the Lord, return to me with all your heart. . . . Return to the Lord, your God, for he is gracious and merciful, slow to anger, and abounding in steadfast love" (2:12–13). Aslan sets out a banquet for them, but they have removed themselves so far from reality that they insist it's barn slop. He can do no more. He leaves them to themselves, the dwarves for the dwarves.

The lion turns abruptly to another task: he calls time, in every sense of the word.[46] Looking through the stable door to the darkness outside it, he

---

Basil's misunderstanding of "the Psalmist" regarding the eighth day, see the footnote on the passage.

45. For more on theosis in Lewis, see Myk Habets, "Mere Christianity for Mere Gods: Lewis on Theosis," in *A Myth Retold: Re-encountering C. S. Lewis as Theologian,* ed. Martin Sutherland (Eugene, OR: Wipf & Stock, 2014), 110–29.

46. Chs. 13–14.

rouses Father Time to blow his trumpet to announce the end of time. In the letters of Paul, a trumpet blasts right before the end of the age (1 Cor. 15:52; 1 Thess. 4:16). After both the biblical and the Narnian trumpets sound, the stars fall. The prophet Joel writes that on the day of the Lord, "The sun and the moon are darkened, and the stars withdraw their shining" (3:15). Jesus says that "in those days, after that suffering, the sun will be darkened, and the moon will not give its light, and the stars will fall from heaven, and the powers in the heavens will be shaken" (Mark 13:24–25). When the apocalyptic Lamb opens the sixth seal, the stars fall, and the "sky was rolled up like a scroll" (Rev. 6:14, a verse Lewis highlights twice in his essay "The World's Last Night").[47]

Then comes the final judgment. Aslan's rational beings stream through what used to be the stable door, and they look him in the face. The divine face, especially in relation to the human face, is a powerful image for Lewis. In *Till We Have Faces*, he sets it at the center of a myth. The main character, Orual, covers her face with a veil because she can't face who she is and what she has done. She deplores the gods for hiding from her, when she is hiding even from herself. In the end she realizes that being face-to-face with anyone, much less the gods, requires honesty and vulnerability.

The face of God is an important image in the Bible. Passages differ on whether anyone can look God in the face, and, if so, who (Gen. 32:30; Exod. 33:11, 20; Num. 6:24–26; Ps. 17:15), but none of that matters here. The Scripture that matters comes from Revelation and Matthew. In Revelation's final judgment, even heaven and earth flee from God's face (20:11), but those who survive judgment will live in the new Jerusalem and gaze upon it forever (22:4). In the same way, as each creature looks Aslan in the face, one of two things happens. Either they join him on his right (this group includes a dwarf who had rejected Aslan in the stable), or they turn away and disappear into darkness on his left. The same thing happens in the judgment of nations in Matthew 25:31–46, the parable of the sheep and the goats. The sheep remain with the Son of Man on his right, and the goats are sent to punishment on his left.

After everyone is judged, dragons and lizards devour Narnia's vegetation, perhaps echoing the burning of grass and trees after the first trumpet blast in Revelation 8:7. When Narnia is barren, waters of chaos rush in—the waters of uncreation. They stop dead at the stable door, lapping at Aslan's paws. It's easy to recall God's words to Job: "Who shut in the sea with doors . . . and prescribed bounds for it, and set bars and doors, and said, 'Thus far you shall come, and no farther?'" (38:9–11).

47. Lewis, "The World's Last Night," in *Essay Collection*, 50, 53.

Narnia's last day dawns with a huge red sun that makes the waters below look like blood. We may remember the water turned to blood in the Exodus plagues, mimicked by the angel with the second bowl who turns the sea to blood in Revelation 16:3. The Narnian moon sidles up to the sun, which turns the moon red and burns it up. Then Father Time extinguishes the sun, and everything goes black, fulfilling Joel 2:30 (a verse taken up in the sixth seal of Rev. 6:12): "I will show portents in the heavens and on the earth, blood and fire and columns of smoke. The sun shall be turned to darkness, and the moon to blood, before the great and terrible day of the Lord comes." Finally High King Peter, fully inhabiting his role as the apostle who holds the keys to the kingdom (Matt. 16:19), locks the door on Narnia.

The "Virtuous Heathen"

But when everyone turns around, they are astonished to see that they're in the same sun-lit land they were before. Aslan immediately dashes off and bids them to follow him west. As they depart, the talking dogs sniff out Emeth, who has survived both the final judgment and a conversation with Aslan.[48] It turns out that Emeth, to use Matthew's language, is a sheep, not a goat. He tells them his story: how he had worshiped Tash his whole life and hated Aslan, so he expected the lion to kill him. Instead, Aslan informed him that the devotion Emeth had given to Tash actually went "to me."[49]

This poignant little phrase comes straight from Matthew's parable. The sheep had no idea they were ministering to the Son of Man, but it didn't matter. He reveals that what they did to the least of these, they did "to me." They receive their reward, life in the new age (Matt. 25:45–46).

"To me" is the tiniest of phrases—only four letters—and an exceedingly common one, but Lewis's own words prove that Aslan is quoting Matthew's parable verbatim. As early as 1941 Lewis wrote, "The parable of the sheep & the goats suggests that [the 'virtuous heathen'] have a very pleasant surprise coming to them."[50] In 1952 he observes, "Every prayer which is sincerely made even to a false god or to a v[ery] imperfectly conceived true God, is accepted by the true God. . . . Christ saves many who do not think they know Him. For He is (dimly) present in the good side of the inferior teachers they follow. In the parable of the Sheep & Goats (Matt. XXV. 31 and following) those who are

48. Ch. 13.

49. Ch. 14.

50. Lewis to Patricia Thomson, Dec. 8, 1941, *CL*, 2:499.

saved do not seem to know that they have served Christ."[51] Thus the fifth quotation of Scripture in the Chronicles is embedded almost invisibly in Aslan's words to Emeth.

Elsewhere Lewis applies another verse, 1 Timothy 4:10, to what he again calls "the virtuous heathen." This verse and the phrase "virtuous heathen" are so important to him that he underlined part of the verse and wrote the phrase in his 1839 King James Bible, one of the few times he marked the New Testament in that book.[52] The KJV reads, "For therefore we both labour and suffer reproach, because we trust in the living God, who is the saviour of all men, specially of those that believe." In 1949 he quotes the verse in a letter: "Our Lord is the saviour 'of all men' though 'specially of those that believe.'"[53]

Let's take a moment to rewrite 1 Timothy 4:10 without the word "specially" (which translates the Greek *malista*): "Our Lord is the saviour of all men, of those that believe." Then put it back in and read the verse again: "Our Lord is the saviour of all men, *specially* of those that believe." "Specially" explodes in the middle of the sentence like a landmine, demolishing any misconception the unwary believer may hold about God's love for his creatures. Not everyone is "saved" in *The Last Battle*, but some unlikely candidates are, and Lewis rightly sees this as biblical.

He presents something of the same idea at the end of *The Great Divorce*. Addressing his psychopomp George MacDonald, the narrator says, "In your own books, Sir, . . . you were a Universalist. You talked as if all men would be saved. And St. Paul, too."[54] Speaking in his own voice, Lewis says much the same thing when he introduces a new translation of Paul's letters. "All the most terrifying texts" about the end come from Jesus, but "all the texts on which we can base such warrant as we have for hoping that all men will be saved come from St Paul."[55] He doesn't specify which Pauline texts he's talking about in either book, but 1 Timothy 4:10 must be one of them.

51. Lewis to Mrs. Johnson, Nov. 8, 1952, *CL*, 3:245–46.

52. He writes "The Virtuous Heathen?" above Jer. 35. C. S. Lewis personal library, Marion E. Wade Center, Wheaton College, Wheaton, IL.

53. Lewis to Bede Griffiths, June 27, 1949, *CL*, 2:948. Writing to Mary Van Deusen, Jan. 31, 1952, *CL*, 3:163, Lewis refers to 1 Tim. 4:10 and Matt. 25:31–46 in tandem. He uses it in *English Literature in the Sixteenth Century, Excluding Drama* (Oxford: Clarendon, 1954), 162, and he underlines the verse and makes a double line next to it in his Moffatt New Testament. He began thinking about it as early as April 4, 1934, writing Bede Griffiths, *CL*, 2:135.

54. *The Great Divorce* (1946; repr., New York: HarperCollins, 2001), 140. Compare Lewis to Greeves, Sept. 22, 1931, *CL*, 1:970.

55. Lewis, "Modern Translations of the Bible," in *God in the Dock: Essays on Theology*

Lewis was not a universalist, a view he makes clear whenever he discusses the "terrifying texts" of Jesus. At the same time, he does say "we may dare to hope," like Julian of Norwich, that "All will be well," and his interest in the "salvation of heathen" continued to the end of his life.[56] In 1963, the year he died, he underlined a quote from the sixteenth-century theologian Sebastian Franck in the newly published *Cambridge History of the Bible*. Franck believed God would save

> all surrendered hearts . . . illuminating and teaching them from the beginning, Adam, Abel, Noah, Lot, Abraham, Job, Trismegistus, Mercury, Plotinus, Cornelius, and all the godly heathen. . . . Wherefore my heart is alien to none. I have my brothers among the Turks, Papists, Jews, and all peoples. Not that they are Turks, Jews, Papists, and Sectaries or will remain so; in the evening they will be called into the vineyard and given the same wages as we. From the East and from the West children of Abraham will be raised up out of the stone and will sit down with him at God's table.[57]

Underlining a text does not mean one agrees with it.[58] Like many Christians, however, Lewis struggled with the question of who will be "saved" and why. Looking at everything he read and wrote on the topic over a lifetime, we see that Lewis hoped for the salvation of as many "surrendered hearts" as possible.

Back in Narnia, Aslan concludes his audience with Emeth with the words, "All find what they *truly* seek" (emphasis mine), another nod to Matthew, this time 7:7–8, and to the underlying meaning of Emeth's name.

---

and Ethics, ed. Walter Hooper (Grand Rapids: Eerdmans, 1970), 232. See David Bentley Hart, *That All Shall Be Saved: Heaven, Hell, and Universal Salvation* (New Haven: Yale University Press, 2019), 94–102, for an argument—with which I agree, and with which it appears Lewis would too—that Paul never envisions eternal punishment.

56. Lewis, "The Psalms," in *Essay Collection*, 226. Reggie Weems, "Universalism Denied: C. S. Lewis' Unpublished Letters to Alan Fairhurst," *Journal of Inklings Studies* 7, no. 2 (2017): 87–98. Lewis responds to Greeves's question "Do you believe in hell?" May 13, 1946, *CL*, 2:710. The New Testament "implies the possibility" of permanent exclusion, but Lewis isn't sure what that means.

57. Quoted by Roland H. Bainton, "The Bible in the Reformation," in *The Cambridge History of the Bible*, vol. 3, *The West from the Reformation to the Present Day*, ed. S. L. Greenslade (Cambridge: Cambridge University Press, 1963), 37.

58. Compare George Sayer, who claims that Lewis underlined "passages of which he approved." *Jack: A Life of C. S. Lewis* (Wheaton, IL: Crossway, 1988), 106.

IT'S (MOSTLY) IN PLATO

Everyone moves on, "always westward." Lewis emphasizes the direction, even having Jill state that they are *not* headed toward Aslan's country, which is in the east. The landscape looks maddeningly familiar to the travelers, but it requires the eyes of Farsight the eagle and the wisdom of Digory the professor to see the truth: they are in Narnia, but now it is the *real* Narnia. The Narnia they had known and loved, the one Aslan had just destroyed, was only a "shadow or a copy" of this one. "It's all in Plato, all in Plato!" Digory cries.[59]

Samuel Taylor Coleridge famously quipped that everyone is born either an Aristotelian or a Platonist, and Lewis joins Team Plato when he takes on the persona of narrator in his fiction.[60] On the first page of *The Great Divorce*, for example, the narrator finds himself in a shoddy gray town with "bookshops of the sort that sell *The Works of Aristotle*." Aristotle's works languish in the bad place, but Plato gets a shout-out in the good place, the new Narnia. The eight kings and queens have already eaten its Platonic fruit, of which any other is a bland imitation. This fruit could grow only in the real Narnia, of which the old Narnia was just a shadow, so it is no accident that the narrator reminds us of that fruit as he struggles to describe the "taste" of that new country.[61]

Paradoxically, however, in a sense the new country *is* the old country. The Platonic Narnia is the original; the previous Narnia, now destroyed, was an imperfect copy. This view comes from Plato, in his concept of "form" or "idea" (Greek *eidos*). A Platonic form may be defined as the perfect exemplar or true essence of an object or concept—or, in this context, a place. Lewis lays out these ideas in *The Allegory of Love* right after he defines allegory. He contrasts allegory and Platonic forms sharply, insisting that "the difference between the two can hardly be exaggerated."[62]

It's all in Plato, but not only in Plato, inasmuch as ideas we call Platonic appear in both testaments of the Bible. In the Hebrew Scriptures, God gives Moses

59. Ch. 15.

60. *Table Talk*, July 2, 1830. Lewis speaks positively of Aristotle to Corbin Scott Carnell, Oct. 13, 1958, *CL*, 3:978.

61. Lewis foreshadows this idea in the last line of "Early Prose Joy" (1931); see Andrew Lazo, ed., "'Early Prose Joy': C. S. Lewis's Early Draft of an Autobiographical Manuscript," *VII: Journal of the Marion E. Wade Center* 30 (2013): 40.

62. *Allegory of Love*, 45; see also Mark Edwards, "Classicist," in *The Cambridge Companion to C. S. Lewis*, ed. Robert MacSwain and Michael Ward (Cambridge: Cambridge University Press, 2010), 58–71, esp. 66.

plans to construct the wilderness tabernacle where the Jews will worship until Solomon builds the first temple. God commands Moses to make it "according to the pattern that is being shown to you" (Exod. 25:40), a verse Lewis underlined in his 1839 Bible.[63] Since God, like an architect, has detailed plans for the earthly tabernacle, some Jews reasoned that its ideal model was in heaven. The tabernacle on earth was a copy of the one in heaven, good enough for now but inferior to its heavenly counterpart. The New Testament book of Hebrews states this explicitly: the Jews worship "in a sketch and a shadow" of the heavenly tabernacle, because God told Moses to "make everything according to the pattern that was shown to you" (8:5). Hebrews 8:5 appears in a rather polemical context, but this doesn't change the fact that both Jews and Christians were proud of Moses's alleged "Platonism." Some of them even said that, since Moses lived before Plato, Plato got his ideas from Moses, and at least one Greek pagan agreed.[64] Lewis was well aware of the claim that Moses was the source of Greek learning, underlining a sentence that said just that in his copy of Origen's *Contra Celsum*.[65]

Several ancient apocalypses, including Revelation, apply the Platonic idea to Jerusalem. That is, there is an earthly Jerusalem here and also a heavenly one with God. At the end of Revelation, the heavenly city descends to earth, melding the boundaries between them, so God dwells on earth with his people. Death must be dead in this new world, and with it "mourning and crying and pain, for the first things have passed away" (21:4). The same holds true in the new Narnia. Digory and Polly, the oldest of the seven, unstiffen, and their pain disappears. Lewis hopes for the same recovery in a letter to a correspondent who complained of the aches of aging. He commiserates with her, reflecting that both of them were breaking down like old cars in need of new parts. They must "look forward to the fine new machines (latest Resurrection model)" waiting for them in the "Divine garage."[66]

Everyone in Narnia has died, but no one is a ghost.[67] They rejoice in their resurrected bodies, which are realer than real. Here Lewis differs from Plato, who disparaged the physical body and believed release from it was a blessing.[68]

63. C. S. Lewis personal library, Marion E. Wade Center, Wheaton College, Wheaton, IL.

64. Numenius as quoted by Clement of Alexandria, *Stromata* 1.22.

65. Henry Chadwick, introduction to *Origen: Contra Celsum*, trans. Henry Chadwick (Cambridge: Cambridge University Press, 1953), ix.

66. Lewis to Mary Willis Shelburne, Sept. 30, 1958, *CL*, 3:975.

67. Lewis, "Weight of Glory," 105.

68. Lewis to Bede Griffiths, Jan. 17, 1940, *CL*, 2:326; *The Problem of Pain* (1940; repr., New York: Macmillan, 1944), 92.

Lewis, in contrast, wrote that the concept of a split between a body in "fetters" and a soul that goes to heaven was an "unfortunate legacy" of the Greeks, an idea "wholly different from the Christian doctrines of man's creation, fall, redemption, and resurrection."[69] Lewis is an orthodox Christian, so for him there can be no ultimate separation of body and soul. There is no "going to heaven" on the eighth day, either in Scripture or in Narnia, if "going to heaven" means vanishing into some misty, disembodied, "spiritual" afterlife. He makes this basic Christian doctrine resoundingly clear in *The Great Divorce*, where the more the ghosts from the gray city take on the image of God (through theosis, "in" purgatory), the more "solid" they grow.

The Great Divorce and *The Last Battle* are fiction, but Lewis includes the idea in his nonfiction, too. Building on Paul, he writes, "If flesh and blood cannot inherit the kingdom of God" (1 Cor. 15:50), it is not because they are "too gross," but rather because they are "too flimsy."[70] Paul would agree with Lewis. The resurrected body in 1 Corinthians 15 is not "spiritual" because it is immaterial; it is "spiritual" because it is a new sort of body, an immortal one, because "Death has been swallowed up in victory" (1 Cor. 15:54).[71] Neither Paul nor Lewis knew what the resurrected body would look like, but only that it would *be*. To Lewis, "*Resurrection* (what ever it exactly means) is so much profounder an idea than mere immortality. I am sure we don't just 'go on'. We really die and are really built up again." When this happens, he says, "old joy, even old power, may come rushing up."[72]

69. *Discarded Image*, 28.

70. Lewis, "Transposition," in *Essay Collection*, 276. He writes almost the same thing in *The Great Divorce*, 114, where George MacDonald tells the narrator that "flesh and blood cannot come to the Mountains. Not because they are too rank, but because they are too weak." Compare *Letters to Malcolm*, 121–23.

71. Ancient authors like Irenaeus saw this. Paul calls resurrected bodies spiritual "because they partake of the Spirit, and not because their flesh has been stripped off and taken away" (Irenaeus, *Against Heresies* 6.1). See also David Bentley Hart, "The Spiritual Was More Substantial Than the Material for the Ancients," *Church Life Journal*, July 26, 2018, https://tinyurl.com/5dpt25zr. Lewis concurs, as he notes in *Miracles*, 92: images of "Spirit" should be "*heavier* than matter."

72. Lewis to Warfield M. Firor, Dec. 5, 1949, *CL*, 2:1006; cf. Lewis to Mary Willis Shelburne, Nov. 26, 1962, *CL*, 3:1384. Lewis underlines a sentence that says much the same thing—"His [Jesus's] was not a miracle of immortality, but one of resurrection"—in his copy of E. L. Mascall, *The God-Man* (Westminster: Dacre, 1940), 101. Like Lewis and Austin Farrer, Mascall was a regular member of the "Zernov Circle" (see chapter 1, p. 20 above).

And that is exactly what happens next in *The Last Battle*. With their resurrected bodies, the citizens of the new Narnia begin to run. At the beginning of chapter 16, "Farewell to the Shadow-Lands," they can "run without getting tired," a quotation with only slight rewording of the middle of Isaiah 40:31: "They will soar on wings like eagles; *they will run and not grow weary*, they will walk and not faint." After his characters swim up a waterfall, Lewis alludes to the first part of Isaiah 40:31, comparing their running to flying, noting that even the eagle couldn't fly faster than the earthbound creatures could run. Their new bodies are fit, in multiple senses of the word, for the new Narnia.

Penultimate Places

As Hebrews 12:1 notes, they had "run with perseverance the race that was set before [them]," and the finish line is a garden on a hill, its trees laden with golden fruit. Just as Polly and Digory had surmised, they were headed for the western garden, the Narnian garden of Hesperides. Everyone dear to them is there, back to the beginning of Narnian time.[73] A reunion of characters is an unexceptional device to wrap up a series, but in the Chronicles it stands for the communion of saints, that "great cloud of witnesses" in Hebrews 12:1, an image that, when we perceive it, confirms the other echo of the verse noted above.

"About half an hour later" Lucy is visiting with her first Narnian friend, Tumnus the faun.[74] Lewis could have chosen any length of time, but "about half an hour" is an exact quote of Revelation 8:1, the duration of the silence that ensues after the lamb opens the seventh seal of his heavenly scroll. Like the phrase "to me," "about half an hour" is common as dirt, and anywhere else one would pass by it oblivious. But at the end of a seventh book based on John's Apocalypse, it should snap us to attention, and we can recognize it as the seventh and final quotation of Scripture in the Chronicles. Lewis underlined "about half an hour" in his Moffatt New Testament, an act that dispels doubt he quoted it purposely.

Tumnus and Lucy's tête-à-tête shares a notable theme with several ancient apocalypses: the end repeats the beginning, but better.[75] The first Narnian scene

73. Everyone except Susan. Neil Gaiman writes a shocking story, "The Problem of Susan," in first-person narration from the point of view of the sister who had to deal with the death of her family. Gaiman, *Fragile Things: Short Fictions and Wonders* (New York: William Morrow, 2006), 181–90.

74. Ch. 16.

75. Cf. the Animal Apocalypse of 1 En. 85–90; Rev. 21–22.

in the first Chronicle, *The Lion, the Witch and the Wardrobe,* brings Lucy and Tumnus together, but all is not well, since he almost betrays her to the White Witch. In the last scene of the last Chronicle, they are together in paradise.

The word "paradise" points to another way the end repeats the beginning. A loanword from Persian, "paradise" means "garden," and the Christian canon of Scripture begins and ends in a garden, as the last chapters of Revelation return to, and redeem, the garden scenes in Genesis 2–3. Lewis's characters are also in a garden, but it is not Eden, and it is not their final home. They are in the west, in the same Hesperian garden that Digory and Polly had visited long ago. In Lewis's thought-world, one may visit the Hesperides but not stay there. In *The Pilgrim's Regress,* after John completes his arduous journey west, he learns that he must turn around and go east again if he wants to meet God. So important is this conversion—a word that literally means "turning around"—that Lewis highlights it as the "regress" of the title. John's guide tells him that "the country will look very different on the return journey."[76] In Lewis's poem "The Landing," a ship's crew thinks they have found the Hesperides, but they have not. It is "Goddesses' country, never men's," so suffering "strenuous longing," they must re-embark.[77] Ransom too must leave his Hesperian isles at the end of *Perelandra.*

References to the Hesperides tumble over each other in chapter 14 of *Surprised by Joy*. The chorus of Euripides's *Hippolytus* that Lewis felt he had to read must be the one beginning in line 742:

> Then to the apple-bearing headland of the Hesperides would I finally arrive, to the land of those singers of songs where the ruler of the sea, with its seething purple stretches of water, no longer gives a path for sailors to proceed any further, and there I would find the revered limit of the sky, which Atlas holds, and there the immortalizing spring waters flow right next to the place where Zeus goes to lie down, and where she who gives blessedness makes things grow. She is the most fertile one.[78]

76. *Pilgrim's Regress,* Wade Annotated Edition, ed. David C. Downing (Grand Rapids: Eerdmans, 2014), 176–77.

77. "The Landing," in *Collected Poems,* 357–58.

78. Euripides, *Hippolytus* 742–750, trans. E. P. Coleridge, rev. Mary Jane Rein, further rev. Gregory Nagy, Center for Hellenic Studies, Harvard University, https://tinyurl.com/bdcnpehu. The fact that the Fox (*Till We Have Faces,* ch. 1) quotes the first few words of the passage with especial happiness confirms the reference. As Michael Ward has shown in ch. 8 ("Venus") of *Planet Narnia* (Oxford: Oxford University Press,

Two pages later Lewis mentions "Asgard, the Western Garden" of Norse mythology, and the page after that he comes right out and names the garden of the Hesperides. *Surprised by Joy* is Lewis's conversion account, and chapter 14, "Checkmate," is the second-to-last chapter of the book, when he is on the verge of giving in and admitting that God is God.[79] To Lewis, "the west" is never the end of the journey. It is a penultimate place, attained just before one must turn around and head toward one's final destination.

And so it is in Narnia. As Lucy and Tumnus gaze across the landscape—which, it is important to note, includes Calormen—they spy the far-off mountains of Aslan's Country. In the ideal Narnia, they can traverse them effortlessly, and just like John in *The Pilgrim's Regress*, they discover that divine mountains circle the earth, so west meets east. That is to say, longing meets fulfillment. For Lewis, the Hesperides embody Joy, the term he uses for the sweet piercing desire that points humanity to something it can never reach in the Shadowlands: the mountains where God dwells.[80] In Aslan's Country, longing meets its end. It is what longing was made for.

The End—and the Beginning

Once they cross the mountains, Aslan tells them they will remain with him forever: "The term is over; the holidays have begun." These are almost the last words Aslan says in the book, and Lucy was the last to speak before him. The constellation of Lucy, Aslan, and the first day of vacation, as Americans call it, takes us back to how Lucy felt the first time she heard Aslan's name: "And Lucy got the feeling you have when you wake up in the morning and realize that it is the beginning of the holidays or the beginning of summer."[81] No one who knows the story of Lewis's childhood will be surprised to see that his metaphor for everlasting joy is the permanent end of school. Other authors might have devised it as a cheap way to appeal to their young readers, but Lewis, who was seared by the pain of his school years, feels the joy truly and

---

2008), the Chronicle that highlights the garden, *The Magician's Nephew*, is connected with Aphrodite and fertility.

79. *Surprised by Joy* (San Diego: Harcourt Brace Jovanovich, 1955), 217, 219, 220. He mentions the garden in the previous chapter to reject it, 203–5.

80. See various references to "the mountains" in *The Great Divorce*, e.g., "Flesh and blood cannot come to the Mountains" (95), and to "the god of the Mountain" in *Till We Have Faces* (Orlando, FL: Harcourt, 1956), 3, 46, 48, 70, 76, 82, 159.

81. *The Lion, the Witch and the Wardrobe* (London: Geoffrey Bles, 1950), ch. 7.

deeply. His placement of the image here is numinous, and he uses it in just the same way in *Surprised by Joy,* where he describes the end of term as "the almost supernatural bliss of the Last Day," marking the last two words with divine capitalization.[82]

Then the narrator writes, "they all lived happily ever after."[83] If we didn't know better, we might view this line as a quick and thoughtless way to wrap up the series. However, we do know better, because "happily ever after" is the classic genre marker that concludes a fairy tale. But it's not the last word, for there is one more biblical allusion. The narrator informs us that the new Narnians have many chapters yet to live in a story that "goes on forever." Thus the last line of *The Last Battle* echoes the last line of the Gospel of John: "But there are also many other things Jesus did; if every one of them were written down, I suppose the world itself could not contain the books that would be written" (21:25).

82. Lewis to Francine Smithline, March 23, 1962, *CL,* 3:1325; Mary Willis Shelburne, July 6, 1963, *CL,* 3:1438; *Surprised by Joy,* 36.

83. Compare Lewis to Joyce Pearce, July 20, 1943, *CL,* 2:585, where Lewis notes that the universe has a "finale in which the good characters 'live happily ever after.'"

17. PAST WATCHFUL DRAGONS

> *The dragon's watch over a spring may run together with his habituation in the sea, his damming of waters, his blockade of a road, and his holding of a sacred precinct.*
>
> —Joseph Fontenrose[1]

In April 1956, a boy named Laurence Krieg read *The Last Battle*, and he liked it so much, he wrote the author. Laurence told him that when he first studied the Apostles' Creed, "I only believed the part about life after death for a short time. But since I read the *Last Battle* I believe it all the time."[2]

Laurence's meditation on *The Last Battle* might have inspired a point in Lewis's essay "Sometimes Fairy Stories May Say Best What's to Be Said," which was published later that year, in November 1956. Lewis recalls that when he was growing up, pressure to feel a certain way about God could backfire. Rather than producing the desired result—piety—it tended to chill pious feelings. By writing stories like the Chronicles, he hoped he might "steal past those watchful dragons."[3] For Laurence, at least, Lewis succeeded.

"Past watchful dragons" has become a catchphrase among Lewis aficionados, but I have never seen anyone place it in its native habitat, the garden of the Hesperides, even though Lewis did so himself in his Ransom trilogy.[4] When

1. Fontenrose, *Python: A Study of Delphic Myth and Its Origins* (1959; repr., Berkeley: University of California Press, 1980), 8.

2. *CL*, 3:744 n. 168.

3. Lewis, "Sometimes Fairy Stories May Say Best What's to Be Said," *New York Times*, Nov. 18, 1956, 310.

4. I have searched Walter Hooper, *Past Watchful Dragons: The Origin, Interpretation, and Appreciation of the Chronicles of Narnia* (New York: Macmillan, 1971); David C. Downing, *Planets in Peril: A Critical Study of C. S. Lewis's Ransom Trilogy* (Amherst: University of Massachusetts Press, 1992); Evrea Ness-Bergstein, "The Garden as Unfinished Narrative of the Good in C. S. Lewis' *Perelandra*," *Journal of Inklings Studies* 2, no. 1 (2012): 49–80; Judith Wolfe and Brendan Wolfe, eds., *C. S. Lewis's "Perelandra":*

Ransom wakes up for the first time on Perelandra, he sees "a small dragon covered with scales of red gold" coiled around a tree, and "he recognized the garden of the Hesperides at once." The creature looked at him "very hard."[5]

Lewis knew about the dragon in the garden long before he wrote *Perelandra*. As a teenager he loved John Milton's poem *Comus*, which he describes in letters to Greeves as a "dream of delight" and "one of the most perfect things in English poetry," and he shares his favorite line with his friend: "the best thing of all is the last song with its allusions to 'Hesperus and his daughters three / That sing about the golden tree.'"[6]

In Milton's poem, the eye of a dragon watches over the garden:

> . . . the fair Hesperian tree
> Laden with blooming gold, had need the guard
> of dragon-watch with uninchanted eye
> To save her blossoms, and defend her fruit . . .[7]

In 1916 Lewis wrote his own Hesperian poem, and he put a dragon in it, too:

> Where, beyond the waters
> Of the outer sea,
> Thy triple crown of daughters
> That guards the golden tree . . .
> And while the old, old dragon
> For joy lifts up his head . . .[8]

When Digory, who in some ways resembles young Lewis, visits the western garden in *The Magician's Nephew*, there is no dragon but rather a bird with "the tiniest slit of one eye" open to watch him, very like the dragon Ransom finds

---

Reshaping the Image of the Cosmos (Kent, OH: Kent State University Press, 2013); Ruth Berman, "Watchful Dragons and Sinewy Gnomes: C. S. Lewis's Use of Modern Fairy Tales," *Mythlore* 30, no. 3/4 (Spring/Summer 2021): 117–27; and more. If someone else has connected Lewis's "watchful dragons" to the little dragon in *Perelandra*, no doubt I will be made aware of it soon.

5. *Perelandra* (1943; repr., New York: Macmillan, 1965), ch. 4.

6. Letters to Greeves: Sept. 27, 1916, *CL*, 1:225; Aug. 4, 1917, *CL*, 1:332–33. See also the poem "Song," appended to his letter to Greeves, May 23, 1918, *CL*, 1:372–73.

7. See also *An Experiment in Criticism* (Cambridge: Cambridge University Press, 1961), 128.

8. "Hesperus," in *Collected Poems*, 111–12.

looking at him another morning in *Perelandra,* with "one eye shut and one open."[9] Lewis didn't make the creature in Digory's garden a dragon, but he had to include some sort of watchful beast. The mythology demanded it.

I didn't mention the bird in the garden in the *Magician's Nephew* chapter because it isn't scriptural. But then again, neither is the garden of the Hesperides itself. Although I have focused on the Bible in part 3 of this book, nonbiblical images kept pushing themselves in, begging for my attention, clamoring that they are too important to ignore, like the Babylonian babies in Psalm 137:9 that Lewis saved with his allegorical interpretation.[10] The nonbiblical images in Narnia are good babies, and I don't want to bash them on the head. I must embrace them, for the paradoxical reason that the Chronicles are not biblical allegory. If I was convinced that they were, I might have been content with calling Digory's garden "Eden" and moved on, thereby cheating myself out of the insight that Lewis wove one of the most fertile images of his life—the Hesperides/the West/longing/Joy—into them.

Lewis was aware of how intemperate allegorizing could reduce a story, shrinking it down to less than its parts. In a letter to Mervyn Peake, the author of *Gormenghast,* Lewis praises his work and then speculates that "fools (I bet) tried to 'interpret' it as allegory." Because they can allegorize *Gormenghast,* they might conclude that Peake composed it as an allegory "and no more." The last three words are important. Allegorical interpretation may be acceptable up to a point, but past that point, it precludes other readings and becomes reductionistic.[11] That is, when readers search for "second meanings," they may miss the author's forest for concentrating on allegedly allegorical trees.

The same caution applies to the Chronicles. A major problem with calling them biblical allegory is that some of the best things in the books don't fit into that box. Favorites will differ, but mine include "the first joke" in *The Magician's Nephew,* the bear in *Prince Caspian* that *would* suck his paws, Lucy's instant friendship with the Sea Girl in *The Voyage of the "Dawn Treader,"* and the moonlit snowball dance in *The Silver Chair.* As much as I might want to, I haven't been able to talk about any of them here because they aren't "biblical." Ironically, our focus on Scripture in the Chronicles puts into relief how much of their magic transcends their biblical imagery.

9. *The Magician's Nephew* (London: Bodley Head, 1955), ch. 13; *Perelandra,* ch. 5.

10. See pp. 67–73 of this book.

11. Lewis to Mervyn Peake, Feb. 10, 1958, *CL,* 3:919; Richard Angelo Bergen, "*The Lion, the Witch and the Wardrobe*: Mere Allegory or More Allegory?," *Journal of Inklings Studies* 9, no. 1 (2019): 50.

Even more ironic is the fact that Lewis's exact quotations of Scripture, the ones we might think would stand out most, are almost always the hardest to spot. He did this purposely, and thus he produced the opposite effect of "clunky biblical allegory." His quotations are so small, and their content so common ("Very good," "Well done," "Come and have breakfast," "Woe, woe, woe," "to me," "run without getting tired," and "about half an hour"), that they elude just about everyone. At the beginning of part 3, I said that the more I read the Chronicles, the more biblical references I discover. But even with this in mind, I was stunned to see how subtly Lewis can employ the Bible when he wants to.[12]

Having teased out biblical references large and small, we are ready to draw conclusions. First, it appears that James Moffatt's idiosyncratic translation of the New Testament occasionally influenced Lewis's use of language in the Chronicles of Narnia. This occurs in two important scenes in *The Horse and His Boy* and one in *The Silver Chair*. Shasta's fear of Aslan as a "ghost" in chapter 11 of *The Horse and His Boy* is surely indebted to Moffatt's translation of *pneuma* in Luke 24:37–39, and Moffatt's version of 2 Peter 2 may have influenced the wording of Rabadash's meeting with Aslan in chapter 15, especially regarding the Calormene's "doom." His unique rendering of Hebrews 11:19, "by what was a parable of the resurrection," may have played a role in Caspian's resurrection scene at the end of *The Silver Chair*. Lewis recommended Moffatt's translation to others and used it himself as he wrote *Reflections on the Psalms*, and now we can see that it probably made a small impact on the Chronicles.

Second, biblical allusions abound in the Chronicles when Aslan is present and tend to be absent when he isn't. References to Scripture in *The Magician's Nephew* appear only in the second half of the book, beginning the moment Aslan enters. In *The Lion, the Witch and the Wardrobe,* other than the jejune phrase "sons of Adam and daughters of Eve," they appear for the first time when Mr. Beaver speaks Aslan's name. There are almost no biblical allusions in *Prince Caspian* until the end, when Aslan finally takes a visible role. *The Silver Chair* offers many allusions in the first part of the book in Aslan's Country, but only a few more until Eustace and Jill return there.

There are exceptions to the pattern. *The Horse and His Boy* contains multiple scriptural allusions that lack the presence of Aslan, almost all of which refer to the Old Testament. New Testament allusions arrive in force only when he does. At the end of the book, we learn that the story, and Aslan's role in it, is different than it seemed. When the lion informs Shasta that he was managing events behind the scenes, we discover that things that didn't appear to refer to

12. See the lists of biblical references in the Chronicles in the appendix to this book.

Aslan actually did. The revelation of Aslan's stealthy moves in *The Horse and His Boy* parallels one of the most popular ways Jesus's followers interpreted the Old Testament—Christologically. Even though Jesus is never mentioned in the Old Testament, every New Testament author reads him back into it, claiming that he was there all along, hidden beneath the surface of the words. Only with the incarnation, they insist, could the true meaning of Scripture be revealed. The same thing happens at the end of *The Horse and His Boy*, where Aslan appears in the flesh, whiskers and all, and reveals to Shasta how he helped them along the way. This scene reflects what the resurrected Jesus said to the disciples on the road to Emmaus at the end of the Gospel of Luke: "Beginning from Moses and all the prophets, he explained to them the things about himself in all the Scriptures" (Luke 24:27). We have seen how Lewis incorporated this passage into *The Horse and His Boy*, and the fact that he later uses it in *Reflections on the Psalms* to argue that Jesus considered himself the fulfillment of Scripture supports the idea that Lewis wrote the same thing into the earlier book.[13] There are "second meanings" in Narnia as well as in psalms interpreted Christologically.

The Voyage of the "Dawn Treader" and *The Last Battle* also break the pattern. Since the unspoken biblical motif of the former is "I am the light of the world," where the light is, so is Aslan, whether he is mentioned or not. The prevalence of Scripture in un-Aslaned places in *The Last Battle* is easy to explain: it is based on Revelation, which is permeated with the Scriptures, but God and the Lamb meet their people face-to-face only at the end.

Other patterns emerge when the biblical references are indexed. (See the charts in the appendix.) Many of Lewis's references to the Hebrew Scriptures come from Genesis, Exodus, Isaiah, and Psalms, which are almost the same books Lewis marks most often in his Gore commentary. Although there are no annotations in the chapter on Genesis, he underlines multiple passages in the sections on Exodus, Isaiah, and Psalms, with only scattered marks on the other Old Testament books. This fact is notable because it sets Lewis squarely within ancient tradition: the authors of the New Testament use these books the most, too. And it isn't just a Christian habit: when one counts biblical manuscripts among the Dead Sea Scrolls, those very titles are the most numerous.[14] The more copies of a manuscript that have survived, the more popular it probably was, like an ancient bestseller list.

13. *Reflections on the Psalms* (New York: Harcourt, Brace & World, 1958), 117, 107.

14. James C. VanderKam, *The Dead Sea Scrolls Today* (Grand Rapids: Eerdmans, 1994), 30–32.

The pattern repeats with surviving manuscripts of New Testament books. We possess more copies of Matthew and John dating to the first centuries of the Christian era than of Mark and Luke, which probably means that Matthew and John were more popular in the early church. As Lewis alludes to the Gospels, he follows his forebears, drawing more from Matthew and especially John than from the others. He relies heavily on John in his characterization of Aslan, and counting his references to it in the Chronicles brings the point home. In these fictional children's books, Lewis works brilliantly with the Gospel, in sharp contrast to his writing on John in his nonfiction.

A few of the scriptural events Lewis highlights in the Chronicles—creation, the death and resurrection of Jesus, and the end of the world—jump out at almost anyone. When readers call the series biblical allegory, these big set pieces are usually what they're talking about. But much of the Scripture he works into the books is hard to see, prompting us to ask why he would want to conceal it. Fortunately, he drops a few hints that answer the question, each one a variation on the same theme.

First, between January 1929 and July 1930, Lewis read Matthew Arnold's book *St. Paul and Protestantism.*[15] As was his habit, he listed topics that caught his attention on the blank flyleaves, and one of them prefigures what he does with Scripture in the Chronicles of Narnia. He writes, "SYMBOLS may be valuable tho' unconscious and unintended—often the only way in wh[ich] the idea can reach the 'general heart of mankind.'"[16]

A second hint comes in a 1943 letter to Sister Penelope. She had asked Lewis for advice about some religious plays she was writing for children, concerned that the symbolism might go over their heads, and his response appears to rephrase and expand upon what he wrote in Arnold: "What they do not understand at the time will go into their semi-conscious mind and help them to understand the Cross years later—will perhaps all the more if they don't remember it. Symbolism exists precisely for the purpose of conveying to the imagination what the intellect is not ready for."[17]

A third hint appears in the lecture Lewis delivered on the literary impact of the Authorized Version in 1950, the same year *The Lion, the Witch and the Wardrobe* was published. Everyone was familiar with the AV in the last few centuries, he said, and anyone would recognize the smallest echo of it. Therefore,

15. I am grateful to Charlie Starr for his assistance in dating Lewis's handwriting.

16. *St. Paul and Protestantism* (London: Smith, Elder, 1892), referring to pp. 153, 160. In the Marion E. Wade Center, Lewis collection.

17. Lewis to Sister Penelope, March 25, 1943, *CL*, 2:565.

he argued, it wielded *less* influence upon them because it could not sink into their minds "through the process of infiltration by which a profound literary influence usually operates. An influence which cannot evade our consciousness will not go very deep."[18]

For decades, then, Lewis thought that symbols that were not recognized were more potent than those that were. For what it's worth, I disagree. Unconscious influences may affect us deeply, but so do influences we are well aware of, particularly things we repeat throughout our lives, such as the words of a liturgy. Through rote repetition, in community, and especially in song, they permeate our being and emerge unbidden at the unlikeliest times and places. Whether one agrees with him or not, however, these hints answer the question of why Lewis wanted to conceal so much of the Scripture that he embedded in the Chronicles so subtly—to get it past those watchful dragons.

18. *The Literary Impact of the Authorized Version*, Facet Books Biblical Series 4 (1950; repr., Philadelphia: Fortress, 1963), 29.

CONCLUSION

> *We start with the original writer, what he said, what he had in mind, and what his contemporaries understood him to mean. But to stop there is the part of a pedant. No great literature will stand such a treatment. All great writers meant more than they knew. They all welcome the imagination of their readers. But it must be instructed imagination, not fantasy. The imagination of the Christian reader of the Bible should be controlled by intelligent study. . . . The new knowledge of the Bible must be assimilated and given its rightful place.*
>
> —C. H. Dodd

Very close to the end of his life, Lewis read this passage in C. H. Dodd's *The Authority of the Bible.*[1] It wasn't directed at him, but it could have been, because it voices both the greatest strength and the most consequential weakness of Lewis's biblical interpretation. As a son who trusted his heavenly father to give him bread, not stones, he never doubted for a moment that the divine author of Scripture, the incarnate Word, welcomed his imagination. But he was less open to "the new knowledge of the Bible" and less sanguine than Dodd about what its rightful place might be. Although he assimilated much of the work of Charles Gore in particular, from *Jesus of Nazareth* and *A New Commentary on Holy Scripture* to Gore's sound guidance on the inspiration and inerrancy of Scripture in *Lux Mundi,* Lewis also tried to

1. Dodd, *The Authority of the Bible* (London: Collins Fontana, 1962), 18–19, a passage Lewis marked in his copy.

put biblical criticism in its place. Never was there a man less likely to allow modern scholarship to control his imagination. He was, and begged his readers to join him in being, skeptical, a stance that sometimes led him to misread and therefore disregard good biblical scholarship in his most Scripture-centric arguments. But the problem is confined to his nonfiction. Lewis's subtle—indeed subliminal and even sublime—use of the Bible in the Chronicles of Narnia succeeds, because there he can let his poet's love of word and image out to play, giving it free rein to frolic without spooking the scholarly horses.

Our work with the Chronicles has illuminated how much Lewis operates out of a Johannine vision of Jesus. It is where he lives and moves and has his Christological being, and it is the lens through which he sees—which makes it an icon of God. In Eastern Orthodox thought, an icon is not something to look *at* but *through*, an earthly window to the divine, so when Lewis contemplates the Gospel of John, it may be more than happy coincidence that his literary output overflows with images that reflect the ancient Christian East. Whether he does this consciously or not, I cannot say, but I do agree with Dodd's observation that all great writers mean more than they know.

That said, many of his misreadings of the Bible also center on John. Lewis's blindness when it comes to good scholarship on the Gospel is unsettling. His biblically infused fiction may soar like an eagle, but his expository arguments fall flat, primarily because he is committed to his self-imposed "principle of noncontradiction" regarding John and the Synoptics. This blind spot cuts off his sight, even when he is reading biblical scholars whom he generally trusts, such as Charles Gore, James Moffatt, and Austin Farrer.[2] The refrain that he is a theological amateur does not always provide him sufficient cover, because sometimes—most overtly in "Modern Theology and Biblical Criticism"—it is clear that Lewis thinks he knows best. But in that essay and in his version of the "liar, lunatic, or Lord" argument, his zeal is not according to knowledge, a fact Farrer recognized early on. Preaching at Lewis's Magdalen College memorial service, he noted that Lewis's "real power was not proof, it was depiction."[3] And he was right.

I wish Lewis were still here among us in the land of the living, ready and eager to jump into the "rough academic arena" where knocks "are given and

2. Farrer provides a gorgeous example of what a Christian who has assimilated modern biblical scholarship on John may offer in "How Far Is Christian Doctrine Reformable?," in *Austin Farrer: Oxford Warden, Scholar, Preacher*, ed. Markus Bockmuehl, Nevsky Everett, and Stephen Platten (London: SCM, 2020), 121.

3. Farrer, "In His Image," in *C. S. Lewis at the Breakfast Table*, ed. James T. Como (New York: Macmillan, 1979), 243.

taken in good part," as he put it.[4] He loved a healthy intellectual brawl, and I would have liked to see how he might respond to this book. I respect his work, even as I critique it. We choose to devote years of our lives to a topic because we love it, but as William Wordsworth, one of the poets who influenced Lewis most, pointedly observed, "We murder to dissect."[5] Digging into a subject we love can turn a bit bloody. Lewis was well aware of the phenomenon, wondering if "analytical understanding must always be a basilisk which kills what it sees and only sees by killing."[6] Nevertheless, like E. M. W. Tillyard, Lewis's interlocutor in *The Personal Heresy*, I too "incline to admire his arguments as much when they seem wrong as when they seem right,"[7] and there is so much he gets right about the Bible: his refusal of biblical inerrancy, his sensitivity to literary genre, his emphasis on myth over doctrine, his subtle use of the Bible in his fiction, and above all his commitment to live the words of Scripture through love of God and neighbor. At the same time, it is great fun to watch Lewis tilt at scholarly windmills in his nonfiction, because there is almost always something to learn from him, and occasionally he scores a hit. Win or lose, it is a fight worth watching.

4. *The Personal Heresy* (1939; repr., New York: HarperOne, 2017), 69.

5. Wordsworth, "The Tables Turned"; Lewis to Bede Griffiths, April 23, 1951, *CL*, 3:111; Mary Ritter, "William Wordsworth, *The Prelude*," in *C. S. Lewis's List: The Ten Books That Influenced Him Most*, ed. David Werther and Susan Werther (New York: Bloomsbury Academic, 2015), 93–112.

6. Lewis, *The Abolition of Man* (1943; New York: Macmillan, 1947), 49. See also Lewis to Sheldon Vanauken, Jan. 5, 1951, *CL*, 3:82–83.

7. *Personal Heresy*, 144–45.

ACKNOWLEDGMENTS

This project has benefited from the support and generosity of many people.

I am grateful to the CS Lewis Company Ltd for granting permissions to quote his work.

Missouri State University awarded sabbatical leave that allowed me to serve as scholar-in-residence at Lewis's former home, the Kilns, and conduct research in the Lewis archive at the University of Oxford. I am grateful to Colin Harris, superintendent of the Special Collections Reading Rooms at Bodleian Libraries, for making material available during the move to the Weston Library in 2014 and to the C. S. Lewis Study Centre at the Kilns. Thanks to Ryan Pemberton, interim warden of the Kilns, and to my fellow scholar-in-residence, Laura Smit, for their friendship, and to Michael Ward, whose advice has been invaluable. I also thank Walter Hooper of blessed memory for his kindness, his assistance via email as the project progressed, and his immense achievement in editing Lewis's letters.

I greatly appreciate Missouri State University's award of a 2016 Summer Faculty Fellowship. Shawn Wahl, dean of the Reynolds College of Arts, Social Sciences, and Humanities; Steve Berkwitz, head of the Department of Languages, Cultures, and Religions; and LCR's budget committee never turned down a request for financial support. I am especially grateful to Dr. Berkwitz and Jane Terry, the department's administrative assistant, for their unceasing encouragement. MSU's Faculty Center for Teaching and Learning sponsored regular writing retreats that facilitated the writing of this book as well as excellent camaraderie among colleagues: thanks to Drs. Etta Madden, Jonathan Newman, and Julia Troche.

Undying gratitude goes to Shannon Conlon, Missouri State University librarian extraordinaire, who worked what appeared to be miracles of interlibrary loan, especially during the height of the Covid pandemic.

It was pure joy to engage in research at the Lewis archive at the Marion E. Wade Center in Wheaton, Illinois, under the expert guidance of Laura Stanifer and Jill Walker. They also introduced me to Aaron Hill, who did outstanding work as a proxy researcher at the Wade among Lewis's annotated books in 2020.

The Wilson Special Collections Library at the University of North Carolina, Chapel Hill, made several books from Lewis's personal library available to me in 2020–2021 when the collections were closed to visitors.

An anonymous reviewer of my application for an NEH grant urged me to analyze Lewis's use of the Bible in the Chronicles of Narnia, which I was not planning to do. I took that advice and am glad I did. I did not receive the grant.

Drafts of material in progress were presented at diverse venues. In the beginning was Hilary Johnson Schmitt's invitation to "say something about Lewis," the seed that grew into this book. Valuable feedback came from members of the Catholic Biblical Association, the Society of Biblical Literature, the Orthodox Theological Society in America, and the Central States Region of the SBL. I enjoyed invitations to speak at the Inklings Festival and the Eighth Day Institute at Eighth Day Books in Wichita, Kansas; Evangel University's Faith and the Arts: Conference on Creativity, Culture, and Calling; the Dean's Series at St. Vladimir's Theological Seminary; the Undiscovered C. S. Lewis Conference at George Fox University; and many church and student groups.

I am grateful to everyone who read portions of the book, cheered it on, and offered constructive criticism, especially Edith M. Humphrey and David Congdon. For over a decade Edith has been my "second friend," as Lewis called Owen Barfield in *Surprised by Joy*. A "second friend" reads the same books you do but sometimes pulls very different things from them. Her opposition sharpens your work, and Edith has flat-out disagreed with me more than anyone else during the writing process. God willing, we'll keep up the conversation until Kingdom come and beyond. David Congdon's scholarship on Bultmann forced me to rethink many things, and his advice has made this book much better than it would have been otherwise.

Other readers of drafts include the students of REL 341 C. S. Lewis, some of whose insights are cited in this book, and generous colleagues and friends: Yonatan Adler, Paul Anderson, David Armstrong, David Artman, Magdalena Berry, Kat Coffin, Brenton Dickieson, Mark Given, Nancy Haught, Andrew Lazo, Amy-Jill Levine, Victor Matthews, Frank Moloney, SDB, Isaac Augustine Morales, OP, Jane O. Newman, John Schmalzbauer, Daniel E. Todd, Cheryl Anne Tuggle, and Peter S. Williamson.

My graduate assistants David Armstrong, Cameron Enochs, Andrew Hickman, Emily Knoppe, and Dakota Nelson made countless library runs, proofread sections in progress, and did some preliminary indexing.

I am not the only one who owes a debt of gratitude to Charlie Starr's published chronology of Lewis's handwriting and to his personal assistance in confirming the dates of specific bits. Some arguments here could not have been made without his expertise.

It has been a true privilege to publish this book with Eerdmans and their splendid team. I thank Michael Thomson, the first to believe in the project, and Andrew Knapp, whose patience, humor, and encouragement helped carry me and the manuscript through the turbulent years in which it was written. Jenny Hoffman and Derek Keefe whipped the final draft into shape and rescued it from many errors. All that may remain are on me. Thanks to Kimberly Benedict, Heather Brewer, Jeff Dundas, Clare Galloway, and Jason Pearson, who have brought it through the final stages.

Words can't express how much I love and appreciate my husband, Tim Baynes, whose life has been almost as intertwined with this project as my own. Thank you most of all.

APPENDIX

Scriptural Allusions in the Chronicles of Narnia

Scriptural Allusions in the Chronicles of Narnia, Listed in Canonical Order

Old Testament

Genesis
1:1–2:4a
1:28
1:31
2–3
2:4b–25
2:7
2:8
3:15
3:19
3:21
4
5:21–24
6:19–20
7
12:1
22:13–14
32:30
37
40–41
49:9

Exodus
2:1–10
2:11–15
2:15–20
3:4
3:14
4:24–26
4:25–26
12:35–36
17:5–7
19:18–19
25:40
32:19
32:30–34
32:33
33:11

Numbers
6:24–26
16:30

Deuteronomy
6:6–7

Judges
11:30–40

1 Samuel
28

2 Samuel
22:14
22:30

1 Kings
19:12

Job
37:5
38:4–7
38:9–11
41

Psalms
5:14
6:5
17:15
18:29

References to Scripture Passages in the Chronicles of Narnia by Book

The Magician's Nephew

Genesis
1:1–2:4a
1:28
1:31
2:4b–25
2:7
2:8
3:19
3:21
4
6:19–20

Job
38:4–7

Matthew
6:9–13
25:21

Luke
11:2–4

John
10:1
11:35

Ephesians
1:4

The Lion, the Witch and the Wardrobe

Genesis
2
3:21

Exodus
32:19

2 Samuel
22:30

Job
41

Psalms
18:29
22:21
23
25:6–10

Isaiah
25:6–10
53:7

Ezekiel
37

Matthew
8:11
13:32–42
15:16–20
16:18
17:22

Mark
6:39
8:11
13:32–42
15:16–20

John
1:1
6:10
20:1–2

Acts
8:32–33

Romans
5:8

Galatians
3:13

Philippians
2:10

Hebrews
1:3
2:14–15
2:17
9:22

1 Peter
3:18–20
4:6

Revelation
1:5–6
11:15

The Horse and His Boy

Genesis

12:1

Exodus

2:1–10

2:15–20

3:14

4:24–26

12:35–36

Judges

11:30–40

1 Kings

19:12

Psalms

45:10

Proverbs

[the book as a whole]

Daniel

4

5:20–21

Hosea

2:14–15

Mark

6:17–29

Luke

16:1–13

24:27

24:37–39

John

20:24–29

Romans

4–5

2 Peter

2:3

2:11

2:12–13

2:15–16

Prince Caspian

1 Samuel

28

Isaiah

8:19–20

49:26

Joel

1:5

3:18

Amos

9:13

Mark

1:29–31

2:4

5:10–19

John

2:1–11

The Voyage of the "Dawn Treader"

Genesis

5:21–24

49:9

Job

38:7

Psalms

74:13

Isaiah

6:1–7

14:12

53:7

Matthew

17:2

John

1:5

1:29

1:36

2:32

5:14

8:12

12:46

13:30

19:14

21:4

21:7–14

21:12

21:15

21:18–19

21:21

Acts

8:32

1 Corinthians

5:7

Galatians

3:27

James

1:17

1 Peter

1:19

Revelation

4:1

4:7

5:1–10

5:5–6

21:23

The Silver Chair

Genesis

3:15

22:13–14

37

40–41

Exodus

3:4

32:33

Deuteronomy

6:6–7

Proverbs

7:23–27

Isaiah

55:1

Joel

2:32

Matthew

1–2

John

4:26

6:44

8:32

11:35

19:34

20:22

Romans

5:9

10:13

Hebrews

11:17–19

2 Peter

3:5–7

1 John

1:7

4:10

Revelation

2:26–28

3:12

7:14

12:9

The Last Battle

Genesis

2–3

7

32:30

Exodus

2:11–15

17:5–7

19:18–19

25:40

32:30–34

33:11

33:20

Numbers

6:24–26

16:30

2 Samuel

22:14

Job

37:5

38:9–11

Psalms

5:14

6:5

17:15

29:3

82:6

88:10

88:12

90:4

119:151

141:7

Isaiah

5:14

14:13–14

40:31

Daniel

7:1–8

Joel

2:11

2:12–13

3:15

Amos

5:18

Habakkuk

2:5

Matthew

7:7–8

16:19

25:23

25:31–46

Mark

13:5–8

13:21–22

13:24–25

Luke

2:16

17:11–19

John

10:33

13:23

20:8

21:25

Romans

8:29

16:7

1 Corinthians

10:4

15:50

15:51–53

15:52

15:54

2 Corinthians

2:15–16

Colossians

1:24

1 Thessalonians

4:16

1 Timothy

4:10

Hebrews

8:5

12:1

2 Peter

1:3–4

3:8

Revelation

1:15

2:7

2:17

6:9–11

6:12–17

6:14

8:1

8:5

8:7

8:13

11:13

11:19

12:9

13:11–15

14:2

16:3

16:5–7

16:12

16:18

19:6

19:20

20:10

20:11

21:4

22:2

22:4

BIBLIOGRAPHY

Allen, Garrick V., ed. *The Future of New Testament Textual Scholarship: From H. C. Hoskier to the Editio Critica Maior and Beyond.* Tübingen: Mohr Siebeck, 2019.

Anscombe, G. E. M. "Some Remarks on C. S. Lewis' *Reflections on the Psalms* (1959)." *Journal of Inklings Studies* 9, no. 2 (2019): 176–77.

"Antisemitism." Glossary of Extremism and Hate. Anti-Defamation League. Feb. 4, 2017. https://tinyurl.com/cdy4njzs.

Arnold, Matthew. *St. Paul and Protestantism: With Other Essays.* London: Smith, Elder, 1892.

Assayas, Michka. *Bono: In Conversation with Michka Assayas.* New York: Riverhead Books, 2005.

Auerbach, Erich. *Mimesis: The Representation of Reality in Western Literature.* Princeton: Princeton University Press, 2003.

Aulén, Gustaf. *Christus Victor: An Historical Study of the Three Main Types of the Idea of the Atonement.* Translated by A. G. Hebert. London: SPCK, 1931.

Avis, P. D. L. "Gore and Theological Synthesis." *Scottish Journal of Theology* 28, no. 5 (1975): 461–76.

Azar, Michael G. "'Supersessionism': The Political Origin of a Theological Neologism." *Studies in Christian-Jewish Relations* 16, no. 1 (2021): 1–25.

Bainton, Roland H. "The Bible in the Reformation." In *The Cambridge History of the Bible,* vol. 3, *The West from the Reformation to the Present Day,* edited by S. L. Greenslade, 1–37. Cambridge: Cambridge University Press, 1963.

Baker, Matthew, and Mark Mourachian, eds. *What Is the Bible? The Patristic Doctrine of Scripture.* Minneapolis: Fortress, 2016.

Ball, David Mark. *"I Am" in John's Gospel: Literary Function, Background, and Theological Implications.* Sheffield: Sheffield Academic Press, 1996.

Barkman, Adam. "Rudolf Otto, *The Idea of the Holy.*" In *C. S. Lewis's List: The Ten Books That Influenced Him Most,* edited by David Werther and Susan Werther, 113–34. London: Bloomsbury Academic, 2015.

Barr, James. *Beyond Fundamentalism.* Philadelphia: Westminster, 1984.

Barron, Andrew. "The Conflicted Jewish Imagination of Joy Davidman." *VII: Journal of the Marion E. Wade Center* 36 (2019): 48–70.

Barton, John. "Source Criticism: Old Testament." In *The Anchor Yale Bible Dictionary*, edited by David Noel Freedman, 6:162–65. New York: Doubleday, 1992.

Bartsch, Hans Werner, ed. *Kerygma and Myth: A Theological Debate*. Translated by Reginald H. Fuller. London: SPCK, 1953; New York: Harper & Row, 1961.

Bass, Clarence B. *Backgrounds to Dispensationalism: Its Historical Genesis and Ecclesiastical Implications*. Grand Rapids: Eerdmans, 1960. Reprint, Eugene, OR: Wipf & Stock, 2005.

Bauckham, Richard. "Are We Still Missing the Elephant? C. S. Lewis's 'Fernseed and Elephants' Half a Century On." *Theology* 116, no. 6 (2013): 427–34.

———. "Moses as 'God' in Philo of Alexandria: A Precedent for Christology?" In *The Spirit and Christ in the New Testament and Christian Theology*, edited by I. Howard Marshall, Volker Rabens, and Cornelius Bennema, 246–65. Grand Rapids: Eerdmans, 2012.

Bauder, Kevin T., Andrew David Naselli, and Collin Hansen, eds. *Four Views on the Spectrum of Evangelicalism*. Grand Rapids: Zondervan, 2011.

Baynes, Leslie. "C. S. Lewis's Use of Scripture in the 'Liar, Lunatic, Lord' Argument." *Journal of Inklings Studies* 4, no. 2 (2014): 27–66.

———. *The Heavenly Book Motif in Judeo-Christian Apocalypses 200 BCE–200 CE*. Leiden: Brill, 2012.

———. "Revelation." In *The Cambridge Companion to the New Testament*, edited by Patrick Gray, 313–30. Cambridge: Cambridge University Press, 2021.

———. Review of *A Hebraic Inkling: C. S. Lewis on Judaism and the Jews*, by P. H. Brazier. *Journal of Inklings Studies* 12, no. 2 (2022): 259–66.

Bebbington, David. *Evangelicalism in Modern Britain: A History from the 1730s to the 1980s*. London: Unwin Hyman, 1989.

Bebbington, David, and David Ceri Jones, eds. *Evangelicalism and Fundamentalism in the United Kingdom during the Twentieth Century*. Oxford: Oxford University Press, 2013.

Benton, Janetta Rebold. *The Medieval Menagerie: Animals in the Art of the Middle Ages*. New York: Abbeville Press, 1992.

Bergen, Richard Angelo. "*The Lion, the Witch and the Wardrobe*: Mere Allegory or More Allegory?" *Journal of Inklings Studies* 9, no. 1 (2019): 43–62.

Berman, Jeffrey. *Companionship in Grief: Love and Loss in the Memoirs of C. S. Lewis, John Bayley, Donald Hall, Joan Didion, and Calvin Trillin*. Amherst: University of Massachusetts Press, 2010.

Berman, Ruth. "Watchful Dragons and Sinewy Gnomes: C. S. Lewis's Use of Modern Fairy Tales," *Mythlore* 30, no. 3/4 (Spring/Summer 2021): 117–27.

Bernier, Jonathan. "Bultmann and Translation." *Critical Realism and the New Testament* (blog), June 7, 2017. https://tinyurl.com/49mcnkdu.

Beversluis, John. *C. S. Lewis and the Search for Rational Religion*. 2nd ed. Amherst, NY: Prometheus, 2007.

Bock, Darrell L. *Blasphemy and Exaltation in Judaism: The Charge against Jesus in Mark 14:53–65*. Grand Rapids: Baker Books, 2000.

Bockmuehl, Markus, Nevsky Everett, and Stephen Platten, eds. *Austin Farrer: Oxford Warden, Scholar, Preacher*. London: SCM, 2020.

Bourke, Myles M. Review of *Reflections on the Psalms*, by C. S. Lewis, and *Les Psaumes Commentés Par La Bible I–II*, by Pierre Guichou. *Blackfriars* (1959): 389–91.

Boyarin, Daniel. *Border Lines: The Partition of Judaeo-Christianity*. Philadelphia: University of Pennsylvania Press, 2004.

———. *The Jewish Gospels: The Story of the Jewish Christ*. New York: New Press, 2012.

Brady, Charles A. "C. S. Lewis: II." *America*, June 10, 1944, 269–70.

———. "Introduction to Lewis." *America*, May 27, 1944, 213–14.

Brazier, P. H. "'God . . . or a Bad, or Mad, Man': C. S. Lewis's Argument for Christ—a Systematic Theological, Historical and Philosophical Analysis of *Aut Deus Aut Malus Homo*." *Heythrop Journal* 51 (2010): 1–30.

———. *A Hebraic Inkling: C. S. Lewis on Judaism and the Jews*. Eugene, OR: Pickwick, 2021.

Brettler, Marc Zvi. "Psalm 137:9—a Verse to Criticize." TheTorah.com, 2015. https://tinyurl.com/53bwew3s.

Brown, Raymond E. *The Death of the Messiah: From Gethsemane to the Grave; A Commentary on the Passion Narratives in the Four Gospels*. 2 vols. New York: Doubleday, 1994.

———. *The Gospel according to John I–XII*. Garden City, NY: Doubleday, 1966.

———. *An Introduction to New Testament Christology*. New York: Paulist, 1994.

Bryan, Christopher. "C. S. Lewis and the Art of Reading Scripture." *Sewanee Theological Review* 55, no. 2 (2012): 180–207.

Bultmann, Rudolf. *Faith and Understanding I*. Translated by Louise Pettibone Smith. Edited by Robert Funk. London: SCM, 1969.

———. *The History of the Synoptic Tradition*. Translated by John Marsh. New York: Harper & Row, 1963.

———. *Jesus and the Word*. Translated by Louise Pettibone Smith and Erminie Huntress Lantero. 1934. Reprint, New York: Scribner, 1958.

———. *Jesus Christ and Mythology*. New York: Charles Scribner's Sons, 1958.

———. "New Testament and Mythology." Translated by Reginald H. Fuller. In *Kerygma and Myth: A Theological Debate*, edited by Hans Werner Bartsch, 1–44. New York: Harper & Row, 1961.

———. "A Reply to the Theses of J. Schniewind." Translated by Reginald H. Fuller. In *Kerygma and Myth: A Theological Debate*, edited by Hans Werner Bartsch, 102–23. New York: Harper & Row, 1961.

———. *Theology of the New Testament*. New York: Charles Scribner's Sons, 1951.

———. *This World and Beyond: Marburg Sermons*. New York: Scribner's Sons, 1960.

———. "View-Point and Method." In *The Historical Jesus in Recent Research*, edited by James D. G. Dunn and Scot McKnight, 50–55. Winona Lake, IN: Eisenbrauns, 2005.

Chapman, Alister. "Evangelical or Fundamentalist? The Case of John Stott." In *Evangelicalism and Fundamentalism in the United Kingdom during the Twentieth Century*, edited by David Bebbington and David Ceri Jones, 192–208. Oxford: Oxford University Press, 2013.

Christensen, Michael J. *C. S. Lewis on Scripture: His Thoughts on the Nature of Biblical Inspiration, the Role of Revelation, and the Question of Inerrancy*. 1979. Reprint, London: Stodder & Houghton, 1988.

Clapton, Ernest, ed. *Our Prayer Book Psalter: Containing Coverdale's Version from His 1535 Bible and the Prayer Book Version by Coverdale from the Great Bible 1539–41 Printed Side by Side*. London: SPCK, 1934.

Clark, Elizabeth A. *The Origenist Controversy: The Cultural Construction of an Early Christian Debate*. Princeton: Princeton University Press, 1992.

Clivaz, Claire. *L'ange et la sueur de sang (Lc 22,43–44) ou comment on pourrait bien encore écrire l'histoire*. Leuven: Peeters, 2010.

Coffin, Kat. "How Do You Solve a Problem Like Susan Pevensie? Narnia Guest Post by Kat Coffin." *A Pilgrim in Narnia* (blog), April 24, 2019. https://tinyurl.com/ycyh7mnxh.

Cohen, Hillel. *Year Zero of the Arab-Israeli Conflict 1929*. Waltham, MA: Brandeis University Press, 2015.

Coleridge, Samuel Taylor. *Aids to Reflection and the Confessions of an Inquiring Spirit*. London: George Bell and Sons, 1890.

———. *Table Talk*, July 2, 1830.

Como, James T., ed. *C. S. Lewis at the Breakfast Table, and Other Reminiscences*. New York: Macmillan, 1979.

Congdon, David W. "Demystifying the Program of Demythologizing: Rudolf Bultmann's Theological Hermeneutics." *Harvard Theological Review* 110, no. 1 (2017): 1–23.

———. "Kerygma and Community: A Response to R. W. L. Moberly's Revisiting of Bultmann." *Journal of Theological Interpretation* 8, no. 1 (2014): 1–21.

———. "Kerygma and History: Bultmann's Hermeneutical Theology in North America Today." In *Rudolf Bultmann und die Neutestamentliche Wissenschaft der Gegenwart*, edited by Lukas Bormann and Christof Landmesser, 79–110. Tübingen: Mohr Siebeck, 2022.

———. *The Mission of Demythologizing: Rudolf Bultmann's Dialectical Theology*. Minneapolis: Fortress, 2015.

———. *Rudolf Bultmann: A Companion to His Theology*. Eugene, OR: Cascade, 2015.

Cooke, G. A. "Walter Lock." *Journal of Theological Studies* 35, no. 137 (1934): 1.

Cootsona, Gregory S. *C. S. Lewis and the Crisis of a Christian*. Louisville: Westminster John Knox, 2014.

Cotter, A. C., SJ. "Alfred Loisy (1857–1940)." *Theological Studies* 2, no. 2 (1941): 242–51.

"C. S. Lewis Letter to Schoolchildren Discussing Narnia Up for Auction." *Daily Mail*, Sept. 7, 2018. https://tinyurl.com/2c5khmax.

Crossan, John Dominic. *Who Killed Jesus? Exposing the Roots of Anti-Semitism in the Gospel Story of the Death of Jesus.* San Francisco: HarperSanFrancisco, 1995.

Culpepper, R. Alan. *Anatomy of the Fourth Gospel: A Study in Literary Design.* Philadelphia: Fortress, 1983.

———. *John, the Son of Zebedee: The Life of a Legend.* Columbia: University of South Carolina Press, 1994.

Cunningham, Richard B. *C. S. Lewis, Defender of the Faith.* Philadelphia: Westminster, 1967.

Dana, H. E., and Julius R. Mantey. *A Manual Grammar of the Greek New Testament.* Toronto: Macmillan, 1927.

Dart, Ron. "C. S. Lewis and Bede Griffiths: Chief Companions on the Contemplative Journey." In *The Inklings and Culture*, edited by Monika B. Hilder, Sara L. Pearson, and Laura N. Van Dyke, 81–94. Newcastle upon Tyne, UK: Cambridge Scholars Publishing, 2020.

Davidman, Joy. *Out of My Bone: The Letters of Joy Davidman.* Edited by Don W. King. Grand Rapids: Eerdmans, 2009.

———. *Smoke on the Mountain: An Interpretation of the Ten Commandments.* Philadelphia: Westminster, 1954.

Davis, Stacy. "Unapologetic Apologetics: Julius Wellhausen, Anti-Judaism, and Hebrew Bible Scholarship." *Religions* 12, no. 8 (2021): 560.

Davis, Stephen T. "Was Jesus Mad, Bad, or God?" In *The Incarnation*, edited by Stephen T. Davis, Daniel Kendall, and Gerald O'Collins, 221–45. Oxford: Oxford University Press, 2002.

DelCogliano, Mark. "Situating Sarapion's Sorrow: The Anthropomorphite Controversy as the Historical and Theological Context of Cassian's Tenth Conference on Pure Prayer." *Cistercian Studies Quarterly* 38, no. 4 (2003): 377–421.

Derrick, Stephanie L. *The Fame of C. S. Lewis: A Controversialist's Reception in Britain and America.* Oxford: Oxford University Press, 2018.

Dibelius, Martin. *From Tradition to Gospel.* Translated by Bertram Lee Woolf. New York: Charles Scribner's Sons, 1971.

Dickieson, Brenton D. G. "Mixed Metaphors and Hyperlinked Worlds: A Study of Intertextuality in C. S. Lewis's Ransom Cycle." In *The Inklings and King Arthur: J. R. R. Tolkien, Charles Williams, C. S. Lewis, and Owen Barfield on the Matter of Britain*, edited by Sørina Higgins, 81–113. Berkeley, CA: Apocryphile Press, 2018.

Dodd, C. H. *The Authority of the Bible.* London: Collins Fontana, 1962.

Dorsett, Lyle W. *Seeking the Secret Place: The Spiritual Formation of C. S. Lewis.* Grand Rapids: Brazos, 2004.

Downing, David C. *Planets in Peril: A Critical Study of C. S. Lewis's Ransom Trilogy.* Amherst: University of Massachusetts Press, 1992.

Drummond, James. *An Inquiry into the Character and Authorship of the Fourth Gospel.* London: Williams & Norgate, 1903.

Dunn, James D. G. *Christology in the Making: A New Testament Inquiry into the Origins of the Doctrine of the Incarnation.* Philadelphia: Westminster, 1980.

———. *The Partings of the Ways: Between Christianity and Judaism and Their Significance for the Character of Christianity.* London: SCM, 1991.

Dunn, James D. G., and Scot McKnight, eds. *The Historical Jesus in Recent Research.* Winona Lake, IN: Eisenbrauns, 2005.

Edwards, Mark. "Classicist." In *The Cambridge Companion to C. S. Lewis,* edited by Robert MacSwain and Michael Ward, 58–71. Cambridge: Cambridge University Press, 2010.

———. "C. S. Lewis and Early Christian Literature." In *C. S. Lewis and the Church: Essays in Honour of Walter Hooper,* edited by Judith Wolfe and Brendan N. Wolfe, 23–39. London: T&T Clark, 2011.

Ehrman, Bart D. "Liar, Lunatic, or Lord? Finding the Historical Jesus." In *Jesus, Interrupted: Revealing the Hidden Contradictions in the Bible (and Why We Don't Know about Them),* chapter 5. New York: HarperCollins, 2009.

———. *The New Testament: A Historical Introduction to the Early Christian Writings.* 7th ed. New York: Oxford University Press, 2020.

Emmet, C. W. "The Modernist Movement in the Church of England." *Journal of Religion* 2 (1922): 561–76.

Farrer, Austin. "Bultmann and All That." In *Austin Farrer: Oxford Warden, Scholar, Preacher,* edited by Markus Bockmuehl, Nevsky Everett, and Stephen Platten, 134–50. London: SCM, 2020.

———. "The Christian Apologist." In *Light on C. S. Lewis,* edited by Jocelyn Gibb and Owen Barfield, 23–43. London: G. Bles, 1965.

———. "An English Appreciation." In *Kerygma and Myth: A Theological Debate,* edited by Hans Werner Bartsch, 212–23. New York: Harper & Row, 1961.

———. *The Glass of Vision.* Westminster: Dacre, 1948.

———. "How Far Is Christian Doctrine Reformable?" In *Austin Farrer: Oxford Warden, Scholar, Preacher,* edited by Markus Bockmuehl, Nevsky Everett, and Stephen Platten, 119–33. London: SCM, 2020.

———. "In His Image." In *C. S. Lewis at the Breakfast Table,* edited by James T. Como, 242–44. New York: Macmillan, 1979.

Feinendegen, Norbert. "*Letters to Malcolm*: The Lost Chapter." *VII: Journal of the Marion E. Wade Center* 34 (2017): 75–82.

Feinendegen, Norbert, and Arend Smilde, eds. *The "Great War" of Owen Barfield and C. S. Lewis: Philosophical Writings, 1927–1930.* Inklings Studies Supplements 1. *Journal of Inklings Studies,* 2015.

Fontenrose, Joseph E. *Python: A Study of Delphic Myth and Its Origins.* 1959. Reprint, Berkeley: University of California Press, 1980.

Fowler, Alastair. "C. S. Lewis: Supervisor." *Yale Review* 91, no. 4 (2003): 64–80.

Fredriksen, Paula. *Jesus of Nazareth, King of the Jews.* New York: Vintage Books, 1999.

———. "Mandatory Retirement: Ideas in the Study of Christian Origins Whose Time Has Come to Go." *Studies in Religion* 35, no. 2 (2006): 231–46.

Frei, Hans W. *The Eclipse of Biblical Narrative: A Study in Eighteenth and Nineteenth Century Hermeneutics.* New Haven: Yale University Press, 1974.

Frey, Jörg. "Anti-Judaism, Philosemitism, and Protestant New Testament Studies: Perspectives and Questions." In *Protestant Bible Scholarship: Antisemitism, Philosemitism and Anti-Judaism*, edited by Arjen Bakker, Yael Fisch, Paula Fredriksen, Hindy Najman, and René Bloch, 149–81. Leiden: Brill, 2022.

———. "Ferdinand Christian Baur and the Interpretation of John." In *Ferdinand Christian Baur and the History of Early Christianity*, edited by Martin Bauspiess, Christof Landmesser, and David Lincicum, 206–35. Oxford: Oxford University Press, 2017.

Friesen, Courtney J. P. *Reading Dionysus: Euripides' Bacchae and the Cultural Contestations of Greeks, Jews, Romans, and Christians.* Tübingen: Mohr Siebeck, 2015.

Fundamentalism: A Religious Problem. London: The Times Publishing Company, 1955.

Gaiman, Neil. "The Problem of Susan." In *Fragile Things: Short Fictions and Wonders*, 181–90. New York: William Morrow, 2006.

Gardner, Helen. *The Business of Criticism.* Oxford: Clarendon, 1959.

———. "Clive Staples Lewis 1898–1963." *Proceedings of the British Academy* 51 (1966): 417–28.

"George Tyrrell Revisited." Jesuits in Ireland (website), Feb. 3, 2009. https://tinyurl.com/25d24tee.

Gibb, Jocelyn, and Owen Barfield, eds. *Light on C. S. Lewis.* London: G. Bles, 1965.

Glasson, T. Francis. "C. S. Lewis on St John's Gospel: A Correction and a Protest." *Theology* 71, no. 576 (1968): 267–69.

———. "Who Were the Liberals?" *Expository Times* 70, no. 11 (1959): 342–44.

Godet, Frédéric Louis. *Commentary on the Gospel of St. John.* Translated by Frances Crombie and M. D. Cusin. Vol. 1. Edinburgh: T&T Clark, 1876.

Gold, Dore. *The Fight for Jerusalem: Radical Islam, the West, and the Future of the Holy City.* Washington, DC: Regnery, 2007.

Gordis, Robert. Review of *Book of Job, a Commentary*, by Solomon B. Freehof, *Reflections on the Psalms*, by C. S. Lewis. *Jewish Social Studies* 21, no. 4 (1959): 247–48.

Gore, Charles. *The Epistles of St. John.* London: John Murray, 1920.

———. "The Holy Spirit and Inspiration." In *Lux Mundi: A Series of Studies in the Religion of the Incarnation*, edited by Charles Gore, 315–62. London: John Murray, 1889.

———. *The Incarnation of the Son of God: Being the Bampton Lectures for the Year 1891.* Edited by Christopher Poore. Galesburg, IL: Seminary Street, 2021.

———. *Jesus of Nazareth.* 1929. Reprint, Oxford: Oxford University Press, 1950.

———. *The New Theology and the Old Religion.* London: John Murray, 1907.

———. *Philosophy of the Good Life.* 1923. Reprint, London: J. M. Dent and Sons, 1938.

Gore, Charles, ed. *Lux Mundi: A Series of Studies in the Religion of the Incarnation.* London: John Murray, 1889.

Gore, Charles, Henry Leighton Goudge, and Alfred Guillaume, eds. *A New Commentary on Holy Scripture, Including the Apocrypha.* New York: Macmillan, 1928.

Graham, Billy. *Just as I Am: The Autobiography of Billy Graham.* Rev. ed. San Francisco: HarperOne, 2007.

Graham, David, ed. *We Remember C. S. Lewis: Essays and Memoirs.* Nashville: Broadman & Holman, 2001.

Graves, Michael. *The Inspiration and Interpretation of Scripture: What the Early Church Can Teach Us.* Grand Rapids: Eerdmans, 2014.

Gray, Patrick. "Screwtape and the Historical Jesus." *CSL: The Bulletin of the New York C. S. Lewis Society* 34, no. 6 (2003): 1–7.

Greenslade, S. L., ed. *The Cambridge History of the Bible: The West from the Reformation to the Present Day.* Cambridge: Cambridge University Press, 1963.

Gregory I, Pope. *Reading the Gospels with Gregory the Great: Homilies on the Gospels, 21–26.* Translated by Santha Bhattacharji. Petersham, MA: St. Bede's, 2001.

Gregory of Nyssa. *Catechetical Discourse: A Handbook for Catechists.* Translated and edited by Ignatius Green. Yonkers, NY: St. Vladimir's Seminary Press, 2019.

Gresham, William. "From Communist to Christian." In *These Found the Way: Thirteen Converts to Protestant Christianity,* edited by David Wesley Soper, 64–82. Philadelphia: Westminster, 1951.

Grossman, Lev. *The Magicians: A Novel.* New York: Viking, 2009.

Grudem, Wayne A. *Systematic Theology.* 2nd ed. Grand Rapids: Zondervan Academic, 2020.

Guite, Malcolm. "Poet." In *The Cambridge Companion to C. S. Lewis,* edited by Robert MacSwain and Michael Ward, 294–310. Cambridge: Cambridge University Press, 2010.

Gunkel, Hermann. *Introduction to Psalms: The Genres of the Religious Lyric of Israel.* Macon, GA: Mercer University Press, 1998.

Habets, Myk. "Mere Christianity for Mere Gods: Lewis on Theosis." In *A Myth Retold: Re-encountering C. S. Lewis as Theologian,* edited by Martin Sutherland, 110–29. Eugene, OR: Wipf & Stock, 2014.

Hammann, Konrad. *Rudolf Bultmann: A Biography.* Translated by Philip E. Devenish. Salem, OR: Polebridge, 2013.

Harding, Anthony John. *Coleridge and the Inspired Word.* Kingston, ON: McGill-Queen's University Press, 1985.

Harnack, Adolf von. *What Is Christianity?* Translated by Thomas Bailey Saunders. 1901. Reprint, Philadelphia: Fortress, 1986.

Harner, Philip B. *The "I Am" of the Fourth Gospel: A Study in Johannine Usage and Thought.* Philadelphia: Fortress, 1970.

Harris, J. Rendel. "Stoic Origins of the Prologue to St. John's Gospel." *Bulletin of the John Rylands Library* 6, no. 4 (1922): 439–51.

Hart, David Bentley. *The New Testament: A Translation*. 2nd ed. New Haven: Yale University Press, 2023.

———. "The Spiritual Was More Substantial Than the Material for the Ancients." *Church Life Journal*, July 26, 2018. https://tinyurl.com/5dpt25zr.

———. *That All Shall Be Saved: Heaven, Hell, and Universal Salvation*. New Haven: Yale University Press, 2019.

Hauerwas, Stanley. "On Violence." In *The Cambridge Companion to C. S. Lewis*, edited by Robert MacSwain and Michael Ward, 189–202. Cambridge: Cambridge University Press, 2010.

Hays, Richard B. *Echoes of Scripture in the Letters of Paul*. New Haven: Yale University Press, 1989.

Heck, Joel. "Alec Vidler's Permanent Opposition: C. S. Lewis." *Sehnsucht* 13 (2019): 57–79.

———. "'Modern Theology and Biblical Criticism' in Context." *VII: Journal of the Marion E. Wade Center* 31 (2014): e123–e39.

Hein, David, and Edward Henderson, eds. *C. S. Lewis and Friends: Faith and the Power of Imagination*. London: SPCK, 2011.

Hengel, Martin. *The Son of God: The Origin of Christology and the History of Jewish-Hellenistic Religion*. Philadelphia: Fortress, 1976.

Henze, Matthias. *Mind the Gap: How the Jewish Writings between the Old and New Testament Help Us Understand Jesus*. Minneapolis: Fortress, 2017.

Herbert, George. *The Poems of George Herbert*. Edited by Helen Gardner. Oxford: Oxford University Press, 1979.

Herford, C. H. "The Elizabethan Age in Recent Literary History." *Quarterly Review* 431 (April 1912): 359.

Heron, Alasdair I. C. "What Is Wrong with Biblical Exegesis? Reflections upon C. S. Lewis' Criticisms." In *Betraying the Gospel: Modern Theologies and Christian Orthodoxy*, edited by A. Walker, 138–59. Wilmore, KY: Bristol Books, 1990.

"The Higher Critic." *Herald and Presbyter*, Feb. 6, 1895, 11.

Hilder, Monika B. *The Feminine Ethos in C. S. Lewis's Chronicles of Narnia*. New York: Peter Lang, 2012.

Hilder, Monika B., Sara L. Pearson, and Laura N. Van Dyke, eds. *The Inklings and Culture: A Harvest of Scholarship from the Inklings Institute of Canada*. Lady Stephenson Library, Newcastle on Tyne, UK: Cambridge Scholars Publishing, 2020.

Hincks, Edward Y. Review of *The Theology of the Gospels*, by James Moffatt. *Harvard Theological Review* 7, no. 4 (1914): 601–3.

Hodge, Archibald A., and Benjamin B. Warfield. *Inspiration*. Princeton: Presbyterian Board of Publication and Sabbath-School Work, 1881.

Holladay, Carl R. *Fragments from Hellenistic Jewish Authors*. Vol. 2, *Poets*. Atlanta: Scholars Press, 1989.

Holmes, Stephen R. "Evangelical Doctrines of Scripture in Transatlantic Perspective." *Evangelical Quarterly* 81, no. 1 (2009): 38–63.

Hooper, Walter. *C. S. Lewis: A Companion and Guide.* New York: HarperSanFrancisco, 1996.

———. *Past Watchful Dragons: The Narnian Chronicles of C. S. Lewis.* New York: Collier Books, 1979.

———. "Preface." In *Fern-Seed and Elephants, and Other Essays on Christianity.* Edited by Walter Hooper, 7–9. Glasgow: Collins, 1975.

———. *Through Joy and Beyond: A Pictorial Biography of C. S. Lewis.* New York: Macmillan, 1982.

Horner, David A. "*Aut Deus Aut Malus Homo*: A Defense of C. S. Lewis's 'Shocking Alternative.'" In *C. S. Lewis as Philosopher: Truth, Goodness, and Beauty,* edited by David Baggett, Gary R. Habermas, and Jerry L. Walls, 68–84. Downers Grove, IL: IVP Academic, 2008.

Houston, James. "Reminiscences of the Oxford Lewis." *Lamp-Post of the Southern California C. S. Lewis Society* 7, no. 2 (1983): 6–12.

———. "Reminiscences of the Oxford Lewis." In *We Remember C. S. Lewis: Essays and Memoirs,* edited by David Graham, 129–43. Nashville: Broadman & Holman, 2001.

Howard-Snyder, Daniel. "Was Jesus Mad, Bad, or God? . . . or Merely Mistaken?" *Faith and Philosophy* 21, no. 4 (2004): 456–79.

Hügel, Friedrich von. *Essays and Addresses on the Philosophy of Religion.* Series 1. London: J. M. Dent and Sons, 1928.

Hummel, Daniel G. *The Rise and Fall of Dispensationalism: How the Evangelical Battle over the End Times Shaped a Nation.* Grand Rapids: Eerdmans, 2023.

Humphrey, Edith M. *Further Up and Further In: Orthodox Conversations with C. S. Lewis on Scripture and Theology.* Yonkers, NY: St. Vladimir's Seminary Press, 2017.

Hurtado, Larry. "Summary and Concluding Observations." In *"Who Is This Son of Man?" The Latest Scholarship on a Puzzling Expression of the Historical Jesus,* edited by Larry W. Hurtado and Paul L. Owen, 159–77. London: T&T Clark, 2011.

Huttar, Charles A. "'Let Grill Be Grill': The Metamorphoses of Rabadash and Others." *VII: Journal of the Marion E. Wade Center* 29 (2012): 17–38.

Hyman, Frieda Clark. Review of *Reflections on the Psalms,* by C. S. Lewis. *Judaism* 8, no. 2 (1959): 187–90.

Irving, Washington. *Life of Mahomet.* London: J. M. Dent and Sons, 1915.

James, Dom Augustine. Review of *Reflections on the Psalms,* by C. S. Lewis. *Downside Review* 78 (1960): 131–34.

James, M. R. *The Apocryphal New Testament.* Oxford: Clarendon, 1924.

James, Richard. "Sister Penelope Lawson CSMV: Her Life, Writings and Legacy." *Inklings Forever: Published Colloquium Proceedings 1997–2016* 10, article 86 (2016): 363–77.

Janson, H. W. *Apes and Ape Lore in the Middle Ages and the Renaissance.* London: Warburg Institute, University of London, 1952.

Jeffrey, David Lyle. "C. S. Lewis, the Bible, and Its Literary Critics." *Christianity and Literature* 50, no. 1 (2000): 95–109.

Joeckel, Samuel. *The C. S. Lewis Phenomenon: Christianity and the Public Sphere.* Macon, GA: Mercer University Press, 2013.

Johnson, Roger A. *The Origins of Demythologizing: Philosophy and Historiography in the Theology of Rudolf Bultmann.* Leiden: Brill, 1974.

Justin. *The First and Second Apologies.* Edited by Leslie W. Barnard. Ancient Christian Writers 56. New York: Paulist, 1997.

Kalvesmaki, Joel. *The Theology of Arithmetic: Number Symbolism in Platonism and Early Christianity.* Washington, DC: Center for Hellenic Studies, 2013.

Käsemann, Ernst. "The Problem of the Historical Jesus." In *Essays on New Testament Themes,* translated by W. J. Montague, 15–47. Naperville, IL: Alec R. Allenson, 1964.

Kay, James F. *Christus Praesens: A Reconsideration of Rudolf Bultmann's Christology.* Grand Rapids: Eerdmans, 1994.

Kenyon, Frederic G. *The Bible and Modern Scholarship.* London: John Murray, 1948.

Khoddam, Salwa. "Balder the Beautiful: Aslan's Norse Ancestor in the Chronicles of Narnia." *Mythlore* 22, no. 3 (1999): 66–76.

King, Don W. *Yet One More Spring: A Critical Study of Joy Davidman.* Grand Rapids: Eerdmans, 2015.

Knust, Jennifer, and Tommy Wasserman. *To Cast the First Stone: The Transmission of a Gospel Story.* Princeton: Princeton University Press, 2018.

Kowalski, Beate. "Selective versus Contextual Allusions: Reconsidering Technical Terms of Intertextuality." In *Methodology in the Use of the Old Testament in the New: Context and Criteria,* edited by David Allen and Steve Smith, 86–102. New York: T&T Clark, 2019.

Kreeft, Peter. *Fundamentals of the Faith: Essays in Christian Apologetics.* San Francisco: Ignatius, 1988.

Law, David R. *The Historical-Critical Method: A Guide for the Perplexed.* London: Continuum, 2012.

Law, Timothy Michael. *When God Spoke Greek: The Septuagint and the Making of the Christian Bible.* Oxford: Oxford University Press, 2013.

[Lawson, Sister Penelope.] A Member of the Community of St. Mary the Virgin, Wantage. *God Persists: A Short Survey of World History in the Light of Christian Faith.* London: Mowbrays, 1939.

[Lawson, Sister Penelope.] A Religious of the Community of St. Mary the Virgin, Wantage. *Windows on Jerusalem: A Study in the Mystery of Redemption.* London: Pax House, 1941.

Lazo, Andrew. "Correcting the Chronology: Some Implications of 'Early Prose Joy.'" *VII: Journal of the Marion E. Wade Center* 29 (2012): 51–62.

———. "'Early Prose Joy': A Brief Introduction." *VII: Journal of the Marion E. Wade Center* 30 (2013): 5–12.

Lelen, J. M. Review of *Reflections on the Psalms,* by C. S. Lewis. *Priest* 15 (1959): 758–59.

Lepojärvi, Jason. "C. S. Lewis on Female Scholars: A Reply to John D. Rateliff." *Journal of Inklings Studies* 14, no. 1 (2024): 69–77.

Levine, Amy-Jill. "Bearing False Witness: Common Errors Made about Early Judaism." In *The Jewish Annotated New Testament: New Revised Standard Version Bible Translation,* edited by Amy-Jill Levine and Marc Zvi Brettler, 2nd ed., 759–63. Oxford: Oxford University Press, 2017.

———. "Supersessionism: Admit and Address Rather Than Debate or Deny." *Religions* 13, no. 2 (2022).

Levine, Amy-Jill, and Marc Zvi Brettler, eds. *The Jewish Annotated New Testament: New Revised Standard Version Bible Translation.* 2nd ed. Oxford: Oxford University Press, 2017.

Levine, Amy-Jill, and Joseph Sievers, eds. *The Pharisees.* Grand Rapids: Eerdmans, 2021.

Lewis, C. S. *The Abolition of Man.* 1943. Reprint, New York: Macmillan, 1947.

———. *The Allegory of Love: A Study in Medieval Tradition.* 2nd corrected ed. Oxford: Clarendon, 1938.

———. "Bluspels and Flalansferes: A Semantic Nightmare." In *Selected Literary Essays,* edited by Walter Hooper. Cambridge: Cambridge University Press, 2013.

———. "Christian Apologetics." In *C. S. Lewis Essay Collection: Faith, Christianity and the Church,* edited by Lesley Walmsley. London: HarperCollins, 2002.

———. *Christian Reflections.* Edited by Walter Hooper. Grand Rapids: Eerdmans, 1967.

———. *The Collected Letters of C. S. Lewis.* Vol. 1, *Family Letters, 1905–1931.* Edited by Walter Hooper. New York: HarperSanFrancisco, 2000.

———. *The Collected Letters of C. S. Lewis.* Vol. 2, *Books, Broadcasts, and the War, 1931–1949.* Edited by Walter Hooper. New York: HarperSanFrancisco, 2004.

———. *The Collected Letters of C. S. Lewis.* Vol. 3, *Narnia, Cambridge, and Joy, 1950–1963.* Edited by Walter Hooper. New York: HarperSanFrancisco, 2007.

———. *The Collected Poems of C. S. Lewis: A Critical Edition.* Edited by Don W. King. Kent, OH: Kent State University Press, 2015.

———. *C. S. Lewis Essay Collection: Faith, Christianity and the Church.* Edited by Lesley Walmsley. London: HarperCollins, 2002.

———. "The Death of Words." In *On Stories, and Other Essays on Literature,* edited by Walter Hooper. New York: Harcourt, 1982.

———. "*De Descriptione Temporum.*" In *They Asked for a Paper,* 9–25. London: Geoffrey Bles, 1962.

———. *The Discarded Image: An Introduction to Medieval and Renaissance Literature.* Cambridge: Cambridge University Press, 1964.

———. "'Early Prose Joy': C. S. Lewis's Early Draft of an Autobiographical Manuscript." Edited by Andrew Lazo. *VII: Journal of the Marion E. Wade Center* 30 (2013): 13–50.

———. *English Literature in the Sixteenth Century, Excluding Drama*. Oxford: Clarendon, 1954.
———. "Ex Libris." *Christian Century*, June 6, 1962, 719.
———. *An Experiment in Criticism*. Cambridge: Cambridge University Press, 1961.
———. Foreword to *Smoke on the Mountain: An Interpretation of the Ten Commandments*, by Joy Davidman, 7–11. Philadelphia: Westminster, 1954.
———. *The Four Loves*. London: Geoffrey Bles, 1960.
———. *George MacDonald: An Anthology*. London: G. Bles, 1946.
———. "George Orwell." In *On Stories, and Other Essays on Literature*, edited by Walter Hooper, 101–4. New York: Harcourt, 1982.
———. *God in the Dock: Essays on Theology and Ethics*. Edited by Walter Hooper. Grand Rapids: Eerdmans, 1970.
———. "God in the Dock." In *God in the Dock: Essays on Theology and Ethics*, edited by Walter Hooper, 240–44. Grand Rapids: Eerdmans, 1970.
———. "The Grand Miracle." In *C. S. Lewis Essay Collection: Faith, Christianity and the Church*, edited by Lesley Walmsley. London: HarperCollins, 2002.
———. *The Great Divorce*. 1946. Reprint, New York: HarperCollins, 2001.
———. "Historicism." In *Christian Reflections*, edited by Walter Hooper, 100–113. Grand Rapids: Eerdmans, 1967.
———. *The Horse and His Boy*. London: Geoffrey Bles, 1954.
———. *Image and Imagination: Essays and Reviews*. Edited by Walter Hooper. Cambridge: Cambridge University Press, 2013.
———. Introduction to *Letters to Young Churches: A Translation of the New Testament Epistles*, by J. B. Phillips, vii–x. New York: Macmillan, 1947.
———. Introduction to *Saint Athanasius: On the Incarnation: The Treatise* De Incarnatione Verbi Dei. Translated and edited by a Religious of C.S.M.V. [Sister Penelope Lawson], 3–10. 1944. Reprint, Crestwood, NY: St. Vladimir's Seminary Press, 1996.
———. "Is Theology Poetry?" In *C. S. Lewis Essay Collection: Faith, Christianity and the Church*, edited by Lesley Walmsley. London: HarperCollins, 2002.
———. "It All Began with a Picture . . ." In *On Stories, and Other Essays on Literature*, edited by Walter Hooper, 53–54. New York: Harcourt, 1982.
———. *The Last Battle*. London: Bodley Head, 1956.
———. *Letters to Malcolm: Chiefly on Prayer*. New York: Harcourt, Brace & World, 1964.
———. "*Letters to Malcolm*: Letter XIIa." *VII: Journal of the Marion E. Wade Center* 34 (2017): 71–74.
———. *The Lion, the Witch and the Wardrobe*. London: Geoffrey Bles, 1950.
———. *The Literary Impact of the Authorized Version*. 1950. Reprint, Philadelphia: Fortress, 1963.
———. *The Magician's Nephew*. London: Bodley Head, 1955.
———. *Mere Christianity*. 1952. Reprint, San Francisco: HarperSanFrancisco, 2001.

———. *Miracles*. 1947. Reprint, New York: Macmillan, 1960.
———. "Modern Theology and Biblical Criticism." In *Christian Reflections*, edited by Walter Hooper, 152–66. Grand Rapids: Eerdmans, 1967.
———. "Modern Translations of the Bible." In *God in the Dock: Essays on Theology and Ethics*, edited by Walter Hooper, 229–33. Grand Rapids: Eerdmans, 1970.
———. "Must Our Image of God Go?" In *C. S. Lewis Essay Collection: Faith, Christianity and the Church*, edited by Lesley Walmsley. London: HarperCollins, 2002.
———. "Myth Became Fact." In *C. S. Lewis Essay Collection: Faith, Christianity and the Church*, edited by Lesley Walmsley. London: HarperCollins, 2002.
———. "On Criticism." In *On Stories, and Other Essays on Literature*, edited by Walter Hooper, 127–42. New York: Harcourt, 1982.
———. *On Stories, and Other Essays on Literature*. Edited by Walter Hooper. New York: Harcourt, 1982.
———. "On Three Ways of Writing for Children." In *On Stories, and Other Essays on Literature*, edited by Walter Hooper, 31–44. New York: Harcourt, 1982.
———. *Out of the Silent Planet*. 1938. Reprint, New York: Macmillan, 1965.
———. *Perelandra*. 1943. Reprint, New York: Macmillan, 1965.
———. "Petitionary Prayer: A Problem without an Answer." In *C. S. Lewis Essay Collection: Faith, Christianity and the Church*, edited by Lesley Walmsley. London: HarperCollins, 2002.
———. *The Pilgrim's Regress*. Wade Annotated Edition. Edited by David C. Downing. Grand Rapids: Eerdmans, 2014.
———. *A Preface to Paradise Lost*. London: Oxford University Press, 1942.
———. *Prince Caspian*. London: Geoffrey Bles, 1951.
———. *The Problem of Pain*. 1940. Reprint, New York: Macmillan, 1944.
———. "The Psalms." In *C. S. Lewis Essay Collection: Faith, Christianity and the Church*, edited by Lesley Walmsley. London: HarperCollins, 2002.
———. *Reflections on the Psalms*. New York: Harcourt, Brace & World, 1958.
———. "Rejoinder to Dr Pittenger." In *God in the Dock: Essays on Theology and Ethics*, edited by Walter Hooper, 177–83. Grand Rapids: Eerdmans, 1970.
———. "Religion and Rocketry." In *C. S. Lewis Essay Collection: Faith, Christianity and the Church*, edited by Lesley Walmsley. London: HarperCollins, 2002.
———. Review of *Principles and Problems of Biblical Translation*, by Werner Schwarz. In *Image and Imagination: Essays and Reviews*, edited by Walter Hooper, 68–72. Cambridge: Cambridge University Press, 2013.
———. *The Screwtape Letters*. London: Geoffrey Bles, 1942.
———. *Selected Literary Essays*. Edited by Walter Hooper. Cambridge: Cambridge University Press, 2013.
———. *The Silver Chair*. London: Geoffrey Bles, 1953.
———. "Sometimes Fairy Stories May Say Best What's to Be Said." *New York Times*, Nov. 18, 1956, 310.
———. *Studies in Words*. 2nd ed. Cambridge: Cambridge University Press, 1967.

———. *Surprised by Joy*. San Diego: Harcourt Brace Jovanovich, 1955.
———. *That Hideous Strength*. 1946. Reprint, New York: Macmillan, 1965.
———. *They Stand Together: The Letters of C. S. Lewis to Arthur Greeves (1914–1963)*. Edited by Walter Hooper. London: Collins, 1979.
———. *Till We Have Faces*. Orlando, FL: Harcourt, 1956.
———. "Transposition." In *C. S. Lewis Essay Collection: Faith, Christianity and the Church*, edited by Lesley Walmsley. London: HarperCollins, 2002.
———. *The Voyage of the "Dawn Treader."* London: Geoffrey Bles, 1952.
———. "The Weight of Glory." In *C. S. Lewis Essay Collection: Faith, Christianity and the Church*, edited by Lesley Walmsley. London: HarperCollins, 2002.
———. "What Are We to Make of Jesus Christ?" In *C. S. Lewis Essay Collection: Faith, Christianity and the Church*, edited by Lesley Walmsley. London: HarperCollins, 2002.
———. "Why I Am Not a Pacifist." In *C. S. Lewis Essay Collection: Faith, Christianity and the Church*, edited by Lesley Walmsley. London: HarperCollins, 2002.
———. "The World's Last Night." In *C. S. Lewis Essay Collection: Faith, Christianity and the Church*, edited by Lesley Walmsley. London: HarperCollins, 2002.
Lewis, C. S., and E. M. W. Tillyard. *The Personal Heresy: A Controversy*. 1939. Reprint, New York: HarperOne, 2017.
Lewis, Warren. "Memoirs of the Lewis Family, 1850–1930." The Lewis Family Papers, vol. 3, p. 101, shelf 1, Warren H. Lewis Papers, Wade-A-110, Marion E. Wade Center, Wheaton College, Wheaton, IL.
Lindsell, Harold. *The Battle for the Bible*. Grand Rapids: Zondervan, 1976.
Lipscomb, Benjamin J. B. *The Women Are Up to Something: How Elizabeth Anscombe, Philippa Foot, Mary Midgley, and Iris Murdoch Revolutionized Ethics*. New York: Oxford University Press, 2021.
Litwa, M. David. *Desiring Divinity: Self-Deification in Early Jewish and Christian Mythmaking*. New York: Oxford University Press, 2016.
Lock, Walter. "The Gospel according to St. John." In *A New Commentary on Holy Scripture, Including the Apocrypha*, part 3, *The New Testament*, edited by Charles Gore, Henry Leighton Goudge, and Alfred Guillaume, 240–72. New York: Macmillan, 1928.
Loisy, Alfred. *Le quatrième Évangile*. Paris: Alphonse Picard et Fils, 1903.
Longenecker, Bruce, and Mikeal C. Parsons, eds. *Beyond Bultmann: Reckoning a New Testament Theology*. Waco, TX: Baylor University Press, 2014.
Louth, Andrew. *Greek East and Latin West: The Church, AD 681–1071*. Crestwood, NY: St. Vladimir's Seminary Press, 2007.
Macaulay, J. C. "One Amateur to Another." *Eternity*, March 1959, 38.
MacDonald, Dennis R. *The Dionysian Gospel: The Fourth Gospel and Euripides*. Minneapolis: Fortress, 2017.
MacDonald, George. *The Miracles of Our Lord*. London: Longmans, Green, 1896.
———. *Thomas Wingfold, Curate*. Vol. 3. London: MacDonald and Tugwell, 1876.
———. *Unspoken Sermons*. Series 2. London: Longmans, Green, 1885.

Macquarrie, John. *The Scope of Demythologizing: Bultmann and His Critics.* Gloucester, MA: Peter Smith, 1969.

MacSwain, Robert. "A Fertile Friendship: C. S. Lewis and Austin Farrer." *Chronicle of the Oxford University C. S. Lewis Society* 5, no. 2 (2008): 22–45.

MacSwain, Robert, ed. *Scripture, Metaphysics, and Poetry: Austin Farrer's "The Glass of Vision," with Critical Commentary*. Farnham Surrey, England: Ashgate, 2013.

MacSwain, Robert, and Michael Ward, eds. *The Cambridge Companion to C. S. Lewis.* Cambridge: Cambridge University Press, 2010.

Marsden, George. *Understanding Fundamentalism and Evangelicalism.* Grand Rapids: Eerdmans, 1991.

Mascall, Eric. *The God-Man.* Westminster: Dacre, 1940.

McDowell, Josh. *The New Evidence That Demands a Verdict.* Nashville: Thomas Nelson, 1999.

McGrath, Alister E. *C. S. Lewis: A Life; Eccentric Genius, Reluctant Prophet.* Carol Stream, IL: Tyndale, 2013.

———. *The Intellectual World of C. S. Lewis.* Chichester, UK: Wiley-Blackwell, 2014.

McKim, Donald K. *The Westminster Dictionary of Theological Terms.* Louisville: Westminster John Knox, 1996.

Meier, John P. *A Marginal Jew: Rethinking the Historical Jesus.* New York: Doubleday, 1991.

Melton, Brian. "The Great War and Narnia: C. S. Lewis as Soldier and Creator." *Mythlore* 30, no. 1/2 (2011): 123–42.

Merrick, J., and Stephen M. Garrett, eds. *Five Views on Biblical Inerrancy.* Grand Rapids: Zondervan, 2013.

Metzger, Bruce M. *The Text of the New Testament: Its Transmission, Corruption, and Restoration.* 3rd ed. New York: Oxford University Press, 1992.

———. *A Textual Commentary on the Greek New Testament.* Stuttgart: Deutsche Bibelgesellschaft/German Bible Society, 1994.

Michaels, J. Ramsey. "John 18:31 and the 'Trial' of Jesus." *New Testament Studies* 36, no. 3 (1990): 474–79.

Miller, Laura. *The Magician's Book: A Skeptic's Adventures in Narnia.* New York: Little, Brown, 2008.

Milward, Peter. "C. S. Lewis on Allegory." *Rising Generation* 114, no. 4 (1968): 227–32.

Mitchell, Christopher W. "Lewis and Historic Evangelicalism." In *C. S. Lewis and the Church: Essays in Honour of Walter Hooper*, edited by Judith Wolfe and Brendan N. Wolfe, 154–73. London: T&T Clark, 2011.

Mitchell, Philip Irving. *The Shared Witness of C. S. Lewis and Austin Farrer: Friendship, Influence, and an Anglican Worldview.* Kent, OH: Kent State University Press, 2021.

M. K. T. "Wise Words in the Psalms." *Amarillo Sunday News-Globe*, Nov. 9, 1958.

Moffatt, James. *The New Testament: A New Translation.* New York: Hodder & Stoughton, 1913.

———. *The Theology of the Gospels.* London: Duckworth, 1912.

"Moffatt, James, 1870–1944." *Journal of Biblical Literature* 64 (1945): xi–xii.

Moody, Dale. "God's Only Son: The Translation of John 3:16 in the Revised Standard Version." *Journal of Biblical Literature* 72, no. 4 (1953): 213–19.

Morris, Leon. *Studies in the Fourth Gospel.* Grand Rapids: Eerdmans, 1969.

Moulton, James Hope. *A Grammar of New Testament Greek.* Vol. 1, *Prolegomena*. 3rd ed. Edinburgh: T&T Clark, 1908.

Muddiman, John. "The Holy Spirit and Inspiration." In *The Religion of the Incarnation: Anglican Essays in Commemoration of "Lux Mundi,"* edited by Robert Morgan, 119–35. Bristol: Bristol Classical Press, 1989.

Musacchio, George. "C. S. Lewis, T. S. Eliot, and the Anglican Psalter." *VII: Journal of the Marion E. Wade Center* 22 (2005): 45–59.

Narborough, F. D. V. "The Synoptic Problem." In *A New Commentary on Holy Scripture, Including the Apocrypha,* edited by Charles Gore, Henry Leighton Goudge, and Alfred Guillaume, part 3, 35. New York: Macmillan, 1928.

Nassif, Bradley. "John Chrysostom on the Nature of Revelation and Task of Exegesis." In *What Is the Bible? The Patristic Doctrine of Scripture,* edited by Matthew Baker and Mark Mourachian, 49–66. Minneapolis: Fortress, 2016.

Nesbit, E. *The Enchanted Castle.* London: T. Fisher Unwin, 1907.

Ness-Bergstein, Evrea. "The Garden as Unfinished Narrative of the Good in C. S. Lewis' Perelandra." *The Journal of Inklings Studies* 2, no. 1 (2012): 49–80.

Newman, Jane O. "The Gospel according to Auerbach." *Publications of the Modern Language Association* 135, no. 3 (2020): 455–73.

Nicholson, Mervyn. "What C. S. Lewis Took from E. Nesbit." *Children's Literature Association Quarterly* 16 (1991): 16–22.

Nickelsburg, George W. E., and James C. VanderKam. *1 Enoch: A New Translation: Based on the Hermeneia Commentary.* Minneapolis: Fortress, 2001.

Nicolson, Adam. *God's Secretaries: The Making of the King James Bible.* New York: HarperCollins, 2003.

Nock, A. D. Review of *Die Kosmologie des Plinius,* by Wilhelm Kroll. *Classical Review* 46, no. 4 (1932): 186.

Noll, Mark A., David Bebbington, and George M. Marsden, eds. *Evangelicals: Who They Have Been, Are Now, and Could Be.* Grand Rapids: Eerdmans, 2019.

Nongbri, Brent. *Before Religion: A History of a Modern Concept.* New Haven: Yale University Press, 2013.

"Notes of Recent Exposition." *Expository Times* 65, no. 4 (1954): 97.

Novak, David. "The Covenant in Rabbinic Thought." In *Two Faiths, One Covenant? Jewish and Christian Identity in the Presence of the Other,* edited by Eugene B. Korn and John Pawlikowski, 65–80. Lanham, MD: Rowman & Littlefield, 2005.

O'Connor, Flannery. *The Habit of Being: Letters of Flannery O'Connor.* Edited by Sally Fitzgerald. New York: Farrar, Straus & Giroux, 1979.

Oesterley, W. O. E. "The Religious Background of the New Testament in Jewish Thought." In *A New Commentary on Holy Scripture, Including the Apocrypha,* edited by Charles Gore, Henry Leighton Goudge, and Alfred Guillaume, part 3, 13. New York: Macmillan, 1928.

Ordway, Holly. *Tolkien's Modern Reading: Middle-earth beyond the Middle Ages.* Park Ridge, IL: Word on Fire Academic, 2021.

Origen. *Contra Celsum.* Translated by Henry Chadwick. Cambridge: Cambridge University Press, 1953.

———. *On First Principles.* Edited and translated by John Behr. Vol. 1. Oxford: Oxford University Press, 2017.

———. *The Philocalia of Origen.* Translated by George Lewis. Edinburgh: T&T Clark, 1911.

Otto, Rudolf. *The Idea of the Holy.* Translated by John W. Harvey. 2nd ed. London: Oxford University Press, 1952.

———. *The Kingdom of God and the Son of Man: A Study in the History of Religion.* Translated by Floyd V. Filson and Bertram Lee-Woolf. London: Lutterworth, 1943.

Ouspensky, Leonid, and Vladimir Lossky. *The Meaning of Icons.* Translated by G. E. H. Palmer and E. Kadloubovsky. 2nd ed. Crestwood, NY: St. Vladimir's Seminary Press, 1982.

Packer, J. I. *"Fundamentalism" and the Word of God: Some Evangelical Principles.* Grand Rapids: Eerdmans, 1958.

Pazdziora, J. Patrick, and Joshua C. Richards. "Balder, Adonis, Bacchus, Aslan: Frazer and Sacrament in *The Lion, the Witch and the Wardrobe* and *Prince Caspian.*" *VII: Journal of the Marion E. Wade Center* 34 (2017): 83–101.

Peppard, Michael. *The Son of God in the Roman World: Divine Sonship in Its Social and Political Context.* Oxford: Oxford University Press, 2011.

Perrin, Nicholas. *Jesus the Temple.* Grand Rapids: Baker Academic, 2010.

Phillips, J. B. *Letters to Young Churches: A Translation of the New Testament Epistles.* New York: Macmillan, 1947.

Phillips, Justin. *C. S. Lewis at the BBC.* London: HarperCollins, 2003.

Pitre, Brant J. *The Case for Jesus: The Biblical and Historical Evidence for Christ.* New York: Image, 2016.

Pittenger, W. Norman. "Apologist versus Apologist: A Critique of C. S. Lewis as 'Defender of the Faith.'" *Christian Century,* Oct. 1, 1958, 1104–7.

———. "The Continuity of Catholic Modernism." *Journal of Religion* 51, no. 2 (1971): 137–41.

Plett, F. Heinrich. *Enargeia in Classical Antiquity and the Early Modern Age: The Aesthetics of Evidence.* Leiden: Brill, 2012.

Poe, Henry Lee. *The Completion of C. S. Lewis: From War to Joy (1945–1963).* Wheaton, IL: Crossway, 2022.

Poirier, J. C. *The Invention of the Inspired Text: Philological Windows on the Theopneustia of Scripture.* London: Bloomsbury, 2021.

Pontifical Biblical Commission. *The Inspiration and Truth of Sacred Scripture: The Word That Comes from God and Speaks of God for the Salvation of the World.* Translated by Thomas Esposito and Stephen Gregg. Collegeville, MN: Liturgical Press, 2014.

Pope, F. Hugh. "Dr. Gore's Bible Commentary." *Blackfriars* 10, no. 11 (1929): 1076–85.

Pope, F. Hugh, and Sebastian Bullough. "The History of the Rheims-Douay Version." In *A Catholic Commentary on Holy Scripture*, edited by Bernard Orchard. Edinburgh: Thomas Nelson and Sons, 1953.

The Prose Edda. Translated by Arthur Gilchrist Brodeur. New York: American Scandinavian Foundation, 1916.

Pullman, Philip. "A Dark Agenda?" SureFish.co.uk (defunct), Nov. 2002. https://tinyurl.com/yhtevsrk (archive). Available at https://tinyurl.com/y567d2a4.

———. *His Dark Materials: The Golden Compass, The Subtle Knife, The Amber Spyglass.* New York: Everyman's Library, 2011.

Purinton, Carl Everett. "*An Anglican Commentary on the Bible*, by Charles Gore, Henry Leighton Goudge, and Alfred Guillaume." *Journal of Religion* 9, no. 3 (1929): 462–65.

Quebedeaux, Richard. *The Worldly Evangelicals.* New York: Harper & Row, 1978.

Quenot, Michel. *The Resurrection and the Icon.* Translated by Michael Breck. Crestwood, NY: St. Vladimir's Seminary Press, 1997.

Quinn, Jerome D. "Saint John Chrysostom on History in the Synoptics." *Catholic Biblical Quarterly* 24, no. 2 (1962): 140–47.

Ramsey, Michael. *An Era in Anglican Theology: From Gore to Temple; The Development of Anglican Theology between "Lux Mundi" and the Second World War, 1889–1939.* New York: Scribner, 1960.

Rancière, Jacques. "Auerbach and the Contradictions of Realism." *Critical Inquiry* 44 (2018): 227–41.

Randall, Ian M. "Billy Graham, Evangelism, and Fundamentalism." In *Evangelicalism and Fundamentalism in the United Kingdom during the Twentieth Century*, edited by David Bebbington and David Ceri Jones, 173–91. Oxford: Oxford University Press, 2013.

Redlich, E. Basil. *Form Criticism*. London: Duckworth, 1939.

"Religion: Don v. Devil." *Time*, Sept. 8, 1947.

Reynolds, Benjamin E. "The Use of the Son of Man Idiom in the Gospel of John." In *Who Is This Son of Man? The Latest Scholarship on a Puzzling Expression of the Historical Jesus*, edited by Larry W. Hurtado and Paul L. Owen, 101–29. London: T&T Clark, 2011.

Ritter, Mary. "William Wordsworth, *The Prelude*." In *C. S. Lewis's List: The Ten Books That Influenced Him Most*, edited by David Werther and Susan Werther, 93–112. New York: Bloomsbury Academic, 2015.

Robertson, E. H. "J. B. Phillips: Translator." *Expository Times* 95, no. 10 (1984): 300–304.

Robinson, John A. T. "The Last Tabu? The Self-Consciousness of Jesus." In *The Historical Jesus in Recent Research*, edited by James D. G. Dunn and Scot McKnight, 553–66. Winona Lake, IN: Eisenbrauns, 2005.

Rollmann, Hans. "Baron Friedrich von Hügel and the Conveyance of German Protestant Biblical Criticism in Roman Catholic Modernism." In *Biblical Studies and the Shifting of Paradigms, 1850–1914*, edited by Henning Graf Reventlow and William Farmer, 197–222. Sheffield: Sheffield Academic Press, 1995.

Runia, David. "God and Man in Philo of Alexandria." *Journal of Theological Studies* 39 (1988): 48–75.

Rupprecht, Arthur. "The Versatile C. S. Lewis: Latin Scholar." *VII: Journal of the Marion E. Wade Center* 18 (2001): 73–92.

Russell, Jeffrey Burton. *Satan: The Early Christian Tradition.* Ithaca, NY: Cornell University Press, 1981.

Ryken, Philip. "Inerrancy and the Patron Saint of Evangelicalism: C. S. Lewis on Holy Scripture." In *The Romantic Rationalist: God, Life, and Imagination in the Work of C. S. Lewis*, edited by John Piper and David Mathis, 39–64. Wheaton, IL: Crossway, 2014.

Sacchi, Paolo. "The 2005 Camaldoli Seminar on the Parables of Enoch: Summary and Prospects for Future Research." In *Enoch and the Messiah Son of Man: Revisiting the Book of Parables*, edited by Gabriele Boccaccini, 499–512. Grand Rapids: Eerdmans, 2007.

Sanders, E. P. *Jesus and Judaism.* Philadelphia: Fortress, 1985.

Sanders, E. P., and Margaret Davies. *Studying the Synoptic Gospels.* Philadelphia: Trinity Press International, 1989.

Santamaria, Abigail. *Joy: Poet, Seeker, and the Woman Who Captivated C. S. Lewis.* Boston: Houghton Mifflin Harcourt, 2015.

Sayer, George. *Jack: A Life of C. S. Lewis.* 2nd ed. Wheaton, IL: Crossway, 1994.

Schakel, Peter. "C. S. Lewis: Reason, Imagination, and Knowledge." In *C. S. Lewis and Friends: Faith and the Power of Imagination*, edited by David Hein and Edward Henderson, 15–34. Eugene, OR: Cascade, 2011.

———. *Imagination and the Arts in C. S. Lewis: Journeying to Narnia and Other Worlds.* Columbia: University of Missouri Press, 2002.

Schwarz, Werner. *Principles and Problems of Biblical Translation: Some Reformation Controversies and Their Background.* Cambridge: Cambridge University Press, 1955.

Schweitzer, Albert. *The Quest of the Historical Jesus.* Translated W. Montgomery. London: Adam and Charles Black, 1910.

Schwenkler, John. "Untempted by the Consequences: G. E. M. Anscombe's Life of 'Doing the Truth.'" *Commonweal*, Dec. 2, 2019.

Smilde, Arend. "C. S. Lewis, St. Jerome, and the Biblical Creation Story: The Background of a Recurring Misattribution." *Journal of Inklings Studies* 4, no. 2 (2014): 115–24.

———. "C. S. Lewis's 'Transposition': Text and Context." *Sehnsucht* 13, no. 1 (2019): 29–56.

Smith, Carol. "What Was in the Scripture Knowledge Syllabus at Bertie Wooster's Prep School?" In *Sense and Sensitivity: Essays on Reading the Bible in Memory of Robert Carroll*, edited by Alastair G. Hunter and Phillip R. Davies, 395–415. Sheffield: Sheffield Academic Press, 2002.

Smith, Stevie. "The Simple Psalms." *Spectator*, Sept. 12, 1958, 352.

Snyder, K. Alan. *America Discovers C. S. Lewis: His Profound Impact.* Eugene, OR: Wipf & Stock, 2016.

Snyder, K. Alan, and Jamin Metcalf. *Many Times and Many Places: C. S. Lewis and the Value of History*. Hamden, CT: Winged Lion, 2023.

Sockness, Brent W. *Against False Apologetics: Wilhelm Herrmann and Ernst Troeltsch in Conflict.* Tübingen: Mohr Siebeck, 1998.

Soulen, R. Kendall. *The God of Israel and Christian Theology.* Minneapolis: Fortress, 1996.

Spearing, A. C. "C. S. Lewis as a Research Supervisor." *Journal of Inklings Studies* 12, no. 1 (2022): 110–17.

Starr, Charlie W. "'Villainous Handwriting': A Chronological Study of C. S. Lewis's Script." *VII: Journal of the Marion E. Wade Center* 33 (2016): 73–94.

Starr, Charlie W., and Crystal Hurd. "C. S. Lewis Manuscripts at the Lanier Theological Library." *Sehnsucht* 15, no. 1 (2021): 15–54.

Stavrakopoulou, Francesca. *God: An Anatomy.* New York: Knopf, 2022.

Stockton, Jim, and Benjamin J. B. Lipscomb. "The Anscombe-Lewis Debate: New Archival Sources Considered." *Journal of Inklings Studies* 11, no. 1 (2021): 35–57.

Stowell, Jerome. Review of *Reflections on the Psalms,* by C. S. Lewis. *Worship* 23, no. 5 (no date): 130.

Streeter, B. H. *The Four Gospels: A Study of Origins.* New York: Macmillan, 1925.

Tanzer, Sarah. "The Historical Jesus." In *The Jewish Annotated New Testament: New Revised Standard Version Bible Translation,* edited by Amy-Jill Levine and Marc Zvi Brettler, 2nd ed., 628–33. Oxford: Oxford University Press, 2017.

Taylor, Vincent. *The Formation of the Gospel Tradition.* London: Macmillan, 1933.

———. *The Gospel according to St. Mark:* London: Macmillan, 1959.

Temple, William. *Readings in St. John's Gospel.* Series 1 and 2. London: Macmillan, 1947.

Theodore of Mopsuestia. *Commentary on the Gospel of John.* Edited by Joel C. Elowsky, Thomas C. Oden, and Gerald L. Bray. Translated by Marco Conti. Ancient Christian Texts. Downers Grove, IL: IVP Academic, 2010.

Tissell, Dwain. "C. S. Lewis's Most Important Message: The Abolition of Man as Lewis's Self-Conscious Struggle for the Value of Human Persons." *Sehnsucht* 18, no. 1 (2024).

Tobin, Thomas. "Logos." In *The Anchor Bible Dictionary,* edited by David Noel Freedman, 4:348–56. New York: Doubleday, 1992.

Toynbee, Polly. "Narnia Represents Everything That Is Most Hateful about Religion." *Guardian,* Dec. 5, 2005. https://tinyurl.com/yf82yp73.

Trible, Phyllis. "A Love Story Gone Awry." In *God and the Rhetoric of Sexuality,* 72–143. Philadelphia: Fortress, 1978.

Tyrrell, George. *Christianity at the Cross-Roads.* London: Longmans, Green, 1910. Republished London: Allen & Unwin, 1963.

VanderKam, James C. *The Dead Sea Scrolls Today.* Grand Rapids: Eerdmans, 1994.

Vanhoozer, Kevin J. "On Scripture." In *The Cambridge Companion to C. S. Lewis,* edited by Robert MacSwain and Michael Ward, 75–88. Cambridge: Cambridge University Press, 2010.

Van Leeuwen, Mary Stewart. *A Sword between the Sexes? C. S. Lewis and the Gender Debates.* Grand Rapids: Brazos, 2010.

Versluis, Arie. "'Knock the Little Bastards' Brains Out': Reception History and Theological Interpretation of Psalm 137:9." In *Violence in the Hebrew Bible*, edited by Jacques van Ruiten and Koert van Bekkum, 373–96. Leiden: Brill, 2020.

Vialon, Martin. "Erich Auerbach und Rudolf Bultmann: Probleme abendländischer Geschichtsdeutung." In *Marburger Hermeneutik zwischen Tradition und Krise*, edited by Matthias Bormuth and Ulrich von Bulow, 176–206. Göttingen: Wallstein Verlag, 2008.

Vidler, Alec R. *Soundings.* Cambridge: Cambridge University Press, 1962.

———. *Windsor Sermons.* London: SCM, 1958.

Waddell, Peter. *Charles Gore: Radical Anglican.* Norwich, UK: Canterbury, 2014.

Walker, Andrew. "Under the Russian Cross: A Research Note on C. S. Lewis and the Eastern Orthodox Church." In *A Christian for All Christians: Essays in Honor of C. S. Lewis*, edited by Andrew Walker and James Patrick, 63–67. Washington, DC: Regnery Gateway, 1992.

Walker, Andrew D. "*Enargeia* and the Spectator in Greek Historiography." *Transactions of the American Philological Association (1974–2014)* 123 (1993): 353–77.

Walsh, Chad. *C. S. Lewis: Apostle to the Skeptics.* New York: Macmillan, 1949.

———. *The Literary Legacy of C. S. Lewis.* New York: Harcourt Brace Jovanovich, 1979.

Walsham, Alexandra. *Catholic Reformation in Protestant Britain.* Surrey: Ashgate, 2014.

Ward, Maisie. *Gilbert Keith Chesterton.* 1942. Reprint, Lanham, MD: Sheed & Ward, 2005.

Ward, Michael. *Planet Narnia: The Seven Heavens in the Imagination of C. S. Lewis.* Oxford: Oxford University Press, 2008.

Ware, Kallistos. "C. S. Lewis, an 'Anonymous Orthodox'?" In *C. S. Lewis and the Church: Essays in Honour of Walter Hooper*, edited by Judith Wolfe and Brendan N. Wolfe, 135–53. London: T&T Clark, 2011.

Warner, Francis. "Lewis' Involvement in the Revision of the Psalter." In *C. S. Lewis and the Church: Essays in Honour of Walter Hooper*, edited by Judith Wolfe and Brendan N. Wolfe, 52–63. London: T&T Clark, 2011.

Weems, Reggie. "Universalism Denied: C. S. Lewis' Unpublished Letters to Alan Fairhurst." *Journal of Inklings Studies* 7, no. 2 (2017): 87–98.

Wellhausen, Julius. *Prolegomena to the History of Ancient Israel.* 1878. Reprint, New York: Meridian Library, 1957.

Werther, David, and Susan Werther, eds. *C. S. Lewis's List: The Ten Books That Influenced Him Most.* New York: Bloomsbury Academic, 2015.

Wheeler, Andrew. *C. S. Lewis: Clarity and Confusion; A Balanced Introduction to His Writings.* Leominster, UK: Day One, 2006.

Williams, Donald T. *Deeper Magic: The Theology behind the Writings of C. S. Lewis.* Baltimore, MD: Square Halo Books, 2016.

Wirt, Sherwood E. "Heaven, Earth, and Outer Space: Part Two of an Interview with C. S. Lewis." *Decision*, Oct. 1963.

Wiseman, Matthew. "A Biblical Scholar's Note on Anscombe's Review of Lewis's *Reflections on the Psalms*." *Journal of Inklings Studies* 9, no. 2 (2019): 178–80.

Wodehouse, P. G. *The Code of the Woosters*. 1938. Reprint, New York: Vintage, 1975.

Wolfe, Brendan. "A Note on the Date of C. S. Lewis's Conversion to Theism." *Journal of Inklings Studies* 9, no. 1 (2019): 68–69.

Wolfe, Judith. "Austin Farrer and C. S. Lewis." In *Austin Farrer: Oxford Warden, Scholar, Preacher*, edited by Markus Bockmuehl, Nevsky Everett, and Stephen Platten, 70–85. London: SCM, 2020.

Wolfe, Judith, and Brendan N. Wolfe, eds. *C. S. Lewis and the Church: Essays in Honour of Walter Hooper*. London: T&T Clark, 2011.

Wolfe, Judith, and Brendan Wolfe, eds. *C. S. Lewis's Perelandra: Reshaping the Image of the Cosmos*. Kent: Kent State University Press, 2013.

Wordsworth, William. *The Letters of William and Dorothy Wordsworth: The Later Years, I: 1821–30*. Edited by Ernest de Selincourt. Oxford: Clarendon, 1939.

———. *The Prelude, or Growth of a Poet's Mind (Text of 1805)*. Edited by Ernest de Selincourt. Revised impression. London: Oxford University Press, 1960.

Worthen, Molly. "John Stott, C. S. Lewis, J. R. R. Tolkien: Why American Evangelicals Love the British." *Religion and Politics*, May 1, 2012. https://tinyurl.com/bdh5ectm.

Wrede, William. *The Messianic Secret*. Translated by J. C. G. Greig. Cambridge: James Clarke, 1971.

Wright, C. J. *Jesus the Revelation of God: His Mission and Message according to St. John.* London: Hodder & Stoughton, 1950.

Wright, N. T. "Jesus' Self-Understanding." In *The Incarnation: An Interdisciplinary Symposium on the Incarnation of the Son of God*, edited by S. T. Davis, D. Kendall, and G. O'Collins, 47–61. Oxford: Oxford University Press, 2002.

———. "Simply Lewis: Reflections on a Master Apologist after 60 Years." *Touchstone: A Journal of Mere Christianity*, March 2007. https://tinyurl.com/3srpehen.

Wright, Ronald Selby, ed. *Asking Them Questions: A Selection from the Three Series.* London: Oxford University Press, 1953.

Yarbro Collins, Adela. "The Charge of Blasphemy in Mark 14.64." *Journal for the Study of the New Testament* 26, no. 4 (2004): 379–401.

———. "Mark and His Readers: The Son of God among Greeks and Romans." *Harvard Theological Review* 93 (2000): 85–100.

———. "Mark and His Readers: The Son of God among Jews." *Harvard Theological Review* 92 (1999): 393–408.

Yarbro Collins, Adela, and John J. Collins. *King and Messiah as Son of God: Divine, Human, and Angelic Messianic Figures in Biblical and Related Literature.* Grand Rapids: Eerdmans, 2008.

Zaleski, Philip, and Carol Zaleski. *The Fellowship: The Literary Lives of the Inklings; J. R. R. Tolkien, C. S. Lewis, Owen Barfield, Charles Williams*. New York: Farrar, Straus & Giroux, 2015.

Zanker, G. "Enargeia in the Ancient Criticism of Poetry." *Rheinisches Museum für Philologie* 124, no. 3/4 (1981): 297–311.

Zernov, Nicolas. *The Reintegration of the Church: A Study in Intercommunion*. London: SCM, 1952.

Zipes, Jack, ed. *The Oxford Companion to Fairy Tales*. 2nd ed. Oxford: Oxford University Press, 2015.

INDEX OF AUTHORS

INDEX OF SUBJECTS

INDEX OF SCRIPTURE AND OTHER ANCIENT SOURCES